ad hoc at home

Thomas Keller with Dave Cruz

Along with Susie Heller, Michael Ruhlman, and Amy Vogler

Photographs by Deborah Jones

ARTISAN

Copyright © 2009 by Thomas Keller

Photographs copyright © 2009 by Deborah Jones

Published by Artisan

A Division of Workman Publishing Company, Inc.

225 Varick Street

New York, NY 10014-4381

www.artisanbooks.com

Library of Congress Cataloging-in-Publication Data

Keller, Thomas.

Ad Hoc at home / by Thomas Keller.

p. cm.

Includes index.

ISBN 978-1-57965-377-4

1. Cookery, American. 2. Ad Hoc (Restaurant). I. Title.

TX715.K29164 2009

641.5973—dc22

2009013258

Design by Level, Calistoga, California

Blackboard art by Dan Bunter and Nick Dedier

Illustrations on pages 63 and 87 by Joleen Hughes

Printed in Singapore

7 9 10 8 6

To my brother Joseph, who in the beginning patiently taught, influenced, and helped shape my career.
I am forever grateful for his guidance and love.
—Thomas Keller

To Sarah, Hendrix, and Jaxon for their unending support, to Mom for her strength,
to the cooks and staff of Ad Hoc, whose belief in this work makes our restaurant truly special.
and in memory of my father, whom I'll miss greatly.
—Dave Cruz

To my mother and her mother for teaching me the joys of cooking and sharing, to my close friends and mentors
Julia, Jacques, and Thomas for the love and support that developed my passion into my profession,
and to Tom, Adam, and Lauren for all the love and encouragement I could ever dream of.
—Susie Heller

CONTENTS

for temporary relief of hunger

ad hoc

THE SECRET EQUATION?

great product
+ great execution
_____
great cooking

It delights me to offer here a big collection of family meals and everyday staples, delicious approachable food, recipes that are doable at home. No immersion circulator required. No complicated garnishes. I promise!

Here is food meant to be served from big bowls and platters passed hand to hand at the table—hearty soups and vegetable salads, potato hash with bacon and onions, braised short ribs, chicken potpie, peaches and cream, and pineapple upside-down cake. This is the food I love to sit down to with my family and friends. It's food that makes you feel good.

The pace of life today is so quick, and we often feel so rushed and disconnected from one another, as well as from the sources of our food, that it's easy to forget how powerful the ritual of eating together can be. To be able to sit around the table, passing food, sharing stories of the day, with the sense that for an hour or so, the outside world can be set aside, is a gift to embrace. Some days life is sweet, other days life can be hard, but the one thing we can always strive to do, is to partake of the comfort and pleasure of sharing a meal with those we hold dear.

Shortly after we set out to write this book, my father died. I was very lucky to have had him just next door to me during the last years of his life and to be able to cook for him. I cooked his last meal, and we shared it together. I remember it happily: his favorite, barbecued chicken with mashed potatoes and braised collard greens. I remember the collard greens especially because I hadn't originally intended to serve them. But when I saw them in the grocery store, they were so big and vivid, I felt compelled to choose them. It was spring, and the first strawberries were in season, so I made strawberry shortcake. It was a good dinner. And now I am unspeakably grateful to have made it—that dinner remains important to me. And so does the food we—friends and family—would have in the following days, brought together in grief, comforted by food.

When we eat together, when we set out to do so deliberately, life is better, no matter your circumstances. Whether it's a sad or difficult time, whether it's an ordinary-seeming day, or whether it's a time of celebration, our lives are enriched when we share meals together.

And that's what the food in this book is all about.

dinner for dad

barbecued chicken with mashed potatoes and collard greens, followed by strawberry shortcake

Bacon (about 4 ounces slab bacon, or lardons, or strips)

About 2 pounds collard greens

Unsalted butter (you'll need at least a stick), at room temperature

Kosher salt

1 pound Yukon Gold potatoes

1 pound strawberries

Sugar

1 to 2 teaspoons Grand Marnier (optional)

One 3- to 4-pound chicken

¾ cup half-and-half

1 cup heavy cream

½ teaspoon vanilla extract

¾ cup barbecue sauce (try to find a sauce with some integrity, preferably from a small producer)

4 shortcake rounds

An hour before you want to eat, preheat the oven to 325°F. If you're grilling over coals, start the fire then too; if you're grilling over propane, know that you'll begin the chicken about a half hour after you start cooking, and preheat the grill (see Grilling Basics, page 345) so it is hot when you're ready to put your chicken on.

Put the bacon in a heavy Dutch oven and set it over medium heat to begin rendering the fat. If you want to serve the bacon with the greens, cut it into lardons; I just wanted the bacon flavor, so I left it whole.

Remove the stems from the collards and discard them. Tear the leaves into large pieces. Wash them in cold water and dry them (use a salad spinner).

Add a couple of tablespoons of butter to the Dutch oven. Add the greens and turn them over in the fat to wilt them. (You may need to do this in batches if they don't all fit in at once, and you might want to turn the heat up a little to speed up the process.) Add a "two-finger pinch" of salt (see page 52), and when the greens are wilted, cover the pot and put it in the oven.

Put your potatoes in a big pot, one that allows them plenty of room, cover them with cold water, add a three-finger pinch of salt, and set over high heat. When the water comes to a simmer, reduce the heat slightly to maintain a gentle simmer, and cook the potatoes until they're tender, meaning they give no resistance to a knife.

Meanwhile, hull the strawberries, cut them into small pieces, and put them in a bowl. Add two three-finger pinches of sugar and, if you like, the Grand Marnier (my dad liked the alcohol in a dessert, but it's optional).

Cut the chicken into 8 pieces (see page 21)—wings (wing tips removed), breast (keep it on the bone, and split it in half down the breastbone), drumsticks, and thighs (discard the back or save it for stock). Season the chicken liberally with salt.

Put the drumsticks and thighs on the grill and cook them for 5 minutes. Add the breasts to the grill, and then the wings. Many variables determine how long the pieces will take to cook. You want a medium-high fire, but you don't want them to burn or have flare-ups from dripping fat. I cooked mine for about 25 minutes that day. The thighs and drumsticks should be cooked through and tender.

Pour the half-and-half into a small pan and add a tablespoon of butter. Just before the potatoes are done, warm the half-and-half over low heat until the butter melts.

After the collards have cooked for 45 minutes or so, you can turn off the oven to finish them gently.

When the potatoes are done, drain them and put them in a bowl, where they will steam. Wash and dry the pot.

When the potatoes have cooled just enough to handle—hold them with a kitchen towel if they're too hot for you—peel them. Press them through a ricer back into the pot. Stir in the warm butter and half-and-half until the consistency is to your liking. Season with salt to taste and partially cover to keep warm.

Put some ice in a large bowl and set a smaller bowl on top of the ice for the whipped cream. Add the cream, two three-finger pinches of sugar, and vanilla to the bowl and whip to soft peaks.

Remove the collards from the oven and keep them warm on the back of the stovetop.

Just before removing the chicken from the grill, baste it all over with the barbecue sauce. Cook it just a little longer to heat the sauce, then transfer to a serving platter.

Open a bottle of Pinot Noir. If you have a back porch and it's a perfect spring evening, serve your meal there.

Finish the potatoes by rewarming them over medium heat and stirring in some more butter (I like butter, so I use a lot—they should be moist and delicious). Taste them and add more salt if they need it.

Toss the collards so that they're evenly coated in the bacon fat and butter. Bring the collards, potatoes, and chicken, with serving utensils, to the table.

When you're ready for dessert, toss the strawberries in the juices they've released, spoon over the shortcakes, and top with the whipped cream.   **SERVES 4**

While developing and testing recipes for this book, we came up with a number of small bright ideas. Some were old kitchen tips that might be new to some home cooks. Others were ingrained habits from years of restaurant cooking that apply equally well at home. We call these bits of wisdom "lightbulb moments" and have designated them here with a hanging lightbulb.

The first lightbulb moment I want to offer is one I was lucky to realize in time, and hope that others will too. It may seem obvious but it's worth repeating: Take care of your parents.

becoming a better cook

I take pleasure in precision—making my knife cuts uniform, in peeling asparagus cleanly, taking off just enough of its outer layer to make it tender while keeping its shape. Naturally, I bring those habits with me into my kitchen at home. But must a home cook strive for the precision we do in restaurant kitchens?

No. When we're cooking at home, we can be and should be more relaxed. Does every piece of diced potato need to be identical? Of course not. Should you throw away half of a carrot in order to achieve six perfect batons? That's probably not the best use of your time or your carrot.

But I'm not saying that you should throw precision out the window. We still need to be precise about time and temperature. When you're sautéing a piece of meat, the pan has got to be hot, and you need to cook the meat for the correct amount of time to bring it to the right temperature. And then you need to let it rest. (For more on these subjects, see pages 40 and 62.)

You must be precise about time and temperature when cooking vegetables too, whether you're roasting them in a hot oven or blanching them in boiling salted water. And sometimes cutting vegetables precisely does matter. If your sliced carrots are different sizes, the small pieces will be overcooked before the big pieces are tender. But if you're making a one-pot meal such as a roast chicken with roasted root vegetables, you don't need to worry about the tips, which will get overcooked—you may even want that caramelized flavor.

The bottom line is this: in order to be a good cook, you have to be aware of everything around you. It's an ongoing process, one you should take pleasure in. The more pleasure you take from cooking, the more fun you have in the kitchen, the better your food will be!

One of the great things about cooking is that no single task is particularly difficult. But cooking can seem difficult when you try to do too much at once, when you attempt several unfamiliar techniques at the same time. Instead, try one new technique in combination with ones you're familiar with. If you've never cooked a duck before, for example, don't also try to make glazed turnips for the first time.

Another way to make cooking more satisfying is to cook the same meal over and over, because practice makes you better and more efficient in your actions. Many home cooks try a new recipe once and then move on to the next, but the fact is, you really only begin to learn the second time you prepare a dish.

Yet another way to improve your kitchen skills is to cook the same kind of fish or cut of meat in different ways. If you like salmon, for example, learn all the various ways you can prepare it, and discover how it's different when it's grilled, sautéed, or poached. The same techniques can be used with any thick cut of fish, from halibut to snapper to bass.

Learn to judge by touch when a piece of meat or fish is done. Pay attention to how it feels when it's rare and when it's cooked through. No one can tell you how to do this. This is something you can learn only by cooking, by touching and remembering. Pay attention to each cooking experience.

If you're a novice or if you simply want to become a better cook, I recommend learning the handful of tasks professional cooks do over and over and naturally get better at over time through simple repetition. Following are a few of those important basics as well as a few particulars helpful to the home cook.

learn to use salt properly Seasoning food is one of the first things we train new cooks to do at the restaurants, and it may be the single most important skill a home cook can develop. Learning both when to salt your food and how much of it to use are critical in achieving maximum flavor in virtually any form of cooking.

Think about what you're salting and what will happen when you salt it. Is it a thick steak or a thin fillet of fish? Is it a sliced raw vegetable or onions in a frying pan? Each responds differently.

Salt used for seasoning (as opposed to a finishing salt) needs time to dissolve. Salt meat well before cooking it; if you don't salt it until just before cooking it, you'll leave a lot of salt in your sauté pan. Salt steaks, chops, and other smaller cuts 15 to 20 minutes before cooking them, and larger cuts (chicken and roasts, for instance) 40 to 45 minutes before cooking.

I'd like to mention pepper here because it's so often grouped with salt. It's important to recognize that salt and pepper are almost opposites, pepper being used for a completely different reason than salt. We use pepper to introduce a new flavor to a dish. You should be able to taste it. By contrast, salt only enhances flavors that are already there—if you can taste the salt in a dish, it's too salty.

See also On Salt, page 52.

learn to use vinegar as a seasoning device Recipes often tell you to season with salt or salt and pepper, but you almost never see the instruction "season with vinegar." In fact, vinegar (or citrus, or any acidic liquid, such as verjus) can be an important way to markedly enhance the impact of a dish. It's always worth considering whether a few drops of vinegar could be added to a soup, sauce, or braising liquid to make the flavors really jump out. You don't necessarily want to taste the vinegar, only to feel its effects. It's an important seasoning tool.

learn how to roast a chicken Knowing how to roast a chicken perfectly is one of those great basic skills (see Whole Roasted Chicken

on a Bed of Root Vegetables, page 22) because it gives you an infinite number of dishes. In the spring, you can serve the chicken with peas and morels. In the height of summer, you can serve the meat cold on a salad; in late summer, with Summer Vegetable Gratin (page 202). In winter, you can roast the chicken with root vegetables. You can season it in any number of ways, or make a great sauce to go with it, or simply top it with some butter and serve it with some mustard on the side. There's a huge amount of variety with just this one technique.

learn how to sauté Recognizing the level of heat you need is the critical part of sautéing food. A duck breast, for example, should be cooked over low heat to render the fat in the skin and make it crisp (see Pan-Roasted Duck Breasts, page 35). A piece of veal or fish that is naturally tender is usually sautéed over high heat to develop flavor on the exterior through browning before the interior is overcooked. (The recipe for Caramelized Sea Scallops, page 88, is an example of high-heat sautéing.) For more on sautéing, see page 40.

learn how to pan-roast Pan-roasting combines two techniques, sautéing and roasting. It's one of the most versatile in the restaurant kitchen, and it's a good technique to use at home. The food is started in a hot sauté pan on the stovetop, then turned and put in a hot oven to finish cooking (see, for example, Pan-Roasted Chicken with Sweet Sausage and Peppers, page 20). The initial sauté helps create a tasty seared exterior, and the ambient heat of the oven cooks the food more uniformly than the heat on the stovetop could. Finishing the food in the oven also frees up the stovetop and allows you to concentrate on other dishes you may be preparing. Pan-roasting requires a frying pan or sauté pan with an ovenproof handle.

learn how to braise Braising is one of my favorite techniques, because of its great transformative ability to develop deep flavor and tenderness in inexpensive, tough cuts of meat. The braising technique is fairly straightforward. The meat is seasoned and browned on the stovetop, then liquid is added and the meat is cooked in the oven at 275° to 300°F for hours, until it is tender. It is then allowed to cool in the liquid and simply reheated to serve (see Braised Beef Short Ribs, page 41). One of the finer points of braising is to cover the pot with a parchment lid (see page 120) rather than a pot lid, to allow some reduction of the cooking liquid, which fortifies the flavors.

learn how to roast There are two types of roasting: high-heat roasting and low-and-slow roasting. High-heat roasting is used for foods that are naturally tender, chicken or a rack of lamb, for instance (see Herb-Crusted Rack of Lamb with Honey Mustard Glaze, page 59). Low-and-slow roasting is used for either of two reasons. We rely on it for meat that needs to be cooked for a long time before it becomes tender, such as a pork shoulder or veal shanks (see Slow-Roasted Veal Shanks, page 76). Slow-roasting these cuts may require some sort of liquid or a covered pot, because collagen, the connective tissue that makes meat tough, needs moisture in order to melt into gelatin. But there are other cuts, especially big ones, that we roast at a very low temperature, not to tenderize them, but rather to ensure that they cook evenly. You can't cook prime rib in a very hot oven without overcooking the outside or undercooking the inside—or both (see Blowtorch Prime Rib Roast, page 56).

learn how to poach Poaching is a gentle form of cooking—the temperature never goes above 200°F. It's usually used for fish, but meats can be poached as well. Poaching allows you to flavor the cooking medium and thereby enhance the flavor of what you're cooking. To poach salmon, we use a court bouillon, water with aromatics, and often an acidic element such as wine (see Poached Salmon, 93). Other stocks can be used as poaching liquids, and fat is an extraordinary poaching medium (see Oil-Poached Sturgeon, page 100, and Duck Confit, page 32).

learn the big-pot blanching technique Most green vegetables and some other vegetables benefit from this simple technique, which results in vividly colored, perfectly seasoned vegetables. Big-pot blanching involves boiling vegetables in what is in effect brine-strength salted water until they are cooked through (see Broccolini Salad with Burrata Cheese, page 144). I use about 1 cup of Diamond Crystal kosher salt per gallon of water. I call it "big-pot blanching" because you need to have enough water so that it doesn't lose the boil when you add the vegetables. That's all there is to it, that and tasting the vegetables to know when they are cooked. If you want to cook the vegetables in advance, you need to stop the cooking as quickly as possible by plunging them into an ice bath until they are thoroughly chilled. Then drain them and store them refrigerated on paper towels, so that they don't soak in water, until you are ready to serve or reheat them.

learn to make one really good soup There's enormous value in making a good soup. If you're going to make chicken soup (see Chicken Soup with Dumplings, page 122), you need a good chicken stock—and it's important to feel comfortable making a simple stock too. But you don't always need a homemade stock to make soup. A good vegetable soup can be made simply with water seasoned with aromatics. A good bean soup can be made with just a thick slice of bacon, tomatoes, carrots, white beans, and water. A vegetable soup, a protein-based soup, and a pureed soup are all an invaluable part of a cook's repertoire.

learn to cook eggs Eggs may be my favorite food to cook and to eat. They can be prepared in so many different ways, can be served at any meal, and can be used in both sweet and savory dishes. Eggs can be featured in a dish or used as a garnish. They can be an ingredient or a tool. They are delicious, inexpensive, and nutritious. Learning to soft-cook, hard-cook, scramble, and poach eggs; prepare an omelet; or use eggs in a custard or a sauce makes you a better, more versatile cook. (See Cooking Eggs, page 342, and Grilled Asparagus with Prosciutto, Fried Bread, Poached Egg, and Aged Balsamic Vinegar, page 156.)

learn to make a pie crust Making a good pie crust gives you the framework for a range of savory and sweet pies and tarts and other pastries from Chicken Potpie (page 24) to Cherry Pie (page 308) to quiche. Baking your own pie crust allows you to choose the type of fat you want to use as your shortening. Butter adds a wonderful richness to pie crusts. Lard is also terrific, especially for savory dishes, where it adds a depth of flavor.

For those who want to improve their skills, my advice is, after learning all the above, to challenge yourself. That is the way anyone—an athlete, a doctor, a musician—improves his or her skills. Set increasingly difficult tasks for yourself. Maybe it's as simple as focusing on slicing an onion thinner, or dicing vegetables more uniformly, or braising short ribs correctly, taking the time to understand the different ways that short ribs look and smell and feel throughout cooking. Or make your own sausage, then a *pâté en terrine*, then a *pâté en croûte*. One of the great things about cooking is that there is no end to the learning.

The second thing I always advise is practice. Do things over and over, every time just a little bit better than the last. Repetition improves the quality of your craft and broadens your capabilities as a cook. The first time you make gnocchi, if it comes out right, it's probably because you got lucky. But if you continue to make it again and again and it comes out right, it's because you've picked up the nuances of the process—how hot the potato is when you mix it with the flour, how moist the potato is, how sticky the dough is when you mix it—all those minute variations that are impossible to articulate precisely and are therefore knowable only through experience, touch, sight, and smell, through repetition and paying attention every step of the way.

INGREDIENTS

We call ingredients "product" in the restaurant kitchen. If you have a better product than I do, you can be a better chef than I am. Perhaps the quickest way you can become a better cook is to buy better ingredients. And there's never been a time in history when such excellent ingredients have been available to so many people. (Remember, too, that the tools of the kitchen are "product" as well.)

For years, chefs have been asking their suppliers for specific ingredients. Do the same thing. This is how we got shiitake mushrooms and cilantro into our grocery stores and supermarkets in the 1980s, and it's how we're going to get humanely raised veal and pork into them in the near future. Develop relationships with the people you buy ingredients from, show them that you care about your ingredients, and ask them for help in finding the best ingredients possible. Ask more questions, work harder to know the source of your food, and understand how it is produced and what the ramifications or results of that production are. If we continue to raise our voices, more products will become available and the products will be better.

Frequent farmers' markets as often as you can. They can be the best source of good food, and we all want to support small-farm agriculture, an important and growing segment of our food production system. We also recommend shopping on the internet, looking for growers and producers creating or harvesting extraordinary products, no matter where they are.

But also let the market tell you what to buy. Be inspired by what you see. I wrote the recipe for what would become one of my signature dishes, "Oysters and Pearls," after a purple box of pearl tapioca caught my eye. Be open to inspiration rather than simply picking up ingredients on a list.

TOOLS AND EQUIPMENT

Cooking is a craft, and a craft requires tools. If you don't have good kitchen tools, you have to be a more skilled cook to compensate for that. If all you have is a flimsy aluminum pan, it's going to be very difficult to sauté a piece of meat well. But the bottom line is that you need only a dozen or so tools for most of the cooking you will do—so buying those few high-quality items should not be prohibitively expensive.

Buy equipment and tools that you find aesthetically pleasing. Your kitchen, your tools, and your equipment can and should express your

DON'T PUT THE SQUEEZE ON

I like to have a variety of tools on hand for turning food. Perforated spoons, spiders, and skimmers allow you to work the food gently; so do palette knives. Too often, tongs crush or tear food. Lifting food from below, rather than clamping onto it, is the way to go.

step away from the tongs

avoid the pinch

say friend, what's the scoop

personality. They should inspire you as much as the food. Here are a few of my essentials.

knives Knives are the cook's fundamental tool, but you need only four of them, and if they're good ones, they'll last your entire lifetime: a 10-inch chef's knife, a 12-inch slicing knife, a paring knife, and a serrated knife, used almost exclusively for cutting bread. The style or specific type of knife is up to you—there are many good brands, and the particular sizes and shapes should be chosen according to your own preferences. Whether you choose a Japanese santoku or a traditional chef's knife is less important than that the quality is excellent and that it feels comfortable in your hand. I use my slicing knife for 50 percent of the cutting I do at the restaurant, though you will likely use a chef's knife more often.

I can do anything I need to in the kitchen with these four knives and a steel. The steel is important to keep your knives sharp, to hone them. Learn how to use it, and steel your knives frequently. You should also buy and learn to use a sharpening stone to keep your knives sharp or find a quality knife-sharpening service. Sharp knives make your work both easier and better, and they're safer to use than dull knives.

cutting board The surface you cut on should be forgiving to the knife: wood or a soft synthetic material that won't hurt your blade. Avoid flimsy cutting boards or, worse, flexible sheets, which are cheap and unstable. Choose a thick surface to work on, and a large one. Small boards are restrictive. If you have the space, buy a large board, at least 12 by 18 inches. It's helpful to put a damp cloth or damp paper towel underneath your cutting board when you work, to prevent it from slipping (see page 195).

pots and pans My favorite pan is a big cast-iron skillet. When I returned from Europe in the mid-1980s, this was the first thing I bought, and I learned to do everything in it. I could roast a chicken in it, with vegetables, for a one-pot meal. I could sauté a steak or a piece of fish in it, I could poach in it, and I could braise in it. It was

the perfect size for cooking a meal for two people, which back then was the most I'd be cooking for at home. In short, it was a workhorse. If you could have only one pan in your kitchen, this is the one I'd give you.

Generally, the same rules of quality and longevity that apply to knives apply to pots and pans—Dutch ovens, roasting pans, saucepans, frying pans, and so on. The outcome of a dish is directly related to the quality of your cookware, especially where heat transfer is critical: sautéing, boiling, braising, frying, and roasting. If you're trying to sauté something in a lightweight aluminum pan, you're not going to get the same result as you would in an All-Clad copper-core sauté pan.

I believe there is a place for nonstick pans in your kitchen, and here quality is especially important. You need good-quality pans with a coating that won't come off in your food. It's useful to have a nonstick pan for cooking some fish and eggs.

the big four: countertop appliances There are four appliances I especially recommend for the home kitchen: a Vita-Mix, a standing mixer, a scale, and a food processor.

> A Vita-Mix, an extremely powerful blender, costs several hundred dollars, but in my opinion it's worth the expense. The fineness with which it can puree soups and sauces is extraordinary. We also use it for other purees and for nut butters. One of its most valuable features is a dial for controlling the mixing speed, from very slow to very fast. And don't ignore the plunger; it's an important part of using the machine (you'll need it for pushing down thicker purees so that they're evenly mixed).

> A standing mixer, such as a KitchenAid, is a workhorse appliance used for whipping egg whites, mixing doughs and batters, and numerous other fundamental tasks. Attachments for other tasks, such as grinding meat, rolling out pasta dough, and making ice cream, are also available.

> A good scale is not expensive and is by far the best way of measuring. Buy one that has both imperial and metric measures. In our restaurant kitchens, we measure most ingredients by weight, but because so few home cooks use a scale routinely, we give traditional volume measurements in most of these recipes.

> A food processor is good for many tasks, such as pulverizing nuts, making bread crumbs, mixing some doughs, and pureeing meat and fish mixtures. Do not use it for mincing onions, garlic, or herbs, because the result will be uneven, from a rough chop to a near puree all in the same bowl.

Other kitchen tools are optional, depending on your needs. I love the All-Clad slow-cooker, which has a much better temperature control than older slow-cookers. It's great for beans, because it cooks them gently (see Slow-Cooker Beans, page 337) without taking up valuable stovetop space.

idiosyncracies All chefs have their own favorite tools, and everyone is different. I want to mention some of the tools I wouldn't want to do without.

Fine-mesh conical and basket strainers are invaluable for achieving a luxurious texture in soups and sauces or simply for straining liquids. They come in all sizes, from very small ones to the large conical strainer called a chinois.

I use *large spoons* all the time when I'm cooking, for stirring, basting, tasting, skimming, and saucing. It's handy to keep a few right by your stove, not just in your silverware drawer.

I need at least one *wooden spoon* or *heatproof spatula* with a flat edge for making risotto, deglazing a pan, and stirring thick sauces and soups, among other tasks.

A *palette knife,* a blunt knife with a rounded tip and a flexible blade, allows you to move or turn food in a pan, whether a steak or a fillet of fish, in a precise and delicate way. (I'm using one to turn the scallops on pages 88–89.) Tongs put pressure on food, and you don't have as much control with them.

A *Japanese mandoline,* such as those made by Benriner, is invaluable for uniform slicing and julienning. Buy the kind that has just a single screw to adjust thickness rather than a wider one that uses two screws; the latter can slice unevenly.

Whenever I travel somewhere to cook, I bring my own *pepper mill.* Too many pepper mills produce only a coarse grind. Finely ground black pepper is a seasoning—I don't want chunks of hot pepper in my food. When you're buying a pepper mill, test it by grinding some pepper in your hand. It should be powdery, not chunky.

Every kitchen should have plenty of *parchment paper.* We use it for making lids (see page 120) for stews and braises, as well as for lining baking sheets so foods don't pick up flavors from the metal itself. All chefs use *baking sheets,* with their raised sides (also known as half sheet pans) for many more uses than making cookies. We use them to transport ingredients, for storage, to top with a cooling rack to drain ingredients (see page 101), etc. In addition to the half sheet pan, which fits in most standard ovens, I use quarter sheet pans for recipes where a traditional 9-x-13-x-2-inch baking pan is too deep (see Note, page 306). Cheap thin sheets will warp in the heat, so go to a restaurant supply store and buy several commercial-weight pans. They'll last you a lifetime.

Kitchen twine is essential for tying meats, trussing birds, and tying up a sachet, a cheesecloth bundle of spices or herbs that will be removed from the pot before you serve the dish.

Last, think about *your kitchen environment.* How does your kitchen feel? I put skylights in the new kitchen at The French Laundry because I know the lighting affects the mood of the brigade. I'm not suggesting that you go out and renovate your kitchen, but let's acknowledge that the environment we cook in matters. It's far more pleasing to work in a clean, well-lighted kitchen than in a dark, cluttered one. And don't forget music—music in the kitchen is an essential ingredient!

be organized

Being organized—as we say in our kitchen, working clean—is a skill to develop. We call it *mise-en-place,* French for, literally, "put in place." The term can be very specific, referring to the ingredients needed to complete a recipe, measured out and ready to use, or it can be more general: are you organized, do you have everything you need to accomplish the task at hand?

Good organization is all about setting yourself up to succeed. It means getting rid of anything that would interfere with the process of making a recipe or preparing an entire meal. If you are in the middle of a preparation, you don't want to have to stop to find the proper pot or dig around

in the cupboard for an ingredient: that opens you up to distractions and errors. When I'm getting ready to make a dish, I make sure everything I need for the entire process is there.

When I peel an onion, I get rid of all the onion skin before I begin slicing it. In our kitchens, we keep bowls or pans out for trimmings; everything is contained. When the cooks peel carrots, they do it over parchment paper so that they can then crumple up the paper with all the peelings and discard it (or use the peelings for compost). I recommend you do the same—use a sheet of newspaper. It saves you time and keeps your work space clean. When you finish with a pot, wash it. (Notice that in the instructions for the mashed potatoes on page 2, one of the steps is to wash the pot you used for cooking the potatoes so that you can then finish them in the same pot.) Clean as you go to avoid clutter; clutter interferes with the cooking process. Things get in your way when you're not organized. Clear your path.

Be organized in your mind too. Think ahead, and think one step at a time. Take sixty seconds to write down a list of the tasks you need to accomplish so that you don't waste time trying to remember what you were going to do next. As you're finishing one task, think about what your next step will be. When preparing a meal, try to set yourself up from beginning to end so that the food that takes the longest is done when the shorter-cooking items are ready. I visualize each step of the way, almost as if I were taking a picture of it in my mind: how much oil should be in the pan as I sauté, how it ought to look, how my cutting board should look, how much liquid should be in the pot when I'm cooking potatoes, what the simmer looks like—anything, everything. Try to visualize what you expect to see as you move through a recipe. Then, if what you see differs from that expectation, try to understand why and adjust if possible.

Being organized is the first and most important part of cooking.

POULTRY

This book is not about restaurant food but rather about the kind of food we eat at home: family meals, fresh healthy food that nourishes body and soul. We're opening the book with the main courses—the birds, meats, and fish—because when we think about what we're going to make for dinner, we tend to think of the main course (the chicken, the steak, the salmon) that will be at the center of the meal and we build from there.

And we're leading off with chicken not just because it's so popular, but because it's somehow emotionally resonant for so many of us, and never more so than when it's fried with a great crunchy crust! I've yet to meet any nonvegetarian who doesn't love fried chicken—not just like it, *love* it. And yet how often do we prepare this adored dish at home? I hope you'll try our version.

I encourage you to buy chicken whole even if you don't intend to cook it whole. It's a way to become more intimate with the act of cooking, and it gives you the most flexibility. You can roast it whole, of course, and that is one of the most satisfying ways to cook a chicken. The overall experience of a whole bird—trussing it, roasting it, appreciating the aromas as it cooks, and the sight of it resting on the cutting board, and, of course, serving and eating it—is among the best in the kitchen.

If you don't want to roast it whole, you can separate the legs from the carcass and braise those for one meal, then use the breast for another. Or you can roast the whole breast on the bone, or take the breasts off the bone and flatten them into cutlets for quick grilling or sautéing. And when you buy a whole bird and cut it up, you'll have the carcass for making a stock—you could make the stock and braise the legs in it. All of these chicken dishes are so simple but so satisfying.

Chicken is also great for one-pot meals, each ingredient enhancing the others with only a single pan to clean afterward. The Crispy Braised Chicken Thighs with Olives, Lemon, and Fennel (page 30), for example, is not just a recipe for a single dish, but an example of a great general technique that can be taken in any number of flavor directions.

Good-quality duck is a little harder to find than good chicken, so it's even more important here to have a relationship with your butcher or grocer. Farmers' markets are a good source for birds beyond chicken, and there are good mail-order sources too (see Sources, page 346).

OVERLEAF: *Buttermilk Fried Chicken (page 16).* **OPPOSITE:** *Whole Roasted Chicken on a Bed of Root Vegetables (page 22).*

buttermilk fried chicken

Two 2½- to 3-pound chickens (see Note on Chicken Size)

Chicken Brine (page 339), cold

FOR DREDGING AND FRYING

Peanut or canola oil for deep-frying

1 quart buttermilk

Kosher salt and freshly ground black pepper

COATING

6 cups all-purpose flour

¼ cup garlic powder

¼ cup onion powder

1 tablespoon plus 1 teaspoon paprika

1 tablespoon plus 1 teaspoon cayenne

1 tablespoon plus 1 teaspoon kosher salt

1 teaspoon freshly ground black pepper

Ground fleur de sel or fine sea salt

Rosemary and thyme sprigs for garnish

If there's a better fried chicken, I haven't tasted it. First, and critically, the chicken is brined for 12 hours in a herb-lemon brine, which seasons the meat and helps it stay juicy. The flour is seasoned with garlic and onion powders, paprika, cayenne, salt, and pepper. The chicken is dredged in the seasoned flour, dipped in buttermilk, and then dredged again in the flour. The crust becomes almost feathered and is very crisp.

Fried chicken is a great American tradition that's fallen out of favor. A taste of this, and you will want it back in your weekly routine.

Cut each chicken into 10 pieces: 2 legs, 2 thighs, 4 breast quarters, and 2 wings (see pages 18–19). Pour the brine into a container large enough to hold the chicken pieces, add in the chicken, and refrigerate for 12 hours (no longer, or the chicken may become too salty).

Remove the chicken from the brine (discard the brine) and rinse under cold water, removing any herbs or spices sticking to the skin. Pat dry with paper towels, or let air-dry. Let rest at room temperature for 1½ hours, or until it comes to room temperature.

If you have two large pots (about 6 inches deep) and a lot of oil, you can cook the dark and white meat at the same time; if not, cook the dark meat first, then turn up the heat and cook the white meat. No matter what size pot you have, the oil should not come more than one-third of the way up the sides of the pot. Fill the pot with at least 2 inches of peanut oil and heat to 320°F. Set a cooling rack over a baking sheet. Line a second baking sheet with parchment paper.

Meanwhile, combine all the coating ingredients in a large bowl. Transfer half the coating to a second large bowl. Pour the buttermilk into a third bowl and season with salt and pepper. Set up a dipping station: the chicken pieces, one bowl of coating, the bowl of buttermilk, the second bowl of coating, and the parchment-lined baking sheet.

Just before frying, dip the chicken thighs into the first bowl of coating, turning to coat and patting off the excess; dip them into the buttermilk, allowing the excess to run back into the bowl; then dip them into the second bowl of coating. Transfer to the parchment-lined pan.

Carefully lower the thighs into the hot oil. Adjust the heat as necessary to return the oil to the proper temperature. Fry for 2 minutes, then carefully move the chicken pieces around in the oil and continue to fry, monitoring the oil temperature and turning the pieces as necessary for even cooking, for 11 to 12 minutes, until the chicken is a deep golden brown, cooked through, and very crisp. Meanwhile, coat the chicken drumsticks and transfer to the parchment-lined baking sheet.

Transfer the cooked thighs to the cooling rack skin-side-up and let rest while you fry the remaining chicken. (Putting the pieces skin-side-up will allow excess fat to drain, whereas leaving them skin-side-down could trap some of the fat.) Make sure that the oil is at the correct temperature, and cook the chicken drumsticks. When the drumsticks are done, lean them meat-side-up against the thighs to drain, then sprinkle the chicken with fine sea salt.

Turn up the heat and heat the oil to 340°F. Meanwhile, coat the chicken breasts and wings. Carefully lower the chicken breasts into the hot oil and fry for 7 minutes, or until golden brown, cooked through, and crisp. Transfer to the rack, sprinkle with salt, and turn skin side up. Cook the wings for 6 minutes, or until golden brown and cooked through. Transfer the wings to the rack and turn off the heat.

Arrange the chicken on a serving platter. Add the herb sprigs to the oil (which will still be hot) and let them cook and crisp for a few seconds, then arrange them over the chicken.

PHOTOGRAPH ON PAGE 13   SERVES 4 TO 6

NOTE ON CHICKEN SIZE *You may need to go to a farmers' market to get these small chickens. Grocery store chickens often run 3 to 4 pounds. They can, of course, be used in this recipe but if chickens in the 2½- to 3-pound range are available to you, they're worth seeking out. They're a little easier to cook properly at the temperatures we recommend here and, most important, pieces this size result in the optimal meat-to-crust proportion, which is such an important part of the pleasure of fried chicken.*

NOTE *We let the chicken rest for 7 to 10 minutes after it comes out of the fryer so that it has a chance to cool down. If the chicken has rested for longer than 10 minutes, put the tray of chicken in a 400°F oven for a minute or two to ensure that the crust is crisp and the chicken is hot.*

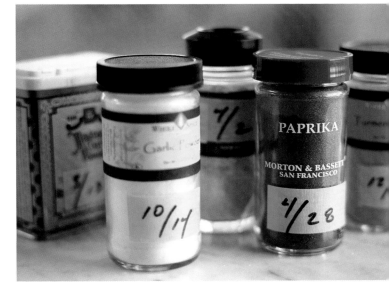

I am a huge proponent of dating products. Spice jars are an example. Unless you go through them very quickly, you're not likely to remember how old they are. Spices are volatile—their power and effectiveness diminish with age. If they're a year old, they won't taste nearly as good as fresh ones.

Find a store that allows you to purchase fresh spices in small quantities. Smell and taste them so you'll be able to recognize, in their cooking, what freshness means. It provides a standard with which to evaluate all the spices that you use.

10 PIECE CUT

Put the chicken breast-side-down on the work surface with the neck facing you. Cut off any excess skin from the neck. Cut out and remove the wishbone.

Using poultry shears, cut down each side of the backbone to remove it; the backbone can be reserved for making stock.

Turn the chicken over. Locate the joint that connects each thigh to the chicken, and cut through the joint with a knife to separate the leg from the bird.

Turn the chicken over again and remove the pointed breastplate (keel bone). Make a shallow cut on each side of the tip of the bone and then run your fingers alongside and under the bone to remove it. Cut through the center of the breast to separate it into 2 pieces.

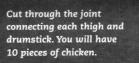

Cut through the joint connecting each thigh and drumstick. You will have 10 pieces of chicken.

Cut off the wings at the joint that attaches them to the breast.

Cut each breast piece crosswise in half.

pan-roasted chicken with sweet sausage and peppers

Two 2½- to 3-pound chickens (see Note)

Chicken Brine (page 339), cold

Kosher salt and freshly ground black pepper

Canola oil

3 sweet Italian sausages (see Sources, page 346)

Peperonata Rustica (page 208)

Extra virgin olive oil

Fleur de sel

About ¼ cup flat-leaf parsley leaves

Here a chicken is cut into pieces, seasoned, and cooked with sausages, then added to a stew of peppers that's seasoned and finished in the oven. This is a wonderfully satisfying dish with the robust flavors of the peppers and sausage.

Cut the chickens into 8 pieces each: 2 legs, 2 thighs, 2 breast halves, and 2 wings (see opposite).

Pour the brine into a container large enough to hold the chicken, add the chicken, and refrigerate for 12 hours (no longer, or the chicken may become too salty).

Preheat the oven to 350°F.

Remove the chicken from the brine (discard the brine) and rinse under cold water, removing any herbs or spices sticking to the skin.

Pat dry with paper towels, or let air-dry. Season the thighs and drumsticks with salt and pepper.

Heat some canola oil in a large ovenproof sauté pan or Dutch oven over medium heat until hot. Add the chicken thighs and drumsticks, skin side down, and cook for 3 minutes. Add the sausage and cook until the chicken is golden and the sausage is browned and crisp, 10 to 12 minutes (it won't be fully cooked); once the chicken is browned, turn the pieces over and sear the other side for 1 minute. Transfer the individual pieces and the sausages to a plate as they are ready.

Season the chicken wings and breasts with salt and pepper, place skin-side-down in the sauté pan, and cook until the skin is crisp and golden and the chicken is almost cooked through, about 8 minutes. Transfer to a plate.

Drain any remaining oil from the pan and return to the heat. Add the peperonata to the pan, bring to a simmer, and add the chicken, tucking it into the peppers. Cut the sausages in half and nestle them in the pan. Transfer to the oven and cook until the chicken is cooked through, about 5 minutes.

Drizzle the chicken with olive oil, sprinkle with fleur de sel, and top with the parsley leaves. Serve directly from the pan.   **SERVES 6**

NOTE *We find these smaller chickens more tender and flavorful, but grocery store chickens are usually larger. For small chickens, you may need to go to a farmers' market.*

8 PIECE CUT

Put the chicken breast-side-down on the work surface. Locate the joint that connects the thigh to the chicken, and cut through the joint to separate the leg from the bird.

Turn the chicken over and make a shallow lengthwise cut, just reaching the bone, down the center of the breast.

Using the knife and your fingers, remove the breast meat from the carcass.

You will have 8 pieces of chicken.

whole roasted chicken on a bed of root vegetables

One 4- to 4½-pound chicken

Kosher salt and freshly ground black pepper

6 garlic cloves, smashed and peeled

6 thyme sprigs

2 large leeks

3 tennis-ball-sized rutabagas

2 tennis-ball-sized turnips

4 medium carrots, peeled, trimmed, and cut in half

1 small yellow onion, trimmed, leaving root end intact,
   and cut into quarters

8 small (golf-ball-sized) red-skinned potatoes

⅓ cup canola oil

4 tablespoons (2 ounces) unsalted butter, at room temperature

This is a perfect one-pot meal, a great fall or winter dish I've made countless times and one of my favorite meals to prepare. Efficient, economical, and delicious, it serves four people (or two people with great leftovers), it pretty much cooks on its own, and you've got only one pan to clean up. The root vegetables make a bed for the chicken, and the rendering fat and juices from the chicken flavor the vegetables. If you have a big cast-iron skillet, use that.

It's important to let the chicken stand at room temperature for about 1½ hours before you roast it. We also often leave it uncovered in the refrigerator for a day or two, which dries the skin and thus helps it to become crisp during the roasting.

Remove the chicken from the refrigerator and let stand at room temperature for 1½ to 2 hours, or until it comes to room temperature.

Preheat the oven to 475°F.

Remove the neck and innards if they are still in the cavity of the chicken. Using a paring knife, cut out the wishbone from the chicken. (This will make it easier to carve the chicken.) Generously season the cavity of the chicken with salt and pepper, add 3 of the garlic cloves and 5 sprigs of thyme, and massage the inside of the bird to infuse it with the flavors. Truss the chicken (see opposite).

Cut off the dark green leaves from the top of the leeks. Trim off and discard any darkened outer layers. Trim the root ends, cutting around them on a 45-degree angle. Slit the leeks lengthwise almost in half, starting ½ inch above the root ends. Rinse the leeks well under warm water.

Cut off both ends of the rutabagas. Stand the rutabagas on end and cut away the skin, working from top to bottom and removing any tough outer layers. Cut into ¾-inch wedges. Repeat with the turnips, cutting the wedges to match the size of the rutabagas.

Combine all the vegetables and the remaining garlic cloves and thyme sprig in a large bowl. Toss with ¼ cup of the oil and season with salt and pepper. Spread the vegetables in a large cast-iron skillet or a roasting pan.

Rub the remaining oil all over the chicken. Season generously with salt and pepper.

Make a nest in the center of the vegetables and nestle the chicken in it. Cut the butter into 4 or 5 pieces and place over the chicken breast.

Put the chicken in the oven and roast for 25 minutes. Reduce the heat to 400°F and roast for an additional 45 minutes, or until the temperature registers 160°F in the meatiest portions of the bird—the thighs, and under the breast where the thigh meets the breast—and the juices run clear. If necessary, return the bird to the oven for more roasting; check it every 5 minutes.

Transfer the chicken to a carving board and let rest for 20 minutes.

Just before serving, set the pan of vegetables over medium heat and reheat the vegetables, turning them and glazing them with the pan juices.

Cut the chicken into serving pieces, arrange over the vegetables, and serve.

PHOTOGRAPH ON PAGE 15

SERVES 4

TRUSSING A CHICKEN

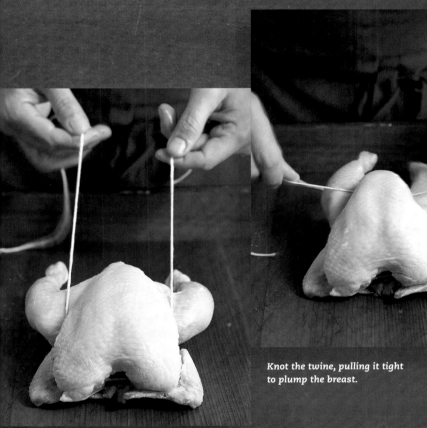

Place the chicken with the legs toward you. Tuck the wing tips under the bird. Cut a piece of kitchen twine about 3 feet long and center it under the neck end of the breast. Pull the twine up over the breast toward you.

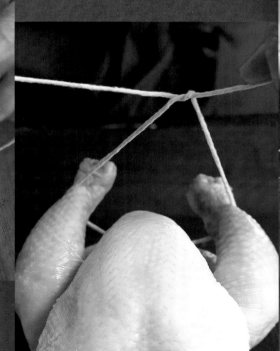

Knot the twine, pulling it tight to plump the breast.

Bring the ends of the twine around the ends of the drumsticks and straight up.

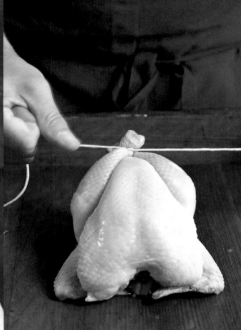

Tie as before to pull the ends of the drumsticks together and form a compact bird. Then tie again to secure the knot.

chicken potpie

Basic Pie Crust (page 338), chilled

FILLING

1 cup ½-inch pieces red-skinned potatoes

1¼ cups ½-inch pieces carrots (cut on the diagonal)

12 white pearl onions

3 bay leaves

3 thyme sprigs

24 black peppercorns

1¼ cups ½-inch pieces celery (cut on the diagonal)

2 cups shredded cooked chicken

BÉCHAMEL

3 tablespoons (1½ ounces) unsalted butter

3 tablespoons all-purpose flour

3 cups whole milk

1 teaspoon kosher salt, or to taste

½ teaspoon freshly ground black pepper, or to taste

1 tablespoon finely chopped flat-leaf parsley

½ teaspoon finely chopped thyme

Pinch of cayenne

1 egg, beaten

Chicken potpie, a relative of the English meat pies and French pâtes en croute, is to me one of those iconic American dishes. I grew up eating Swanson's frozen potpies—that kind of food is how a big family with a working mom survived during the week in the 1960s and '70s. While it may have reached icon status due to the ingenious convenience food industry, its origins as a wonderful dish are why I value it now. I wanted to include it here because of its powerful association with home meals, and to show how good it can be when made at home.

Roll out the dough, place one piece in a 9- or 10-inch pie plate and the second on a baking sheet, and refrigerate as directed on page 338.

Put the potatoes, carrots, and onions in separate small saucepans with water to cover and add 1 bay leaf, 1 thyme sprig, and 8 peppercorns to each pan. Bring to a simmer over medium-high heat and simmer until just tender, 8 to 10 minutes.

Drain the vegetables, discard the bay, thyme, and peppercorns, and spread on a baking sheet. Cut the onions in half.

Bring a large pot of salted water to a boil. Fill a medium bowl with ice water. Blanch the celery until just crisp-tender, 1 to 1½ minutes. Drain, transfer to the ice bath, and chill just until cold. Drain and add to the baking sheet with the other vegetables.

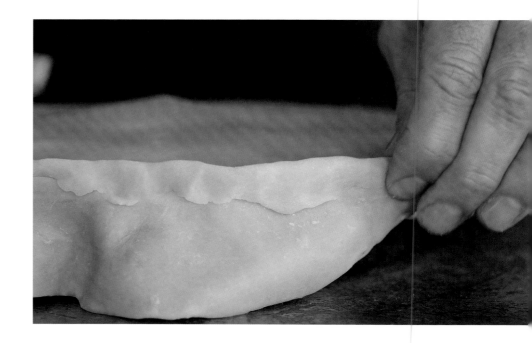

Melt the butter in a medium saucepan over medium heat. Whisk in the flour and cook for 2 to 3 minutes; adjust the heat as needed so that the mixture does not brown. Whisk in the milk, lower the heat to keep the béchamel at a gentle simmer (use a diffuser, such as a Flame Tamer, if necessary), and cook, whisking often, until the sauce has thickened and reduced to about 2 cups, 30 to 40 minutes; move the whisk over the bottom and into the corners of the pan to be sure the béchamel doesn't burn.

Position the oven racks in the lower third and center of the oven and preheat the oven to 375°F.

Strain the béchamel through a fine-mesh conical strainer into a spouted measuring cup. Season with salt, pepper, parsley, thyme, and cayenne.

Remove both doughs from the refrigerator.

Scatter the vegetables and chicken into the pie shell. Pour the béchamel over them. At this point, if the top crust is too hard to shape, let it rest at room temperature for a few minutes. Moisten the rim of pie shell with some of the beaten egg. Cover the filling with the top crust and press the edges of the dough together to seal. Trim away the excess dough that overhangs the rim. Brush the top crust with the egg. Cut a small vent in the center of the dough with a small cutter or the tip of a paring knife to allow steam to escape.

Bake on the lower oven rack until the crust is a rich golden brown, 50 minutes to 1 hour. If necessary, move the pie to the center rack during the last 10 minutes of baking to brown the crust. Transfer to a cooling rack and let rest for 10 minutes.

Cut the potpie into 6 wedges and serve warm. **SERVES 6**

roast poussins or cornish hens

Six 1¼-pound poussins or Cornish game hens

GREMOLATA BUTTER

1 teaspoon black peppercorns

Finely grated zest of 2 lemons

2 large garlic cloves, grated (with a Microplane grater) or minced

12 tablespoons (1½ sticks; 6 ounces) unsalted butter, at room temperature

2 tablespoons fresh lemon juice

2 tablespoons finely chopped flat-leaf parsley

1 teaspoon kosher salt

Kosher salt and freshly ground black pepper

Canola oil

6 garlic cloves, smashed, skin left on

1 bunch thyme

Fleur de sel

We love the young chickens known as poussins for their tenderness. They're usually less than a month old and weigh about a pound. Of course, you can use Cornish game hens, which are older and a little larger; even an ordinary chicken is delicious prepared with this method. The birds can be stuffed with the gremolata butter up to 2 days ahead and refrigerated; bring to room temperature before proceeding.

Remove the poussins or hens from the refrigerator and set aside while you make the butter.

Using the pestle, grind the peppercorns in a mortar (or put them in a heavy-duty plastic bag and crush with a meat pounder or heavy pan). Add the lemon zest and garlic and mix and mash to a paste. Put the butter in a medium bowl and mix in the pepper mixture, followed by the lemon juice. Stir in the parsley and salt.

Remove the neck and innards if they are still in the cavities of the poussins or game hens, and discard. Rinse the inside of the birds and dry well with paper towels. Season the inside of the birds with salt and pepper. Cut out the wishbones. Leave any fat or skin at the neck attached, and trim any other excess fat.

Starting at the cavity end of each bird, carefully run your fingers between the skin and flesh of the breasts and then the thighs to loosen the skin. Spread about ½ tablespoon of the butter under the skin of each thigh and spread the remaining 1 tablespoon of butter under the skin on each side of the breast.

Truss the birds (see page 23). Let stand at room temperature for 30 minutes, or until they come to room temperature.

Preheat the oven to 450°F.

Brush the birds with canola oil and season with salt. Place the birds on their backs in a roasting pan that will hold the birds in a single layer. Scatter the garlic and thyme evenly around them.

Transfer to the oven and roast for 25 to 30 minutes; the temperature should register 160°F in the meatiest portions of the bird (the thighs and under the breast where the thigh meets the breast), and the juices should run clear. If necessary, baste the birds, return to the oven, and roast; check every 5 minutes.

Set a cooling rack over a baking sheet. Transfer the birds, along with the garlic and thyme to the rack. Baste the birds with the pan juices, and let rest for 15 minutes.

Serve the birds whole, or cut into halves or quarters. Arrange on a serving platter, garnish with the thyme and garlic, and sprinkle with fleur de sel.

SERVES 6

NOTE *The gremolata butter is not only great for spreading under the skin of chicken but is also a terrific all-purpose technique. Think of a compound butter like this as a simple sauce: parsley and lemon butter melting on hot grilled steak or steamed asparagus is delicious. You might make a citrus butter for poached salmon, or a Parmesan butter for finishing an omelet.*

sautéed chicken breasts with tarragon

1 teaspoon sweet paprika

1 teaspoon Yellow Curry Powder (page 336) or Madras curry powder

6 large (about 6 ounces each) or 12 small (about 3 ounces each) boneless, skinless chicken breasts

Kosher salt

Canola oil

3 tablespoons (1½ ounces) unsalted butter

1 tablespoon minced shallot

¼ cup dry white wine, such as Sauvignon Blanc

1 cup Chicken Stock (page 339)

1 tablespoon coarsely chopped tarragon, plus 1 tablespoon tarragon leaves

Freshly ground black pepper

A chicken breast—flattened, seasoned, sautéed, and served with a simple pan sauce—can be delicious and very easy to prepare. The curry brings a lot of flavor to the chicken, and the tarragon butter sauce blends beautifully with that flavor. The Summer Vegetable Gratin (page 202), Puree of Garlic Potatoes (page 223), and Romano Beans with Mint (page 203) are all excellent accompaniments.

This basic method works with other lean, tender cuts of meat as well, such as pork loin or veal.

Mix together the paprika and curry in a small bowl. Season the chicken breasts on both sides with the mixture. Cover and refrigerate for 2 hours.

Lay 2 pieces of chicken on a large piece of plastic wrap, cover with a second piece of plastic wrap, and, using a meat pounder, pound to about ¼ inch thick. Transfer to a plate and repeat with the remaining chicken. (The chicken can be wrapped and refrigerated for up to 12 hours.)

Preheat the oven to 200°F. Set a cooling rack over a baking sheet.

Season the chicken on both sides with salt. Heat some canola oil in a large frying pan over medium-high heat. Working in batches, without crowding, add the chicken to the pan, presentation (smooth) side down, and cook, adjusting the heat if necessary, until the bottom is golden brown, 1 to 1½ minutes. Turn to the second side and cook until golden, another 1 to 1½ minutes. Transfer to the rack and keep warm in the oven. Add oil to the pan as needed as you cook the remaining chicken.

Pour any remaining oil from the pan and wipe out any burned bits. Melt 1 tablespoon of the butter over medium-high heat. Add the shallot to the pan, reduce the heat to medium, and cook for 30 seconds, swirling the pan to coat the shallot with the butter. Pour in the wine, increase the heat to medium-high, and cook until the wine has reduced by half, about 1 minute. Add the chicken stock, bring to a boil, and cook until slightly reduced and thickened, 1 to 2 minutes. Stir in the chopped tarragon, the remaining 2 tablespoons butter, and any juices that have accumulated on the baking sheet and swirl to melt the butter. Season to taste with salt and pepper.

Arrange the chicken on a platter, pour the sauce over it, and garnish with the tarragon leaves.

SERVES 6

chicken mar i muntanya

with shrimp, mussels, green beans, piquillo peppers, and chorizo

One 4-pound chicken

½ recipe Chicken Brine (page 339), cold

12 extra-large shrimp (12–15 count), shells on

Kosher salt and freshly ground black pepper

Piment d'Espelette (see page 208)

Canola oil

Saffron Rice (page 220), warm

3 piquillo peppers (see Lightbulb Moment, page 183), cut lengthwise into
    ¼-inch-wide strips

1 cup thin green beans (haricots verts), blanched (see page 147)

½ cup Chicken Stock (page 339), warm

1 Spanish chorizo sausage (about 4 ounces), cut into ¼-inch-thick slices

¼ cup dry white wine, such as Sauvignon Blanc

18 small mussels, preferably Bouchot or PEI (Prince Edward Island)

Flat-leaf parsley leaves

Fleur de sel

We like to combine chicken with big ingredients, here in a Spanish surf-and-turf preparation—the words for "sea" and "mountain" are used in the recipe title in fact—with mussels (try to use smaller mussels, as the larger ones can overpower the stew with their flavor), shrimp, and Spanish chorizo, a spicy smoked sausage.

Cut the chicken into 10 pieces (see pages 18–19).

Pour the brine into a container large enough to hold the chicken, add the chicken, and refrigerate for about 12 hours (no longer, or the chicken may become too salty).

Preheat the oven to 400°F.

Remove the chicken from the brine and rinse under cold water, removing any herbs or spices sticking to the skin. Pat dry with paper towels, or let air-dry. Set aside.

Without removing the shells, using a small pair of scissors or a paring knife, make a shallow cut down the back of each shrimp from head to tail. Gently open up the shrimp and, with your fingers or the paring knife, remove the vein. Rinse the shrimp under cold water.

Combine 4 cups water and ½ cup plus 2 tablespoons salt in a medium bowl and stir to dissolve the salt. Add the shrimp to the brine and let stand at room temperature for 10 minutes. Remove from the brine, rinse, and drain on paper towels.

Season the chicken with salt, pepper, and a sprinkling of Espelette. Heat some canola oil in a large frying pan over medium-high heat. Add the dark meat skin-side-down, lower the heat to medium-low, and cook until the skin is a rich golden brown and crisp, about 8 minutes. (If you turn the chicken too early, more moisture will be released from the meat and you will not get the crisp caramelized surface you are looking for.) Turn the pieces and brown for another 6 minutes, or until golden brown on the second side. Remove from the heat, transfer the dark meat to a plate, and set aside.

Return the pan to medium-high heat and add more oil as needed. Add the breasts skin-side-down and cook until the skin is crisp and golden brown, about 8 minutes. Turn the chicken and cook for about 5 minutes, until almost cooked through. Remove from the heat.

Spread the rice in the bottom of a large heatproof serving dish or baking dish. Arrange half the piquillos and half the green beans over the rice. Tuck the dark meat and the breasts into the rice, pour the stock over the ingredients, and put the dish in the oven.

Heat some oil over medium heat in a frying pan large enough to hold the mussels in one layer. Add the chorizo and cook until browned and crisp on the edges, 2 to 3 minutes. Transfer the chorizo to a plate and pour off the excess fat, leaving just a coating in the pan. Add the shrimp to the pan and sauté until just cooked through, 1½ to 2 minutes per side. Transfer the shrimp to a plate.

Add the wine to the pan, bring to a boil, and boil for 30 seconds. Add the mussels, cover the pan, and cook until the mussels have opened, 2 to 3 minutes. Remove from the heat.

When the mussels are finished, take the baking dish out of the oven. Arrange the chorizo, shrimp, and mussels in the dish; set aside in a warm spot.

Return the frying pan to the heat, add the remaining peppers and green beans, and heat through. Arrange them over the chicken and shellfish, garnish with parsley leaves, and sprinkle with fleur de sel.

SERVES 6

crispy braised chicken thighs

with olives, lemon, and fennel

3 large fennel bulbs

12 chicken thighs

Kosher salt

Canola oil

1 cup coarsely chopped onion

1 tablespoon finely chopped garlic

¼ cup dry white wine, such as Sauvignon Blanc

1 cup Ascolane or other large green olives, such as Cerignola

¼ teaspoon red pepper flakes

4 fresh or 2 dried bay leaves

4 strips lemon zest—removed with a vegetable peeler

8 thyme sprigs

1 cup Chicken Stock (page 339)

About ¼ cup flat-leaf parsley leaves

Olives, here big fleshy green Ascolanes from Italy, and fennel are an extraordinary pairing with chicken. In this one-pot dish, we use only the thighs, the most flavorful part of the chicken. The seared chicken is braised in chicken stock on a bed of fennel, onion, and garlic, with strips of lemon zest. The stock picks up the lemon and fennel flavors and becomes concentrated and rich. Here the flavors are Mediterranean, but the technique itself can be taken in any number of seasoning directions.

Cut off the fennel stalks. Trim the bottom of the bulbs and peel back the layers until you reach the core; reserve the core for another use. Discard any bruised layers, and cut the fennel into 2-by-½-inch batons. You need 3 cups fennel for this recipe; reserve any remaining fennel for another use.

Preheat the oven to 375°F. Set a cooling rack on a baking sheet.

Season the chicken thighs on both sides with salt. Heat some canola oil in a large ovenproof sauté pan or roasting pan that will hold all the thighs in one layer over medium-high heat. Add the thighs skin-side-down and brown on the skin side, about 4 minutes. Turn the thighs over and cook for about 1 minute to sear the meat. Transfer to the cooling rack.

Reduce the heat to medium-low, add the onion to the pan, and cook for 1½ minutes. Add the garlic and cook for 1 minute. Cook, stirring often, until the onion is translucent, about 5 minutes. Stir in the fennel, turn the heat up to medium, and cook, stirring often, until the fennel is crisp-tender, about 10 minutes.

Pour in the wine and simmer for about 2 minutes to burn off the alcohol. Stir in the olives, red pepper flakes, bay leaves, lemon zest, and thyme, then pour in the chicken stock. Increase the heat, bring the liquid to a simmer, and cook until the fennel is tender, about 1 minute.

Taste the stock and season with salt as needed. Return the chicken to the pan skin-side-up, in a single layer. When the liquid returns to a simmer, transfer to the oven and cook for about 20 minutes, until the chicken is cooked through.

Turn on the broiler, and put the pan under the broiler for a minute or two to crisp and brown the chicken skin. Remove from the oven, and transfer to a serving platter. Garnish with the parsley leaves. SERVES 6

quail with lemon and herbs

Quail makes a wonderful first course, one per person. It can be grilled or pan-seared (methods for both follow). This mild game bird takes well to marinades, and we offer two marinades here. This one is a simple lemon and herb marinade. Serve the quail with Caramelized Savoy Cabbage (page 197), Rainbow Chard with Raisins, Pine Nuts, and Serrano Ham (page 205), Mushroom Conserva (page 260), or Sweet Potato Chips (page 232).

MARINADE

⅓ cup thinly sliced scallions

1 teaspoon finely minced rosemary

1 tablespoon minced thyme

⅓ cup chopped flat-leaf parsley

2 bay leaves

4 small garlic cloves, smashed and peeled

⅓ cup fresh lemon juice

¾ cup olive oil

Freshly ground black pepper

6 semiboneless quail (see Sources, page 346)

Canola oil

Fleur de sel

Combine all the marinade ingredients in a bowl. Blot any moisture from the quail and put them in a large resealable bag. Pour in the marinade and seal, removing as much air as possible from the bag. Refrigerate for 6 hours.

Remove the quail from the marinade and drain on paper towels. Remove any marinade ingredients clinging to the quail, since they could burn as the quail cooks. Pour about ¼ inch canola oil into a shallow bowl.

TO COOK THE QUAIL ON THE GRILL: Preheat a grill to medium heat. (See Grilling Basics, page 345, and Lightbulb Moment, page 51.)

Dip the quail in the oil, place breast-side-down on the grill, and cook until there are golden brown grill marks on the breast and the skin is crisp, about 3 minutes. Turn the quail over and cook on the second side for about 2 minutes, until cooked through. Sprinkle with fleur de sel.

TO COOK THE QUAIL IN A SKILLET: Heat a large heavy skillet, preferably cast iron, over medium heat until very hot. Dip the quail in the oil, place breast-side-down in the skillet, and cook for 2 to 3 minutes, adjusting the heat as necessary to brown and crisp the skin. Turn and brown the second side, 1 to 2 minutes, until cooked through. Sprinkle with fleur de sel. **SERVES 6 AS AN APPETIZER**

pomegranate-glazed quail

The marinade in this quail recipe is based on chile peppers and pomegranate "molasses" (reduced pomegranate juice), which gives the skin a nice glaze. Again, the birds can be either grilled or pan-seared. For serving suggestions, see the headnote at the left.

MARINADE

½ cup pomegranate juice

½ cup pomegranate molasses (see Sources, page 346)

2 tablespoons chopped serrano chile, including seeds

4 small garlic cloves, crushed and peeled

¼ cup chopped shallots

2 tablespoons chopped sage

4 strips lemon zest—removed with a vegetable peeler

6 semiboneless quail (see Sources, page 346)

Canola oil

continued

Combine all the marinade ingredients in a bowl. Blot any moisture from the quail and put them in a large resealable bag. Pour in the marinade and seal, removing as much air as possible from the bag. Refrigerate for 6 hours.

Remove the quail from the marinade and drain on paper towels. Pour the marinade into a small saucepan, bring to a simmer over medium heat, and simmer until reduced to a glaze. Strain through a fine-mesh basket strainer into a bowl. If grilling the quail, reserve a couple of tablespoons of the glaze for brushing the birds, and pour the rest into a small serving bowl.

Remove any marinade ingredients clinging to the quail, since they could burn as the quail cooks. Pour about ¼ inch of canola oil into a shallow bowl.

TO COOK THE QUAIL ON THE GRILL: Preheat a grill to medium heat.

Dip the quail in the oil, turning to coat, place breast-side-down on the grill, and cook until there are golden brown grill marks on the breasts and the skin is crisp, about 3 minutes. Brush the top sides of the quail with the glaze, turn the quail over, and cook on the second side for about 2 minutes, until cooked through; brush again with the glaze as the quail cook.

TO COOK THE QUAIL IN A SKILLET: Heat a large heavy skillet, preferably cast iron, over medium heat until very hot. Dip the quail in the oil, place breast-side-down in the skillet, and cook for 2 to 3 minutes, adjusting the heat as necessary to brown and crisp the skin. Turn and brown on the second side, 1 to 2 minutes, until cooked through.

Serve the quail with the glaze on the side for dipping.

SERVES 6 AS AN APPETIZER

duck confit

HERB SALT

½ cup kosher salt

2 tablespoons light brown sugar

2 bay leaves, broken into pieces

2 tablespoons chopped thyme

¼ cup packed flat-leaf parsley leaves

1 teaspoon black peppercorns

Eight 8-ounce whole Pekin (Long Island) duck legs
  (see Sources, page 346)

6 to 8 cups rendered duck fat (see Sources, page 346), melted

Confit is hard to resist straight out of the oven, but it's even better cooled in its fat and refrigerated for up to 6 months, then reheated before serving. We like to serve it with a sweet condiment such as Red Onion–Cranberry Marmalade (page 248) or Tangerine-Kumquat Marmalade (page 249), or a sweet vegetable, such as English peas or sugar snap peas. We use it for the Frisée and Duck Confit Salad (page 167), and it's also excellent with Sautéed Red and Green Cabbage (page 198).

The duck legs are cured with an herbed salt, which contains a little brown sugar to balance the salt. This cure, along with the cooking and storing of the duck submerged in fat (protected from the harmful effects of oxygen and light), is what allows you to store it for so long.

Combine the salt, sugar, bay leaves, thyme, parsley, and peppercorns in a small food processor and process until well combined. Set aside.

Pull away and discard any excess fat from the duck legs. With scissors, trim the excess skin near the bottom of the legs and around the edges, leaving at least a ¼-inch overhang of skin.

It is important to know the weight of the duck legs when salting them, so that you do not oversalt them; the correct ratio is 2 tablespoons of herb salt to 1 pound of duck legs. Rub about 1 tablespoon herb salt over each leg, rubbing a little extra on the thicker parts and around the joint. Put the legs flesh side up in a single layer in a baking dish that holds them comfortably (use two if necessary), cover with plastic wrap, and refrigerate for 24 hours.

Position an oven rack in the center of the oven, put an oven thermometer on the rack, and preheat the oven to 190°F (it is important to check the heat from time to time while the legs cook to be certain that the oven maintains the proper temperature).

Rinse the legs well under cold water and dry thoroughly with paper towels. Layer the duck legs (no more than 2 deep) in a 9- to 10-inch heavy ovenproof pot with a lid. Add enough melted duck fat to cover the legs and heat over medium heat just until the fat is warm.

Cover the pot, transfer to the oven, and cook for 8 to 10 hours. Check a duck leg by carefully lifting it from the fat and piercing it with a paring knife: the meat should be meltingly tender. If necessary, return the duck to the oven for up to 2 hours longer, checking the legs frequently (if they cook for too long, they may fall apart when they are sautéed). Remove from the oven and let the duck cool in the fat.

Gently lift the legs from the fat and place in a storage container (see Note). Strain the fat over the legs (but not the juices, which will have sunk to the bottom). They should be completely submerged in fat; if necessary, transfer them to a smaller container. Cover and refrigerate for up to 2 weeks. To store for up to 6 months, see Note.

When you are ready to serve the duck legs, remove the container from the refrigerator and allow it to sit at room temperature for an hour or two to soften the fat enough to remove the legs without breaking them apart, or microwave them just long enough to soften the fat.

Preheat the oven to 350°F. Set a cooling rack over a baking sheet.

Pour some duck fat into each of two large frying pans and heat over high heat until very hot. (If you have only one large skillet, brown the legs in 2 batches.) Arrange 3 legs in each pan, skin-side-down, and cook, without moving them, for 1 minute. Reduce the heat to medium and cook until the skin is richly browned, about 3 minutes.

Carefully transfer the duck legs, skin-side-up, to the cooling rack and put in the oven to heat through, about 10 minutes.

SERVES 6 AS AN APPETIZER OR LIGHT MAIN COURSE

NOTE ON STORING DUCK CONFIT *You can keep the confit for months if you remove all the meat juices from the fat. After cooking, transfer the legs to a container and refrigerate. Refrigerate the fat separately; as it solidifies, the meat juices will settle to the bottom of the container, where they will jell. When the fat has solidified, carefully spoon it off, without disturbing the jell; the jell can be frozen and added to soups. Melt the fat and pour it through a strainer over the duck.*

DUCK CONFIT WITH SAUTÉED RED AND GREEN CABBAGE
If you'd like to serve the cabbage on page 197 with the duck, sauté the duck legs as directed and remove them from the pans; leave a coating of fat in one pan to cook the cabbage. Prepare the cabbage while the duck heats through in the oven. Arrange the cabbage on a serving platter and top with the duck legs. If desired, spoon about ⅓ cup Tangerine-Kumquat Marmalade (page 249), warmed, over the legs.

pan-roasted duck breasts

Six 10- to 12-ounce Pekin (Long Island) duck breasts
   (see Sources, page 346), preferably with tenderloins still attached
Kosher salt and freshly ground black pepper
Grated nutmeg
1 orange
Balsamic vinegar
6 thyme sprigs
6 bay leaves
Canola oil
Gray salt or other coarse sea salt

One of the keys to an excellent duck breast is crisping the skin properly, resulting in great texture and flavor. The first step is to score the skin and season it in advance, preferably 12 hours before cooking it. In this dish, the breasts get what amounts to a cure, rich with spices, aromatics, and citrus. The second step is cooking the breasts very slowly, over medium heat, skin side down, to render out the fat, pouring off the fat as they cook. When the skin is crisp, after 20 to 25 minutes, it's simply a matter of briefly cooking the flesh side so that the meat is medium-rare. For a fall or winter dish, you might try this with Butter-Braised Radishes, Kohlrabi, and Brussels Sprouts (page 196), or with Scallion Potato Cakes (page 230). Other great side dish choices include Leek Bread Pudding (page 211).

Line a baking sheet with parchment paper. Using a sharp knife, cut a ¼-inch crosshatch pattern in the skin of each breast, being careful not to pierce the meat. (Do this while the duck is cold, since it's difficult to make such precise cuts at room temperature.) Turn the duck breasts skin-side-down on the baking sheet. If the tenderloins, the smaller piece of meat that runs along the bottom of the breast, are still attached, leave them on the breasts. Use a paring knife to remove the small white tendon that runs through each tenderloin. You will see a vein that runs the length of each breast. Run your finger down the length of each vein, and if any blood comes out, wipe it away with a paper towel.

Season the flesh side of each breast with salt and pepper and a grating of nutmeg. Using a Microplane or other grater, grate a little orange zest over each breast. Sprinkle a few drops of vinegar over the meat. Lay a sprig of thyme running lengthwise down the center of each breast and cover with a bay leaf. Turn over and season each breast with a generous pinch of salt and a grating of nutmeg. Refrigerate, uncovered, for at least 1 hour, or up to 12 hours.

Preheat the oven to 400°F.

Set a cooling rack over a baking sheet. Set a metal bowl or other container near the stove. With a paper towel, blot any moisture from the duck breasts. Season both sides of each breast with a pinch of salt.

Pour some canola oil into each of two large ovenproof frying pans over medium-low heat. (If you have only one large pan, cook the duck in 2 batches.) Add the duck skin-side-down. Move the duck breasts every few minutes to help them brown evenly. As the fat is rendered, carefully remove the excess (leaving about ⅛ inch) from each frying pan: move the pan away from the heat when you remove the fat, since if any fat hits the flame, it will cause a flare-up; tilt the pan, remove the fat with a large kitchen spoon, and transfer it to the metal bowl. Cook the duck for a total of 20 to 25 minutes, until the skin is an even rich brown and very crisp; the internal temperature of the breasts should be about 115°F. Flip each breast and just "kiss" the meat side for about 30 seconds.

Put the duck skin-side-down in the oven and cook for about 5 minutes. The internal temperature should be 125°F for a rosy medium-rare. (If you cooked the duck in batches, the first batch may take up to 8 to 10 minutes to reheat.)

Put the duck breasts skin-side-down on the cooling rack and let rest for 5 to 10 minutes before slicing. Cut each piece of duck lengthwise into 3 slices. Sprinkle the meat with gray salt and pepper.   **SERVES 6**

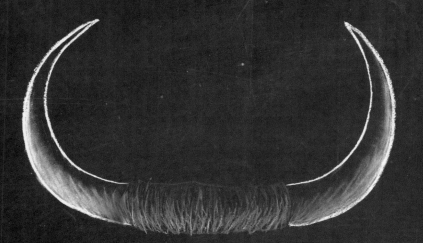

MEATS

Although there's nothing better than a well-aged Prime sirloin steak, the humble hamburger, when it's got the optimal ratio of fat to lean meat, can be extraordinary. And I even have fond memories of the Swiss steak my mom made me with the beef that had been sent through the automatic tenderizer. She'd sear it, heat a can of cream of mushroom soup to pour over it, and serve it with rice. It was delicious.

The main thing I look for when I buy beef is the fat—I want plenty of good marbling. A pork chop for pan-frying or a tough short rib for braising should also have a good proportion of fat. Though I applaud the smaller farmers who are raising livestock responsibly, I still prefer the flavor and the quality of fat in beef from steers finished on grain rather than from those fed exclusively on grass.

How you cook meat is determined primarily by the cut. If it comes from a lesser-used muscle, such as the loin or tenderloin, we cook it quickly, typically in a very hot pan or on a hot grill, to develop a flavorful sear. If it comes from one of the heavily worked muscles, from the shank or shoulders, which have developed a lot of connective tissue, it will need to be tenderized by long, gentle cooking. Even these cuts benefit from a good initial sear. I sear meat in plenty of oil. Don't worry about using too much—you're using it only to brown the meat (see page 40).

Perhaps the most critical part of cooking meat is allowing it to rest once it has been removed from the heat. Resting allows the heat to equalize and the juices to be redistributed evenly throughout the cut. The effect on beef is especially vivid. You can't really achieve that perfect medium-rare without a resting period. Steaks should generally be allowed to rest for about the same amount of time they took to cook; big roasts should rest for 20 or 30 minutes.

Humanely raised animals usually means better-tasting meat. Again, develop a relationship with your butcher or grocer, who can help you find the best.

OVERLEAF: *Herb-Crusted Rack of Lamb with Honey Mustard Glaze (page 59).* **OPPOSITE:** *Marinated Skirt Steak (page 53).*

how much oil?

When I sauté, I want plenty of oil in the pan. I've never felt comfortable with a recipe that specifies how much oil to use to sauté a piece of meat or fish. Volume measurements—say, so many teaspoons—are dependent on the size of the pan, and depth measurements are impractical and fail to take into account all variables. Many people fear using fat and so try to use as little oil as possible. Actually, using too little oil leads to more problems for the home cook than using too much oil.

It's important to understand what's happening when you put meat into a pan. The meat cools the oil and the pan, so you need enough oil to carry enough heat to compensate for what this cooler item will do to it. If there's not enough oil, the food can cool the oil to the point that it won't sear the meat and may lead to the meat's sticking to the pan. For items that are not uniformly flat (for instance, scallops), parts of the surface of what you're sautéing may not even be touching the pan or the oil if you use too little oil.

By contrast, when you use more oil than you need, you can simply pour it off after you have a good sear. Regardless of how much oil you use, you're not consuming appreciably more or less oil. And the cost of adding a little more oil is not extraordinary.

It's always a good idea to heat your pan before you add the oil—that way, you're not in danger of forgetting about the pan and letting it get too hot and even igniting. Once you've added your oil to the pan, you need to allow the oil to get hot. If you inadvertently let the oil become too hot, simply add some more oil to cool the pan down.

Sautéing involves many points of finesse, one of the most important of which is adding the right amount of oil to your pan. It's one of the most common acts we do as cooks, so it's important that you feel comfortable judging the amount of oil by sight.

How do you judge how hot oil is? Mainly by sight. Oil is viscous—sluggish when it hits a cold pan—but as it gets hotter, it appears thinner. For sautéing you want to see the oil rippling, which means it's very hot. Any hotter and the oil begins to smoke and starts degrading. Heating it further will increase the risk of accidental flaming, as vapors coming off smoking oil can ignite.

braised beef short ribs

RED WINE REDUCTION

1 (750-ml) bottle dry red wine, such as Cabernet Sauvignon

1 cup diced (½-inch) yellow onion

1 cup ½-inch-thick slices peeled carrots

1 cup ½-inch-thick slices leeks (white and light green parts only)

1 cup thinly sliced shallots

1 cup thinly sliced button mushrooms and/or mushroom stems

3 thyme sprigs

6 flat-leaf parsley sprigs

2 bay leaves

½ teaspoon black peppercorns

3 large garlic cloves, smashed, skin left on

BRAISE

1 piece (about 2½ pounds) boneless chuck short rib

Kosher salt and freshly ground black pepper

All-purpose flour

Canola oil

1 cup diced (½-inch) yellow onion

⅔ cup ½-inch-thick slices peeled carrots

1½ cups ½-inch-thick slices leeks (white and light green parts only)

2 garlic cloves, smashed, skin left on

3 thyme sprigs

2 bay leaves

About 5 cups Beef Stock (page 340)

Braising is such a satisfying process for the cook. First, you brown the ribs in fat, then cook them in a rich braising liquid—until they're tender but still have some body to them, not until they're falling apart—then cool them in the braising liquid. The flavor improves with time, so these are actually best cooked at least a day before you plan to serve them.

Ask your butcher for a cut called "boneless chuck short rib." Cooking it whole off the bone allows you to cut portions as you wish after it has cooked and cooled. Serve this with a rich, creamy side dish, such as Polenta (page 218), Puree of Garlic Potatoes (page 223), or Celery Root with Melted Onions (page 199). These short ribs are also the base for the Beef Stroganoff (page 42) and Catalan Beef Stew (page 46).

Combine all the ingredients for the red wine reduction in a large Dutch oven or other heavy ovenproof pot that will hold the meat comfortably. Bring to a simmer over high heat and reduce the heat to maintain the simmer for 45 to 50 minutes, until the wine has reduced to a glaze.

Meanwhile, trim any pieces of sinew from the top of the short ribs; leave the layer of fat and silverskin. Remove any remaining connective tissue from where the bones were removed. Season all sides of the meat generously with salt and pepper and coat in flour, patting off any excess.

Heat some canola oil in a large sauté pan over high heat until it shimmers. Add the meat fat-side-down, reduce the heat, and brown the meat for 3 minutes. Turn the meat and brown the other side. Transfer the meat to a tray.

Preheat the oven to 350°F.

Add the onion, carrots, leeks, garlic, thyme, and bay leaves to the wine reduction and toss together. Cut a piece of cheesecloth about 4 inches larger than the diameter of the pot. Moisten the cheesecloth and wring dry, place over the vegetables, and fold over the edges to form a "nest" for the meat. (The cheesecloth will allow the liquid to flavor and cook the meat but prevent bits of vegetable and herbs from clinging to it.) Put the meat on the cheesecloth and add the stock; it should come just to the top of the meat. Cut a parchment lid (see page 120) and place it over the meat.

continued

Transfer the pot to the oven, reduce the heat to 325°F, and braise the beef for 1½ to 2 hours, until very tender. To check, uncover the meat and press on it: the fibers should separate as you press down, but the meat shouldn't be falling apart.

Transfer the meat to a heatproof container. Strain the braising liquid twice through a fine-mesh conical strainer into a bowl, then strain into a fat separator or deep bowl and allow the fat to rise to the top. Skim off the fat and strain the liquid over the meat. (The meat can be refrigerated in the liquid for up to 3 days, then finished as follows. Or it can be used to make Beef Stroganoff or Catalan Beef Stew.)

To get ready to serve, preheat the oven to 400°F.

Remove any solidified fat from the surface of the liquid. (If the liquid has gelled, place the container in the oven or microwave and heat until the liquid melts and you can remove the meat without breaking it.) Put the meat fat-side-down in an ovenproof sauté pan and pour in about ¼ inch of the braising liquid. Pour the remaining liquid into a saucepan, bring to a simmer, and simmer until reduced to a sauce consistency. Remove the sauce from the heat.

Meanwhile, put the pan of short ribs over medium heat and bring to a simmer, spooning the juices over the meat. Transfer the uncovered pan to the oven to heat through, about 15 minutes, basting with the juices once or twice. Turn the meat over and baste generously with the juices. Return to the oven for another 5 minutes or so, basting two more times, until the meat is hot and richly browned with the sauce.

Cut the short ribs against the grain into slices about ½ inch thick (see Cutting Meat Across the Grain, page 54). Keep checking the meat as you slice, as the grain will not follow a straight line, and adjust your knife to keep cutting against the grain. Arrange the meat on a platter and spoon the sauce over it.   **SERVES 4**

beef stroganoff

CREAM SAUCE

1 pound cremini mushrooms, trimmed and cut in ¾-inch pieces

1 tablespoon (½ ounce) unsalted butter

⅔ cup chopped onion

Kosher salt and freshly ground black pepper

3 cups heavy cream

1 Sachet (page 342), without the garlic

⅓ cup crème fraîche

MUSHROOMS

4 tablespoons (2 ounces) unsalted butter

2 tablespoons canola oil

1 pound small or medium cremini mushrooms, trimmed and sliced ¼ inch thick

Kosher salt and freshly ground black pepper

Braised Beef Short Ribs (page 41), chilled, braising liquid reserved for another braise if desired

Pappardelle, homemade (see pages 215 and 338) or store-bought

2 tablespoons (1 ounce) unsalted butter, at room temperature

Coarsely chopped flat-leaf parsley

Gray salt or coarse sea salt

Beef stroganoff made with Campbell's cream of mushroom soup was a mainstay of the 1970s that I still feel some nostalgia for. This interpretation of that all-American version of stroganoff calls for braised beef short ribs with a mushroom cream sauce, enriched with crème fraîche. This is just as much about the mushrooms as it is the beef. Some of the cremini are pureed to use in the sauce, and some are sliced and sautéed to toss with the noodles.

Working in a couple of batches, process the mushrooms for the sauce in a food processor, scraping down the sides as necessary, until finely chopped. Transfer to a bowl.

Melt the butter in a medium saucepan over medium heat. Add the onion and cook until translucent, about 5 minutes. Season with salt and pepper. Add the chopped mushrooms, increase the heat to medium-high, and cook, stirring occasionally, until all the liquid has evaporated, 10 to 15 minutes.

Pour in the cream, add the sachet, and bring to a boil. Reduce the heat to keep the cream at a simmer and simmer for about 35 minutes, until the cream is reduced by about one-third and infused with the mushroom flavor.

Meanwhile, set a cooling rack over a baking sheet and line the rack with paper towels. Heat a large frying pan over medium heat. Add 2 tablespoons of the butter and 1 tablespoon of the canola oil and heat until the butter melts. Add half of the mushrooms, season with salt and pepper, and cook, without stirring (if you toss or move the mushrooms too early, they will steam rather than brown), for about 3 minutes, until the first side is golden brown. Turn the mushrooms and cook for another minute or two, until golden brown. Transfer to the lined baking sheet to drain and cook the remaining mushrooms in the remaining 2 tablespoons butter and 1 tablespoon oil.

It is easiest to cut the short ribs into pieces while the meat is cold. Cut into 2-inch cubes and let sit at room temperature for 30 minutes.

When the sauce is ready, discard the sachet, pour the sauce into a blender, and blend until smooth. Strain the sauce into a medium saucepan, set over medium-low heat, and stir in the crème fraîche until incorporated. Reserve about ¼ cup of the sautéed mushrooms, and add the remaining mushrooms to the sauce. Season to taste with salt and pepper. The sauce will be on the thick side. Keep warm on the back of the stovetop or on a diffuser over very low heat.

Preheat the oven to 350°F. Set a cooling rack over a baking sheet.

Bring a large pot of salted water to a boil for the pasta.

Meanwhile, heat some oil in an ovenproof frying pan over medium-high heat. When the oil is hot, add the meat, presentation (nicest) side down, and brown for 2 to 3 minutes, until richly caramelized. Turn the meat over, transfer to the oven, and heat through, about 10 minutes.

Add the pappardelle to the boiling water and cook until al dente, about 2 to 4 minutes if fresh. Reserve a cup of the cooking water, and drain the pasta. Transfer to a large bowl and toss with the butter.

Meanwhile, if necessary, reheat the cream sauce over low heat. Reheat the reserved sautéed mushrooms in a small pan.

Toss the noodles with the cream sauce. If the sauce seems too thick, add a bit of the reserved cooking water to thin. (The cooking water will have some starch in it from the pasta and will maintain the silkiness of the sauce while thinning it.) Add half of the sautéed mushrooms to the noodles and arrange them on a platter. Arrange the short ribs and the remaining mushrooms on the top. Sprinkle with gray salt and garnish with parsley. **SERVES 4**

BEEF STEW

CATALAN

2 medium fennel bulbs →

12 baby leeks →

12 fingerling potatoes →

1 sachet →

braised beef short ribs

½ c. soffritto

orange zest

⅔ c. spanish olives

fennel fronds

catalan beef stew

8 baby fennel bulbs, about 1 inch in diameter, or 2 medium fennel bulbs (about 10 ounces each)

12 baby leeks, about ½ inch in diameter, or 3 small leeks (about 8 ounces each)

Kosher salt

12 fingerling potatoes, about 2 inches long (about 1 pound total)

1 Sachet (page 342)

Braised Beef Short Ribs (page 41), chilled

½ cup Soffritto (page 263)

⅔ cup pitted oil-cured Spanish olives

2 large strips orange zest—removed with a vegetable peeler

Gray salt or coarse sea salt

Short rib braises can be taken in numerous directions. Here we use ingredients common in Catalonian cuisine—black olives, orange, and fennel—along with fingerling potatoes. The soffritto, a combination of slow-cooked onions and tomato puree, reduced to almost a jammy consistency, adds great depth to virtually any stew or braise.

If you cannot find baby fennel and leeks, substitute larger ones, cut into smaller pieces.

If using baby fennel, trim the root ends. Cut off the stalks, and reserve the fronds for garnish. If using larger fennel bulbs, trim off the stalks; reserve the fronds for garnish. Peel off the tough outer layer of each fennel bulb. Trim the root ends, keeping the bulbs intact. Cut the bulbs lengthwise in half, then cut each half into 3 wedges.

Trim the roots and dark green leaves from the leeks. The baby leeks should be about 4 inches long. Cut larger leeks into 4-inch sections, then quarter each piece lengthwise. Rinse well to remove any dirt.

Blanch the fennel wedges and leeks separately in a large pot of boiling salted water (see page 147). The fennel will take about 4 minutes, the leeks 3 to 4 minutes. Chill in an ice bath, drain, and transfer to paper towels to drain. Once they are cooled, peel off the wilted outside layer of the leeks.

Put the potatoes and sachet in a medium saucepan, add enough water to cover, and season with a generous pinch of salt. Bring to a simmer, and simmer until the potatoes are tender, 12 to 15 minutes. Drain, discard the sachet, and transfer the potatoes to a tray.

Preheat the oven to 350°F. Set a cooling rack over a baking sheet.

Remove the short ribs from the braising liquid and set aside. (If the liquid has gelled, place the container in the oven or microwave and heat until the liquid melts and you can remove the meat without breaking it.) Strain the braising liquid through a fine-mesh conical strainer into a large measuring cup; discard any solids. Allow the fat to rise to the top, then pour off and discard.

Cut the short ribs into pieces about 2 inches by 1 inch; you will need at least 8 pieces. Put the pieces presentation (nicest) side down in an ovenproof sauté pan that will hold them in a single layer with room enough to baste them. Add enough of the braising liquid to come ½ inch up the sides of the pieces and bring to a simmer over medium heat. (Reserve the remaining braising liquid.)

Transfer the pan to the oven and cook until the short ribs are hot, about 10 minutes. Turn the ribs, baste with the pan juices, and return to the oven for 5 minutes. Baste with the pan juices again and return to the oven for 5 more minutes. Carefully transfer the short ribs to a plate and set aside. Strain the braising liquid in the pan through a fine-mesh conical strainer into a measuring cup. You need 2 cups liquid; if necessary add some of the reserved braising liquid to make up the difference (see Note).

Put a large Dutch oven over medium heat, add the soffritto and braising liquid, and bring to a simmer. Stir in the olives and orange zest and simmer for 5 minutes, to allow the flavors to marry and the sauce to reduce.

Add the potatoes and stir to coat. Add the short ribs, tucking them in and around the potatoes, and baste the meat with the sauce (the sauce should be thickening and beginning to glaze the meat). Put the leeks and fennel on the top, and spoon a light coating of sauce over them. Turn the heat to low, cover, and cook for 5 minutes. Baste the meat and vegetables again, cover, and simmer for 5 minutes longer.

Garnish the stew with the reserved fennel fronds, sprinkle with gray salt, and serve directly from the Dutch oven. **SERVES 4**

NOTE *If you have any leftover braising liquid, it can be reduced and used as a flavorful sauce, or it can be frozen and used for another braise.*

peppercorn-crusted beef tenderloin

¼ cup black peppercorns, preferably Telicherry
Canola oil
Six 8-ounce beef tenderloin steaks, 1½ inches thick, trimmed if necessary
Kosher salt
Gray salt or coarse sea salt

A hearty coating of peppercorns that have been steeped in oil to soften their bite offers a contrast to the delicate texture of this tender, lean muscle. If you want to lessen the bite further, double the amount of oil you steep them in. Honey-Glazed Cipollini Onions (page 203) go well with this, as does Horseradish Cream (page 57). (Save leftover oil for vinaigrettes.)

Put the peppercorns in a small saucepan, cover them with 1½ cups canola oil, and bring to a simmer over medium heat. Remove from the heat and let the peppercorns steep in the oil for 1 hour.

Drain the peppercorns and reserve the oil for another use (see Note). Coarsely crush the peppercorns in a mortar with a pestle or use the bottom of a heavy pan. Spread them on a work surface, coat both sides of the steaks, and let stand at room temperature for 30 minutes.

Preheat the oven to 350°F. Set a roasting rack in a roasting pan.

Heat some canola oil in 2 large frying pans over medium-high heat. Season the steaks with kosher salt and add 3 steaks to each pan, without crowding (if the meat is crowded, it will steam instead of sear). Sear for 1½ to 2 minutes on each side, until richly browned. When you turn the steaks, move them to a different part of the pan (see Lightbulb Moment, page 89). Transfer to the rack.

Transfer the steaks to the oven and cook for about 18 minutes, or until the center registers 125° to 128°F. Remove from the oven and allow the steaks to rest for about 10 minutes for medium-rare before serving. Sprinkle with gray salt. **SERVES 6**

NOTE *The pepper oil can be refrigerated for up to 1 month.*

hamburgers

1½ pounds beef sirloin

12 ounces beef brisket

12 ounces beef chuck

1 teaspoon kosher salt

½ teaspoon freshly ground black pepper

Gray salt or coarse sea salt

The way to ensure a great burger is to use the proper cuts of meat, with a good amount of fat; to season it before grinding it; and to combine all the ingredients without overworking the mixture. I like a combination of sirloin, brisket, and chuck, for flavor and for a succulent burger. If you don't have a grinder, ask your butcher or the meat department of your grocery store to grind the meat for you, all together, first through a large die and then through a small die, alternating quantities of each meat through the grinder so they are mixed. Besides great flavor, there's an important safety reason to grind meat from whole cuts. Some meat ground at processing plants has been found to carry a harmful strain of E. coli. When you grind your own, the possibility of bacterial contamination is considerably reduced, so that you can serve your hamburgers medium-rare without worrying about bacteria.

Add seasonings to your own taste, such as sautéed (and chilled) sliced garlic, onions, and/or chiles. Try the burgers with Fingerling or Sweet Potato Chips (page 232).

Trim any excess fat or sinew from the meat, leaving about ¼ inch of fat. Cut all the meat into 1-inch pieces and put in a bowl. Season with salt and pepper. (The amounts listed for salt and pepper will give you a moderately seasoned hamburger; if you'd like, add more or less.)

Set up a grinder with the ⅜-inch die. Fill a large bowl three-quarters full with ice water, and put a bowl on top of the ice for catching the ground meat. Grind the meat, alternating pieces of sirloin, brisket, and chuck. Run a piece of plastic wrap or parchment through the grinder to pass all the meat through. (see Every Last Bit, page 49). Change the die to the smaller one and run the meat through again.

Divide the meat into 6 portions. Handling it gently, form it into ¾-inch- to 1-inch-thick burgers. Do not squeeze, mash, or overwork the meat—try to keep the strands intact.

Prepare a charcoal or gas grill for two-temperature cooking, with one area for medium-high heat and the other for medium heat (see Grilling Basics, page 345).

Put the hamburgers over medium-high heat and cook, without moving, for 2 minutes, or until they are well marked. (Do not move them too early; they need to cook long enough to prevent sticking to the grate.) Turn the hamburgers 90 degrees to make a crosshatch pattern, and grill for 2 minutes. Flip the hamburgers over, move to medium heat, and grill, without moving them, for 5 minutes. Turn the hamburgers 90 degrees and cook for another 4 to 5 minutes, transfer to a platter, and let rest in a warm spot for about 10 minutes for medium-rare.   SERVES 6

EVERY LAST BIT A good trick for pushing the last chunks of meat through a meat grinder is to tear off about a foot or so of plastic wrap and feed it into the grinder, holding on to the end to ensure it's traveling the length of the auger (you should feel it tugging as it moves toward the blade). The plastic wrap will push the meat through the blade and die, but the blade won't cut the wrap.

It is almost always better to grind your own meat than to buy it preground from the grocery store. First, it allows you to choose precisely what cuts you want to use, such as flavorful chuck, brisket, and sirloin for these hamburgers, or to include veal and well-marbled pork butt, as we do in the meatballs on page 50. Fat is essential in any ground meat preparation, and when you grind your own meat, you can make sure to include enough fat so the results won't be dry. For a juicy burger with good texture, you need to keep the meat and fat you're grinding cold. One way is to grind them into a bowl set over an ice bath.

Be sure to have your blades sharpened regularly or buy new ones on a regular basis—dull blades can ruin the texture of ground meat.

meatballs with pappardelle

2 tablespoons canola oil

1 cup chopped onion

2 teaspoons minced garlic

Kosher salt and freshly ground black pepper

12 ounces boneless beef sirloin

12 ounces boneless beef chuck

8 ounces boneless pork butt

8 ounces boneless veal shoulder or top round

¼ cup Dried Bread Crumbs (page 273)

3 tablespoons chopped flat-leaf parsley

1 large egg

4 ounces fresh mozzarella cheese

1 pound pappardelle, homemade (see pages 215 and 338) or store-bought

4 tablespoons (2 ounces) unsalted butter, melted

Juice of ½ lemon

Oven-Roasted Tomato Sauce (page 333), warmed

Fried oregano sprigs (see page 342)

This was one of my dad's favorite meals at Ad Hoc—meatballs stuffed with fresh mozzarella and served over oven-roasted tomato sauce, alongside big hearty noodles. The meatballs can also be served with many side dishes for a festive family meal. Or serve them as a first course or even an hors d'oeuvre. Instead of the tomato sauce, they can be served in a broth with potatoes and other vegetables. Or you can pan-fry them for a crisp crust and serve them as a tapas plate or part of a mezze platter, with some tomato sauce for dipping.

If you don't have a meat grinder, ask the butcher to grind the meats for you (see page 49), alternating quantities of each meat as they go through the grinder so that they are well mixed. Or, if necessary, buy ground meat.

Heat the canola oil in a large sauté pan over medium heat. Add the onion and garlic, season with salt and pepper, and reduce the heat. Cook gently for about 20 minutes, to soften the vegetables without browning them. Remove from the heat and set aside.

Meanwhile, trim any sinew from the meat. Cut all of the meat into 1-inch pieces and place in a bowl. Toss with 1 tablespoon salt.

Set up a meat grinder with a ⅜-inch die. Fill a large bowl with ice water and nestle a smaller bowl in it to catch the ground meat. Grind the meat, alternating the types of meat. (To get every bit of meat out of the grinder, see Every Last Bit, page 49.) Change the die to ³⁄₁₆ inch and run the meat through again.

Add the onion and garlic, bread crumbs, 2 tablespoons of the parsley, and the egg to the meat and mix gently to incorporate evenly; do not overwork the mixture. To check the seasoning, put a small patty of the meat on a plate and cook in the microwave for 30 seconds, then taste and add more salt if desired.

Divide the mixture into 12 equal balls, using a scant ½ cup (4 ounces) for each.

Cut the cheese into 12 cubes, about ¾ inch. Shape the meatballs, stuffing a cube of cheese into the center of each one (see Note).

Preheat the oven to 425°F. Set a cooling rack over a baking sheet.

Bring a large pot of salted water to a boil for the pasta.

Put the meatballs on the cooling rack and bake for 15 to 18 minutes, until cooked through but still juicy. Remove from the oven and let the meatballs rest on the rack for a few minutes before serving.

Meanwhile, cook the pappardelle; drain and put in a large bowl. Toss with the melted butter, the remaining 1 tablespoon parsley, and the lemon juice.

Spoon the tomato sauce into a gratin dish or shallow serving dish. Top with the meatballs and garnish with the oregano. Serve the pappardelle on the side. **SERVES 4 TO 6**

NOTE *Once the meatballs are stuffed, they can be placed on a baking sheet and frozen uncovered, then stored in a sealed plastic bag. Spread the meatballs on a tray and defrost in the refrigerator before cooking.*

porterhouse steak

Three 1½-inch-thick porterhouse steaks (about 1½ pounds each)

Canola oil

Kosher salt and freshly ground black pepper

About 1 cup Herb and Shallot Butter (page 334), at room temperature

Gray salt or coarse sea salt

It's fun to serve a porterhouse steak because it gives you two different cuts of meat, the flavorful strip loin and the delicate tenderloin. We grill this for flavor, but carefully—we don't want it overly charred. It's delicious topped with the Herb and Shallot Butter and served with Creamed Baby Spinach (page 206).

Trim the excess fat from the steaks, including the "tail" if it is very fatty. Let the steaks sit at room temperature for at least 30 minutes, or up to 1 hour. Just before grilling, coat the steaks with canola oil and season both sides generously with salt and pepper.

Prepare a charcoal or gas grill for two-temperature cooking with one area for medium-high heat and the other for medium heat (see Grilling Basics, page 345).

Grill the steaks over medium-high heat, without moving, for 2 to 3 minutes, or until they are well marked. (For a nice crust, and to prevent the meat from sticking to the grate, do not move the steaks too early.) Rotate the steaks 90 degrees to make a crosshatch pattern, and grill for 2 to 3 minutes. Flip the steaks over, move to medium heat, and grill, without moving them, for 3 minutes. Rotate the steaks 90 degrees and cook for another 8 to 12 minutes (timing can vary greatly, depending on the heat level), brushing the steaks 2 or 3 times with the herb butter, until the center of the meat registers 125°F to 128°F. Transfer the steaks to a carving board, brush with herb butter, and allow to rest for at least 15 minutes for medium-rare.

Slice the meat away from the bones, and cut against the grain into ½-inch-thick slices (see page 54). Arrange the meat around the bones on a serving platter and sprinkle with gray salt. **SERVES 6**

You can clean and oil a grill grate with just an onion. Cut a large yellow onion crosswise in half. Spear the root end with a grill fork. Pour about ¼ inch of canola oil into a shallow bowl just slightly larger than the onion. Heat the grill to high, dip the cut side of the onion in the oil, and rub it against the grate. It will smoke as it cleans and coats the grill. Once it is clean, set the onion aside, and adjust the heat as needed. As soon as you finish grilling, quickly repeat the technique with the onion. For the best results, use the onion one last time before the grill is completely cool.

on salt

A mortar and pestle are enormously useful for grinding sea salts that may be a little too coarse. We also use them to grind peppercorns, whole fresh or toasted spices, fresh herbs, preserved lemon, or nuts. They're also fantastic for making sauces such as pesto, salsas, and aioli. On top of this, they're beautiful objects; I have all kinds in different sizes.

For most of our cooking, we use kosher salt, and I recommend you do too. The brand is less important than using the same kind consistently so that you become accustomed to its effects, to the feel of it between your fingers, and learn to gauge how much you are adding. The two major brands are Morton's and Diamond Crystal. Morton's is considerably heavier than Diamond Crystal; a cup of Morton's weighs about 8 ounces; a cup of Diamond Crystal weighs about 5 ounces. We prefer Diamond Crystal because it gives you a little more control, has a cleaner flavor, and doesn't contain any anticaking agents.

Because of the wide variations in salt densities, we recommend you weigh salt when you're using a lot of it, as in a brine. But when using small amounts of salt to season food, I recommend you learn your own "pinch volumes"—that is, the amount of salt you pick up when you pinch salt between your thumb and three fingers, two fingers, or one finger. You will be able to pick up about a teaspoon of salt or perhaps a little less if you gather as much as you can between thumb and three fingers, about ½ teaspoon between thumb and two fingers, and ¼ teaspoon between thumb and one finger. You should use salt all the time in your cooking, seasoning as you go. Measuring by hand and sight is not difficult to learn, and it makes you a more efficient cook.

While kosher salt is our basic seasoning, we use a few other salts too. Fleur de sel is a lovely sea salt from Brittany that we use to finish fish and white meats. It has a mild flavor and crunch. Sel gris, gray salt, from the same region, has a more mineraly flavor and decidedly more crunch; we use it to finish red meats.

Maldon salt, a flaky sea salt produced in Essex, England, is a favorite for its delicate texture. It's excellent for fish and vegetables and flatbreads, where we don't want it to dissolve too quickly. While all these salts have nuances of flavor, finishing salts are used primarily for the texture they give a dish.

Another technique we use is to grind high-quality sea salts that are a little too coarse for some purposes in a mortar and pestle. We do this for salads and for other dishes, or even fruits, when we want to add a nice mineral burst but don't want crunchy pieces of salt. Sometimes we chop coarse sea salt very fine in a food processor and use it for finishing certain dishes. Salt isn't oil-soluble, so we use finely chopped salt to finish dishes like fried chicken, or the roasted nuts that we toss with a little oil (larger flakes of salt wouldn't dissolve).

And we occasionally use special salts for their unique flavor. Sometimes we flavor the salt ourselves, as in the lime salt for Corn on the Cob (page 188).

marinated skirt steak

MARINADE

6 thyme sprigs

Two 8-inch rosemary sprigs

4 small bay leaves

1 tablespoon black peppercorns

5 garlic cloves, smashed, skin left on

2 cups extra virgin olive oil

Six 8-ounce trimmed outer skirt steaks (see headnote)

Kosher salt and freshly ground black pepper

Canola oil

2 tablespoons (1 ounce) unsalted butter

4 thyme sprigs

2 garlic cloves, smashed, skin left on

Skirt steak, part of the diaphragm, is a very flavorful cut. There are two sections of the skirt, an outside muscle and an inside muscle. The inside muscle is smaller, a little more uneven, and a little tougher than the outer skirt, which we prefer. The outer skirt is still a tough cut of meat and, because it's served medium-rare, not tenderized through long cooking, you need to slice it across the grain, straight down (thereby shortening the long muscle fibers that otherwise make it tough), to ensure that it's tender (see Cutting Meat Across the Grain, page 54). The marinade we use here, with abundant herbs and garlic, is excellent for all cuts of beef.

Combine the thyme, rosemary, bay leaves, peppercorns, garlic, and oil in a medium saucepan and bring to a simmer over medium heat. Remove from the heat and let the marinade cool to room temperature.

Pull away the excess fat from the skirt steak and discard. If necessary, trim the steak of any silverskin. Cut crosswise into 6 equal pieces. Put in a dish or a resealable plastic bag, add the marinade, and cover the dish or seal the bag, squeezing out excess air. Marinate for at least 4 hours, or for up to a day, in the refrigerator.

Remove the meat from the marinade and let sit at room temperature for about 30 minutes before cooking; discard the marinade. Dry the meat with paper towels. Season with salt and pepper.

Preheat the oven to 350°F. Set a roasting rack in a roasting pan.

Heat some canola oil in a large frying pan over high heat. When it shimmers, add half the meat and quickly brown the first side. Turn the meat and, working quickly, add 1 tablespoon of the butter, 2 thyme sprigs, and 1 garlic clove and brown the meat on the second side, basting constantly; the entire cooking process should take only about 1½ minutes. Transfer the meat to the rack and spoon the butter, garlic, and thyme over the top. Wipe the pan and repeat with the remaining steaks.

Transfer the baking sheet to the oven and cook for 8 to 10 minutes, or until the center of the meat registers about 125°F. Remove from the oven and let the meat rest on the rack in a warm place for about 10 minutes for medium-rare.

Arrange the steak on a serving platter, or slice each piece against the grain, cutting straight down, and arrange on the platter. Garnish with the garlic and thyme.

PHOTOGRAPH ON PAGE 39   **SERVES 6**

santa maria–style tri-tip

One 2½-pound tri-tip roast, about 3 inches thick at its thickest point

½ teaspoon freshly ground black pepper

½ teaspoon piment d'Espelette (see page 208)

1 teaspoon sweet paprika

Kosher salt

Canola oil

1 tablespoon (½ ounce) unsalted butter

1 rosemary sprig

1 garlic clove, smashed, skin left on

5 very thin lemon slices, preferably Meyer lemon, seeds removed

The tri-tip is a cut from the very bottom of the sirloin section of the cow, between the ribs and the rump. It's a single triangular-shaped muscle—there's one on either side of the animal—sometimes called the sirloin tip; cuts vary throughout the country, and sometimes the tri-tip is included as part of another cut.

Accounts of the history of the tri-tip suggest that because it could quickly become tasteless and flavorless when cooked for too long, it was usually given to the workers on the ranches of the central California coast. But cooks eventually discovered that properly barbecued, it was delicious, every bit as flavorful as meat from the rib and loin, and Santa Maria, north of Santa Barbara, became known for its tri-tip barbecues.

We like to serve this with succotash made from our local corn. Start the recipe a day ahead to allow the spices to penetrate the meat.

One day ahead, trim the meat of all silverskin. Combine the black pepper, Espelette, and paprika and rub all over the meat. Wrap the meat tightly in plastic wrap and refrigerate.

Thirty minutes before cooking, remove the meat from the refrigerator.

Preheat the oven to 300°F. Set a roasting rack in a roasting pan.

Pat the meat dry with paper towels and sprinkle on all sides with salt. Heat some oil in a large frying pan over high heat. When the oil shimmers, add the meat and sear, without moving it, for 1 to 1½ minutes to brown the bottom. Turn the meat over, add the butter, rosemary, garlic, and lemon slices, and brown the second side of the meat, another 2 minutes or so; as it browns, tilt the pan from time to time and baste the top of the meat with the butter mixture. Transfer the meat to the rack and arrange the lemon slices, rosemary sprig, and garlic clove on top.

Put the roasting pan in the oven and roast for 40 to 60 minutes, depending on the thickness of the roast, until the temperature in the center of the meat is about 135°F. Let the meat rest on the rack in a warm spot (such as the back of the stove) for about 30 minutes for medium-rare, allowing the juices to redistribute.

Cut the roast into thin slices: the grain in the tri-tip does not follow a straight line, so adjust the angle of the knife as you carve to continue cutting against the grain. Arrange the meat on a platter and garnish with the lemon slices, rosemary, and garlic.

SERVES 6

CUTTING MEAT ACROSS THE GRAIN Meat is muscle. The muscles of land animals are composed of fibers that are very thin (about the width of a human hair, according to Harold McGee) and long, sometimes as long as the entire muscle. These fibers are wrapped in bundles, like cables; the sheathing for the cable is the connective tissue. The more a muscle is worked, the bigger those fibers get, and the more connective tissue there is. The bundles of fibers that compose muscle are tough to separate, and thus can be tough to chew. We make tougher meats more tender by long, slow cooking, which melts the connective tissue, and also by the way we cut it. Slicing meat across the grain shortens the long strands and makes them easier to separate from one another. You can see the grain—the way the fibers are running—in any piece of meat. Cut across the grain. Some cuts, such as the tri-tip sirloin, don't have one straight grain throughout, so keep an eye on the grain as you proceed.

braised oxtail and mushroom tartine

9 pieces (about 10 ounces each) oxtail

Kosher salt and freshly ground black pepper

Canola oil

About 5 cups Beef Stock (page 340)

12 ounces (about 5 cups) oyster mushrooms, cut into 1½-inch pieces

2 tablespoons minced shallots

1 teaspoon finely chopped thyme

2 tablespoons (1 ounce) unsalted butter

One 1-pound loaf rosemary ciabatta or other thick flat bread

Extra virgin olive oil

½ cup thinly sliced white onion

When you have leftover braised meat—short ribs, osso buco, pot roast—from a previous dinner, it makes amazing sandwiches. But it's worth cooking extra just for this purpose. Oxtails (which are more commonly beef tails) contain meat, bone, and cartilage, making them ideal for braising. The meat gives flavor to the cooking liquid, and the bone and cartilage add great body. Here we make a thick ragù with them, add some oyster mushrooms, and serve it all on ciabatta bread, topped with sliced onions (pickled vegetables would work well too). It's simple, and it's really, really good. (You could probably put it between slices of Wonder Bread and it would still be delicious.) The ragù would also be a great sauce for pasta, or serve it for breakfast with eggs and hot sauce.

Preheat the oven to 400°F. Set a cooling rack over a baking sheet.

Generously season both sides of the oxtails with salt and pepper. Pour some canola oil into a large ovenproof sauté pan that will hold the oxtails in one layer, and heat over medium-high heat until hot but not smoking. Reduce the heat to medium, add about half the oxtails, and cook, adjusting the heat if necessary, until the first side is richly browned, 5 to 7 minutes. Flip and brown the second side, about 5 minutes more. Transfer to the cooling rack. Repeat with the remaining oxtails.

Pour off the fat and return the oxtails to the pan. Add enough beef stock to come halfway up the oxtails. Bring to a simmer, cover, transfer to the oven, and cook until the oxtails are tender, 2½ to 3 hours.

Turn the oxtails over and let rest on top of the stove for at least 30 minutes, or up to 1 hour.

Remove the oxtails from the cooking liquid, and strain the cooking liquid through a fine-mesh conical strainer; set aside. Remove the meat from the bones, discarding the fat and tough connective tissue, and put the meat in a bowl. Season to taste with salt and pepper. (The meat can be covered with the strained cooking liquid and refrigerated overnight. The cooking liquid will solidify; when you reheat the oxtails, it may be necessary to add about ¼ cup water.)

Heat some canola oil in a large sauté pan over medium heat until hot but not smoking. Add half the mushrooms and cook, without moving them, until golden brown, about 2 minutes. Stir and cook for another 2 minutes, or until browned on all sides. Season with salt and pepper and transfer to a bowl. Cook the remaining mushrooms in the same way.

Return all the mushrooms to the sauté pan, add the shallots and thyme, and cook for 1 to 2 minutes, until the shallots soften. Add the butter and cook, stirring, until the liquid the mushrooms release has cooked off and they are glazed with butter, about 2 minutes. Stir in the oxtails, then pour in the reserved cooking liquid, bring to a simmer, and simmer until the liquid has reduced considerably and glazed the meat and mushrooms, about 8 minutes.

Meanwhile, preheat the broiler.

Slice off the top of the loaf of bread and reserve for another use. Brush the bread generously with olive oil, and toast under the broiler. Transfer to a serving platter.

Spoon the meat and mushrooms over the bread and scatter the onion slices over the top. Cut into 6 pieces and serve.

SERVES 6 AS AN APPETIZER, FOR LUNCH, OR AS A LIGHT MAIN COURSE

blowtorch prime rib roast

One 2-bone center-cut rib roast (about 4½ pounds), trimmed of excess fat

Kosher salt

Coarsely ground black pepper

Gray salt or coarse sea salt

Horseradish Cream (recipe follows)

I cook rib roast in a very low oven to ensure that it is a rosy medium-rare from the very center almost to its outer edges. But we like the dark caramelized surface, for flavor and for visual appeal, which is typically achieved through roasting at high heat. We discovered that if you start by giving meat a quick heating using a blowtorch, though it won't look particularly brown after the toasting, it will develop a beautifully browned surface even in that very low oven.

Propane torches are inexpensive and easy to use. Available at most hardware stores, they usually cost less than $20; replacement cylinders are usually less than $5. Avoid the smaller butane-fired torches sold at gourmet shops; propane torches are more effective. You can use a torch for caramelizing sugar on crème brûlee, browning meringue, and, as we do, giving a crust to your roast beef. Be sure to store your torch in a safe place.

Position an oven rack in the lower third of the oven and preheat the oven to 275°F.

Put the roast on a roasting rack in a roasting pan. Hold a blowtorch about 1 inch from the roast and turn to lightly brown the fat on all sides; the idea is to start the fat rendering and to torch the meat just until the surface begins to turn gray. Season the roast generously with salt and pepper.

Transfer to the oven, with the meat toward the back of the oven, and cook until the roast registers 128°F in the center. The total cooking time will be about 2 hours, but begin to check the temperature after 1½ hours. Remove from the oven and let rest in a warm spot for at least 30 minutes for medium-rare.

To carve, cut the meat away from the bones. Separate the bones and put them on a serving platter. Cut the roast in half through the center, turn each piece cut side down, and slice straight down into slices that are about ½ inch thick. Arrange the meat on the platter and sprinkle with gray salt and pepper. Serve with the horseradish cream on the side.

SERVES 6

horseradish cream

½ cup very cold heavy cream

2 tablespoons sherry vinegar

About ¼ cup drained prepared horseradish

½ teaspoon fleur de sel, or to taste

½ teaspoon freshly ground black pepper, or to taste

This is a basic, and very easy, horseradish sauce—prepared horseradish and cream, seasoned with salt and pepper and a little bit of sherry vinegar. It goes especially well with grilled or roasted beef, like this prime rib roast, and the Peppercorn-Crusted Beef Tenderloin (page 47).

Put the heavy cream and vinegar in a medium bowl and whisk until the cream holds a soft shape. Whisk in the horseradish, salt, and pepper. Refrigerate in a covered container for up to 1 week.   **MAKES ABOUT 1 CUP**

When you season food with salt (or other seasonings, for that matter), whether the food is raw or cooked, always season from high above the food to ensure an even distribution. By contrast, when you hold your hand right over the food as you sprinkle the salt, the seasoning winds up concentrated in a smaller area.

sautéed lamb loin chops

2 lemons, halved

18 baby artichokes (about 2 pounds)

Kosher salt

Twelve 1¼-inch-thick lamb loin chops (about 4 ounces each)

Freshly ground black pepper

Canola oil

4 thyme sprigs

4 garlic cloves, slightly crushed, skin left on

3 tablespoons capers

1 cup oil-cured black olives

18 Oven-Roasted Tomatoes (page 262)

Gray salt or coarse sea salt

The flavor of lamb is showcased in this cut, the loin chop. But the loin chops are often cut too thin to be cooked perfectly medium-rare, the temperature I prefer most sautéed or grilled red meat, so it's a good idea when you order these from your butcher or meat department to specify the thickness. Artichokes and lamb are a great springtime combination. Here we also include roasted tomatoes, capers, and olives.

Fill a large bowl with cold water and squeeze in the juice of the lemons. Add the lemon halves. Working with one artichoke at a time, snap off the outer leaves until you reach the pale inner leaves. With a paring knife, trim the bottom of the artichoke, starting from the top of the heart and slicing down to create a smooth line. Cut off the bottom of the stem. Cut off the top of the artichoke at the point where the leaves begin to take on a pink hue, and put the artichoke in the lemon water.

Remove the artichokes, drain them, and put them in a saucepan that will hold them in a single layer. Cover with water and add 2 tablespoons of the lemon water and a generous pinch of salt. Lay a clean, dampened kitchen towel over the artichokes to keep them submerged. Bring to a simmer over medium-high heat and simmer until the artichokes are tender, about 15 minutes.

Using a slotted spoon, transfer the artichokes to a small bowl, and pour in just enough cooking liquid to cover. Let cool. The artichokes can be refrigerated for up to 2 days.

Remove the lamb chops from the refrigerator and let sit at room temperature for 30 minutes.

Preheat the oven to 350°F. Set a cooling rack over a baking sheet.

Season the lamb chops generously with salt and pepper. Heat some canola oil in a large frying pan over medium-high heat until hot but not smoking. Add 6 of the chops and cook until well browned on the first side, 3 to 4 minutes. Turn the chops, add half the thyme and garlic, and cook, basting the meat with its own fat, until browned on the second side, 2 to 3 minutes. Transfer to the cooling rack, along with the thyme and garlic. Repeat with the remaining chops, thyme, and garlic. Pour off the excess fat and set the pan aside.

Transfer the chops to the oven and cook for 7 to 8 minutes, or until the internal temperature of the meat is 128° to 130°F. Remove from the oven and let the meat rest in a warm spot for 15 minutes for medium-rare.

Meanwhile, drain the artichokes, cut them lengthwise in half, add to the skillet, and heat over medium heat for about 1 minute. Add the capers and olives and cook for 30 seconds. Add the tomatoes and cook just to warm through, 30 seconds to 1 minute. Season to taste with salt and pepper.

Arrange the chops on a serving platter, top with the vegetables, sprinkle with gray salt, and garnish with the thyme and garlic. **SERVES 6**

herb-crusted rack of lamb

with honey mustard glaze

2 frenched 8-bone racks of lamb (2 to 2¼ pounds each)
    (see headnote, page 60)

Kosher salt and freshly ground black pepper

Canola oil

¼ cup Dijon mustard

3 tablespoons honey

6 tablespoons (3 ounces) unsalted butter, at room temperature

4 cloves Garlic Confit (page 266) or 1 tablespoon Garlic Puree (page 266)

3 to 5 anchovy fillets, salt packed or oil packed, rinsed, dried, and minced

1½ cups Dried Bread Crumbs (page 273) or ground panko crumbs

3 tablespoons finely chopped flat-leaf parsley

1 tablespoon minced rosemary

Gray salt or coarse sea salt

Rack of lamb is a special dish—impressive to bring to the table and carve, tender, and delicious. We coat the racks with buttered bread crumbs seasoned with anchovy, rosemary, and garlic. The anchovies add a salty, savory depth, rather than an anchovy taste, to the breading. You can omit them if you don't like anchovies or, if you love anchovies, you could add more. The racks can be seared and coated with the crumbs up to 6 hours ahead, then roasted when you are ready. This would be good with a potato gratin and braised endive.

Score the fat covering the lamb in a ½-inch crosshatch pattern; be careful not to cut into the meat. Season the racks on all sides with salt and pepper.

Set a roasting rack in a roasting pan. Heat some canola oil in a large frying pan over medium-high heat until it shimmers. Put 1 rack fat-side-down in the pan and sear until golden brown, 1½ to 2 minutes; carefully move the lamb as it sears to brown as much of the fat as possible. (It is best to sauté 1 rack at a time, so the temperature of the pan doesn't drop dramatically.) Transfer the lamb to the roasting rack, meat-side-up. Drain off the fat, reheat the pan, adding fresh oil, and sear the remaining rack.

Combine the mustard and honey in a small bowl; set aside. Combine the butter, garlic, and anchovies in a small food processor and puree until smooth. Transfer the puree to a medium bowl and stir in the bread crumbs, parsley, and rosemary to combine. Do not overmix; the mixture should be moist, but it may not all come together.

Brush the mustard mixture over the fat and meat (do not coat the underside of the racks). Spread the bread crumbs evenly over the racks, pressing gently and patting them so the crumbs adhere. (The lamb can be refrigerated, on the rack in the roasting pan, for up to 6 hours; remove it from the refrigerator 30 minutes before roasting it.)

Position an oven rack in the bottom third of the oven and preheat the oven to 425°F.

Put the lamb in the oven, with the meat side toward the back, and roast for 25 to 35 minutes, until the temperature in the center of the meat registers 128° to 130°F. Let the racks rest on the rack in a warm place for about 20 minutes for medium-rare.

Carve each rack into four 2-bone chops and arrange on a platter. Sprinkle with gray salt and serve.

PHOTOGRAPH ON PAGE 37   SERVES 8

roasted spring leg of lamb

One 6½-pound trimmed leg of lamb, bone frenched (see headnote)

5 garlic cloves, halved lengthwise

4 rosemary sprigs

½ cup canola oil

Kosher salt and freshly ground black pepper

Gray salt or coarse sea salt

L eg of lamb marinated with canola oil and garlic and thyme, studded with more garlic, and coated with plenty of aromatic herbs is a traditional dish. We insert the garlic cloves so that the meat is evenly flavored and the lamb is appealing when carved, and we use rosemary instead of thyme. It's important to remove the fell, the membrane covering the fat, because it has a very gamy flavor; you can ask your butcher to do this if necessary. Also ask him to french it—clean the end of the bone—which makes a nicer presentation and also provides a "handle" for carving. Be sure to allow this big cut to come to room temperature before roasting it. We cook the leg to medium, rather than medium-rare, so that it becomes a little more tender. A long resting time is also important with a big cut such as this.

Try this with artichokes or asparagus, Butter-Poached Marble Potatoes (page 223), and some Tomato-Basil Marmalade (page 248).

Set a roasting rack in a roasting pan. If the fell, the thin membrane over the outer layer of fat, is still intact, carefully remove it with a sharp knife. (Don't be concerned if some of the fat is removed with the fell.) Make ten ½- to 1-inch-deep incisions in the thickest parts of the leg, where the garlic will be visible when the lamb is sliced, and insert a piece of garlic in each. Make another incision in the meat just above the frenched bone and insert 1 sprig of rosemary in the incision. Lay another 2 sprigs in the groove of the sirloin.

Turn the leg over and rub ¼ cup of the oil over the meat. Season generously with salt and pepper. Turn the meat back over, tuck the flap of sirloin under the roast, and place on the rack. Rub the top of the roast with the remaining ¼ cup oil and season generously with salt and pepper. Pull off the leaves of the remaining rosemary sprig and scatter them over the roast. Let sit at room temperature for 1 hour or until it has reached room temperature.

Preheat the oven to 325°F.

Put the lamb in the oven and roast for 1 hour.

Turn the pan around and roast for 30 minutes, or until the very center of the top round registers 135°F.

Remove from the oven and let the meat rest on the rack for 45 minutes.

To carve the roast, hold the exposed bone, stand the lamb up on a cutting board, and slice the meat vertically, against the grain, until you reach the bone. Turn the roast around and carve the other side in the same manner until you reach the bone. Finally, slice across the sirloin. Arrange the meat on a serving platter and sprinkle with gray salt.

SERVES 8 TO 10

on lamb *I love lamb for its unique flavor, as well as for the diversity of cuts you get from lamb. I especially like to cook whole cuts, such as rack of lamb—very tender, and delicious and special—or a leg of lamb, which gives you all kinds of textures and variations in doneness and will serve a big group. We raise wonderful lamb in the United States and I find that it has a subtler flavor than that of New Zealand or Australian lamb, which tends to be more assertive. I have a strong relationship with a lamb farmer in Pennsylvania, Keith Martin, who sells his lamb under the brand name Pure Bred. He raises the best lamb I've ever tasted, and it's worth finding out if it's available in your area (see Sources, page 346).*

tempering & resting

Two of the most important parts of cooking are "tempering" meats and fish that have come out of the refrigerator (letting them come to room temperature) and resting meats and some fish after you remove them from the heat. Tempering happens on the countertop away from the stove, and resting takes place in a warm spot such as the top of your stove. They should be considered critical parts of the cooking process.

If you put a piece of meat, poultry, or fish straight from the refrigerator into a hot pan or oven, it can't possibly cook evenly. To ensure even cooking, you must allow it to come to room temperature.

The bigger the item, the more necessary this is. A whole chicken or a prime rib should sit at room temperature for at least an hour, even longer for a large roast. But smaller cuts all benefit from being allowed to come to room temperature before going into the heat.

Equally significant is the resting period after the food has been removed from the heat. Everything continues to cook once it's out of the heat, an effect called carryover cooking. But, even more important, as meat rests, the juices can redistribute throughout the meat. The meat fibers also firm up a little as they rest and are able to hold more juices. Allow a good long rest for big roasts, 30 minutes or so, and for whole birds, at least 20 minutes. Don't worry about the food getting cold; the dense flesh stays hot for a long time. The smaller the item, the less time it needs to rest. The only items you should not let rest are thin fillets of fish, which lose moisture easily and can dry out.

shh...
The lamb is resting.

brined pork tenderloin

Pork Brine (page 339), cold

2 pork tenderloins (about 1¼ pounds each), silverskin and excess fat removed

Canola oil

Kosher salt and freshly ground black pepper

2 tablespoons (1 ounce) unsalted butter

2 garlic cloves, smashed, skin left on

6 thyme sprigs

2 rosemary sprigs

8 slices Cured Lemons (page 263)

Gray salt or coarse sea salt

Pork tenderloin is inexpensive, very tender, and flavorful. Here we brine it, then sear it, adding plenty of flavor by caramelizing slices of cured lemon in the pan, and finish it in the oven, covered with the lemon slices. Serve this with something hearty, like braised chard or chicory, and with something rich, like the Polenta (page 218), to balance the lean meat.

Pour the brine into a container large enough to hold the pork and add the pork. Refrigerate for 4 hours (no longer, or the pork may become too salty).

Remove the pork (discard the brine) and rinse under cold water. Pat dry with paper towels, or let air-dry. Let the tenderloins sit at room temperature for 30 minutes.

Preheat the oven to 350°F. Set a roasting rack in a roasting pan.

Pour some canola oil into a large frying pan or small roasting pan large enough to hold the pork and heat over medium-high heat until hot. Season the tenderloins with kosher salt and pepper, add to the pan, and sear, turning them occasionally, until golden brown on all sides, about 6 minutes. Add the butter, garlic, thyme, rosemary, and lemon slices and cook, tilting the pan and using a spoon to baste the pork with the pan juices, for 2 minutes.

Transfer the meat to the roasting rack. Overlap the lemon slices down the length of the tenderloins and top with the garlic, rosemary, and thyme. Roast until the internal temperature is 135° to 140°F (use the latter if you prefer your pork less pink), about 20 minutes. Remove from the oven and let the meat rest for 15 minutes for medium-rare to medium.

Slice the pork on the diagonal into ½- to ¾-inch-thick slices. Arrange the slices on a serving platter and garnish with the garlic, rosemary, and lemons. Sprinkle gray salt over the top. **SERVES 6**

rack of pork arista

Pork Brine (page 339), cold

One 6-bone center-cut rack of pork (about 4 pounds), bones frenched (see headnote, page 60)

½ teaspoon whole cloves

½ teaspoon black peppercorns

6 garlic cloves

1 lemon

Kosher salt

1 tablespoon minced rosemary

1 tablespoon minced sage

3 tablespoons canola oil

Gray salt or coarse sea salt

According to a perhaps apocryphal story, a church council in Florence had convened dignitaries from Greek and Roman churches to smooth out their differences, and when they were served a dish of roasted pork—heavily seasoned with cloves, pepper, garlic, fresh herbs—the dignitaries were heard to murmur, *"Arista, arista!"* (This is terrific, the best!) And so it was called.

We almost always brine pork loin, pork racks, and most cuts of pork, which both seasons the meat and keeps it juicy. For the arista, the brined pork is rubbed with a paste of aromatic spices, herbs, garlic, and lemon juice, which creates a beautiful crust during roasting. Sometimes we serve a little jus with the loin, but it goes well with any of the prepared mustards (see page 251), along with a side of Celery Root with Melted Onions (page 199); in late summer, serve it with Tomato-Basil Marmalade (page 248).

Ask your butcher or meat department for a center-cut rack of pork, with a large fat cap. The fat cap is the fat and well-marbled exterior of the loin; it adds flavor and succulence to the finished dish.

Pour the brine into a container large enough to hold the pork and submerge the pork in the brine. Refrigerate for 10 hours (no longer, or the pork may become too salty).

Remove the pork from the brine (discard the brine) and rinse under cold water. Pat dry with paper towels or let air-dry. Score the fat, making shallow cuts about 1 inch apart in a crosshatch pattern; be careful not to cut into the meat.

Tying the roast keeps it in a compact shape and helps to cook it more evenly. Cut 5 pieces of twine about 15 inches long. Stand the roast on a baking sheet, meat side down and facing you. Position a piece of twine under the meat, bring up the ends between the first and second bones, and tie into a knot. The twine should hold the meat but not be pulled so tight that it cuts into the meat. Repeat between the second and third bones and then continue in the same manner. Trim any excess twine.

Make the rub just before using it for the most intense flavor: Grind the cloves and peppercorns with a mortar and pestle until pulverized. (Alternatively, put the cloves and peppercorns in a heavy-duty plastic bag and crush with a meat pounder or heavy pan.) Using a Microplane or box grater, grate the garlic and then the zest of the lemon directly into the ground peppercorns. Add a big pinch of salt and mash to a paste. Add the herbs and mash to a paste. Transfer to a bowl. Juice the lemon and stir the juice and oil into the paste.

Set a roasting rack in a roasting pan, put the roast on the rack, and massage the rub all over the roast and into the scored cuts. Let the meat stand at room temperature for 1 hour.

Preheat the oven to 350°F.

Roast the meat for about 1 hour and 15 minutes, until the temperature in the center of the roast is 135° to 140°F (use the latter if you prefer your pork less pink). Remove the pan from the oven, cover the meat with a foil tent, and let rest on top of the stove for 30 minutes for medium-rare to medium.

Carve the meat into chops, arrange on a platter, and sprinkle with gray salt.

SERVES 6

roasted pork short ribs

3 racks pork short ribs (1½ to 1¾ pounds each)
Kosher salt and freshly ground black pepper
Canola oil
Gray salt or coarse sea salt

Short ribs are the first three ribs, those closest to the shoulder of the pig. They are fatty and contain some white meat, the beginning of the loin, but the prize is the dark meat close to the bone. Short ribs aren't tender, like back ribs, so they require long, slow cooking. We sear them in fat first and then roast them for about 2 hours, until they're tender. We serve this in winter with sides like Borlotti Bean Ragù (page 210) or Caramelized Savoy Cabbage (page 197), and maybe something sweet like the Honey-Glazed Cipollini Onions (page 203) or stewed fruit.

Remove the short ribs from the refrigerator and let sit at room temperature for 30 minutes.

Preheat the oven to 350°F. Set a cooling rack over a baking sheet.

Generously season both sides of the short ribs with salt and pepper. Sauté the racks in batches to avoid crowding. In a frying pan that will easily hold 2 racks, heat some canola oil over medium-high heat until hot but not smoking. Add 2 racks of short ribs, fat-side-down, and cook, turning occasionally, until golden brown on all sides, about 15 minutes. Transfer the short ribs to the rack, bone side down. Clean the pan, add oil as needed, and brown the remaining short ribs.

Transfer to the oven and roast until the meat is very tender, about 2 hours. Remove from the oven and let the short ribs rest in a warm place for 30 to 45 minutes. (The longer resting time will yield slightly more tender meat.)

Slice the meat from the ribs and cut against the grain into thin slices. Arrange the slices and a stack of the bones on a serving platter. Sprinkle with gray salt. **SERVES 6**

rubbed and glazed pork spareribs

RUB

1 cup packed light brown sugar
2 tablespoons kosher salt
2 teaspoons sweet pimentón (Spanish smoked paprika)
2 teaspoons cayenne
2 teaspoons garlic powder
1 teaspoon ground allspice
1 teaspoon red pepper flakes

2 slabs pork spareribs (each about 3 pounds), cut into 3-bone portions

I love finger food, and spareribs are among the best finger food I know—seared over a hot grill, then cooked over indirect heat until tender, with a smoky spicy sweet flavor. We coat them in a flavorful dry rub and allow them to stand for 2 to 6 hours before cooking so that the flavor penetrates the meat. If you like to smoke with wood chips, extra smokiness works perfectly here. Serve the ribs with summery side dishes such as Smashed Roasted Marble Potatoes (page 224), Creamed Summer Corn (page 189), Coleslaw (page 198), and/or Red Potato and Green Bean Salad with Creamy Pepper Dressing (page 228).

Combine all of the rub ingredients in a medium bowl.

Line a baking sheet with parchment paper. Rub the spareribs on all sides with the spice rub. Put on the baking sheet and wrap in plastic wrap. Refrigerate for at least 2 hours, or up to 6 to allow the flavors to develop. (The rub will also help tenderize the meat.)

Prepare a charcoal or gas grill for direct-heat cooking followed by indirect-heat cooking (see Grilling Basics, page 345). To use an onion to clean and oil the grill, see Lightbulb Moment, page 51.

If your grill is small, sear the meat in batches. Place the ribs meat side down, without crowding, on the hot section of the grill and cook for about 2 minutes, until grill marks appear. Turn the ribs 90 degrees to create a crosshatch pattern and cook for another 2 minutes, or until well marked.

Transfer the ribs, meat side up, to the cool section of the grill, close the lid, and cook until tender but not falling off the bones, about 2 hours; move the ribs around after the first hour so they cook evenly. The temperature of the grill should remain at about 250°F; if the grill doesn't have a thermometer, put an oven thermometer next to the meat to check the temperature, and adjust the heat as necessary.

Cut the spareribs into individual ribs if desired, and arrange on a serving platter.   **SERVES 4 TO 6**

on pork *Its fat is one of the things that makes pork so special. It's got a flavor and creaminess that's unlike any other kind of fat. Another reason chefs love pork is its sheer versatility, with all the various fresh cuts, from the rack to the shoulder to the belly, and all the cured products made from pork, including great bacon and hams, such as the very special dry-cured ibérico ham from Spain. We have come so far in this country. So many of us grew up eating ham sandwiches without any idea at all where ham came from! We've finally come to realize how great a part pigs have played in our culinary heritage.*

Pork Brine (page 339), cold

One 2½-pound pork loin roast

1 large fennel bulb

Canola oil

½ cup ½-inch cubes ciabatta or other artisan bread

1 teaspoon minced garlic

1 tablespoon finely chopped shallot

1 cup Fig and Balsamic Jam (page 246)

¼ cup Chicken Stock (page 339)

½ teaspoon finely chopped thyme

Kosher salt and freshly ground black pepper

Gray salt or coarse sea salt

A stuffing is a good way to introduce flavors into the pork. You can stuff the pork by hand, as described here, or use a piping bag. We sear the loin to brown and crisp the fat layer, then roast it to an internal temperature of 135°F, so that the interior is pale pink and juicy. Side dish possibilities include roasted parsnips, Caramelized Fennel (page 194), Sautéed Broccoli Rabe with Garlic and Chile Flakes (page 195), and Glazed Sweet Potatoes (page 232); you might also accompany it with Fennel Mustard (page 251).

Pour the brine into a container large enough to hold the pork loin and add the pork. Refrigerate for 10 hours (no longer, or the pork may become too salty).

Remove the pork loin from the brine (discard the brine) and rinse under cold water. Pat dry with paper towels, or let air-dry.

Using a long thin knife, make a horizontal lengthwise cut all the way through the center of the loin. (Instead of making one long slit, you may find it easier to cut halfway into the meat, working from either end.) Turn the knife and make a vertical cut through the meat (the two cuts should intersect like a plus sign). Let the meat rest at room temperature while you prepare the stuffing.

Cut the stalks from the fennel and trim the root end. Remove the thicker outer layers. Separate the bulb into individual layers and cut into batons about 1¼ inches long and ½ inch wide (see photo, page 30); you need ½ cup fennel. Reserve the remaining fennel for another use.

Set a cooling rack over a small baking sheet and line it with paper towels.

Heat some canola oil in a medium frying pan over medium heat. Add the bread cubes and cook, tossing to brown on all sides, 1 to 2 minutes. Transfer the bread cubes to the lined rack.

Pour off any excess oil, leaving just a light film in the pan, return the pan to the heat, and add the fennel. Cook until tender with just a little bite left, 2 to 3 minutes. Add the garlic and shallot and cook for 1 minute. Stir in the jam and warm through, then add the bread cubes, chicken stock, thyme, and salt and pepper to taste, stirring until thoroughly combined. Transfer to a bowl and let cool completely.

Preheat the oven to 350°F. Put a roasting rack in a small roasting pan and put it in the oven.

Meanwhile, use your fingers to widen the cavity in the meat enough to hold the stuffing, working from either end of the loin. Place the filling into a pastry bag fitted with a large plain tip and pipe it into the opening on one side of the pork, pushing the filling into the center of the roast. Turn the loin around and finish stuffing it from the other end. Tie the roast with kitchen twine (see next page), being careful not to pull the string so tight that it pushes out the filling.

Season the loin on all sides with salt and pepper. Heat some canola oil in a large frying pan over medium-high heat until smoking. Add the loin to the pan and brown on all sides, moving it to a different area of the pan with each turn (see Lightbulb Moment, page 89), for 2 to 3 minutes per side.

Transfer the pork to the roasting pan and roast for 30 to 40 minutes, or until the internal temperature is 135° to 140°F (if you prefer your pork less pink). Remove from the oven and let rest in a warm spot for 30 minutes for medium-rare to medium.

Remove the string and cut the loin into ¼-inch-thick slices. Arrange on a platter and sprinkle with gray salt.   SERVES 6

TYING A BONELESS ROAST

This pork loin could simply be tied with several pieces of kitchen twine an inch apart, but this method allows the meat to maintain its shape without the twine cutting into the meat.

Put the loin fat-side-up on the work surface. Loop the twine around one end of the loin, leaving several inches of twine hanging at the end.

Pull off more twine from the spool and twist the twine to make a loop over the other end of the loin.

Bring the twine back to the other end of the loin, about ¾ inch or so from the first loop.

Tighten to secure, without cutting into the loin, adjusting the loop as necessary so it is in the center of the meat. Continue to pull off more twine, twisting it into loops and moving down the length of the loin until you have tied the entire loin.

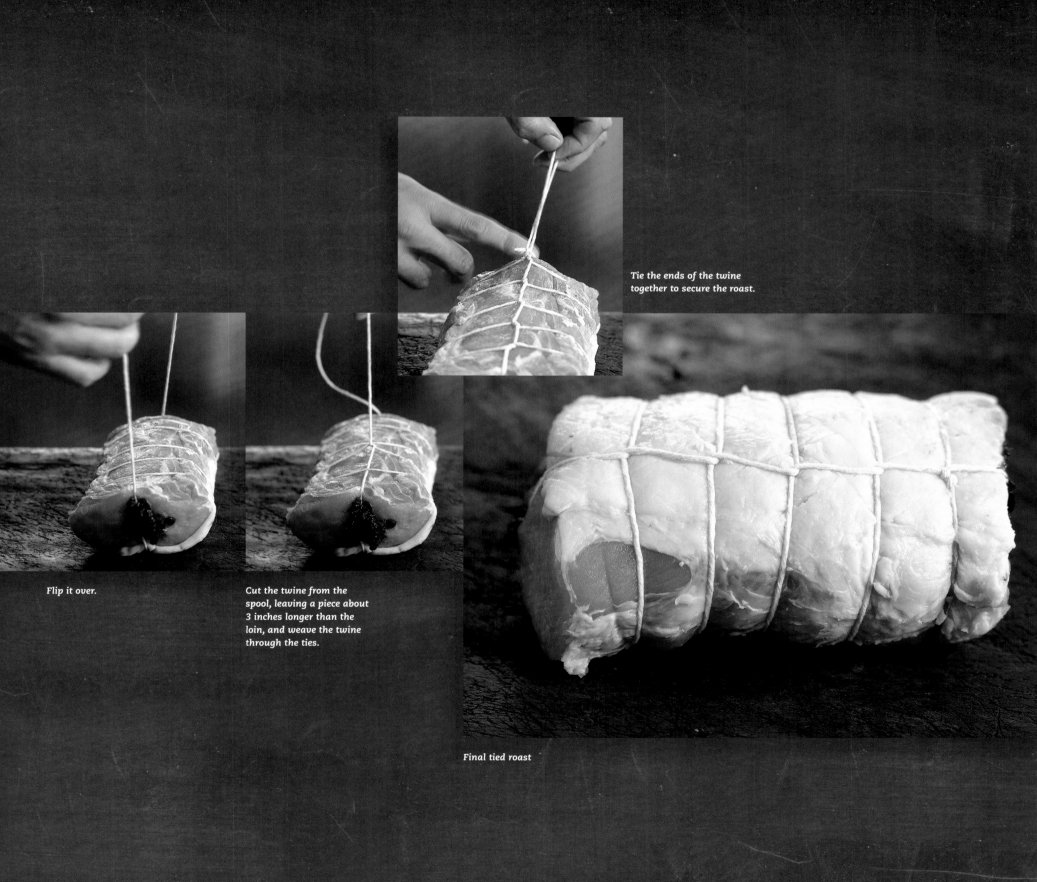

Tie the ends of the twine together to secure the roast.

Flip it over.

Cut the twine from the spool, leaving a piece about 3 inches longer than the loin, and weave the twine through the ties.

Final tied roast

fresh pork belly Pork belly is simply wonderful. It gives us bacon and pancetta. It can be braised or turned into confit. Because it's so rich, with a nearly even ratio of fat to meat, you wouldn't want to serve big portions. Instead you might combine it with something else, such as big sea scallops. Ask your butcher or supermarket for the center cut of the belly, which will have the best proportion of meat to fat (if you buy it from a supermarket, you'll probably need to order it ahead of time).

Pork belly is a tough muscle, so it must first be braised or confited for hours to tenderize it; both methods follow. Then it can be sliced into smaller pieces and sautéed to develop a lovely crisp exterior while the center remains succulent and tender.

After cooking the pork belly, we like to press it, weighting it down, as it cools, for a more uniform shape and a better texture, but, strictly speaking, it's not essential; you can simply allow the belly to cool submerged in the fat or cooking liquid. Then it can be cut in different ways—sliced lengthwise, for example, almost like bacon, and served at brunch. If you want to serve it with scallops, cut it into pieces roughly the same size as the scallops. Sautéed Broccoli Rabe with Garlic and Chile Flakes (page 195) would make a good side dish in that case.

Pork Brine (page 339), cold
One 2½-pound slab pork belly with skin
About 6 cups (3 pounds) lard
Canola oil
Gray salt or coarse sea salt

Pour the brine into a container large enough to hold the pork belly and add the pork. Refrigerate for 10 hours (no longer, or the pork may become too salty).

Remove the pork belly (discard the brine) and rinse under cold water. Pat dry with paper towels, or let air-dry.

Preheat the oven to 200°F.

Choose an ovenproof pot, such as a 12-quart Dutch oven, that is only slightly larger than the pork belly and has a lid; the pot should be just large enough that the pork will be surrounded by the lard. Put the belly in the pot and cover with the lard; the lard should cover the pork by ½ to ¾ inch.

Heat the pot over low heat until the lard registers 190°F. Cover, transfer to the oven, and cook until the pork is meltingly tender; this will probably take 5½ to 6 hours, but start checking after 4 hours. As the belly cooks, it will lose fat and shrink; it is best to transfer the meat and fat to a smaller pot, always keeping the belly covered by fat. Remove the pot from the oven and let cool to room temperature.

The belly can simply be refrigerated in its fat, but we prefer to press it to compress the internal layers of connective tissue and force out some of the excess fat, resulting in a better texture and appearance. To press it, transfer it to a deep baking dish. Pour enough fat into the dish to just cover the belly. Cover with plastic wrap, top with a smaller baking dish, and weight it down with a brick or large can. Refrigerate for at least 12 hours; reserve the extra fat.

Once it's been pressed, the pork belly can be refrigerated, covered by fat (add some of the reserved fat if necessary), for up to 1 week.

To serve, remove the pot from the refrigerator and let sit in a warm spot to soften the fat for 2 to 3 hours. You want to soften the fat enough so you can scrape it from the belly while keeping the belly as cold as possible so it will be easier to slice.

continued

Remove the pork belly from the fat, and wipe off any cooking fat that clings to the meat. Remove the skin and score the fat on the belly in a crosshatch pattern. The belly can be cut into any shape. Slice it or cut it into squares, and let sit at room temperature for 20 to 30 minutes before sautéing. (The fat can be reused to confit pork belly several more times as long as it does not taste too salty. Pour it into a pot and heat gently to liquefy, then strain through a fine-mesh conical strainer into a storage container. Refrigerate for up to 2 months or freeze for up to 6 months.)

Preheat the oven to 350°F.

Heat some canola oil in a large ovenproof frying pan over medium-high heat just until smoking. Put the pieces of belly fat-side-down in the skillet, reduce the heat to medium-low, and cook until the excess fat is rendered and the fat side is browned, about 18 minutes; pour off excess fat about halfway through the cooking.

When the pork is browned, transfer the pan to the oven to heat through, about 10 minutes. Remove from the oven, sprinkle with gray salt, and serve.   **SERVES 6 AS AN APPETIZER**

braised pork belly

Pork Brine (page 339), cold
One 2½-pound slab pork belly, skin removed
Kosher salt and freshly ground black pepper
2 to 3 cups Beef Stock (page 340), warmed

Pour the brine into a container large enough to hold the pork belly and add the pork. Refrigerate for 10 hours (no longer, or the pork may become too salty).

Remove the pork (discard the brine) and rinse under cold water. Pat dry with paper towels, or let air-dry.

Preheat the oven to 325°F.

Season the pork belly with salt and pepper. Put the belly fat-side-down in an ovenproof sauté pan that is just large enough to hold it comfortably. Set over medium-low heat and cook until it begins to render out the fat. Cook until the fat is golden brown, about 15 minutes; pour off the excess fat several times as the belly cooks.

Remove the belly from the pan and pour off all of the remaining fat, then return the pork to the pan, fat side down. Ladle in enough stock to come about halfway up the belly and bring to a simmer. Cover with a parchment lid (see page 120), transfer to the oven, and cook, checking it once an hour, until tender, about 2½ hours.

Turn the belly over, baste with the pan juices, and return to the oven, uncovered, to glaze the pork, about 10 minutes. Remove the pan from the oven and let cool to room temperature.

The belly can simply be stored in its liquid, but we prefer to press it to compress the internal layers of connective tissue and force out some of the excess fat, resulting in a better texture and appearance. To press it, transfer it to a deep baking dish. Pour enough braising liquid into the dish to just cover the belly. Cover with plastic wrap, top with a smaller baking dish, and weight it down with a brick or large can. Refrigerate for at least 12 hours. Reserve the extra liquid.

Once it's been pressed, the belly can be refrigerated, completely covered by liquid (add some of the additional reserved liquid if necessary), for up to 3 days.

To serve, preheat the oven to 400°F.

Remove any fat that may have solidified on the surface of the liquid. Put the belly fat side down in an ovenproof sauté pan and add enough of the liquid to come about ¼ inch up the meat. Bring to a simmer over medium heat, spooning the juices over the meat. Transfer the (uncovered) pan to the oven and cook, basting the meat once or twice, until heated through, about 15 minutes. Turn the meat over and baste several times, then return to the oven for another 5 minutes, basting every 2 minutes, until the meat is richly browned and glazed with the braising liquid.

Meanwhile, pour the remaining braising liquid into a saucepan, bring to a simmer, and reduce to the consistency of a sauce.

Carve the meat into ½-inch slices, sprinkle with gray salt, and serve with the reduced sauce on the side.

SERVES 6 AS AN APPETIZER OR 4 AS A MAIN COURSE

brining meats & fish

Brining is a powerful tool. It can cure chicken, pork, other meats, and fish, as well as change their texture, flavor, and juiciness. It also allows us to season meat or fish uniformly.

We brine chicken and pork long enough to introduce flavors into the meat. This is especially noticeable in Buttermilk Fried Chicken (page 16)—in fact, the brining is what distinguishes this preparation. A seasoned crust is easy (flour is flour), but the herb-infused brine gives the meat a wonderful aromatic flavor. Pork also absorbs flavors well and, because of the nature of the osmotic effect of the salt, the meat actually retains more moisture after cooking.

We don't flavor the brine for fish as we do for meat brines because we don't brine them long enough for flavor to penetrate. So it is simply salt in solution and it works well for all fish that will be cooked. The brine is usually a solution of one part salt to ten parts water. The quick brining seasons the flesh, gives it a little firmer texture, and, most important, prevents its soluble protein from coagulating into unsightly white masses on its surface as it cooks.

As a rule thin fillets, such as sole, should be brined for 3 to 5 minutes. Pieces that are 1 inch thick or more can be brined for 10 minutes. And we almost always give clams and mussels a brine, or a series of short brines, to help purge them of sand.

Brining fish, chicken, and pork also ensures uniform and perfect seasoning, perhaps the most important factor in the quality of a finished dish.

From a technique standpoint, the one critical thing to remember is that the brine needs to be completely chilled before you add the meat or fish. Therefore, it's a good idea to make your brine the day before you'll need it. Brine times are important—so stick to them—but keep in mind that the brined food does not have to be cooked immediately: it has in effect been cured by the brine, so once it's removed from the brine it can be refrigerated for a day before being cooked.

Finally, discard the brine after it's used—never reuse it.

slow-roasted veal shank

2 whole veal shanks (about 4 pounds each)

1 large onion, cut into 1-inch pieces

3 large carrots, cut into 1-inch pieces

3 large celery stalks, cut into 1-inch pieces

Kosher salt and freshly ground black pepper

Canola oil

Gremolata (recipe follows)

gremolata

⅓ cup Dried Bread Crumbs (page 273)

1 to 2 teaspoons extra virgin olive oil

3 tablespoons finely chopped flat-leaf parsley

1 lemon

1 medium garlic clove, or to taste

Kosher salt and freshly ground black pepper

Rather than buying veal shank pieces to make osso buco, a common preparation for this muscle, try slow-roasting the whole shank. The meat acquires a texture like the long-cooked and pulled pork you might enjoy at a barbecue. Veal has a subtle flavor, but the long cooking time helps it to develop some complexity, enhanced in the end by the gremolata, the traditional garlic-parsley-lemon-zest garnish. This would be excellent with Polenta (page 218).

Remove the veal shanks from the refrigerator and let sit at room temperature for 45 minutes.

Preheat the oven to 275°F.

Toss the onion, carrots, and celery together and spread out in a small roasting pan or baking dish large enough to hold the shanks.

Season the shanks generously on all sides with salt and pepper. Heat some canola oil in a frying pan over medium-high heat until shimmering. Put 1 shank in the pan and cook, turning occasionally, until golden on all sides, about 6 minutes. Place on the vegetables, and repeat with the remaining shank.

Transfer the pan to the oven and cook for 7 to 8 hours, turning the shank 3 or 4 times during the cooking to brown evenly. Cook until the meat is extremely tender and can be pulled off the bones with a meat fork. Remove from the oven and let rest in a warm spot for 30 minutes.

Stand the shanks on end on a platter to present at the table. With two meat forks, pull the meat from the bones. Sprinkle each serving with gremolata.

SERVES 6

Gremolata, a mixture of lemon zest, finely minced garlic, and chopped parsley, brings a lemony freshness to any number of dishes. It's traditionally used with braised dishes as a bright counterpoint to the deep rich flavor of, say, osso buco or braised short ribs, but its lemonyness makes it a perfect garnish for fish. Traditionally gremolata does not have bread crumbs, but I love the crunch that they add.

Put the bread crumbs in a small bowl and toss with just enough olive oil to lightly coat. Toss in the parsley. Using a Microplane grater, grate the lemon zest and then the garlic into the bowl (if you don't have a Microplane, zest the lemon with a box grater and finely mince the garlic). Season to taste with salt and pepper. The gremolata is best served shortly after it is made. **MAKES A GENEROUS ½ CUP**

FLAT OR CURLY Parsley plays an important role in cooking whether used fresh or cooked. Like most chefs I know, I prefer flat-leaf parsley to curly, because it is less assertive and has a more gently herbaceous quality. In this gremolata, the fresh flat-leaf parsley imparts vivid color and fresh taste. Parsley also falls into a category of ingredient we call aromatics, those herbs, spices, and vegetables—thyme, bay leaves, peppercorns, garlic, onions, and leeks, for example—that we add to stocks, soups, stews, and braising liquids for their aromatic qualities.

breaded veal cutlets

2 pounds trimmed veal top round, cut across the grain into
    twelve ½-inch-thick slices

3 small or 2 medium fennel bulbs

About 3 cups panko crumbs

All-purpose flour for dredging

2 to 3 large eggs

Kosher salt and freshly ground black pepper

Peanut or canola oil for shallow-frying

6 ounces (about 8 loosely packed cups) arugula, rinsed and dried

1 lemon, cut into 8 wedges

3 tablespoons extra virgin olive oil

Instead of buying presliced cutlets, consider slicing the meat yourself. It's always better to cut thicker cutlets and pound them thin, as opposed to cutting them thin to start, because pounding tenderizes the meat. You can do this with other meats for cutlets too. When it comes to veal, we prefer cutlets cut from the top round.

As with all meats, try to find humanely raised veal. It will be a little darker in color and have a richer, more complex flavor than other veal.

Lay 2 pieces of veal on a large piece of plastic wrap, cover with a second piece of plastic wrap, and, using a meat pounder, pound to ¼ inch thick. Transfer to a plate and repeat with the remaining veal. (The cutlets can be wrapped and refrigerated for up to 12 hours.)

Fill a large bowl with ice water. Remove the stalks from the fennel bulbs. Using a Japanese mandoline, vegetable slicer, or a very sharp knife, thinly shave the fennel crosswise. Transfer to the ice water to keep the fennel crisp. Set aside.

Place the panko crumbs in a food processor and pulse until finely ground.

Set up a dipping station: Put about ½ inch of flour in a shallow bowl wide enough to hold the cutlets. Lightly beat 2 eggs in a second bowl. Spread ½ inch of panko crumbs in the third. Replenish each bowl as needed.

Line a baking sheet with parchment paper. Season the meat with salt and pepper and coat each piece, one at a time: Dip both sides of a cutlet in the flour, patting off any excess, then dip into the eggs, letting any excess drip back into the bowl, and then coat on both sides with panko crumbs, patting them so they adhere; transfer to the baking sheet.

Preheat the oven to 200°F. Set a cooling rack over a baking sheet.

Pour just under ½ inch of peanut oil into a large frying pan and heat to 350°F. Add 2 cutlets to the hot oil and cook for about 1 minute on each side, until crisp and golden. Transfer to the rack, and keep warm in the oven. With a skimmer, remove any pieces of coating remaining in the oil. (Do not allow the oil to get too hot, or any bits of coating will burn and give the oil an off taste.) Fry the remaining cutlets in batches, transferring them to the oven.

Drain the fennel and pat dry. Toss with the arugula in a large bowl. Squeeze 2 of the lemon wedges over the greens. Drizzle the olive oil around the sides of the bowl (see photo, page 134), season with salt and pepper, and toss.

Arrange the cutlets on one side of a platter, overlapping them. Arrange the greens on the other side of the platter. Garnish the platter with the remaining lemon wedges.   **SERVES 6**

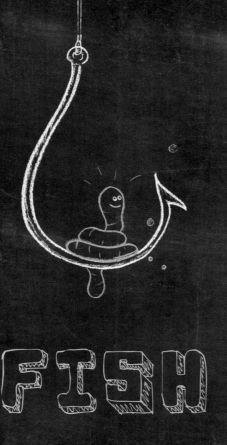

FISH

How well you cook fish depends on how well you buy fish. The quality of fish varies wildly, so learn how to choose it well. Develop a relationship with your fishmonger and enlist his or her help. Look for the three obvious signs of freshness. You want whole fish with clear bulging eyes, not eyes that are sunken and cloudy. Aroma is critical—your fish should smell clean, like the fresh ocean, not fishy like low tide. And the flesh should have elasticity—

in other words, be resilient to the touch. Don't be afraid ask your fishmonger if you can smell and touch the fish to check for all of these. When buying fillets, the same rules for aroma and firmness apply. Fillets should look moist, not dried out, and if it's a white fish, there should be almost a translucence to the flesh.

As with chicken, I encourage you to buy fish whole and to butcher it yourself, to learn about fish in that way. Snapper, bass, trout, and Arctic char are all commonly available whole. But whether you buy it whole or in fillets or steaks, I hope you think of cooking fish as fun, because there are so many ways to do it: over high heat in a sauté pan or with low heat in the oven, packed in salt, or poached in oil. One way to think of fish is to divide it into two categories, thicker fish (salmon and halibut, for example) and thin fish (sole and trout, for example). Learning how each type responds to moist or dry heat, to low or high heat, teaches you how most of the other fish in the same category will behave.

As far as buying bivalves—clams, oysters, and mussels—and other shellfish, again, the source is important, especially for any you will serve raw. Plan to buy these on the day you want to cook them; shellfish should not be stored at home for more than a day.

Sustainability truly is an issue now with fish and seafood, and we need to pay attention to our choices. You can keep track of sustainable choices through groups that monitor the health of our oceans, such as the Monterey Bay Aquarium and its Seafood Watch program (www.mbayaq.org/cr/seafoodwatch.aspx).

OVERLEAF: *New England–Style Clambake (page 90).* OPPOSITE: *Soft-Shell Crabs with Sweet-and-Sour Cherry Gastrique (page 82).*

soft-shell crabs with sweet-and-sour cherry gastrique

6 prime soft-shell crabs (about 2 ounces each),
    preferably cleaned by the fishmonger
Peanut or canola oil for deep-frying
¼ to ⅓ cup cornstarch or potato starch
12 baby Bibb lettuce leaves, washed and dried
Extra virgin olive oil
Kosher salt
Cherry Gastrique (page 336)
½ red onion, thinly sliced
About 2 teaspoons coarsely chopped chives

There's something very special about soft-shell crabs: they're available only during one small window of the year, late spring into summer; they're impressive to serve; and they're fun to eat, especially because of their unique texture. I ate them growing up in Maryland, and I have great memories of soft-shell crab sandwiches. We serve them two ways, in little lettuce cups with a sweet-sour cherry sauce, or as open-faced sandwiches with a spicy aioli; see the variation.

Soft-shell crabs should be bought live and cooked the day they are purchased. You can have the fishmonger clean them or do it yourself; see the instructions. Soft-shell crabs are graded by size; prime crabs are about 4½ to 5 inches across.

If the crabs haven't been cleaned, using a pair of scissors, cut off the face of each crab just behind the eyes. Pull off the apron, the pointed piece on the underside of the crab. Remove the lungs and any other matter beneath the top shell.

Put the crabs upside down on a cutting board and cut each crab into 4 pieces: First cut straight down the center to divide the crab in half. Then cut each half in half, so that the three bottom legs are on one piece and the claw and first leg are on the other. Rinse the pieces and pat dry thoroughly with paper towels (excess moisture will cause the oil to splatter), then put on a paper-towel-lined baking sheet.

Preheat the oven to 200°F. Set a cooling rack over a baking sheet and line with paper towels.

Fill a large, deep pot with 2 inches of peanut oil and heat the oil to 350°F. Put a thin layer of cornstarch in a large bowl. Place 8 pieces of crab (2 crabs) in the bowl and turn and roll just to lightly coat. Lift up the crabs by the ends of the legs, holding all of the pieces of crab at once, and carefully add them to the hot oil. Using a spider or slotted spoon, turn the pieces as necessary to brown them on all sides, for 2 to 2½ minutes. Transfer to the towel-lined rack and keep warm in the oven. Repeat with the remaining crabs.

Arrange the lettuce leaves on a platter. Drizzle the greens with olive oil and season with salt. Top with the crab pieces and garnish with the onions. Put the gastrique in a small bowl, sprinkle with the chives, and serve on the side.

PHOTOGRAPH ON PAGE 81

SERVES 6 AS AN APPETIZER OR
FOR LUNCH OR 3 AS A MAIN COURSE

SOFT-SHELL CRABS ON TOAST WITH PIMENT D'ESPELETTE AIOLI
Omit the gastrique, onion, chives, olive oil, and salt. Toast 12 slices of brioche or other egg bread. Cook the crabs as directed. Spread the toasts with Piment d'Espelette Aioli (page 333) and top with the lettuce leaves. Arrange 2 pieces of the crab on each toast, and garnish with Pickled Red Onions (page 257).

crab cakes

1½ teaspoons (¼ ounce) unsalted butter

2 tablespoons finely diced onion

2 tablespoons finely diced red bell pepper

1 garlic clove

1¼ pounds lump and/or jumbo crabmeat, such as Dungeness or
Maryland Blue crab, picked over for shells and cartilage

¼ cup Piment d'Espelette Aioli (page 333)

1 teaspoon Worcestershire sauce

1 teaspoon Dijon mustard

1 teaspoon finely chopped flat-leaf parsley

1 teaspoon Old Bay seasoning, or to taste

1 teaspoon kosher salt

1 tablespoon fresh lemon juice

2½ cups panko crumbs (see Note)

1 large egg

Canola oil

Piquillo Pepper Vinaigrette (page 182)

Crab cakes are traditionally made with the blue crabs that are abundant on the Eastern Seaboard, but the most important thing is to use good crabmeat. We make ours from Dungeness crab, more available on the West Coast. Buy the best crabmeat you can get, regardless of the type, with plenty of big chunks of meat for a great texture. The cakes are served with a vinaigrette seasoned with piquillo pepper, a sweet smoky pepper—which could also dress a garnish of bitter or spicy greens, such as frisée or endive.

Position two oven racks in the lower and upper thirds of the oven and preheat the oven to 350°F.

Melt the butter in a small saucepan over medium heat. Reduce the heat to medium-low and add the onion and pepper. Grate the garlic with a Microplane grater directly into the pan (or mince it and add it). Cook, stirring often, until the onion and pepper are tender, about 5 minutes. Remove from the heat and let cool completely.

continued

Using your hands to measure is more efficient and satisfying than using measuring spoons. Figure out how much salt you pick up when you take a pinch between your thumb and three fingers, two fingers, and one finger. Take a pinch of salt, put it in the palm of your hand, and then transfer the salt to a ¼ or ½ teaspoon measure to see *exactly* how much you pick up. You might also measure out a teaspoon of salt and put it in your palm so that you know what a teaspoon of salt *looks* like. (For more on salt and pinch volumes, see page 52.)

Place the cleaned crabmeat in a fine-mesh basket strainer and drain well.

In a large bowl, whisk the aioli with the Worcestershire, mustard, parsley, Old Bay, salt, and lemon juice to combine well. Stir in ½ cup of the panko crumbs and the onion mixture. Gently fold in the crab. Lightly whisk the egg in a small bowl, and gently fold it into the mixture.

Put the remaining 2 cups panko crumbs in a shallow bowl. Divide the crab mixture into 12 equal portions. One portion at a time, gently shape the mixture into a ball (the mixture is very delicate because there is only a small amount of panko in it), roll gently in the panko to coat, and shape into a slightly flattened ball about 2 inches in diameter and 1 inch thick. Add a bit more panko as needed to coat, and set on a plate.

Heat some canola oil in each of two large ovenproof frying pans over medium heat until it shimmers. (If you don't have two pans, cook the cakes in batches and transfer to a rack set over a baking sheet, then finish in the oven.) Add the cakes, pat down gently, still maintaining the rounded shape, and cook until golden brown on the first side, about 5 minutes. With a spatula, gently turn each crab cake over and cook on the second side for another 5 minutes, or until golden brown. Transfer the pans to the oven and cook for 2 to 3 minutes, to ensure that the crab cakes are hot throughout.

Line a small baking sheet with paper towels. Transfer the crab cakes to the towels to briefly drain. Arrange the crab cakes on a serving platter and serve the vinaigrette on the side.

SERVES 6 AS AN APPETIZER OR 4 AS A MAIN COURSE

NOTE ON PANKO *Panko is a special kind of bread crumb made in Japan and available at most grocery stores. The crumbs are large, coarse, and very hard; they don't absorb cooking oil the way other bread crumbs do, which means you wind up with a wonderfully crisp crust. Therefore, we prefer panko when food is being fried, as here; but it can also be used in any other preparation where bread crumbs are called for.*

1½ pounds (about 4 cups) cooked lobster (see Note)

3 to 4 tablespoons mayonnaise

2 tablespoons minced red onion

2 tablespoons finely chopped peeled celery

2 teaspoons finely chopped tarragon

2 teaspoons finely chopped flat-leaf parsley

2 teaspoons finely chopped chives

Kosher salt and freshly ground black pepper

½ lime

6 New England–style (top-slit) hot dog buns or other hot dog buns, preferably unsliced

4 tablespoons (2 ounces) unsalted butter, melted

1 celery stalk

1 head butter lettuce, leaves separated, rinsed, dried, and torn into pieces

Pickled Red Onions (page 257)

I leave the chunks of lobster large, ¾ inch or so, to appreciate its texture and give a juicy, luxurious feel, and then bind them with an herb mayonnaise. Find hot dog buns that are slit down the top or uncut, so that you can slice them that way, and then grill the outsides for color and flavor. We garnish this seashore classic with mildly acidic pickled red onions and, for crunch, ribbons of celery. A summery side dish, such as Corn on the Cob with Lime Salt (page 188), would also go well.

Put the lobster meat in a large bowl, add the mayonnaise, and stir gently to coat. Add the onion, celery, tarragon, parsley, chives, and salt and pepper to taste and stir gently to mix. Squeeze the lime over the salad and fold in the juice. Cover and refrigerate.

If using top-slit buns, brush butter on both outer sides of each bun. If using unsliced buns, slit them open from the top, then trim each long side to create a flat surface and brush with melted butter. If using regular hot dog buns, open the buns and brush with butter. Heat a frying pan over medium-high heat. Just before serving, put the rolls in the pan and brown the buttered sides.

To serve, peel the strings from the celery with a vegetable peeler. Using a Japanese mandoline or other vegetable slicer, or a sharp knife, slice the celery lengthwise into thin ribbons. Line each bun with a couple of small pieces of lettuce. Mound the lobster salad in the buns and garnish with the celery and pickled red onions.

PHOTOGRAPH ON PAGE 86   **SERVES 4 TO 6**

NOTE *For this quantity of lobster meat, you will need five 1¼-pound lobsters. Lobsters that have grown too big are not as tender. To cook the lobsters yourself, see page 342.*

Here's a tip to extract more meat from a lobster. Pull off the legs from a cooked lobster. Cut off the wider end of each leg. Lay the legs down on the counter, with the pincers facing you. Using a rolling pin, roll from the pincers toward the cut end: the pressure will cause a strand of lobster meat, "spaghetti," to emerge from each leg. (Makes a great cook's snack.)

OPPOSITE: *Maine Lobster Rolls (page 84)*

caramelized sea scallops

1 cup (5 ounces) Diamond Crystal kosher salt, plus more to taste

2 cups boiling water

8 cups cold water

12 U7 sea scallops (about 1¾ pounds; see headnote),
    preferably dry-packed, tough side muscle removed from each one

About 2 tablespoons (1 ounce) Clarified Butter (page 335)

½ lemon (optional)

I always buy big scallops, graded U7, meaning there are 7 of this size in a pound, and for this dish, we brine them to season them all the way through. Scallops are great with sweet, earthy, or salty things, such as the Braised Pork Belly (page 74) or Melted Leek Rounds (page 337).

Line a small baking sheet with paper towels. Combine the salt with the boiling water in a large bowl, stirring to dissolve the salt (if using another brand, use 5 ounces—see page 52). Add the cold water.

Add the scallops to the brine and let stand for 10 minutes (no longer, or the scallops may become too salty).

Drain the scallops, rinse under cold water, and arrange in a single layer on the paper towels.

Heat the clarified butter in a large stainless steel frying pan over medium-high heat until it ripples and begins to smoke. (Although you may be tempted to use a nonstick pan, a stainless steel pan will produce a more beautiful caramelized exterior.) Sprinkle the scallops lightly with salt and add them to the pan, without crowding. (If necessary, cook the scallops in two pans or in 2 batches; if they touch, they will steam rather than caramelize.) Cook, without moving the scallops, until the bottoms are a rich golden brown, 3 to 3½ minutes. Turn the scallops and caramelize the second side.

Transfer the scallops to a serving platter and serve with a squeeze of lemon juice on top, if desired.   SERVES 6

The best way to sear a piece of fish or meat is over high heat. After you put the fish or meat into the pan, don't try to move it—let it cook until the bottom browns and releases on its own. When it is ready to turn over, turn it and, if possible, put it in a different part of the pan. The surface there will be hotter and give the best sear to the second side.

new england–style clambake

Kosher salt

2 pounds clams, preferably steamers or Manila

18 extra-large (16–20 count) shrimp

2 pounds mussels, preferably Bouchot, scrubbed and debearded

1½ pounds Red Bliss or other red potatoes, about 1½ inches in diameter

Canola oil

Fleur de sel

8 ounces andouille sausage, cut into 3- to 4-inch-long pieces

6 ears corn, shucked, ends trimmed, and cut in half

Three 1- to 1¼-pound lobsters

2 large eggs

Melted butter

Malt vinegar

Lemon wedges

Old Bay seasoning

OTHER MATERIAL

Enough clean rocks to cover the bottom of a 20-quart pot

1 pound seaweed (from the fishmonger), rinsed well in hot water

A clambake is one of the great family-style American regional meals—fun to put together, festive, and impressive, especially when everything is served spilled out across the table, in all its abundance. This one includes potatoes, corn, lobster, sausage, shrimp, mussels, and, of course, steamers. Buy Bouchot mussels if you can; they are very small and tasty. The key to a good clambake is making sure everything is done at the same time. We wrap the different ingredients separately in cheesecloth bundles so we can control their cooking.

You can cook this on an outdoor grill or use the indoor method described here; both methods use rocks and seaweed.

The clams, mussels, and shrimp are all soaked in a salt brine, to clean any grit from the clams and mussels and flavor the shrimp. We use a ratio of 10 parts water to 1 part salt by weight; this translates as 8 cups water to 1¼ cups salt for a basic brine. Begin by mixing up one batch, stirring to dissolve the salt, then make more brine if needed.

Scrub the clams and mussels with a clean scouring pad to remove any sand from the shells.

Put the clams in a medium bowl. Add enough of the brine to cover them and let soak for 5 minutes. Lift from the brine and discard it. Soak the clams in brine two more times, then rinse under cold water.

Put the shrimp in a bowl, add enough brine to cover, and let stand for 10 minutes. Lift out the shrimp and rinse under cold water.

Put the mussels in a medium bowl. Add enough of the brine to cover and let soak for 5 minutes. Lift from the brine and discard it. Meanwhile, using a small pair of scissors (such as nail scissors) or a sharp paring knife, cut a slit down the back of each shrimp, beginning at the head and stopping before the last tail segment, and cutting just slightly into the flesh. Carefully open the shell just enough to find the intestinal tract; remove it with a paring knife and discard.

Meanwhile, arrange the rocks in an even layer in the bottom of a 20-quart stockpot and cover with half the seaweed spread in an even layer. Add water to come to just below the top of the seaweed (the ingredients will be steamed and should not come in contact with the water). Set the pot over high heat and bring to a boil.

Toss the potatoes with canola oil to coat and season generously with fleur de sel. Put the potatoes in the center of a double layer of cheesecloth about 18 inches square, bundle the cloth around the potatoes, and tie with kitchen twine.

Wrap the mussels and clams together in a slightly larger cheesecloth square and tie it. Wrap the shrimp and sausage in separate bundles.

Add the potatoes to the pot, cover, and cook for 12 minutes. Add the corn and the sausage to the pot, and tuck in the lobsters and shellfish bundles. Tuck in the eggs—they will let you know when the clambake is cooked. Cover and cook for 15 minutes. Remove 1 of the eggs and crack it open. When the clambake is ready, the egg will be hard-cooked. If it is not, cover and cook for about 3 minutes longer, then check the second egg.

Transfer the bundles and other ingredients to a tray. Arrange the remaining seaweed in the bottom of a large deep platter. Open all the bundles and cut the lobsters lengthwise in half. Arrange all the ingredients on the platter, interspersing them. Tuck in the hard-boiled egg. Serve with melted butter, malt vinegar, lemon wedges, and Old Bay seasoning on the side.

PHOTOGRAPH ON PAGE 79　　　　　　　　　　　　　　　SERVES 6

Mussels and clams should be closed tightly when you buy them. If they're open and you squeeze them, they should close tightly and remain closed. If a mussel or clam doesn't close, discard it.

When cooking mussels and clams, they should all open; those that don't open should be discarded.

pan-roasted halibut

2 pounds halibut fillet, cut into 12 rectangular pieces

Kosher salt

Canola oil

Extra virgin olive oil

Fleur de sel

Halibut stands up well to heat and so is good for pan-roasting. It has a beautiful flake, and serving this very white fish with vivid-green pea shoots and yellow chanterelles (see page 206) is visually appealing. Other sides might include Butter-Poached Marble Potatoes (page 223), Asparagus and Tomato-Bacon Stew (page 193), or Buttered Farro (page 219).

Remove the fish from the refrigerator and let stand for 15 minutes.

Position oven racks in the lower and upper thirds of the oven and preheat the oven to 350°F.

Check the halibut to be sure all bones were removed. Season on both sides with salt. Add some canola oil to two large ovenproof frying pans and heat over high heat until it shimmers. (If you don't have two pans, cook the fish in batches and transfer to a rack set over a baking sheet, then finish in the oven.) Add 6 pieces of halibut to each pan, presentation (nicer) side down, lower the heat to medium-high, and cook for 4 to 5 minutes, until the bottom of the fish is golden. Lower the heat to medium-low and cook for 2 more minutes.

Transfer the pans to the oven and cook for about 2 minutes, until just cooked through.

Remove the pans from the oven, flip the fish over, and "kiss" the second side for about 30 seconds. Transfer to a platter, and serve with a drizzle of olive oil and a sprinkling of fleur de sel.   **SERVES 6**

poached salmon

Court Bouillon (page 341)

One 2½- to 3-pound side of salmon, any pinbones removed

Maldon salt or other flaky sea salt

Small dill sprigs

Extra virgin olive oil

Salmon is a wonderfully flavorful fish, and it's very versatile. You can grill it, steam it, poach it, cure it, slow cook it in oil . . . the only thing you shouldn't do with salmon is overcook it. We provide the option of serving it hot or cold. The salmon is poached in a court bouillon, which basically translates as "quick stock," water flavored with aromatic vegetables, herbs, and some white wine or another acidic element. Poaching fish in court bouillon infuses it with flavor, and the gentle cooking keeps it moist. (The court bouillon can be strained, refrigerated, and used one more time.)

Try this as a hot main course on Caramelized Savoy Cabbage (page 197) and with a vinaigrette, such as Garden Herb Vinaigrette (page 182). Or serve it cold for brunch or lunch with a salad and a classic creamy sauce, such as aioli, with dill and capers and lemon. If you have a fish poacher, it makes a beautiful presentation, but the salmon can also be poached in a roasting pan.

Strain the court bouillon into a saucepan (reserve the vegetables) and heat over medium-high heat to 200°F.

If you don't have a fish poacher, you can poach the salmon in a deep roasting pan—put a rack in the pan if you have one, since that will make removing the salmon easier. Put the fish skin side down on the rack in a fish poacher (or in a large deep roasting pan), and add enough court bouillon to cover the fish completely. If space allows, add some of the reserved vegetables to the court bouillon. Set the pan over medium-high heat and bring the liquid to 200°F. Adjust the heat as necessary to maintain a temperature of 190° to 200°F.

IF THE FISH IS TO BE SERVED COLD: Remove the pan from the heat when the center of the fillet reaches 110°F, about 10 minutes. Allow the fish to cool in the liquid, then refrigerate in the liquid for up to 1 day. If you have used a rack, just lift up the rack with the fish on it to remove from the pan at serving. If you did not use a rack, use the largest spatulas you have (or your hands) to gently lift the salmon from the liquid. Drain well and place on a serving platter.

IF THE FISH IS TO BE SERVED HOT: Remove the pan from the heat when the center of the fillet reaches 120°F. Let the salmon sit in the liquid until the temperature reaches 125°F, then use the rack or two large spatulas to lift the salmon from the liquid, and place on a serving platter.

Sprinkle the fish with Maldon salt and dill, and drizzle with olive oil.

SERVES 6

wild cod en persillade

One 2-pound piece skinless cod top loin

½ cup Dried Bread Crumbs (page 273)

2 teaspoons finely chopped flat-leaf parsley

About 1 tablespoon Dijon mustard

Kosher salt

Canola oil

Fleur de sel

Ask your fishmonger for cod cut from the top loin, the best part (you may need to order in advance). This is the thickest and densest part of the fish. You could also use another white flaky fish, such as halibut, for this simple dish. A *persillade* is a combination of chopped parsley and bread crumbs, here held to the fish by a thin coating of mustard. The fish is sautéed to brown the crust, then finished in the oven. Serve it, as shown in the photograph, with Asparagus Coins (page 192) and Nantes Carrot Stew (page 190).

Remove the cod from the refrigerator and let stand for 15 minutes.

Preheat the oven to 325°F.

Check the cod to be sure that all bones were removed. Cut crosswise into 6 pieces. Combine the bread crumbs and parsley in a shallow bowl. Put the mustard in a small bowl and fill a second small bowl with cold water.

Season the cod fillets on both sides with salt. Dip a brush into the water and then into the mustard (this small amount of water will thin the mustard slightly, making it easy to brush only a thin coating on the fish). Brush the top of each fillet with a light coating of mustard, then dip the mustard side of the fish into the bread crumb mixture to make an even coating; shake the bowl of crumbs slightly before coating each piece so that the crumbs are in an even layer.

Pour some canola oil into an ovenproof frying pan that will hold the pieces of cod without them touching and heat over medium-high heat until the oil just begins to smoke. Lower the heat to medium, put the fish crumb side down in the pan, and cook until the crust is golden brown, about 1 minute.

Transfer the pan to the oven and cook until the fish just begins to flake when prodded with a fork, 8 to 9 minutes.

Arrange the fish on a platter, sprinkle with fleur de sel, and serve.

SERVES 6

roasted monkfish

Four 8-ounce monkfish tail fillets

Canola oil

Kosher salt

4 tablespoons (2 ounces) unsalted butter

4 garlic cloves, smashed, skin left on

6 medium rosemary sprigs

Romesco Sauce (page 333), warmed

24 Baby Leeks (page 214) or Melted Leek Rounds (page 337)

Extra virgin olive oil

Maldon salt or other flaky sea salt

Monkfish is a dense, meaty fish that cooks almost like a roast, so you can pan-roast it, like a pork loin. The herb-infused butter used to baste it flavors the fish and helps it both to cook evenly and to stay moist. As you baste, allow the butter to brown, adding more flavor to the monkfish. The final and important stage is resting the fish. Don't rest very delicate fish because they lose moisture quickly, but monkfish benefits from a rest. The monkfish is perfection with a piquant, acidic romesco sauce or an aioli and sweet leeks, as pictured here.

Remove the fish from the refrigerator and let sit at room temperature for 30 minutes.

Heat some canola oil in a large frying pan over medium-high to high heat just until it smokes. Season 2 of the fillets with salt, add to the pan presentation (rounded) side down, and cook until the first side is pale golden, about 3 minutes. (The monkfish should not be crowded in the pan, so it is best to cook it in 2 batches.) Add 1 tablespoon of the butter to the pan and let it melt, then add a second tablespoon (adding all of the butter at once could bring down the temperature in the pan too quickly and the butter will not brown as well). Once the butter has browned, tilt the pan and baste the fish as you continue to cook it until it is a rich golden brown on the first side, 1 to 2 more minutes.

Turn the fish over, and cook, basting continuously with the butter, until it is a rich golden brown on the second side, 4 to 5 minutes. Add half of the garlic and rosemary to the pan and cook, continuing to baste as the aromatics flavor the butter, until the temperature in the center of the fish is 145°F, about 2 more minutes. Transfer the fish, with the garlic and rosemary, to a plate and keep in a warm spot. Clean the pan and cook the remaining fish in the same manner.

Spread the sauce on a platter and arrange the leeks on top. Top with the fish. Drizzle the fish with olive oil and season with Maldon salt. Garnish with the rosemary and garlic. SERVES 6 TO 8

BASTING WITH BUTTER AND OTHER FATS Basting, spooning hot flavorful fat over the food you are cooking, adds flavor and helps the food cook more quickly and evenly. When we're sautéing a piece of fish, we continue to cook the top of it after we turn it by basting it with that hot fat. We add aromatics such as rosemary or thyme and garlic to the fat to flavor it. We often use a finishing fat, usually butter, for more flavor. Very few foods that are cooked at high temperature are not improved by basting.

salt-crusted striped bass

One 4-pound striped bass, gutted and scaled, fins cut off with scissors

4 cups kosher salt

8 large egg whites

About ½ bunch flat-leaf parsley

Fronds from 1 fennel bulb (reserve the bulb for another use)

2 thin lemon slices

2 thin orange slices

Extra virgin olive oil

Roasting a whole fish in a salt crust makes a very impressive presentation—cracking the crust is an event. And the technique results in very moist fish that's perfectly seasoned (not at all salty). If you have a large ovenproof platter, you can bake it on that and deliver it straight to the table. Saffron Rice (page 220) would be an elegant side dish, with a bowl of Gremolata (page 76) or Lemon Aioli (page 333) as a garnish.

Remove the fish from the refrigerator and let stand for 15 to 30 minutes.

Preheat the oven to 425°F.

Stir together the salt and egg whites in a medium bowl.

On a large ovenproof platter or a baking sheet, make a layer of the salt crust mixture just over ¼ inch thick and slightly larger than the fish, patting the mixture down into an even layer.

Stuff the back end of the cavity of the fish with the parsley and fennel, using twice as much parsley as fennel. Lay the citrus slices next to them, inside the cavity, following the shape of the belly. Center the fish on the salt crust. Working from the bottom to the top of the fish, pat the remaining crust mixture over it in a thin coating, covering it completely. (You may have more of the salt mixture than you need.) Using a paper towel, pat the crust to remove any excess moisture.

Roast for about 40 minutes, turning the pan around once after 20 minutes, until the thickest part of the fish registers about 125°F (insert the thermometer through the crust). Remove from the oven and let rest for 10 minutes.

To serve the fish, have on hand a serving platter and a tray to hold the crust and bones. Crack the crust with a wooden spoon or mallet, breaking it into large pieces, and carefully remove it. Push back the skin and, using a palette knife or narrow spatula, lift the top fillet, in large pieces, from the frame of bones that runs down the center of the fish and place on the serving platter. Then, starting at the tail end, lift the frame out in one piece. Discard the fennel and parsley, and reserve the citrus slices to use as a garnish. Check the bottom fillet for any visible bones and remove them, then lift out the fillet in large pieces and transfer to the platter.

Garnish with the citrus slices and drizzle with olive oil.

SERVES 4 TO 6

oil-poached sturgeon

¼ cup plus 3 tablespoons kosher salt

6 sturgeon fillets (about 6 ounces each)

About 6 cups extra virgin olive oil

4 thyme sprigs, tied together with kitchen twine

1 head garlic, cut in half through the equator

Fleur de sel

Delicate fish can be oil-poached at a gentle heat (120° to 125°F) without breaking up, and a meaty fish prepared in the same way stays very moist. Most fish can be oil-poached this way. Sturgeon is a rich fish with dense, meaty flesh. Pair it with accompaniments that have big flavors, such as the Bacon Vinaigrette (page 179), the sweet intense Peperonata Rustica (page 208), Rainbow Chard with Raisins, Pine Nuts, and Serrano Ham (page 205), or Curried Cauliflower-Chickpea Salad (page 152).

Mix the salt and 2½ cups cold water together in a large bowl, stirring until the salt dissolves. Add the fish and let stand for 10 minutes. Remove the fish from the brine and drain on paper towels; pat dry.

Pour 1 inch of oil into an 11- to 12-inch sauté pan or deep frying pan, add the thyme and garlic, and heat the oil to 140°F over medium heat. Use a diffuser, if you have one, to keep the heat low enough for poaching the fish. Add the fish to the oil: the oil temperature will immediately drop. The idea is to poach the fish at 120° to 125°F, so adjust the heat as necessary. After about 10 minutes, when the fish has whitened, gently turn it and cook for another 5 minutes, or until opaque throughout.

Set a rack over a baking sheet. Transfer the fish to the rack, discarding the thyme and garlic, and let drain for about 1 minute.

Transfer to a platter and serve sprinkled with fleur de sel. **SERVES 6**

crispy fried fish

BATTER

1½ cups whole milk

8 tablespoons (1 stick; 4 ounces) unsalted butter, cut into 8 pieces

½ cup warm water

1 package (¼ ounce; 2¼ teaspoons) active dry yeast

1¾ cups plus 2 tablespoons all-purpose flour

½ teaspoon kosher salt

1 tablespoon granulated sugar

2 large eggs, lightly beaten

¼ teaspoon baking soda

6 fillets petrale or other sole (5½ to 6 ounces each)

¼ cup plus 3 tablespoons kosher salt

Peanut oil for deep-frying

Flour for dredging

Susie Heller came up with the batter for this crispy fried fish. We'd been developing waffle recipes and had invented some great versions, among them buckwheat waffles, waffles lightened with egg white, and cornmeal waffles. Susie changed the proportion of flour in a yeast-leavened batter and used it as a coating for fried fish. It's a great first course or main course—fried fish with a good malt vinegar and aioli, and some fried fingerling chips, little thumb-sized potato chips. You could even use it to make fish tacos, rolled up in flour tortillas with some shredded cabbage, Piment d'Espelette Aioli (page 333), crème fraîche, and a squeeze of lime juice.

A white flaky fish, such as sole or cod, is best. We cure the fish briefly in a strong brine, both to season it and to draw out some of the albumin and firm up the texture a little. This recipe makes more batter than you'll need (it's difficult to reduce the proportions), so if you want to increase the amount of fish by another pound or so, you'll have enough batter.

Combine the milk and butter in a small saucepan and heat over medium heat until the butter melts. Remove from the heat and let cool while you proof the yeast.

Pour the warm water into a small bowl and sprinkle with the yeast. Let sit for 10 minutes, then stir to dissolve the yeast.

Combine the flour, salt, and sugar in a large bowl. Whisk in the dissolved yeast and the milk and butter. Cover tightly with plastic wrap and let sit at room temperature for 1½ hours. The mixture will bubble.

Stir the eggs and baking soda into the yeast mixture; set aside.

Cut each fillet lengthwise into 2 pieces, cutting along either side of the natural line running down the center length of the fillet, to avoid the small bones and blood lines; discard the center piece. Cut the larger piece of each fillet in half on the diagonal, and trim the ends of the pieces on the diagonal as well.

Mix the salt and 2½ cups cold water together in a large bowl, stirring until the salt dissolves. Add the pieces of fish and let sit for 3 to 5 minutes, then remove the fish and drain well on paper towels.

Meanwhile, pour two inches of peanut oil into a large deep pot and heat the oil to 350°F. Preheat the oven to 175°F.

Set a cooling rack over a baking sheet and line the cooling rack with paper towels. Put another baking sheet with a rack in the oven.

Spread ½ inch of flour in a shallow bowl. Have a skimmer ready.

When the oil has reached the proper temperature, dredge 3 pieces of fish in the flour, patting off any excess, then one at a time, dip the fish into the batter, letting excess batter drip off, and slip into the oil. Check the temperature of the oil and adjust the heat as necessary to maintain the temperature. The fish will float to the top of the oil; cook for about 2 minutes, or until a rich golden brown on the bottom, then turn the fish and brown the second side, about 2 minutes. Use the skimmer to lift the fish from the oil and drain on the paper towels; then turn over to drain the second side and transfer to the rack in the oven to keep warm. Skim any pieces of batter from the oil and cook the remaining fish in batches. Serve hot. **SERVES 6 AS A MAIN COURSE**

We love racks. We cool food on them and we also use them to keep food warm in the oven—the rack allows the heat to circulate around the cooked food. We put them in baking sheets to drain blanched vegetables and foods that have been sautéed or deep-fried.

Never leave food sitting in water or cooking fat.

the accidental restaurant

ad hoc (ad häk') [L, to this] *created for a specific situation, without concern for the long term. Synonyms: informal, impromptu, extemporized.*

For fifteen years I'd wanted to open a restaurant featuring burgers, so when a former diner in Yountville became available, not far from The French Laundry and Bouchon, I grabbed it. It would be perfect for the casual restaurant I'd been envisioning.

But our restaurant group was very busy when we bought the property, and I didn't have time to design and build the new restaurant, nor did I have the people—my team was already engaged in other projects. It quickly became clear that my idealized burger restaurant would have to wait. And yet we were paying for this property—we had to put it to use somehow.

So I thought of the simplest restaurant possible, one founded on a style of cooking we do for ourselves every day, if not twice a day, at all our restaurants: preparing the family (staff) meal. Maybe we could create a restaurant that fed our community in the same way we feed ourselves, just for the time being, just until we could design what I had in mind. And so with Jeffrey Cerciello, now director of casual dining for our group, we put together an ad hoc restaurant that would serve family style, a single new menu each day, no choices; whatever Jeffrey and chef Dave Cruz were serving, that's what you'd get. We'd focus on dishes that represented the most important food of all to me, the food from our childhood, food that we eat with our families—hearty soups, beef stews, spaghetti and meatballs—only these dishes would be prepared by truly engaged chefs who would make the best beef stews, the best spaghetti and meatballs possible. We could deepen our understanding of this food, we could try to perfect the family meal while bringing new dishes to the table and exploring family meals from other cultures, most notably those of Italy and Spain. And we called it what it was: Ad Hoc.

It turned out to be a lot of fun—serving platters of fried chicken, tender boneless beef short-ribs, meatballs with papperdelle and mushroom sauce, big beautiful salads—and the people who came to eat connected to this style of service and had fun eating the food. So much so that nobody wanted us to close the restaurant. It became such a surprising success we simply couldn't, and so we decided in September 2007 to keep it open. Ad Hoc is no longer ad hoc, it's permanent. And I can't express how gratifying it is to have a restaurant that serves the kind of food that is so important to me, the food that embodies the pleasures, support, and nourishment we get from family. Sharing this kind of food with family and friends is one of the great pleasures of life.

From: Thomas Keller
To: French Laundry Restaurant Group
Sent: Saturday, April 01, 2006 11:22 PM
Subject: **A fun idea!**

Hello all,

What if we did a temporary restaurant at the Wine Garden?

FUN, Simple, Affordable, 1 Service, No Menu, 4–5 nights a week. Maybe supper on Sunday.

Here it is!

Ad Hoc

Opening as soon as we can

Wed–Sun

Wed–Sat 6:30–9:00

Sunday Supper 3–7

NO MENU

4 courses

Salad course served family-style

Protein (roast, slice, and serve), Starch, and Vegetable.

Old style, SIMPLE

Cheese

Dessert

50.00 plus beverage, tax, and tip

25.00 corkage

40 wines top

All wines will be from our friends and can possibly rotate.

Staff = 1 manager type, 1 wine guy, 1 chef type (maybe me), servers, cooks, and porters. May be a good way to utilize our Bouchon private dining staff.

60 covers a night, 75.00 check average.

What do you think????

Let me know,

T

JEFFREY CERCIELLO None of us knew what to think when we got the e-mail from Thomas about opening a temporary restaurant. A fun idea? Was this just a spur-of-the-moment impulse, or was this something we could really do? He had sent it on April Fools' Day, after all.

He said it was going to be fun. We all wrote back to each other saying, Thomas doesn't do fun. Thomas does complex, refined.

But he was serious, and that weekend a group of us sat around: the directors, Laura Cunningham, Jim Brockman (CFO), Eric Lilivois (COO), Paul Roberts to discuss wines, Thomas, and me. And we all agreed we could do it. I could take Dave Cruz, a Bouchon executive sous-chef, and bring him over to assist me at Ad Hoc for three to six months—it was just temporary. And at the end of the meeting, we said, "OK, let's do this."

I went home that night really, really charged. I'd been focused on Bouchon for about eight years by then, had been at The French Laundry before that, so I'd been involved exclusively in high-end classical technique and French cuisine. This would allow us to stretch way beyond French food. I could experiment with and explore the influences that had shaped me, Thomas could continue his work, Dave could do the same with the influences that had

shaped him, and we could both pursue dishes or techniques that we were simply curious about. It wasn't going to be French. It could feature American regional dishes, it could even be Italian regional, with food from Puglia, where my family originated, and le Marche, both parts of Italy that are largely overlooked. It could offer Spanish and Catalonian meals. And it was all intended to be achieved within the casual home-style cooking that we all loved. I could serve corn on the cob if I wanted! I'd never been

a part of a restaurant like that.

As culinary director for casual dining, I've moved out from behind the line on an everyday basis, so I actually have the energy and inclination to cook at home for my wife and daughters. What was so exciting for me about Ad Hoc was that we could take not only that affection for home cooking techniques, but also our love of rustic home cooking vessels and tools and make them a part of the restaurant.

Because it was to be temporary, we wanted

to spend as little money as possible. Also, we wanted to get it up and running fast. The space had been a restaurant called the Wine Garden, so we cleaned it up, figured out how we'd use the available equipment, bought a few stainless steel tables for work surfaces and a few other necessities for the kitchen. For the dining room, we went to a consignment store, where we bought a bench to put near the entrance, rented a big butcher block table for the center of the room, and picked up a window frame for a piece of etched glass we had. We bought two cast-iron pigs for decoration. Thomas gave us an antique butcher block table from his house, which had been a gift from Susie Heller. A maitre d' stand, originally part of the restaurant Bouchon took over, was hauled out of storage and placed at the front door. We bought some chalkboards on which we'd post the daily menu, some mirrors, and a few other pieces that gave the place a rustic, casual edge. This makeshift decor was OK, because it was temporary—but its being temporary was refreshing, even energizing. Not just for me, but for everybody involved.

Despite the patchwork nature of it all, it still had Thomas's name on it, so it wasn't without the pressure or the necessity to make it the best it could be, in terms of food and service. But that too was part of the excitement.

What I got most excited about were all the plates and the earthenware cooking vessels and serving vessels. Deborah Jones had told me about a store that sold great old cookware in San Francisco, called Cookin. Packed with old and antique cookware, it turned out to be a jackpot. I found some enameled orange cooking/serving dishes that were the same as my grandmother's Descoware from Belgium; she gave them to my mom, and my mom gave them to me, and I've been using them for nearly twenty years. I love them. You can sear chicken thighs in them, then take the chicken out and start building your dish: put in some chopped onion, some tomato, some garlic, and cook that down slowly; add some broth, return the chicken, maybe toss in some olives, some sausage, some fennel, whatever you have on hand; and let it braise on the stovetop until the chicken is tender, then crisp the skin under a broiler—a one-pot meal, so satisfying. I love this kind of cooking. And we were going to cook like that at the restaurant.

So as I was setting up the kitchen, the food, and the work flow, I kept thinking, how would I do this at home? I didn't want the chefs to be cooking with hotel pans and big stockpots—I wanted them to feel, as much as possible, that

this was home cooking. One-pot, economical, efficient, delicious.

The single-menu format does put a certain kind of pressure on us: we've got to nail each dish. You can't have a dish that doesn't work perfectly. Because everybody is getting the same meal, it had to work 100 percent of the time.

Often cookbooks talk about bringing restaurant techniques and styles to home cooking. Ad Hoc is a reflection of the reverse—applying home cooking to a restaurant—and the result is really good home cooking for everyone. Food that's fun to cook, fun to eat and to share. Thomas was right. Ad Hoc was a lot of fun to open—and it still is.

DAVE CRUZ In July 2006, Jeffrey Cerciello asked me what I thought about helping at Ad Hoc. "It would be temporary," he said. "The place will only be around for six or eight months and your spot here at Bouchon will still be here for you." My duties as executive sous-chef at Bouchon included being in charge of the day-to-day operations of the kitchen: running services, leading the sous-chefs and chefs de partie, the entire kitchen. Ad Hoc would be the same, he said, only "temporary,"

and the food would be "American food reminiscent of what Thomas ate as a kid growing up": fried chicken, beef stroganoff, meat loaf. Fried chicken? Beef stroganoff? These are dishes we make for family meal before service. I didn't want to leave my post at an elegant restaurant serving French classics to go make "family meal." I was grateful for the offer, but I respectfully declined.

A couple of weeks passed, and the subject rose again during a meeting between Jeffrey, me, and Joshua Schwartz, the chef de cuisine at Bouchon at the time, and it was decided unilaterally that I would go to Ad Hoc for a couple of

The staff meal cook is a low man in the kitchen hierarchy. You cook meals from scraps for people who work in the kitchen. . . .

Staff meal was first about the fundamentals of cooking and how to work with by-products, using scraps to make something tasty, eye-appealing, and satisfying. But the message underlying that was "Can you be passionate about cooking at this level?" Staff meal. Only the staff sees it. If you can make great food for these people, create that habit, have that drive, that sincerity, and keep that with you and take it to another level in the staff meal, then someday you'll be a great chef. Maybe.

—THE FRENCH LAUNDRY COOKBOOK

months. I would define the systems or protocol for ordering, production, and general operations. It was, they reminded me, *temporary.*

I looked for positives in the situation. I'd have the opportunity to spend more time with Jeff, whom I'd exploit for ideas and inspiration. And for almost three months, I was able to really learn from him. One of his ideas was that if we were going to serve food reminiscent of what someone grew up with in Maryland and south Florida, why not explore what it would have been in Texas, in California, in Pennsylvania, in New England? Or, for that matter, in a particular region of Spain or Italy, or France? Why not serve a Catalan Beef Stew (page 46), a Santa Maria–Style Tri-Tip (page 54), a Clam Chowder with Bacon (page 126), or a Wild Cod en Persillade (page 95)? Now here was something I could get excited about. The food would have a tether to real lives and cultures. Reference points and tethers are important ideas I'd learned from my mentors, Jeffrey and Thomas.

And then one day, while reading through my small library of books at home, looking for inspiration for the menus, I came across an essay that I was sure I'd read before, but never taken much note of.

Right then the whole picture became clear for me. This was what cooking was all about, and I'd been resisting where I most wanted to be. I've come to deeply love and respect the food represented by the recipes in this book. It's some of the best food I know. Preparing a meal for your family is not just a matter of following recipes, but rather a continual, thoughtful process that begins when you ask yourself "What should I make?," carries through the cooking and the eating, and ends when the kitchen is clean (and you begin to think about what you want to cook next).

SOUPS

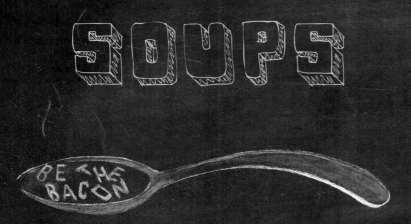

Soup may be the quintessential family meal, a true social dish as we serve ourselves from the same pot. Soup gives us a sense of comfort and warmth, soothes us when we're ill, lifts us when we're down. Soup is generous. When soup is cooking on the stove, the whole house knows it.

My favorite soups are those made from beans and other legumes. But I also love chilled summer soups, which are light and refreshing. The soups here are big and hearty, stew-like creations packed

with ingredients, and they can be a great start to a meal or a meal in themselves.

When making big soups, one technique to keep in mind is the sweating of aromatic vegetables, which deepens and intensifies their sweetness. Once the liquid is in and brought up to temperature, skim the fat and impurities on the surface. You always want to be removing what you don't want in the finished dish, so frequent skimming is a constant in my kitchen. It applies to almost any liquid that's being cooked. It's especially important to skim stocks so that when they are finished and strained, they taste as clean and light as possible. (By setting your pot half off the burner, you create a current that pushes impurities to one side of the pot, making it easier to skim them away.)

Similarly, any vegetable that's been in the soup for, say, 45 minutes or longer has imparted all its flavor to the liquid. You wouldn't want to add flavorless ingredients to a soup before you served it, would you? So remove or strain out vegetables that have no flavor and add new ones that can be served perfectly cooked.

OVERLEAF: *Spring Vegetable Garbure (page 112).* **OPPOSITE:** *Chicken Soup with Dumplings (page 122).*

spring vegetable garbure

3 tablespoons canola oil

2 cups thinly sliced carrots

2 cups coarsely chopped leeks

2 cups coarsely chopped onions

Kosher salt and freshly ground black pepper

A 12-inch square of skin from smoked bacon
    (or 2 inches larger than the diameter of your soup pot) (optional)

8 cups Chicken Stock (page 339)

3 yellow creamer potatoes

3 red creamer potatoes

2 Sachets (page 342)

2 cups oblique-cut carrots (see Lightbulb Moment, page 191)

1 teaspoon honey

8 ounces pencil-thin asparagus

1 pound fava beans, in the pod (medium favas are preferable
    to smaller ones)

1 cup sliced thin green beans (haricots verts)—stem ends removed and
    cut on the diagonal into thirds

1 cup English peas

1 small head Savoy cabbage, cut into 6 wedges

2 cups cooked cannellini, garbanzo, or white beans

Red wine vinegar

Extra virgin olive oil

Flat-leaf parsley leaves

Escoffier's dictum is that a garbure should be so packed with ingredients that a ladle won't sink when set down onto its surface. A critical step, as in many of our stews and soups, is the long, slow sweating of the vegetables. Here we cover them with a slab of skin from smoked bacon, which adds flavor, richness, and, more important, in an otherwise vegetable soup, abundant collagen and therefore body to the broth; you may have to order this from the butcher. An alternative is a parchment lid (see page 120).

Heat the canola oil in an 8- to 10-quart stockpot over medium heat. Add the carrots, leeks, and onions, and stir to coat in the oil. Season with salt and pepper. Lay the piece of bacon skin fat side down over the vegetables, pushing it down so it rests on them (see photo, opposite); the skin will come up the sides of the pot at first, but it will shrink as the vegetables cook. Cook, lifting the skin and stirring occasionally, for 30 to 35 minutes, until the vegetables are cooked through but not falling apart. Remove the bacon skin and discard (or make into dog treats—see opposite).

Add the chicken stock, and increase the heat to medium-high. Bring to a simmer and simmer for 20 minutes. Strain the broth into another pot and discard the vegetables; set aside.

Meanwhile, peel the potatoes, quarter lengthwise, and cut crosswise into medium pieces. Put the potatoes, 1 sachet, and 2 teaspoons salt in a large saucepan, add cold water to cover, bring to a simmer, and cook until the potatoes are just tender, about 10 minutes. Drain and spread on a tray to cool; discard the sachet.

Put the oblique-cut carrots, honey, the second sachet, and a pinch of salt in a medium pot, cover with cold water, and bring to a simmer. Cook for 4 to 5 minutes, or until the carrots are tender but slightly resistant to the tooth. Drain and discard the sachet.

Bring a large pot of salted water to a boil (see page 147). Prepare an ice bath. Meanwhile, hold an asparagus spear and bend it to break off the less tender bottom end. Trim all of the asparagus to the same length. Cut them on the diagonal into 1-inch pieces. You will need 1 cup of asparagus pieces; reserve any leftover for another use. Shell the fava beans and peel the skins from the beans (peeling the beans before cooking them prevents gases that could cause discoloration from being trapped between the beans and their skins). Working with small batches at a time, put the fava beans in a large fine-mesh basket strainer, immerse the strainer in the boiling water, and blanch the favas for 1 minute. Remove and plunge the strainer into the ice bath to cool the favas (see photos, page 145), then remove and drain on paper towels. Repeat with the green beans, 2 minutes; the peas, 1½ minutes; and the asparagus, 1 minute. Then add the cabbage to the boiling water and blanch just until tender. Chill in the ice bath, then drain.

Bring the broth to a simmer. Add the carrots, potatoes, and cannellini beans and stir in vinegar, salt, and pepper to taste. (At this point, the soup can be held for up to 1 hour.)

To serve, bring the soup back to a simmer, add all the blanched vegetables, and return to a simmer. Remove from the heat and serve, drizzled with olive oil and garnished with parsley leaves.

PHOTOGRAPH ON PAGE 109   **SERVES 8 (MAKES ABOUT 4 QUARTS)**

When we slow-cook, we often want some evaporation and reduction of the liquid, but we still want partial covering. A parchment lid (see page 120) is what we use most often, but in a soup where pork would enhance the flavor, you can ask the butcher to cut you a piece of skin from smoked bacon that is slightly larger than the diameter of your pot—it will shrink once it hits the heat.

As a bonus, the skin can then be made into wonderful treats for your dog. Dry the skin on a paper towel, and cut it into pieces of a size appropriate for your dog. Preheat the oven to 300°F. Line a baking sheet with parchment paper and set a cooling rack over it. Put the skin on the rack and bake until the fat is rendered and the skin is crisp, 30 minutes or longer; timing will vary depending on the thickness of the pieces, and some pieces will curl while others remain flat. Remove the pieces as they become dry and crisp. Store in an airtight container for up to 1 week.

sun gold tomato gazpacho

1 cup cold water

2 medium garlic cloves, crushed and peeled

¼ cup coarsely chopped onion

2 pounds ripe Sun Gold or other yellow cherry tomatoes, stemmed and halved, any juices reserved

2 Armenian cucumbers (about 12 ounces total) or 1 English cucumber, peeled

1 large yellow bell pepper, cored, seeded, and cut into large pieces

1 red bell pepper

1 tablespoon sherry vinegar, or to taste

½ teaspoon piment d'Espelette (see page 208)

Kosher salt

Freshly ground white pepper

¾ to 1 cup extra virgin olive oil, as needed

2 tablespoons minced chives

Sun Gold tomatoes have an intense flavor and a balance of acidity and sweetness that makes them perfect for this summer gazpacho, which is a little different from traditional gazpachos in that the pureed tomatoes are strained and then the olive oil is emulsified into them, making the soup very rich and creamy.

Armenian cucumbers are long and narrow, with pale green stripes. They have very few seeds and are sweet. If you can't find them, you can substitute an English cucumber.

Pair this tomato soup with the Grilled Cheese Sandwich (page 288) for a familiar and comforting combination.

Pour the water into a large bowl and add the garlic and onion. Reserve 1 cup of tomatoes for the garnish, and add the remaining tomatoes and their juices to the bowl.

Peel the cucumbers. If using Armenian cucumbers, cut 1 cucumber lengthwise in half, put cut side down on the cutting surface, and cut into large half circles. If using an English cucumber, cut it lengthwise in half and scrape out the seedy centers, then cut one half into large half circles. Add the sliced cucumbers to the tomatoes. Add the yellow pepper and let all the vegetables marinate, tossing once or twice, for 5 minutes.

Meanwhile, cut the remaining cucumber into small dice for garnish. Core, seed, and finely dice the red pepper for garnish. Refrigerate until serving.

Transfer the vegetables, with their marinade, to a Vita-Mix and, starting on low speed and then increasing the speed, blend until completely smooth. Strain through a fine-mesh conical strainer into a bowl. (If you have trouble passing the soup through the strainer, blend it again. Only the tomato skins should remain in the strainer.)

Rinse out the blender jar and return the strained tomato mixture to it. Add the vinegar and Espelette, season with salt and white pepper to taste, and blend to combine. With the blender running on medium-high speed, gradually add the oil, blending until the gazpacho is velvety smooth. Taste and add additional vinegar and/or Espelette if desired. Refrigerate the gazpacho until cold, or for up to 2 days.

If the gazpacho has separated into two layers, pour it into the blender and blend to recombine. Pour the gazpacho into a large serving bowl and garnish with a sprinkling of the diced red pepper and cucumber, a few tomato halves, and some of the chives. Serve the remaining garnishes in small bowls on the side. **SERVES 6 (MAKES ABOUT 6 CUPS)**

heirloom bean and escarole soup

3 tablespoons canola oil

2 cups diced (about ½-inch) carrots

2 cups diced (about ½-inch) leeks

2 cups diced (about ½-inch) onions

1½ teaspoons finely minced garlic

Kosher salt

1 smoked ham hock (about 1 pound)

8 cups Chicken Stock (page 339)

2 heads (about 12 ounces each) escarole

7 cups cooked white beans (see page 337)

Freshly ground black pepper

1 tablespoon red wine vinegar, or to taste

This is a big rustic soup, the kind you'd find in the Italian countryside, and a great example of why bean soups are my favorite. You've got the protein-rich beans, the healthful greens and aromatic vegetables, and a delicious broth given depth from a ham hock and deft seasoning with some red wine vinegar. If you have good stock on hand, it's very quick and easy.

Heirloom beans are now widely available and easily found in stores and via the internet. My favorites come from Steve Sando's Rancho Gordo (see Sources, page 346), in nearby Napa. He grows some of the best beans in the world, and he also tracks down other great products such as dried corn, dried chiles, spices, and herbs.

Heat the canola oil in an 8- to 10-quart stockpot over medium heat. Add the carrots, leeks, onions, garlic, and a generous pinch of salt. Reduce the heat to low, cover with a parchment lid (see page 120) and cook very slowly, stirring occasionally, for 30 to 35 minutes, until the vegetables are tender. Remove and discard the parchment lid.

Add the ham hock and chicken stock and bring to a simmer. Cook for about 1 hour, or until the ham hock is tender. Remove from the heat, remove the ham hock, and let cool enough so you can handle it.

Meanwhile, bring a large pot of salted water to a boil (see page 147). Set up an ice bath. Trim away and discard any very dark or bruised greens from the escarole. One at a time, hold the end of each head together at the top, cut off the core, and cut crosswise into 3 sections. Separate the pieces of escarole and trim away any large tough ribs. Rinse in a large bowl of cold water to remove any dirt, lift the greens from the water, and blanch in the boiling water for 30 seconds. (Blanching helps remove any bitterness from the escarole.) Drain and cool in the ice bath, then drain again and squeeze dry.

Pull away and discard the skin and fat from the ham hock. Shred the meat and return it to the soup. Add the beans and season the soup with salt, pepper, and the red wine vinegar. At this point, the soup can be refrigerated for up to 2 days.

Add the escarole to the soup and bring to a simmer. Serve.

SERVES 6 (MAKES 10 CUPS)

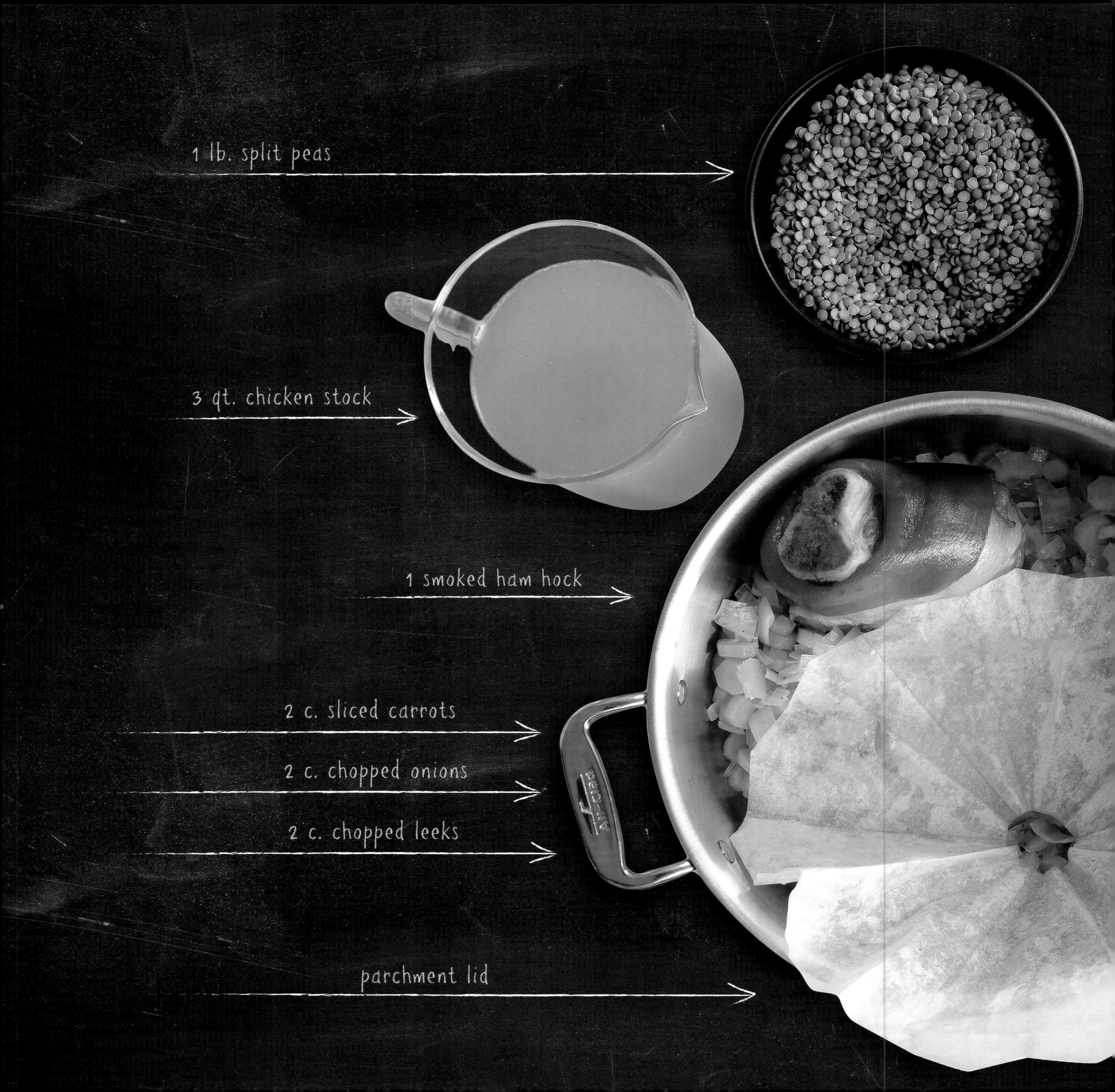
1 lb. split peas
3 qt. chicken stock
1 smoked ham hock
2 c. sliced carrots
2 c. chopped onions
2 c. chopped leeks
parchment lid
All-Clad

1 to 2 Tbsp. red wine vinegar

½ c. crème fraîche

mint leaves

2 c. peas

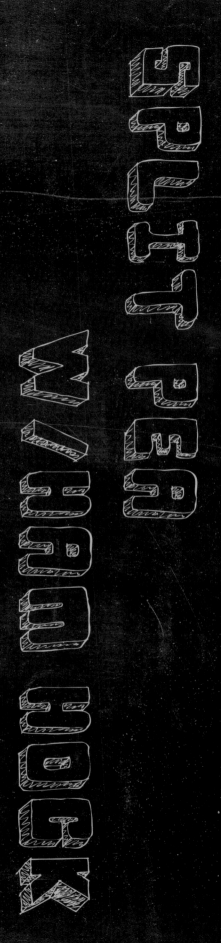

SPLIT PEA w/HAM HOCK

split pea soup
with ham hock, fresh peas, and mint

3 tablespoons canola oil

2 cups thinly sliced carrots

2 cups coarsely chopped leeks

2 cups coarsely chopped onions

Kosher salt

1 smoked ham hock (about 1 pound)

3 quarts Chicken Stock (page 339)

1 pound (about 2 cups) split peas, small stones removed, rinsed

1 to 2 tablespoons red wine vinegar

Freshly ground black pepper

2 cups peas (2 pounds in the pod), blanched (see page 147)

½ cup crème fraîche

Mint leaves

This is at heart a classic split pea soup, with a big ham hock to flavor the stewing split peas, but rather than serving it as a rustic dish, it is pureed so that it's smooth and velvety. Fresh peas, along with chunks of the ham hock and fresh mint, are part of the garnish. Serve this soup in the spring when peas are very, very sweet.

Heat the canola oil in an 8- to 10-quart stockpot over medium heat. Add the carrots, leeks, onions, and a generous pinch of salt. Reduce the heat to low, cover with a parchment lid (see page 120), and cook very slowly, stirring occasionally, for 35 to 40 minutes, until the vegetables are tender. Remove and discard the parchment lid.

Add the ham hock and chicken stock, bring to a simmer, and simmer for 45 minutes. Prepare an ice bath. Strain the stock into a bowl, discard the vegetables, and reserve the ham hock. Place the bowl of stock over the ice bath to cool. (The split peas will cook more evenly when started in a cold liquid.)

Return the cold stock and ham hock to the pot, add the split peas, and bring to a simmer. Simmer for 1 hour, or until the split peas are completely soft (do not worry if the peas begin to break apart, as they will be pureed).

Remove the soup from the heat, and remove and reserve the ham hock. Season the soup with 1 tablespoon vinegar and salt to taste. Transfer some of the split peas and liquid to a Vita-Mix, filling it only about one-third full, and blend on very low speed until pureed. (If you blend it on high speed, the steam could pop the lid off and send the soup shooting out in all directions.) Transfer to a bowl, and puree the remaining soup in batches. Taste for seasoning, adding additional vinegar, salt, and/or pepper to taste if necessary. (The soup can be refrigerated for up to 2 days. It will continue to thicken as it stands; add a bit of water or stock when reheating if it becomes too thick.)

Pull away and discard the skin and fat from the ham hock. Trim the meat and cut into ½-inch dice. (Refrigerate if not serving immediately; bring to room temperature before serving.)

To serve, reheat the fresh peas in a little water if needed. Drain and stir half the peas into the soup. Put the remaining peas, the crème fraîche, ham hock meat, and mint leaves in separate serving bowls, and serve the soup with the garnishes. **SERVES 6 (MAKES 8 CUPS)**

mushroom soup

with cavolo nero and yukon gold potatoes

Canola oil

1 cup diced (about ½-inch) carrots

1 cup diced (about ½-inch) leeks

1 cup diced (about ½-inch) onion

Kosher salt

1½ teaspoons finely minced garlic

1 small bunch (4 to 5 ounces) cavolo nero (Tuscan kale)

1¼ pounds (2 to 3 large) Yukon Gold potatoes

1 Sachet (page 342)

⅔ pound hen-of-the-woods mushrooms

1½ tablespoons (¾ ounce) unsalted butter

¼ cup minced shallots

1 tablespoon minced thyme

8 cups Mushroom Stock (page 341)

Freshly ground black pepper

5 to 6 tablespoons Garlic Puree (page 266)

1 to 2 teaspoons red wine vinegar

Extra virgin olive oil

Cavolo nero, also called Tuscan kale, has a very deep flavor that pairs beautifully with the earthiness of mushrooms. If you can't find hen-of-the-woods mushrooms, you can use oyster mushrooms. We keep this completely vegetarian by using mushroom stock as the base.

Heat 3 tablespoons of canola oil in an 8- to 10-quart stockpot over medium heat. Add the carrots, leeks, onion, and a generous pinch of salt, and reduce the heat to low, cover with a parchment lid (see page 120), and cook very slowly for about 25 minutes; the vegetables will have released their liquid but the carrots will not yet be tender. Lift the parchment lid, add the garlic, and cook for 10 minutes, or until the carrots are tender. Remove and discard the parchment lid

Meanwhile, remove and discard the ribs from the kale leaves. Rinse the leaves under cold water, drain, and cut them into pieces about 1 inch by 3 inches. Set aside.

Peel the potatoes, quarter lengthwise, and cut crosswise into large pieces. Put the potatoes, sachet, and 2 teaspoons salt in a large saucepan, add cold water to cover, bring to a simmer, and cook until the potatoes are just tender, about 10 minutes. Drain and spread on a tray to cool; discard the sachet.

Trim any woody ends from the clusters of mushrooms and break them apart into bite-sized clusters.

Set a cooling rack over a baking sheet and line with paper towels. Heat some canola oil in a large skillet over high heat until the oil shimmers. Add half the mushrooms, season with salt, and cook, without stirring, for about a minute to allow the mushrooms to absorb the oil. Add half the butter, shallots, and thyme, toss, and sauté until the mushrooms are lightly browned and tender, 6 to 8 minutes total. Transfer the mushrooms to the towel-lined rack. Wipe out the skillet with paper towels, heat additional canola oil in the pan, and cook the remaining mushrooms in the same way.

Add the mushroom stock to the stockpot and bring to a simmer. Season generously with salt and pepper. (The soup is best served just after it is finished, but it can be refrigerated at this point for up to 2 days.) Meanwhile, blanch the kale in a large pot of boiling salted water (see page 147) until wilted and just tender, 1½ to 2 minutes. Drain the kale.

To serve, stir the garlic puree into the soup. Add the mushrooms, kale, and potatoes. Season with salt, pepper, and vinegar. Pour into a serving bowl and drizzle with olive oil.   **SERVES 6 (MAKES ABOUT 10 CUPS)**

Using parchment paper as a lid for soups, stews, and braises allows some evaporation because of the small steam hole cut in it. But because it covers the meat, it keeps the liquid from reducing too quickly and prevents the surface from becoming caramelized as it cooks. It's like having a lid and not having a lid at the same time. For step-by-step instructions, see Making a Parchment Lid, opposite.

lentil and sweet potato soup

8 ounces applewood-smoked slab bacon, (see Sources, page 346)

3 tablespoons canola oil

2 cups thinly sliced carrots

2 cups coarsely chopped leeks

2 cups coarsely chopped onions

¾ to 1 teaspoon Yellow Curry Powder (page 336) or Madras curry powder

Kosher salt

1½ pounds sweet potatoes

2 Sachets (page 342)

2 cups (about 8 ounces) Spanish Pardina lentils (see Sources, page 346),
   or French de Puy lentils, small stones removed, rinsed

8 cups Chicken Stock (page 339)

1 to 2 tablespoons red wine vinegar

Freshly ground black pepper

Cilantro leaves

The sweet potatoes make this a rich soup. The curry powder sharpens the flavor, and the cilantro brightens the rich ingredients. The bacon and cilantro used as garnish could be served on the side and added at the table if you prefer.

Cut the bacon into lardons that are 1 inch long and ½ inch thick (see page 150).

Heat the canola oil in an 8- to 10-quart stockpot over medium heat. Add the bacon, reduce the heat to low, and render the fat for 20 to 25 minutes. The bacon should color but not crisp. Using a slotted spoon, remove the bacon and set aside.

Add the carrots, leeks, onions, and curry powder to the pot and stir to coat in the bacon fat. Season with salt, reduce the heat to low, cover with a parchment lid (see opposite), and cook very slowly for 30 to 35 minutes, until the vegetables are tender. Remove and discard the parchment lid.

Meanwhile, peel the sweet potatoes. Trim them and cut them into ½-inch dice. Put the potatoes, one of the sachets, and 2 teaspoons salt in a large saucepan, add cold water to cover, bring to a simmer, and cook until the potatoes are just tender, about 10 minutes. Drain and spread on a tray to cool; discard the sachet.

Add the lentils, second sachet, and stock to the vegetables, bring to a simmer, and simmer for 30 to 40 minutes, until the lentils are tender. (At this point, the soup can be refrigerated for up to 2 days.)

Spread the bacon in a small frying pan and crisp over medium-high heat.

Add the vinegar to taste to the soup, then add the potatoes and heat through. Season to taste with salt and pepper.

Serve the soup garnished with the bacon and cilantro leaves.

SERVES 6 (MAKES 10 CUPS)

MAKING A PARCHMENT LID Fold a length of parchment paper in half to give you a piece bigger than the pot to be covered. Place the crease to your right. Folding away from you, fold in half again to make a crease in front of you. Fold this bottom crease up to make a narrow triangle. Continue to fold the triangle over until you have reached the opposite side of the parchment paper.

To gauge the size, place the tip over the center of the pot to be covered and mark the edges of the pot with your thumb, then cut the end off there. With a pair of scissors, cut ¼ inch off the narrow tip of the triangle. Trim the pointed edges of the triangle to form a smooth rounded edge. Unfold the triangle. It will be a circle the size of your pot with a steam hole in the center. Put the paper lid in the pot so that it rests gently on the food you're cooking.

chicken soup with dumplings

1 tablespoon (½ ounce) unsalted butter

1 cup thinly sliced carrots

1 cup coarsely chopped celery

1 cup coarsely chopped onion

1 cup coarsely chopped leeks

Kosher salt

DUMPLINGS

½ cup water

4 tablespoons (2 ounces) unsalted butter

1½ teaspoons kosher salt

⅔ cup all-purpose flour

1 teaspoon Dijon mustard

2 large eggs

1 tablespoon plus 1 teaspoon minced chives

4 quarts Chicken Stock (page 339)

5 stalks celery

3 large carrots

1 teaspoon honey

1 bay leaf

2 thyme sprigs

1 large garlic clove, crushed, skin left on

Kosher salt and freshly ground black pepper

½ cup (about 4 ounces) Roux (page 334)

2 cups cooked shredded chicken (dark or white meat)

¼ cup minced chives

1 tablespoon champagne vinegar

Flat-leaf parsley leaves

This simple, satisfying soup is all about texture. A roux is used to thicken the stock to achieve a luxurious satiny feel on the palate. And we add refinement to it by making the dumplings with pâte à choux (cream puff dough) rather than the standard biscuit dough. This is a great soup to make when you have leftover roast chicken. If you start off with a nice rich chicken stock, you can't go wrong.

Melt the butter in an 8- to 10-quart stockpot over medium heat. Add the carrots, celery, onions, and leeks, season with salt, and cover with a parchment lid (see page 120). Reduce the heat to low and cook very slowly, stirring occasionally, 30 to 35 minutes, until the vegetables are tender. Remove and discard the parchment lid.

MAKE THE DUMPLINGS: Fill a wide deep pot with salted water and bring to a simmer. Set up a stand mixer fitted with the paddle attachment.

Combine the water, butter, and 1 teaspoon of the salt in a medium saucepan and bring to a simmer over medium-high heat. Reduce the heat to medium, add the flour all at once, and stir rapidly with a stiff heatproof or wooden spoon until the dough pulls away from the sides of the pan and the bottom of the pan is clean. The dough should be glossy and smooth but still moist; enough moisture must evaporate from the dough to allow it to absorb more fat when the eggs are added. Continue to stir for 4 to 5 minutes, adjusting the heat as necessary to prevent the dough from coloring; a thin coating of dough will form on the bottom and sides of the pan. When enough moisture has evaporated, steam will rise from the dough and the nutty aroma of cooked flour will be noticeable.

Immediately transfer the dough to the mixer bowl. Add the mustard and the remaining ½ teaspoon salt and mix for a few seconds to incorporate the ingredients and release some of the heat. With the mixer on the lowest speed, add the eggs one at a time, beating until the first egg is completely incorporated before adding the second and incorporating it. Then add the chives and incorporate. Remove the bowl from the mixer.

Line a baking sheet with parchment paper. Shape the dumplings using two soupspoons to make a quenelle shape (see Note), dropping them into the simmering water. Cook the dumplings in batches of about 6 to avoid crowding the pot and allow them to cook evenly. Once the dumplings rise to the surface, it will take about 5 minutes for them to cook; remove one and break it open to make sure it is cooked. With a slotted spoon, transfer the dumplings to the baking sheet, and cook the remaining dumplings. (You will have about 18 dumplings.)

Once the dumplings have cooled, trim any uneven edges with scissors.

FINISH THE SOUP: Add the chicken stock to the vegetables and bring to a simmer. Simmer for 30 minutes, then strain the soup base into another pot and discard the vegetables.

Peel the celery stalks with a peeler. Cut each stalk crosswise on the diagonal into thin slices about 1½ inches long. As you get to the wider lower part of the stalk, adjust the angle of your knife to keep the pieces relatively the same size. You need about 1½ cups celery for this recipe (reserve any extra for another use). Cook the celery in a large pot of boiling salted water (see page 147) until just tender. Drain, cool in an ice bath, and drain again.

Cut the carrots lengthwise into quarters and then crosswise into bite-sized pieces. As each carrot widens, adjust the size of the cut to keep the pieces bite sized. You need about 1½ cups carrots for this recipe (reserve any extra for another use).

Put the carrots in a saucepan, add the honey, bay leaf, thyme, garlic, and a pinch of salt and pepper, and cover with cold water. Bring to a simmer and cook for 4 to 5 minutes, or until the carrots are tender but slightly resistant to the tooth. Drain and transfer to paper towels.

Bring the soup base to a simmer and whisk in the roux a little at a time until thick enough to coat the back of a spoon; you may not use all the roux. Simmer for 30 minutes, skimming often—this is necessary to remove all impurities from the roux. (The soup will continue to thicken as it simmers.)

Add the dumplings, chicken, carrots, celery, and chives to the soup and heat through. Season with the vinegar and salt and pepper to taste. Transfer to a large serving bowl and sprinkle with parsley leaves.

PHOTOGRAPHS ON PAGES 111 AND 124   **SERVES 6 (MAKES ABOUT 8 CUPS)**

NOTE *To form a three-sided quenelle using two soupspoons, start by using one spoon to scoop up a portion of dough that is slightly smaller than the bowl of the spoon. Hold the second spoon in your other hand, place the side of the spoon against the far side of the dough, and scoop it onto the second spoon, forming one smooth long side. Continue transferring the dough between the spoons until you have the desired oval football shape. (With practice, this should take no more than three transfers, but it may require more when you are first getting started.) Before you begin, set up a container of hot water in which to regularly dip the spoons—this will make it easier to form the quenelles.*

Chicken Soup with Dumplings (page 122)

I DO
LOVE TO SPOON

I love spoons the way I love eggs, for the beauty of their shape and their multiple uses.

Spooning hot, flavorful fat over the food as you cook adds flavor and helps it cook more quickly and evenly.

clam chowder with bacon

8 ounces applewood-smoked slab bacon (see Sources, page 346)

Canola oil

2 cups coarsely chopped leeks (white and light green parts only)

2 cups coarsely chopped onions

5 garlic cloves

Kosher salt

2 pounds Yukon Gold potatoes, cut into ½-inch dice

1 Sachet (page 342)

CLAMS

4 pounds littleneck or Manila clams

1¼ cups kosher salt

2 tablespoons (1 ounce) unsalted butter

⅓ cup chopped shallots

2 thyme sprigs

Kosher salt and freshly ground pepper

½ cup dry white wine, such as Sauvignon Blanc

4½ tablespoons (2¼ ounces) unsalted butter

¼ cup all-purpose flour

3 cups whole milk

3 cups heavy cream

3 tablespoons finely chopped chives

This is a classic chowder, with potatoes, cream, and fresh clams, but we use littlenecks or Manila clams, rather than big quahogs ("chowder clams"), because they're a little sweeter and tastier. The bacon is essential, because the smokiness of the pork pairs so well with the sweet clams.

Cut the bacon into lardons that measure 1 inch by ½ inch thick (see page 150).

Heat some canola oil in an 8- to 10-quart stockpot over medium heat. Add the bacon, reduce the heat to low, and let the fat render for 20 to 25 minutes, stirring from time to time; the bacon should color but not crisp. Using a slotted spoon, remove the bacon from the pan.

Add the leeks, onions, and garlic to the pan and stir to coat with the bacon fat. Sprinkle with salt, cover with a parchment lid (see page 120), and cook very slowly for 30 to 35 minutes, until the vegetables are tender. Remove and discard the parchment lid.

Put the potatoes, sachet, and 2 teaspoons salt in a large saucepan, add cold water to cover, bring to a simmer, and cook until the potatoes are just tender, about 10 minutes. Drain and spread on a tray to cool; discard the sachet.

Use a clean scouring pad to scrub any sand from the shells of the clams. Put the clams in a large bowl. Mix 8 cups water and the salt in another bowl, stirring to dissolve the salt. Pour enough of the water over the clams to cover, and soak for about 5 minutes, to purge them of any sand.

Lift the clams from the water, drain the water, and repeat the soaking one more time. Drain the clams and rinse under cold water.

When the vegetables are tender, increase the heat to medium and add the butter. Once the butter has melted, stir in the flour to coat the vegetables and cook for 2 to 3 minutes to take away the raw flour taste. Whisk in the milk and cream, season to taste with salt and pepper, and bring to a very low simmer.

Melt the 2 tablespoons butter in a large sauté pan over medium-high heat. Add the shallots and thyme sprigs, season with salt and pepper, and cook, stirring, for about 1 minute, until the shallots are tender. Add the wine, bring to a boil, and cook for 2 minutes to evaporate some of the alcohol. Add the clams, cover the pan, and cook for about 4 minutes, removing the clams as they open. Strain all the clam liquid through a fine-mesh conical strainer into a bowl.

Shell the clams and set aside.

Gently stir clam liquid to taste into the soup (avoid any sand that may have settled in the bottom of the bowl). Season the chowder with salt and pepper to taste. Gently stir in the potatoes, and add about two-thirds of the clams.

Spread the bacon in a small frying pan and crisp over medium-high heat.

Garnish the soup with the bacon, the remaining clams, and the chives. **SERVES 6 (MAKES 3 QUARTS)**

cream of cauliflower soup with red beet chips

2 heads cauliflower (4 to 5 pounds total)

4 tablespoons (2 ounces) unsalted butter

¾ cup coarsely chopped onion

¾ cup coarsely chopped leeks (white and light green parts only)

¼ teaspoon Yellow Curry Powder (page 336) or Madras curry powder

Kosher salt

2 cups milk

2 cups heavy cream

2 cups water

Peanut or canola oil for deep-frying

1 medium red beet

1 teaspoon distilled white vinegar

Torn Croutons (page 274)

Extra virgin olive oil

Freshly ground black pepper

The unctuous, velvety, creamy texture of this soup is so elegant and satisfying. Curry offsets the richness and cauliflower florets, croutons, and beet chips give the soup some body and crunch.

Remove the leaves from the cauliflower, and cut out the core. Trim off the stems and reserve them. For the garnish, trim 2 cups florets about the size of a quarter and set aside.

Coarsely chop the remaining cauliflower and the stems into 1-inch pieces so that they will cook in the same amount of time. You need 8 cups of cauliflower (reserve any extra for another use).

Melt 3 tablespoons of the butter in a large saucepan over medium heat. Add the onion, leeks, curry, and coarsely chopped cauliflower, season with 2 teaspoons salt, cover with a parchment lid (see page 120), and cook, stirring occasionally, until the vegetables are almost tender, about 20 minutes. Remove and discard the parchment lid.

Pour in the milk, cream, and water, increase the heat to medium-high, and bring to a simmer. Simmer for 30 minutes, skimming off the foam from time to time.

Working in batches, transfer the cauliflower mixture to a Vita-Mix (leave an opening in the lid for the steam to escape). Begin pureeing the cauliflower on the lowest speed and blend, slowly increasing the speed, until smooth and velvety. Check the seasoning and add more salt if needed. Transfer to a large saucepan and keep warm. (The soup can be refrigerated for up to 2 days.)

Fill a small deep pot with 1 inch of peanut oil and heat over medium heat to 300°F. Set a cooling rack over a baking sheet. Line the rack with paper towels.

While the oil heats, peel the beet and slice off about ½ inch from the top. Using a Japanese mandoline or other vegetable slicer, slice the beet into rounds that are slightly thicker than paper-thin. Reserve only the full rounds.

Carefully add a few beet rounds to the oil and fry, turning them with a wire skimmer or slotted spoon as the edges begin to curl and pressing gently on the chips to keep them submerged. You will see a great deal of bubbling around the beets as the moisture in them evaporates; when the bubbling stops, after 1 to 1½ minutes, the beets will be crisp. Transfer the beets to the paper-towel-lined rack and season with salt. Fry the remaining chips in batches. The chips can be kept warm in a low oven.

Bring a medium saucepan of salted water to a boil. Add the vinegar and the reserved cauliflower florets and blanch until tender, 4 to 6 minutes. The vinegar will help keep the cauliflower white. Drain.

Melt the remaining 1 tablespoon butter in a medium frying pan over medium-high heat, swirling the pan occasionally, until the butter turns a rich golden brown. Add the florets and sauté until a rich golden brown. Set aside.

To serve, reheat the soup. This is a thick soup, but if it seems too thick, add water to thin it to the desired consistency. Season with salt and pepper to taste.

Pour the soup into a serving bowl or soup tureen. Top each serving with a few cauliflower florets, several torn croutons, and a stack of beet chips. (If the beet chips sit in the soup, they will become soggy and discolor it.) Drizzle with olive oil and sprinkle with pepper. Serve the remaining florets, croutons, and chips in separate bowls on the side.

PHOTOGRAPH ON PAGE 129   **SERVES 6 (MAKES ABOUT 2 QUARTS)**

Cream of Cauliflower Soup with Red Beet Chips (page 127)

SALADS

I recall a time when salad was always served with the meal, which was the custom when I was growing up. But really, salads can be served at any point in the meal. At home I almost always serve salad after a meal—olive oil and balsamic on fresh greens—along with some cheese. When a salad begins a meal, I like that salad to be substantial with lots of vegetables and hardier ingredients, with or without greens. My favorites are beet

salads and tomato salads. I also love beans and chickpeas and fennel featured in salads. It's not that I shy away from greens, but I like greens at the end of the meal.

In these pages we discuss salad basics—our thoughts on how to combine ingredients in a salad and how to season them, dress them, and serve them. Such salad issues may seem obvious, but small matters make big differences. We also include recipes for special salads, ones often referred to as composed salads: wonderful combinations of greens and other vegetables, fruits, nuts, meats, fish, cheeses, and vinaigrettes that work well together.

Our salads show off the garden. In the spring, we pair peas with asparagus, and leeks with almonds. In late summer, it's cucumbers, marinated and served with cherry tomatoes and a citrus vinaigrette. When we're heading out of tomato season, we oven-roast the tomatoes to intensify their flavor, using them on salads, as the base for a vinaigrette, for sandwiches, and as a garnish to fish and meat. In the fall, we like shredded radicchio with apple wedges or sweet grilled figs.

And baby greens—spicy tatsoi, mizuna, chicory, red oak—can be found almost year-round.

Soup and salad are natural partners. A salad and a big hearty soup with lots of ingredients is a wonderful meal.

OVERLEAF: *Endive and Arugula Salad with Peaches and Marcona Almonds (page 140).*

salad basics

A surprising amount of finesse goes into making a great salad. You have to know when to salt it, how to dress it, when to pepper it. What's appropriate as ingredients? Are the greens bright and fresh? Is the dressing balanced in flavor, the garnish vivid?

If you can put your fork into any part of the salad and have in that one forkful all its components—some piquillo pepper, pickled carrot, red onion, and greens, say—that's an important quality. Is every leaf evenly dressed? Are the fresh herbs strewn throughout? These are some of the things that define a great salad.

Our method follows just a few rules. We season all the components separately and then bring them together—meaning that if we're making a Cobb salad, all the ingredients, from the avocado to the tomatoes, are seasoned separately with salt. When we're ready to mix the salad, we place the leaves in a shallow bowl, drizzle the oil or vinaigrette around the sides of the bowl, and then toss the leaves gently. Oiling the bowl, rather than pouring the oil directly on the greens, ensures that all the greens pick up the same amount of oil when you toss them. We then salt the greens and toss again. We may dress the greens with something acidic, or we may serve a dressing on the side, depending on how delicate the greens are. The leaves are often so delicious that we want to feature them and serve them simply with salt and olive oil, and perhaps a little vinaigrette on the side.

The final step in building a salad is to finish it with fresh herbs, either whole leaves or torn: mint, basil, chervil, tarragon. The only herbs we cut are chives. I find you lose too much flavor on the cutting board when you chop herbs.

And that's it—all very simple, but each step is important.

Below are the key steps in a nutshell, followed by suggestions for interesting combinations.

For a mixed green salad, select the greens, just one type or a combination, and other components that will complement them. Figure on about 2 cups of greens per person. Remove limp or bruised leaves and trim the greens of any dark spots. Wash the greens with cold water. If they are very dirty, wash them twice, place them in a bowl of cold water and let stand briefly, then lift the greens from the water. (If you drain the greens and water into a colander, you will be reintroducing any dirt that's fallen to the bottom of the bowl.) Spin the greens in a salad spinner to dry them thoroughly.

Put the greens in a wide bowl. Pour the oil or dressing around the sides of the bowl, rather than directly on the greens. Lift and toss the greens so the oil or dressing lightly coats them. If we use a dressing on the greens, rather than just oil, we add it sparingly and serve more dressing on the side. Sprinkle the greens with salt and freshly ground pepper and toss.

For multicomponent salads, choose a shallow serving platter, so that you can layer the additional ingredients and intersperse them with the greens, both creating a beautiful presentation and making it easy for everyone to sample all the ingredients in the salad. As you layer the ingredients, think about their weight, and save lighter, more delicate ingredients for the top.

some salad combinations to try

pickled salad Pickled Carrots (page 255), Pickled Baby Leeks (page 255), and Pickled Red Onions (page 257) with salami, Torn Croutons (page 274), shaved Parmesan cheese, and Anchovy Dressing (page 183)

fall salad (ingredients pictured on pages 138–39): Mixed greens with blanched baby leeks, Parmesan cheese, Fuyu persimmon, pine nuts, prosciutto di San Daniele, and Sherry Vinaigrette (page 179)

waldorf salad Mixed greens with Honeycrisp apples, toasted walnuts, celery batons, and Blue Cheese Dressing (page 182)

cobb salad (ingredients pictured below): Mixed greens with avocado, bacon lardons (see page 150), shaved red onion, hard-cooked eggs, black olives, Torn Croutons (page 274), Oven-Roasted Tomatoes (page 262), and Buttermilk Dressing (page 182)

valencian salad (ingredients pictured on pages 138–39): Frisée and watercress with Marcona almonds, Spanish olives, Valencia oranges, piquillo peppers, and Roasted Garlic Vinaigrette (page 179)

succotash salad Belgian endive with fava beans, red bell peppers, sweet corn, slices of fingerling potato, sliced serrano ham, and Spicy Herb Vinaigrette (page 179)

caesar salad Little Gem lettuce with marinated anchovies, Torn Croutons (page 274), Pecorino Romano, and Anchovy Dressing (page 183)

moroccan salad Baby spinach with cold roast lamb, Medjool dates, Garlic Chips (page 266), pistachios, and Mustard Vinaigrette (page 179)

spring salad Butter lettuce, Braised Artichokes (page 221), Pickled Carrots (page 255), blanched pearl onions, blanched English peas, and citrus vinaigrette

smoked trout salad Mixed chicories, Green Grapes with Green Curry (page 258), smoked trout, toasted pecans, and Creamy Pepper Dressing (page 183)

\+   \+   \+   =   *cobb salad*

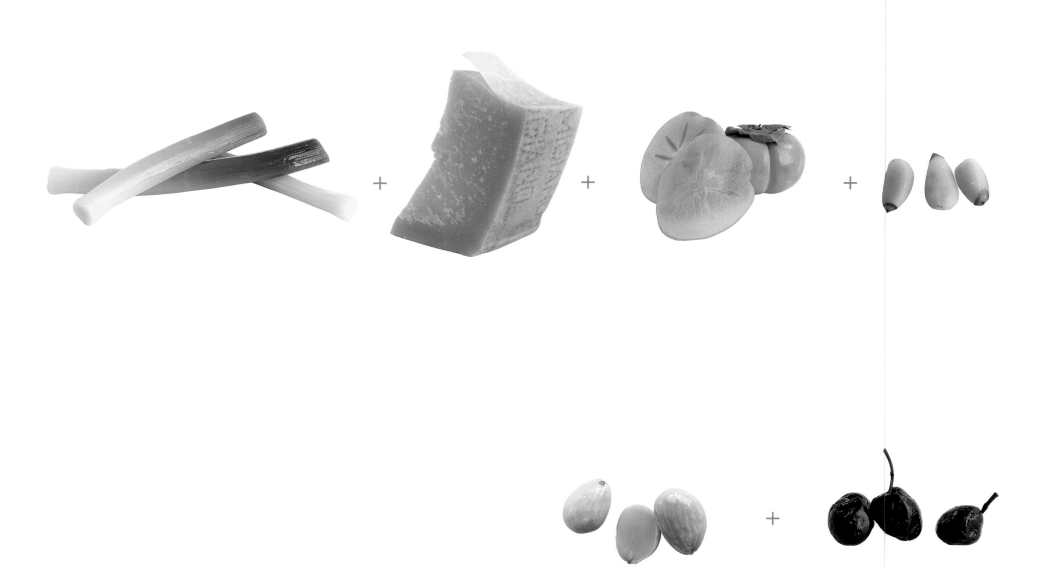

+  = *fall salad*

+  +  = *valencian salad*

endive and arugula salad
with peaches and marcona almonds

3 heads white Belgian endive

3 heads red Belgian endive

2 tablespoons Peach Puree (page 249)

1 tablespoon finely chopped shallot

1 tablespoon finely chopped flat-leaf parsley

¼ cup sherry vinegar

¾ cup extra virgin olive oil

1½ pounds (about 5) medium-size ripe freestone peaches

Kosher salt and freshly ground black pepper

1 tablespoon minced chives

1½ ounces arugula (about 2 cups)

½ cup salted, roasted Marcona almonds

In this summer salad, the soft sweetness of the peaches plays off the crisp bitterness of the endive and the nutty crunch of Marcona almonds. In the fall, pears could be substituted for the peaches, replacing the peach puree with a pear puree, for the base for a pear vinaigrette.

Cut about ½ inch from the bottom of each head of endive: the outer leaves will naturally fall away. Cut the base again and continue to remove the leaves in the same way until you reach the core (I like to eat the core as a chef's snack). Put all of the leaves in a large bowl of cold water and let stand for 5 minutes to crisp and refresh.

Drain the endive and spin dry in a salad spinner. Transfer to a large bowl.

Put the peach puree in a medium bowl. Stir in the shallot, parsley, and vinegar. Slowly whisk in the oil.

Cut the peaches in half and discard the pits. Put each peach half cut-side-down on a cutting board and slice crosswise into ¼-inch slices. Repeat with the remaining peaches.

Finely dice enough of the peach trimmings to make ¼ cup and stir them into the dressing. Season the dressing with salt and pepper to taste.

Drizzle half of the dressing around the sides of the bowl of endive and toss lightly to coat the endive with the dressing. Season with salt and pepper, and toss in the chives. Toss the arugula and the peach slices with a light coating of dressing.

Arrange the salad on a serving platter, layering the endive with the peaches, arugula, and almonds. Drizzle a little vinaigrette over the top and serve the remaining dressing on the side.

PHOTOGRAPH ON PAGE 131

SERVES 6

mediterranean melon salad

2 tablespoons pine nuts

About 5 pounds assorted small melons (see headnote),
    at room temperature

1 head frisée

4 lemon cucumbers or 1 English cucumber (about 1 pound total), peeled

12 small French breakfast radishes

¼ cup extra virgin olive oil

2 tablespoons balsamic vinegar

Kosher salt

3 ounces firm feta cheese, preferably Mt. Vikos,
    drained and cut into ½-inch cubes

¼ cup pitted Kalamata olives, quartered lengthwise

Small mint leaves

Olives and feta take this melon and cucumber salad in a Mediterranean direction, and the frisée adds a bitter counterpoint to the melon. Use some red watermelon for color and an assortment of other seasonal melons, such as Crane, Charentais, honeydew, Sharlynne, Galea, and Ambrosia.

Buy the smallest melons you can find and save the extra melon for another use.

Preheat the oven to 375°F.

Line a small baking sheet with parchment paper and spread out the pine nuts. Toast in the oven 6 to 7 minutes, until a rich golden brown. Transfer the nuts to a plate and cool.

Cut away the rinds from all the melons as you would citrus (see photo, page 142). Cut each melon open and remove any seeds. Cut the melons into thin slices, cubes, melon balls, or any other desired shape. They can be somewhat free-form and vary melon to melon.

Use scissors to trim off the dark tops of the frisée and discard. Pull apart the leaves and soak them in a large bowl of cold water for 5 minutes to refresh. Spin dry in a salad spinner, and wrap in damp paper towels until ready to assemble the salad.

Cut the lemon cucumbers lengthwise in half. Scoop out and discard the seeds. Cut the halves into 1-inch-wide wedges.

Cut the tops and bottoms from the radishes and cut them into small wedges, 4 to 6 per radish. (These can be cut ahead and held in cold water; drain and dry on paper towels before using.)

Toss together the frisée, radishes, and pine nuts in a medium bowl. Pour the oil and vinegar into a bowl and just swirl together to make a broken vinaigrette. Drizzle about half the vinaigrette around the sides of the bowl of frisée. Toss the salad to coat lightly with the dressing. Season with salt to taste.

Arrange slices of one type of melon on a serving platter. Drizzle with a small amount of vinaigrette. Then add slices of the other melons, drizzling them with vinaigrette as you build the salad. Once you have arranged an assortment of melons on the platter, arrange some of the salad loosely over the melons. Scatter with some of the feta cheese and olives. Continue to build the salad with the remaining ingredients, and garnish with mint leaves.   **SERVES 6**

To cut away the peel from citrus or melons, lay the fruit on its side and cut away both ends. Stand the fruit upright and cut away the peel, following the curve of the flesh to remove as little fruit as possible but all of the white pith. This method also works well with vegetables such as turnips and rutabagas.

little gem lettuce salad
with citrus, pomegranate, and honey vinaigrette

4 heads Little Gem lettuce (about 10 ounces each)

1 pomegranate

2 ruby red grapefruits

2 blood oranges

3 Satsuma oranges

¾ cup walnuts

Kosher salt

Honey Vinaigrette (recipe follows)

Freshly ground black pepper

Tarragon leaves

Flat-leaf parsley leaves

This salad, which uses a wonderful lettuce called Little Gem, something like a cross between romaine and butter lettuce, is all about bright flavors and colors: suprêmes of blood oranges, tangerines, and grapefruit, the ruby red pop of pomegranate, and fresh tarragon and parsley, all tied together with a honey vinaigrette

Fill a deep bowl with cold water. Remove any loose outer leaves (they can be reserved for another salad) and trim the root, leaving enough of it to hold the leaves together. Hold each head of lettuce by the root and dip into the cold water several times, shaking it gently as you lift out the lettuce to remove any dirt. Cut each head of lettuce into 4 wedges, and drain on paper towels.

To remove the seeds from the pomegranate, follow the instructions in the Lightbulb Moment opposite.

Preheat the oven to 350°F. Line a baking sheet with parchment paper.

Cut off the tops and bottoms from the grapefruit and oranges. Stand each one up and use a very sharp knife to cut away the peel and pith in wide strips, working from top to bottom of the fruit. To cut the suprêmes, cut down one side of a grapefruit segment to release it from the membrane; when you reach the center of the fruit, turn the blade over and just push the segment off the other membrane (this will yield more fruit than cutting down each side of the segment). Cut the suprêmes from the rest of the grapefruit, and repeat with the remaining fruit (see photo, page 139).

Spread the walnuts out on the baking sheet and toast in the oven, turning the pan around after 5 minutes, for 10 minutes, or until lightly toasted. Remove from the oven, transfer the nuts to a plate, sprinkle with salt, and let cool.

To serve, put half the wedges of lettuce cut side up in a large bowl. Sprinkle with half the pomegranate seeds. Spoon some dressing over the wedges, sprinkle with salt and pepper, and toss to coat. Arrange the lettuce wedges cut side up on a serving platter, and scatter half the citrus segments over them. Toss the remaining lettuce with enough dressing to coat, then toss with the remaining pomegranate, the walnuts, and salt and pepper to taste. Arrange on the serving platter, and scatter the remaining citrus segments over the top. Garnish with tarragon and parsley. Serve with any remaining dressing on the side.

SERVES 6

To remove the seeds from a pomegranate, cut the pomegranate in half through the equator. Hold one half over a bowl and hit the back of the pomegranate with a rolling pin to release the seeds. Add cold water. The membranes will float to the top. Remove any membranes from the water and drain the seeds.

honey vinaigrette

½ cup canola oil

½ cup extra virgin olive oil

⅓ cup champagne vinegar

3 tablespoons honey

Combine the canola and olive oil in a measuring cup. Put the vinegar and honey in a Vita-Mix and blend to combine. With the machine running on low speed, stream in the oil. Refrigerate in a covered container for up to 1 month.

MAKES ABOUT 1½ CUPS

pickled radish and red onion salad
with baby carrots, lemon cucumbers, and torn croutons

2 medium lemon cucumbers or ½ English cucumber

¼ cup extra virgin olive oil, plus more for dressing the greens

¼ cup champagne vinegar

¼ teaspoon red pepper flakes

Kosher salt and freshly ground black pepper

12 baby carrots, about 3 inches long

1 teaspoon honey

1 bay leaf

2 thyme sprigs

1 large garlic clove, crushed, skin left on

12 cups mixed greens

¼ cup Pickled Red Onions (page 257)

5 Pickled Icicle Radishes (page 257)

1 Pickled Watermelon (or other) Radish (page 257)

Torn Croutons (page 274)

When you have vegetables in abundance give them a quick pickling to feature them in salads, such as this one. The pickling liquid from the vegetables creates a preliminary vinaigrette.

Peel the cucumbers, trim the ends, and cut lengthwise in half, then cut into 1-inch-thick wedges. Slice off the seedy portion of each wedge and discard.

Whisk together the oil, vinegar, and red pepper flakes in a medium bowl and season to taste with salt and pepper. Add the cucumbers and marinate for at least 30 minutes, or for up to 4 hours.

Peel the carrots, trim the stems to about ½ inch, and cut lengthwise in half. Put them in a pot and cover with cold water. Add the honey, bay leaf, thyme, garlic, and a pinch each of salt and pepper, bring to a simmer, and cook for 4 to 5 minutes, until the carrots are crisp-tender. Drain on paper towels.

Put the greens in a large bowl, drizzle a little olive oil around the sides, and toss to coat lightly. Season with salt and pepper. Line a platter with the greens. Layer the cucumbers, carrots, onions, and radishes with the greens, and tuck the croutons in and around the greens.   **SERVES 6**

broccolini salad
with burrata cheese

2 pounds broccolini

3 large cremini mushrooms, about 2 inches in diameter

1 red onion

1 cup black Cerignola olives, or other cured olives

About ½ cup Sherry Vinaigrette (page 179)

Kosher salt and freshly ground black pepper

One 8-ounce burrata cheese (see Sources, page 346)

Extra virgin olive oil

Fleur de sel

Burrata is a pouch of fresh mozzarella with a creamy center that's very rich and buttery. It's from Apulia, the heel of Italy's boot, and can be found in Italian markets and cheese shops (see also page 187). Here it's served with broccolini, cremini mushrooms, red onion, and Cerignola olives. Cerignolas are great-tasting, big meaty olives from Puglia, Italy. They are only lightly cured, so you get good olive flavor as well as a little sweetness.

Bring a large pot of salted water to a boil (see page 147). Prepare an ice bath. Set a cooling rack over a baking sheet and line the rack with paper towels.

With a paring knife, cut off the thick ends of the broccolini stalks and peel the remaining stalks. Blanch the broccolini in batches in the boiling water until crisp-tender, 3 to 4 minutes. Transfer to the ice bath to stop the cooking, and drain on the paper towels.

Cut off the stems of the mushrooms flush with the caps and discard. Cut the caps into paper-thin slices using a Japanese mandoline or other vegetable slicer or by hand, and transfer to a small bowl.

Cut the onion in half through the equator. Slice one half of the onion into paper-thin rings on the mandoline. Select about 20 of the nicest rings, and reserve the remaining onion for another use.

Cut the flesh of the olives away from the pit (see photo, page 146). Lay the pieces cut-side-down and cut lengthwise into thin slices.

Line a baking sheet with parchment paper. Line up the broccolini stalks side by side on the parchment paper (this will allow you to dress

and season the broccolini evenly), drizzle with about ¼ cup of the vinaigrette, and toss to coat. Season to taste with salt and pepper.

Toss the mushroom slices with about 2 tablespoons of the vinaigrette and season with salt and pepper (do not overdress the mushrooms).

Cut away the top nub of the burrata and put it in a shallow serving bowl that just holds it. Holding a pair of scissors vertically, snip an X into the top of the burrata, reaching the soft center. Open the top slightly and drizzle olive oil over and around the cheese. Sprinkle with fleur de sel and pepper, and place on a serving platter.

Arrange the broccolini, mushrooms, olives, and onions on the platter.   **SERVES 6**

To make it easy to retrieve small batches of vegetables from boiling water, we put smaller green vegetables, such as peas and fava beans, in a fine-mesh basket strainer and submerge it in the water to cook, then just lift it and submerge it in an ice bath to stop the cooking. The strainer also makes it easy to remove the vegetables from the ice water.

big-pot blanching

I want green vegetables to be bright, bright green so their color can launch the flavor and impact of the entire dish. The old saying "We taste first with our eyes" is true. The faster a vegetable is cooked, the greener it becomes. So blanching green vegetables in a big pot with a lot of water and a lot of salt until they are thoroughly cooked is critical to the finished product, whether the vegetable is to be pureed for soup, served whole, or transformed into a sauce.

Raw green vegetables appear dull because a layer of gas has developed between the skin and pigment. Heat releases this gas, and the pigment floods to the surface. But this happens fast, and pretty soon, as the vegetable cooks, the acids and enzymes in it are released, dulling the color. At the same time, pigment begins to leach out into the water. So the challenge is to fully cook a vegetable before you lose that color, which means cooking it as quickly as possible.

There are three key factors in achieving this. First, use a large quantity of water relative to the amount of vegetables you're blanching, so you won't significantly lower the boiling temperature when you add the cold vegetables. If you lose the boil, not only will the vegetables cook more slowly, but the water will become a perfect environment for the pigment-dulling enzymes to go to work (these enzymes are destroyed only at the boiling point). Furthermore, using a lot of water means the pigment-dulling acids released by the vegetables will be more diluted.

Second, use a lot of salt—about a cup of salt per gallon of water; the water should taste like the ocean. Salt helps prevent the color from leaching into the water. A side benefit is that the vegetables will be uniformly seasoned when they are done.

The final critical step: Stop the vegetables from cooking by plunging them into a large amount of ice water. Leave them there until they are chilled through, then drain them. Once dried, you can store them on a layer of paper towels in a container, covered, for up to a day in the refrigerator.

You may need to be patient if your stove isn't strong and your pot is big, or you may have to do your vegetables in small batches. But it's not hard—you only have to decide to do it. And the results are dramatic.

While we give approximate times for big-pot blanching in the recipes, timing can vary depending on the size and quality of the vegetable. There is only one certain way to tell if a fava or a green bean or a pea is done: put it in your mouth and eat it.

tomato and handmade mozzarella salad

MOZZARELLA

8 cups water

¼ cup kosher salt

2 pounds mozzarella curd (see Sources, page 346),
    cut into ½-inch or smaller pieces, at room temperature

SALAD

3¾ pounds assorted medium to large tomatoes

½ pound assorted cherry and/or grape tomatoes,
    such as Sweet 100s and Sun Gold

½ medium Armenian cucumber or ¼ English cucumber,
    peeled and thinly sliced

¼ cup heavy cream (optional)

2 tablespoons Basil Oil (optional; page 265)

Extra virgin olive oil

Kosher salt and freshly ground black pepper

¼ cup thinly sliced red onion

12 to 15 small basil leaves, such as Italian, opal, and/or lemon lime

Fleur de sel

Make the mozzarella as close as possible to serving. To make a brine, combine the water and salt in a small pot and heat the water to 175°F, stirring to dissolve the salt. If you are making the cheese ahead, prepare an ice bath.

Put the curd in a large bowl. Ladle just enough of the hot brine over it to cover and let it sit for a minute to soften the curd. (You want to leave the curd in the water for as short a period of time as possible and work it as little as possible.) Stir gently with a wooden spoon, lifting the curd with the spoon as it melts. It is important to keep the entire mass of curds in the warm brine so that they don't stiffen. Once the curds have melted into a mass, use your hands to fold the cheese under itself to make a smooth round ball.

The cheese is ready to be shaped. It can be left in one piece or pulled into a log and sliced. Move it in and out of the brine as necessary to keep it pliable, and add more hot water if the brine cools down. Or you can make bocconcini: squeeze a small ball of cheese (about 1 inch in

T his salad features the tomato in all its late-summer glory, but the fun part of it is making the mozzarella.

Here, pieces of cow's milk curd are warmed in a hot brine, then kneaded until they become pliable and stretched until tender. The mozzarella can be formed into any shape you wish. We usually make our mozzarella fresh, but it can be made ahead and refrigerated. Curd is simply milk solids that are coagulated by treating with heat and acidity. You can buy it or make your own from whole milk, as described on numerous internet sites.

Use a variety of heirloom or other ripe tomatoes in a range of colors and sizes.

diameter) between your thumb and index finger, and pinch those to make the ball. As you shape each piece, return it to the brine or, if not serving the cheese immediately, chill it in an ice bath (it would become misshapen if left in the warm brine), then transfer to a container, cover with the cooled brine, and refrigerate. (The cheese should be served the day it is made.)

When ready to serve, put the mozzarella in a serving bowl and strain some brine over it.

Core the large tomatoes and cut into ½-inch slices. Halve or quarter the small tomatoes, depending on their size; leave some of the small stems attached. Peel the cucumber and cut into desired shapes.

To make the basil cream, if desired, whip the cream in a medium bowl until it just holds soft peaks. Fold in the basil oil. (The cream should not be refrigerated, or the texture will change.)

Spread the tomato slices on a baking sheet or work surface, with the wider side of the tomatoes facing up, and drizzle lightly with olive oil.

Turn the slices over, brush lightly with the basil cream, and season with salt and pepper. (The basil cream will add just a small amount of hidden flavor to the dish.) Drizzle olive oil over the small tomatoes and the cucumber.

Arrange the sliced tomatoes on a large platter, basil cream side down. Layer the cucumber slices and small tomatoes on top, and drizzle with olive oil. Scatter the onion and basil over the salad and sprinkle fleur de sel around the platter.

Serve with the mozzarella and remaining basil cream on the side.

SERVES 6

iceberg lettuce slices

with blue cheese dressing, oven-roasted tomatoes, bacon, and brioche croutons

8 ounces applewood-smoked slab bacon (see Sources, page 346)

4 heads baby iceberg lettuce (about 9 ounces each)

Extra virgin olive oil

Kosher salt and freshly ground black pepper

8 pieces Oven-Roasted Tomatoes (page 262)

Brioche Croutons (page 273)

Flat-leaf parsley leaves

Blue Cheese Dressing (page 182)

W e've added the intense flavors of oven-dried tomatoes, bacon, and blue cheese to this classic American salad and introduced additional crunch with elegant brioche croutons. Try to find baby heads of iceberg, which are tender and sweet.

Cut the bacon into lardons about 1 inch long and ½ inch thick (see photos below). Pour 2 tablespoons water into a medium saucepan and set over medium heat (the water will keep the bacon from crisping as the fat begins to render). Add the bacon, reduce the heat to medium-low, and let the bacon render its fat for 30 minutes. The bacon will color but not become completely crisp. Transfer to paper towels to drain.

Remove the outer couple of leaves from each head of lettuce (reserve for another use if desired). Cut out the core end and discard. Cut each head crosswise into 3 rounds. Place the slices on a tray, drizzle with olive oil, and season with salt and pepper.

Arrange the lettuce on a platter. Tuck the tomatoes in and around the lettuce. Sprinkle with the croutons, lardons, and parsley. Spoon some of the dressing over the salad and serve the remaining dressing on the side.   SERVES 6

Cut a slab of bacon crosswise into slices that are ½ inch thick.
Stack a few slices and cut them lengthwise into ½-inch-thick strips.
Cut the strips crosswise to form 1-inch-long lardons.

curried cauliflower-chickpea salad

CHICKPEAS

1 cup (about 6 ounces) dried chickpeas (garbanzo beans) or ½ cup dried
 chickpeas plus 1 cup shelled, blanched (see page 147) fresh chickpeas

1 Sachet (page 342)

½ medium carrot, split lengthwise

1 medium leek (white and light green parts only), split lengthwise and
 washed well

A 1-inch wedge of yellow onion, with root end intact

1 tablespoon red wine vinegar

Kosher salt and freshly ground black pepper

CAULIFLOWER

1 medium head (about 2 pounds) cauliflower

Kosher salt

1 tablespoon distilled white vinegar

¼ cup pine nuts

Kosher salt

5 ounces (1 to 2 heads) white Belgian endive

5 ounces (1 to 2 heads) red Belgian endive

4 ounces (about ¾ cup) pitted oil-cured Spanish black olives

½ cup Pickled Red Onions (page 257)

¼ cup Wine-Steeped Golden Raisins (page 258)

1 tablespoon minced chives

Curry Vinaigrette (page 182)

Freshly ground black pepper

¼ cup fried parsley leaves (see page 342)

Cauliflower and hearty chickpeas, tossed with an abundance of plumped sultana raisins, black olives, red onion, julienned endive, and toasted pine nuts are then seasoned with a curried vinaigrette. Spanish olives are oil-cured black olives, slightly bitter and salty, with a puckered appearance from the cure.

In the spring and early summer, you can sometimes find fresh chickpeas, which are a real treat. They must first be shelled, then blanched and chilled in an ice bath to preserve their beautiful green color.

Put the dried chickpeas in a large bowl, cover with 4 cups of water, and let soak for 12 hours.

Drain the soaked chickpeas and put in a pot. Add the sachet, carrot, leek, onion, and about twice the depth of cold water to the pot to cover the chickpeas and bring to a gentle simmer. Cook for 30 to 40 minutes until the chickpeas are tender.

Transfer the chickpeas (with their liquid) to a bowl, remove the sachet and vegetables, and stir in the vinegar and salt and pepper to taste. Let cool to room temperature. (The chickpeas can be refrigerated in their liquid for up to 3 days.)

Cut out the core of the cauliflower and remove the leaves. Cut the cauliflower into florets and trim the stems; the florets should not be larger than a 50-cent piece or smaller than a quarter.

Bring 8 cups of salted water to a rapid boil in a large saucepan. Add the vinegar and the cauliflower and cook for 4 to 5 minutes, until tender but not at all mushy. Lift out the florets with a slotted spoon and spread on a tray to cool, then refrigerate.

Preheat the oven to 375°F. Line a baking sheet with parchment paper.

Spread the pine nuts on the baking sheet and toast in the oven for 6 to 7 minutes, until a rich golden brown. Remove from the oven, transfer to a plate, sprinkle with salt, and let cool.

Cut off about ¼ inch of the bottom of each endive and remove the leaves that start to fall away from core. Cut away a bit more of the base and continue to remove the leaves until you reach the core (I like to eat the core as a chef's snack). Stack the leaves a few at a time on a cutting board, with the outside facing up, and cut on a 45-degree angle into thin slices. Put the endive in a bowl of cold water for 10 minutes to help prevent it from turning brown and to crisp it. Drain and dry in a salad spinner.

Put the cauliflower and endive in a large bowl and add the olives, pickled onions, pine nuts, raisins, and 2 teaspoons of the chives. Toss with ¼ cup of the dressing, then season with a sprinkling of salt and a few grinds of black pepper.

Drain the chickpeas, add to the salad, and toss with another ¼ cup dressing. Taste the salad and add additional dressing if needed.

Arrange the salad on a serving platter. Scatter the remaining 1 teaspoon chives and the fried parsley over the top.   **SERVES 6**

a garden of one's own

When Jean-Louis Palladin, the Michelin-starred chef, arrived in Washington, D.C., in 1979 to open Jean-Louis in the Watergate Hotel, he had a hard time finding the quality of produce he was used to in France. And so he searched the outlying areas of Virginia, Delaware, and Maryland and said to people, "I know you've got great products here—where are they?" He was one of the first chefs to initiate and develop relationships with farmers and fishermen. We need to continue to do this, both at the restaurant level and at home, via the produce managers of our grocery stores.

When asked to put a monetary value on what the French Laundry garden produces, I say it's not possible. How can you put a monetary value on the knowledge and respect for food that's gained by my staff and my customers from having our own garden? It's a huge benefit to all of us. For that reason, beyond the extraordinary bounty it produces, and the quality of it, the garden more than pays for itself. Now I can't imagine our restaurant *not* having a garden, though there was a time not long ago that it didn't even occur to me. Of course, not every chef or home owner can have a garden, but all of us can support small farms and bring gardeners into our lives and support them. For those with restaurants on farmable land, I encourage you to find gardeners to help you develop a growing program.

grilled asparagus

with prosciutto, fried bread, poached egg, and aged balsamic vinegar

2 tablespoons white wine vinegar

6 large eggs

2 bunches pencil-thin asparagus

Canola oil

Kosher salt and freshly ground black pepper

3 ounces thinly sliced prosciutto

2 cups Torn Croutons (page 274)

Extra virgin olive oil

Aged balsamic vinegar

Fleur de sel

Asparagus at its peak, bright green, tender, and sweet, can't be beat. Here we add poached eggs to enrich it, along with some ham, which goes great with the egg, of course. We balance the richness with some vinegar and add fried croutons for texture.

To poach the eggs, bring 6 to 8 inches of water to a boil in a large deep saucepan. Prepare an ice bath. Add the vinegar to the boiling water and reduce the heat to a simmer. Crack 1 egg into a small cup or ramekin. Using a wooden spoon, stir the water at the edges of the pan twice in a circular motion to get the water moving, then add the egg to the center of the pan and simmer gently for 1½ minutes, or until the white is set but the yolk is still runny. With a slotted spoon, carefully transfer the egg to the ice bath. Skim and discard any foam that has risen to the top of the water, and cook the remaining eggs one at a time. (The eggs can be poached several hours ahead and stored in ice water in the refrigerator.)

Prepare a charcoal or gas grill for cooking over medium heat (see Grilling Basics, page 345), or heat a grill pan over medium-high heat when you are ready to cook the asparagus. Line a baking sheet with parchment paper.

Hold an asparagus spear and bend it to break off the less tender bottom end. Trim all of the asparagus to the same length. If using medium or large asparagus, peel the stalks with a vegetable peeler. Spread the asparagus out on the parchment-lined pan, generously coat with canola oil, and season with salt and pepper.

Arrange the asparagus on the grill, or cook in batches in the grill pan. Cook for 1½ to 2 minutes per side, flipping with a palette knife or narrow spatula, until tender. Arrange the asparagus on a platter.

Meanwhile, bring a large pot of water to a simmer. With a small pair of scissors, trim any uneven edges from the poached eggs. Lower the eggs into the simmering water for about 30 seconds, just to reheat. Remove the eggs with a skimmer or slotted spoon and blot the bottoms with paper towels. Season the eggs with salt and pepper and arrange around the asparagus.

Arrange the prosciutto and croutons on the platter. Drizzle the salad with olive oil and balsamic, and sprinkle with fleur de sel and pepper.

SERVES 6

green bean and potato salad
with mission figs and ibérico ham

1½ pounds thin green beans (haricots verts)

1 pound fingerling potatoes (12 to 14), about 1 inch in diameter (see Note)

1 Sachet (page 342)

Kosher salt

1 cup (about 4 ounces) walnuts

Ground fleur de sel or fine sea salt

3 radishes, about 1 inch in diameter

¼ cup minced shallots

About 1 cup Sherry Vinaigrette (page 179)

Freshly ground black pepper

2 tablespoons minced chives

4 Black Mission figs, halved

Splash of fresh lemon juice

16 very thin slices Ibérico ham (see Sources, page 346) or prosciutto
   (about 3 ounces)

Extra virgin olive oil

This is a beautiful salad, beans and potatoes with walnuts and a sherry vinaigrette and, for salty-savoriness, dry-cured ham. Jamon Ibérico is a Spanish dry-cured ham made from the leg of the black Iberian pig, which forages on acorns. The flavor of the meat is sweet and nutty, and the supple unctuousness of the fat is extraordinary. Prohibited in the United States until just recently, it's now available through several internet sources. Because of its uniqueness, it's very expensive—feel free to substitute good-quality prosciutto.

Bring a large pot of salted water to a boil for blanching the beans (see page 147). Prepare an ice bath. Set a cooling rack over a baking sheet and line the rack with paper towels.

Meanwhile, hold the beans a handful at a time with the ends facing the same direction and, using scissors, cut off the stem ends (see photo, page 229). Add the beans to the boiling water and cook for 2 to 3 minutes, until just tender. Drain and cool in the ice bath, then drain on the paper towels.

Cut the potatoes into ¼-inch slices; discard the end slices. Put the potatoes, sachet, and 2 teaspoons salt in a large saucepan, add cold water to cover, bring to a simmer, and cook until the potatoes are just tender, about 10 minutes. Drain and spread on a tray to cool; discard the sachet.

Preheat the oven to 375°F.

Line a baking sheet with parchment paper, spread the walnuts on the pan, and toast in the oven, for 10 minutes, or until lightly toasted. Turn the pan around midway through the 10 minutes. Remove from the oven, transfer to a plate, sprinkle with fleur de sel, and let cool.

Fill a small bowl with ice water. Trim the ends from the radishes. Using a Japanese mandoline or other vegetable slicer, slice the radishes, making them just thick enough to keep the outer edges intact. Transfer the slices to the bowl of water to keep them crisp. Drain and dry the slices on paper towels before serving.

To serve, transfer the beans to a large bowl and add the potatoes, shallots, and walnuts. Whisk the dressing and spoon it over the salad. Season with salt and pepper, sprinkle with about half the chives, and toss well.

Arrange about half the salad on a platter. Place half the figs over the salad. Toss the radishes with the remaining salad, and arrange over the first layer of salad. Add the remaining figs, and sprinkle with the remaining chives and a few drops of fresh lemon juice.

Arrange the ham on a small plate and drizzle with olive oil. Serve with the salad.   SERVES 6

NOTE *Look for potatoes that are even in diameter and have minimal tapering at the ends. You'll get more usable slices per potato.*

mushroom and leek salad

with oven-roasted tomatoes and radishes

8 medium leeks, 1 to 1½ inches in diameter

1 tablespoon (½ ounce) unsalted butter

Kosher salt and freshly ground black pepper

10 Oven-Roasted Tomatoes (page 262), finely diced

1 tablespoon minced shallot

1 cup oil from the Oven-Roasted Tomatoes or olive oil, or a combination

1 tablespoon plus 1 teaspoon sherry vinegar

Fleur de sel

3 red radishes

1 small (golf-ball-sized) black radish

Mushroom Conserva (page 260)

6 slices country bread, toasted

Fleur de sel

1 bunch chervil, leaves only

This salad pairs wild mushrooms steeped in a flavorful oil with the sweetness of leeks, the savory acidity of oven-dried tomatoes, and the spicy crunch of radishes, all tied together with a tomato vinaigrette. Serve the salad with slices of toasted crusty country bread. The mushrooms, leeks, and tomatoes can all be prepared a day ahead of time.

Preheat the oven to 350°F.

Trim the root ends from the leeks, leaving enough of the ends intact to keep the leaves attached. Cut off the dark green tops of the leaves. Cut the leeks lengthwise in half and rinse under warm water to remove any dirt.

Arrange the leeks cut side up in an ovenproof sauté pan that just holds them in a single layer. Add enough water to come halfway up the sides of the leeks, add the butter and salt and pepper to taste, and bring to a simmer. Cover the pan with a lid, transfer to the oven, and cook for 12 minutes. Pierce a leek with a paring knife: it should be just tender, with no resistance. If necessary, return the leeks to the oven, and check them often. Remove the leeks from the pan and let cool enough to handle. Set a cooling rack over a baking sheet and line the rack with paper towels. Cut off the root ends of the leeks and discard the tougher outer leaf from each leek. Spread the leeks on the paper towels to drain.

Put the tomatoes and shallot in a small bowl and add enough of the tomato oil to cover (reserve any remaining oil). Stir in the vinegar and a sprinkling of fleur de sel.

Fill a small bowl with ice water. Trim the ends from the radishes. Using a Japanese mandoline or other vegetable slicer, slice the red and black radishes, making them just thick enough to keep the outer edges intact. Transfer the slices to the bowl of water to keep them crisp. Drain and dry the slices on paper towels before serving.

Remove the mushrooms from the oil and arrange them on a platter (the herbs can be left in or removed as desired). Arrange the leeks and radishes around the mushrooms. Spoon a bit of the reserved tomato oil over the dish. Using a slotted spoon, arrange small spoonfuls of the tomatoes on the platter. Place the slices of bread around the salad, sprinkle the salad with fleur de sel, and garnish with chervil leaves.

Serve the remaining tomato vinaigrette in the bowl on the side.

SERVES 6

farro and black rice
with roasted autumn squash

3 tablespoons canola oil

3 tablespoons chopped onion

Kosher salt

1 cup farro (see Sources, page 346, and Note, page 163)

½ cup sweet Asian black rice (see Sources, page 346)

1 small (12 ounces) Delicata squash

1 small (about 1½ pounds) butternut squash

1 small (12 ounces) Kabocha squash

4 tablespoons (2 ounces) unsalted butter

Freshly ground black pepper

2 ounces (about ½ large bunch) small dandelion or other spicy greens

4 ounces applewood-smoked slab bacon (see Sources, page 346)

VINAIGRETTE

3 tablespoons champagne vinegar

1 teaspoon Dijon mustard

About ⅓ cup canola oil

½ teaspoon whole-grain mustard

Kosher salt and freshly ground black pepper

Extra virgin olive oil

Fleur de sel

Squash sautéed in brown butter and bitter dandelion greens, dressed with a sharp mustard vinaigrette and served atop farro and black rice, make for a rich, hearty salad to serve warm in the fall. Farro, a type of wheat that looks like barley, has an amber hue and firm texture—it almost pops when you chew it. Black sticky rice is nutritious and high in fiber and gluten, with a wonderful nutty flavor. In Asia, it is primarily used for breakfast, puddings, and other desserts, but it makes a great bed for cooked Asian fruit and vegetable recipes.

Heat 2 tablespoons of the canola oil in a medium saucepan over medium heat. Add 2 tablespoons of the chopped onion with a pinch of salt and cook until translucent, about 3 minutes. Meanwhile, heat the remaining tablespoon oil in a small saucepan over medium heat. Add the remaining tablespoon chopped onion with a pinch of salt and cook until translucent, about 3 minutes.

Stir the farro into the medium saucepan and the rice into the small saucepan and cook, stirring occasionally to toast the grains, about 2 minutes.

Stir 2 cups of water into the farro, bring to a simmer, and stir once, then partially cover, reduce the heat to low, and simmer for 25 to 50 minutes (see Note). Stir 1 cup of water into the black rice, bring to a simmer, stir once, then partially cover, reduce the heat to low, and simmer for about 30 minutes. The farro and rice should be tender but not at all mushy. Add salt to taste. Drain the farro if necessary and spread on a tray to cool. Drain the rice and spread on another tray to cool.

continued

Position oven racks in the lower and upper thirds of the oven and preheat the oven to 350°F.

Cut off the ends of the Delicata squash and peel it. Cut lengthwise into quarters and remove the seeds. Cut each quarter lengthwise into 3 pieces. Put each piece seed side down on a cutting surface and cut on a sharp diagonal into ⅜-inch-thick slices about 1½ inches long; discard the end pieces. You need about 1½ cups squash for this recipe (reserve any extra for another use).

Peel the butternut squash. Cut the neck from the bulb, trim the neck, and cut into ½-inch cubes. Cut the bulb end lengthwise in half and remove the seeds. Cut each half lengthwise in half. Trim the ends, lay seed side down on a cutting surface, and cut into thin crescents.

Peel the Kabocha squash and cut into thin crescents as you did the butternut squash.

Put two large baking sheets into the oven to heat. You will be cooking the squash in 4 separate batches.

Heat a large skillet over medium-high heat. Remove the pan from the heat and add 1 tablespoon of the butter, swirling the pan to melt and brown it, then add the cubes of butternut squash and return to the heat. Season with salt and pepper and cook, stirring to coat evenly with the butter and seasoning, for about 1½ minutes. Spread on one of the hot baking sheets in a single layer and roast for about 10 minutes, stirring once, until completely tender. Test a few pieces to be certain, then transfer to a tray to cool.

Meanwhile continue to cook the remaining squash, using the remaining 3 tablespoons butter. There is no need to clean the pan between batches. Cook the Kabocha squash and transfer to the second baking sheet to roast for about 12 minutes, until tender. Repeat with the butternut and Delicata crescents, which will take about 10 minutes. (Turn the oven down to 200°F.)

Trim any woody stems from the dandelion greens. You should have about 3 cups loosely packed greens.

Cut the bacon into lardons 1 inch long and about ½ inch thick (see page 150). Put the lardons in a frying pan in a single layer and cook over medium heat for 10 to 12 minutes, turning to color all sides and adjusting the heat as necessary, until crisp on the outside but still soft inside. Transfer to paper towels to drain. Pour the fat from the frying pan into a liquid measuring cup; you should have 2 to 3 tablespoons.

Set up the Vita-Mix, preferably with the small bowl, and add the vinegar and Dijon mustard. Add enough canola oil to the reserved bacon fat to equal ½ cup. Blend the vinegar and mustard and then, with the machine running, drizzle in the oil mixture until emulsified and smooth. Transfer to a small bowl and whisk in the whole-grain mustard. Season to taste with salt and pepper.

To serve, put the squash in the oven to heat through.

Meanwhile, toss the farro, rice, and bacon with a light coating of the vinaigrette in a large bowl.

Transfer the warm squash to another large bowl, and toss gently with the dandelion greens and a light coating of vinaigrette.

Arrange a bed of the farro mixture on a large platter, followed by layers of the squash mixture and remaining farro. Drizzle with olive oil and sprinkle with fleur de sel. Serve the remaining dressing on the side.

SERVES 6

NOTE *Most farro is semipearled, which means that part of the hull has been removed and the grain will cook more quickly. Farro that is not pearled will take about twice as long to cook. Because farro is often sold without labeling that specifies cooking times, it is important to check it frequently during cooking.*

roasted beet and potato salad

with soft-cooked egg, smoked salmon, and mustard vinaigrette

BABY BEETS

8 baby golden beets, 1 to 1½ inches in diameter

8 baby red beets, 1 to 1½ inches in diameter

8 baby Chioggia beets, 1 to 1½ inches in diameter

3 tablespoons canola oil

Kosher salt and freshly ground black pepper

POTATOES

6 ounces marble potatoes, about 1 inch in diameter

6 ounces purple marble potatoes, about 1 inch in diameter

6 ounces Bintje creamer potatoes or small Red Bliss potatoes,
   about 1 inch in diameter

3 Sachets (page 342)

Kosher salt

4 Soft-Cooked Eggs (see page 342)

Extra virgin olive oil

1 tablespoon minced shallot

Mustard Vinaigrette (page 179)

About 1½ cups chicory leaves

12 slices (about 4 ounces) smoked salmon (see Sources, page 346),
   cut into strips about 4 inches long and 1 inch wide

Minced chives

A lot of big ingredients come together here in a salad that's a meal in itself: beets, potatoes, soft-cooked eggs, and smoked salmon. We use small potatoes about 1 inch in diameter and baby beets that are approximately the same size. All the ingredients can be prepared ahead of time and the salad can be assembled just before serving.

Preheat the oven to 375°F.

Trim the stems of the beets to about ½ inch and trim any root ends. Put 3 pieces of aluminum foil (each large enough to encase one type of beet) on a work surface. Put the beets in the center of the pieces of foil and top each with 1 tablespoon of canola oil and a sprinkling of salt and pepper. Wrap the beets in the foil, crimping the edges of the foil and rolling them over to ensure that there is a good seal.

Put the packets on a baking sheet and roast for 30 minutes, or until the beets are tender when pierced with the tip of a knife. Carefully open the packets and let the beets sit until cool enough to handle.

Meanwhile, cut the potatoes into quarters. Put each type of potato in a separate saucepan, add 1 sachet and 2 teaspoons salt to each, and cover with cold water. Bring to a simmer and cook just until the potatoes are tender, about 10 minutes. Drain the potatoes and spread on a tray to cool; discard the sachets.

Cut off both ends of each beet, and rub the beets with a paper towel to remove the skin (see Lightbulb Moment, page 241). Refrigerate the beets until chilled.

Cut the beets in half or quarters so you have pieces of approximately the same size, and put each type in a small bowl.

To serve, cut the eggs lengthwise in half and drizzle them with a bit of olive oil. Put the potatoes in a large bowl, add the shallot, and toss with about two-thirds of the dressing. Toss the beets with a drizzle of olive oil and season with salt and pepper.

Arrange about one-third of the potatoes on a platter. Scatter one-third of the beets and about one-third of the chicory over them. Continue layering, adding the slices of smoked salmon as you go; reserve a few chicory leaves. Arrange the eggs around the salad. Top with the remaining chicory, drizzle with olive oil, and sprinkle with the chives. Spoon the remaining dressing around the salad.   SERVES 6

saffron rice salad

with summer squash and maine lobster

6 ounces thin green beans (haricots verts)

5 baby pattypan squash (about 3 ounces total)

5 baby yellow squash (about 3 ounces total)

6 baby zucchini (about 4 ounces total; see Note)

Saffron Rice (page 220), cold

½ cup lightly packed red onion julienne

Sherry Vinaigrette (page 179)

8 piquillo peppers (see Lightbulb Moment, page 183), drained and
   cut into thin julienne

Kosher salt and freshly ground black pepper

Three 1-pound lobsters, cooked (see page 342), meat removed from shells,
   and refrigerated

Extra virgin olive oil

Fresh lemon juice

T his lobster salad was developed when we had paella rice left over from a previous night's dinner. Here the saffron rice is the base for abundant summer vegetables, green beans and squash, with some vivid piquillo peppers (you could substitute roasted red bell peppers). In the spring, use English peas or snap peas or asparagus. It's a great dish to make on its own, but it's a lesson to remember—the economy of turning leftovers into a salad by adding some fresh vegetables and a vinaigrette.

Bring a large pot of salted water to a boil (see page 147). Prepare an ice bath. Set a cooling rack over a baking sheet and line with paper towels.

Blanching the vegetables will brighten their color. Trim off the stem ends of the green beans (see photo, page 229). Trim the pattypan and yellow squash and halve lengthwise; trim the zucchini but leave whole.

Add the green beans to the boiling water and blanch until crisp-tender, 2 to 3 minutes. Transfer to the ice bath to cool, then drain on the paper towels. Add the zucchini to the pot and cook for 1 minute, or until crisp-tender. Transfer to the ice bath. Repeat with the pattypan and summer squash; the squash may take up to 2 minutes. Cool in the ice bath, then drain well on the paper towels.

Cut the zucchini into thirds on a diagonal. Cut the beans in half on a diagonal.

To serve, combine the rice, green beans, squash, and red onions in a large bowl. Add ½ to ¾ cup of the dressing, just enough to coat the ingredients, and stir to combine. Add the peppers and toss well. Season to taste with salt and pepper. Mound the rice on a long narrow platter. Drizzle the lobster with olive oil and season again with salt and pepper. Tuck the pieces of lobster into the rice. Drizzle with a little olive oil and finish with a sprinkle of lemon juice.   SERVES 6

NOTE *If you can't get the baby vegetables, buy the same weight of larger squash and cut into cubes.*

frisée and duck confit salad

½ cup sliced blanched almonds

4 legs Duck Confit (page 32)

2 heads frisée, any bruised and tough outer leaves removed,
    washed, and dried

4 cups (about 2 ounces) loosely packed mâche

Roasted Garlic Vinaigrette (page 179)

Kosher salt and freshly ground black pepper

1 cup pitted oil-cured Spanish olives

½ cup piquillo peppers (see Lightbulb Moment, page 183),
    cut into small diamonds

Duck confit, like bacon lardons, combines beautifully with bitter greens in this classic salad along with olives, crunchy almonds, and a garlic vinaigrette. We use warm duck in the salad; it's great in the fall. You could make it even more substantial by topping it with poached eggs.

Preheat the oven to 350°F. Line a baking sheet with parchment paper.

Put the almonds on the baking sheet and toast in the oven for 3 minutes. Turn the pan around and toast for 3 to 4 minutes longer, or until a rich golden brown. Remove from the oven, transfer to a plate, and let cool.

Remove the skin from the duck legs, keeping the skin in pieces as large as possible. Pull the meat from the legs and shred it.

Heat a large nonstick frying pan over low heat. Add the skin and cook slowly for about 25 minutes, flipping the skin once the first side is golden brown and then continuing to flip it from time to time; drain off the fat as it renders. When the skin is browned and the fat has been rendered, remove the skin from the pan and drain on paper towels. Coarsely chop the skin and reserve.

To serve, add the duck to the pan in a single layer and warm over medium heat for 2 to 3 minutes while you build the salad.

Put the frisée and half the mâche in a large bowl. Drizzle enough Garlic Vinaigrette around the sides of the bowl to lightly coat the greens; toss the greens. Season the greens with salt and pepper to taste. Add the olives, peppers, and all but a small handful of the almonds, and toss gently to combine.

Arrange about half the salad on a platter. Top with about half the warm duck confit. Layer with the remaining greens and duck. Sprinkle the salad with the reserved almonds and duck skin. Serve the remaining dressing on the side. **SERVES 6**

fresh tuna salad

1 pound trimmed center-cut tuna loin (ask the fishmonger for a block of loin about 4 inches by 4 inches by 2 inches), room temperature

3 heads Bibb lettuce

Kosher salt and freshly ground black pepper

Canola oil

6 ounces thin green beans (haricots verts), stem ends trimmed, blanched (see page 147)

Simple Vinaigrette (page 179)

4 ounces cherry tomatoes, halved

½ cup pitted Kalamata olives

4 Medium-Cooked Eggs (see page 342)

Extra virgin olive oil

1 Hass avocado

Tarragon leaves

Chervil leaves

This is essentially salade Niçoise using fresh tuna rather than canned. The tuna is briefly seared so it's still very rare and served, sliced, with Bibb lettuce, green beans, olives, avocado, cherry tomatoes, and medium-cooked eggs, in a standard red wine vinaigrette. We use center-cut big-eye albacore tuna, sushi-grade. You may have to order the tuna ahead.

Cut the tuna loin into 2 rectangular blocks about 4 inches long and 2 inches thick. Set aside.

Twist off the core of each head of lettuce and discard any bruised outer leaves. Submerge the lettuce in a large bowl of cold water. The leaves will separate naturally. Remove and dry in a salad spinner.

Season the tuna on all sides with salt and pepper. Heat some canola oil in a large sauté pan over high heat until hot. Add the tuna and lightly brown on all 4 sides, 20 to 30 seconds per side. When you turn the tuna, move it to another section of the pan, which will be hotter (see Lightbulb Moment, page 89). You can gauge the cooking process if you look at the ends of the pieces—allow only about ¼ inch of the tuna to cook on each side. The tuna will be very rare. Drain on paper towels and let rest for 5 minutes.

Slice each piece of tuna crosswise into 6 slices.

Put the lettuce in a large bowl. Drizzle a light coating of the dressing around the sides of the bowl and toss to coat lightly. Season with salt and pepper and toss again.

Cut the beans in half on a diagonal. Put the beans, tomatoes, and olives in a second bowl. Season with salt and pepper and toss with a light coating of dressing.

Cut the eggs lengthwise into quarters. Drizzle lightly with olive oil and sprinkle with salt and pepper.

Peel and pit the avocado and cut into 8 wedges. Season with salt and pepper.

Arrange a layer of lettuce on a platter. Scatter some of the beans and tomatoes over the lettuce. Arrange the eggs and tuna on top and continue to build the salad. Garnish the salad with tarragon and chervil, and serve the remaining dressing on the side.   **SERVES 6**

shellfish salad

with endive, watercress, and spicy herb vinaigrette

Court Bouillon (page 341)

One 1-pound lobster

12 extra-large (12–15 per pound) shrimp

18 bay scallops, muscle removed

12 ounces Bouchot or PEI (Prince Edward Island) mussels

1 tablespoon (½ ounce) unsalted butter

¼ cup dry white wine, such as Sauvignon Blanc

2 large heads red Belgian endive

1 large head white Belgian endive

Spicy Herb Vinaigrette (page 179)

Kosher salt and freshly ground black pepper

4 cups loosely packed watercress

Maldon salt or fleur de sel

Bouchot mussels, a small variety we get from Maine, are very sweet and flavorful. The mussels are cooked separately from the other shellfish, in order to retain their juices, but the other shellfish are cooked one after the other in the same court bouillon, the lobster flavoring it for the shrimp, which in turn flavor it for the scallops. The dressing is packed with herbs and spices, and we use spicy greens—endive and watercress—to balance the richness of the shellfish.

Bring the court bouillon to a boil in a large pot. Prepare the lobster as directed on page 342.

Using a small pair of scissors (such as nail scissors), cut a slit down the back of each shrimp, cutting just slightly into the flesh of the shrimp. Leaving the shell on the shrimp, gently separate the flesh to check for the intestinal tract; remove it with a paring knife, and discard. (The flavor of the shrimp will be better if they are cooked in the shell.) Rinse the shrimp.

Return the court bouillon to a boil, then turn off the heat and add the shrimp. Move them around so they cook evenly. After 1½ minutes, lift one out with a skimmer to check it. It should just be cooked all the way through. If it is still translucent, continue to cook up to another 30 seconds. Remove the shrimp, spread on a tray, and chill in the refrigerator.

Return the court bouillon to a boil. Put the scallops in a large strainer, turn off the heat, and dip the strainer with the scallops into the court bouillon. As the scallops float in the liquid, move them around so they cook evenly. Cut a scallop open after 1 minute. If the scallop is not cooked through, continue to cook for up to another 30 seconds. Lift the strainer to drain the scallops, spread on a tray, and chill in the refrigerator.

Wash the mussels well under cold running water; if necessary, scrub them to remove any sand. If there is a beard protruding from the shell, pull it out from each mussel and discard. If any of the shells are not completely shut, squeeze and release them, like playing castanets; if the shell does not close tightly, the mussel is dead and should be discarded.

Combine the butter and white wine in a sauté pan that will hold the mussels in one layer and bring to a simmer over medium-high heat. Add the mussels, cover, and cook for 1½ to 2 minutes; check frequently, transferring the mussels to a bowl as they open. If any mussels have not opened after several minutes, discard them. Strain the liquid over the mussels and refrigerate until cold.

Peel the shrimp and return them to the refrigerator.

Shortly before serving, cut about ½ inch from the bottom end of each head of endive; the outer leaves will naturally fall away. Cut the base again and continue to remove the leaves in the same way until you reach the core (I like to eat this as a chef's snack). Stack the leaves a few at a time on a cutting board with the outside facing up and cut on a 45-degree diagonal into fine slices. Put the endive in a bowl of cold water for 10 minutes to help prevent it from turning brown and to crisp it. Drain and dry in a salad spinner before using.

Put all the shellfish in a large bowl, with the mussel liquid, and toss with a light coating of vinaigrette. Let marinate for about 2 minutes. Season with salt and pepper to taste.

Arrange the endive and watercress in the center of a serving bowl. Arrange the shellfish around the greens (discard any empty mussel shells). Sprinkle with Maldon salt. Serve the remaining dressing on the side.

SERVES 6

deep-frying

The most important factor in deep-frying is your pot. It needs to be sturdy, for good heat distribution, and big enough to hold enough oil to cook the food without filling the pot more than a third full. If you fill it higher than that, you run the risk that the oil will bubble over when you add the ingredients.

For a big 7-quart Dutch oven, which has a base of 10 inches, you will need about 4 quarts of oil to achieve a depth of 3 inches. A pan with a diameter of 8 inches will require about 2½ quarts.

Use a deep-fry thermometer for consistent results. Deep-frying is usually done at temperatures between 320° and 375°F. When the oil goes above 400°F, it will begin to smoke and break down.

We prefer peanut oil for deep-frying because of its flavor and high smoking point; canola oil is also acceptable. The oil can be reused several times, but eventually it will begin to break down and affect the flavor of what you're cooking.

The basics of deep-frying are simple: To reiterate, don't overfill your pot with oil. Don't add too much food at a time, or the temperature of the oil will drop too much. Add the food carefully, lowering it into the oil rather than tossing it in; or use a slotted spoon or spider if you prefer. When you first add the food, it will release voluminous bubbles as the surface moisture vaporizes. The bubbling will subside as there is increasingly less moisture in the food. If no bubbles are being released, you have probably overcooked the food. Pay attention, and watch the food as it cooks. When you remove the food, shake off some of the excess oil and drain it on paper towels or a kitchen towel, giving it ample space— if you crowd the food or pile it up, its own steam can make it soggy. We drain many foods on paper towels spread on a rack, so that the towels don't become saturated with oil.

fritto misto

BATTER

2 cups all-purpose flour

½ teaspoon sweet paprika

½ teaspoon cayenne

1 tablespoon kosher salt

¾ cup extra virgin olive oil

1½ cups cold water, or as needed

CHOOSE 6 OF THE FOLLOWING

1 cup broccolini florets and tender stems (2½ to 3 inches long)

1 cup ½-inch-thick half-rounds Japanese eggplant

1 cup ½-inch-thick slices small zucchini

1 cup 2-inch-by-¼-inch carrot batons

1 cup 2½- to 3-inch by ¼-inch strips fennel
    (cut from the outer layers of the bulb)

6 mini peppers, halved, cored, and seeded

1 cup small clusters hen-of-the-woods mushrooms

1 cup 2½- to 3-inch-long asparagus tips

1 cup cleaned calamari rings and tentacles

6 fresh sardine fillets, halved lengthwise, bones removed

Peanut or canola oil for deep-frying

Kosher salt

¼ to ½ cup Piment d'Espelette Aioli (page 333)

Chopped chives

Mix the flour, paprika, cayenne, and salt together in a large bowl with a fork. Stir in the olive oil until smooth. Mix in the water. The mixture should be slightly thinner than pancake batter. If necessary, add more water to reach the right consistency. Let rest for 1 hour in the refrigerator.

Pour 3 inches of peanut oil into a Dutch oven or heavy stockpot; ideally, the oil should come no more than one-third of the way up the sides of the pot, but it should be deep enough to allow the ingredients to float freely. Heat the oil to 375°F.

Preheat the oven to 175°F. Set a cooling rack on a baking sheet and put it in the oven. Set another rack over a second baking sheet and top the rack with paper towels.

Make sure all of the ingredients, particularly the calamari, are dry, to prevent splattering. Fry each type of vegetable or fish separately. Dip into the batter and add to the pot. Use a spider or wire skimmer to move the ingredients in the oil and separate them if any stick together, turning them as necessary to brown evenly. Carefully monitor the temperature, turning the heat up or down as necessary. Cook all the ingredients, in the order given below, until golden brown, following the times listed here:

Broccolini, 3 to 4 minutes	Peppers, 3 to 4 minutes
Eggplant, 3 to 4 minutes	Mushrooms, about 3 minutes
Zucchini, 3 to 4 minutes	Asparagus, 2 to 3 minutes
Carrots, 4 to 5 minutes	Calamari, about 2 to 3 minutes
Fennel, 3 to 4 minutes	Sardines, 2 to 3 minutes

This dish is so festive—put it in the middle of the table and everybody will dive in. The batter begins with a kind of slurry—olive oil and seasoned flour—to which cold water is added. The result is a crisp, lacy crust, one you can almost see through. Serve it with Aioli (page 333), Olive or Sweet Onion Tapenade (page 250), or Artichoke Mustard (page 251).

This recipe can be expanded to feed a large group of people. Choose the vegetables and fish you like best, allowing about 1 cup total per person.

As they are cooked, transfer the ingredients to the paper towels to drain briefly. Season with salt, and transfer the ingredients to the cooling rack on the baking sheet in the oven to keep warm. Use a skimmer to remove any bits of fried batter that remain in the oil after each batch, and be sure to let the oil reach the proper temperature before frying the next batch.

Line a large serving platter with brown paper to absorb any remaining oil. Arrange the fritto misto on a platter, sprinkle with chives, and serve with aioli on the side.　　　　　　　SERVES 6

mezze platter Instead of opening a meal with a salad, consider
this festive course composed of several small dishes. When you set
out a series of plates and everyone starts reaching and sharing,
there's more socializing, more talk, because there's such a variety of
foods and flavors. Put a mezze platter together in the same way you
would put a meal together, a balance of flavors and textures, proteins,
starches, and vegetables, with a mix of acidity and sweetness and of
spicy and savory flavors complementing one another. Sautéed shrimp
with garlic, marinated feta cheese with olives, lamb meatballs, and a
little quinoa salad with confit of duck is one great combination. But
there's no set formula—just have a good variety. The dishes can be as
elaborate as those pictured here or as simple as flatbreads with assorted
tapenades or nut butters. Other mezze combinations might be:

Fritto Misto (page 173) made with or without seafood and served
    with Aioli (page 333)

Assorted sausages with Artichoke Mustard (page 251), Eggplant-
    Raisin Mustard (page 251), Fennel Mustard (page 251), and
    Pickled Vegetables (page 254) or Potted Bing Cherries with
    Cherry Balsamic Vinegar and Tarragon (page 242)

Garlic Toast (page 280) with Soffritto (page 263), Herbed Toasted
    Walnuts (page 238), and Cipollini Onion Chutney with Almonds
    (page 242)

marinated feta with olives

3 ounces feta, cut into ½-inch cubes
¼ cup extra virgin olive oil
¼ teaspoon finely chopped thyme
One 2-inch rosemary sprig
½ teaspoon chopped chives
1 piquillo pepper (see Lightbulb Moment, page 183), cut into thin strips
1 cup mixed olives

Put the feta in a small bowl. Pour the oil over, add the herbs and pepper,
and gently stir to combine. Let sit at room temperature for 1 to 2 hours.
    Just before serving, add the olives, mixing them in gently.

CLOCKWISE FROM TOP LEFT: *Quinoa with Duck Confit (page 176); Sautéed Shrimp with Garlic (page 177); Marinated Feta with Olives (page 174); Lamb Meatballs (page 176).*

quinoa with duck confit

Canola oil

½ cup quinoa

1 cup water

1 carrot, cut into 3-inch pieces

½ medium leek, outer leaves removed,
    cut in half lengthwise, and cleaned

1 large onion wedge, root end still intact

1 Sachet (page 342)

Kosher salt

1 leg Duck Confit (page 32), at room temperature

1 tablespoon currants, plumped in ¼ cup hot water

1½ cups loosely packed trimmed escarole

1 tablespoon extra virgin olive oil

2 teaspoons white balsamic vinegar

Freshly ground black pepper

Heat some canola oil in a medium saucepan over medium heat until warm. Add the quinoa and toast, stirring, for 2 to 3 minutes; the quinoa should have a very nutty aroma. Pour in the water, add the carrot, leek, onion, sachet, and a sprinkling of salt, increase the heat, and bring to a simmer. Simmer for 20 to 25 minutes, until tender.

Drain the quinoa and place in a mixing bowl, discarding the vegetables and sachet. Let the quinoa cool to room temperature, then complete, or cover and refrigerate. (The quinoa can be refrigerated for up to 2 days; bring to room temperature before completing.)

To serve, remove the skin and fat from the duck leg and pull the meat into shreds. Add the duck, currants, escarole, olive oil, and vinegar to the quinoa, mixing gently. Season with salt and pepper and transfer to a serving bowl.

PHOTOGRAPH ON PAGE 175

lamb meatballs

2 teaspoons extra virgin olive oil

1 tablespoon finely chopped onion

1 teaspoon finely chopped garlic

Kosher salt and freshly ground black pepper

¼ cup plus 2 tablespoons finely diced zucchini

1 tablespoon lightly rinsed, dried, and finely chopped Cured Lemons
    (page 263) or Preserved Whole Lemons (page 263)

8 ounces ground lamb shoulder

1 large egg yolk

1 teaspoon Dried Bread Crumbs (page 273)

1 tablespoon coarsely chopped mint

6 Oven-Roasted Tomatoes (page 262), halved lengthwise,
    at room temperature

Heat a small frying pan over medium heat. Pour in the oil and heat until warm. Add the onion and garlic, season with salt and pepper, and cook until translucent, about 1 minute. Add the zucchini and cook until tender, 3 to 4 minutes. Remove the pan from the heat and stir in the lemons. The residual heat will bring out the flavor of the lemons. Transfer to a medium bowl and let cool.

Preheat the oven to 450°F. Line a baking sheet with parchment paper.

Add the lamb, egg yolk, bread crumbs, and mint to the zucchini mixture, and season with salt and pepper. Sauté a small patty to check the seasoning; add more salt and/or pepper to the lamb mixture if needed. Shape the meat into twelve 1-inch meatballs.

Put the meatballs on the baking sheet and bake for 12 to 15 minutes, or until they are cooked through. Arrange the meatballs and tomatoes on a serving plate.

PHOTOGRAPH ON PAGE 175

sautéed shrimp with garlic

12 extra-large shrimp (12–15 count), peeled,
    leaving tail shell intact, and deveined
Kosher salt
1 tablespoon (½ ounce) unsalted butter
1 garlic clove, thinly sliced
¼ cup dry white wine, such as Sauvignon Blanc
2 tablespoons chopped chives

Put the shrimp in a medium bowl.

Mix together 4 cups cold water and ½ cup plus 2 tablespoons of salt in another bowl, stirring to dissolve the salt. Pour over the shrimp. Let stand at room temperature for 10 minutes. Drain the shrimp, rinse under cold water, and pat dry on paper towels.

Melt the butter in a frying pan that will hold the shrimp in a single layer over medium heat. When the butter just starts to foam, add the garlic and shrimp. Swirl the pan and cook, turning once, until the shrimp are browned on both sides and cooked through, 1½ to 2 minutes per side. Transfer the shrimp to a tray and keep in a warm spot.

Add the wine to the pan and simmer to reduce to a glaze. Swirl about 2 teaspoons of the chives into the glaze, and remove from the heat.

Sprinkle a serving platter with the remaining chives, arrange the shrimp on the platter, and spoon the glaze over the shrimp.

PHOTOGRAPH ON PAGE 175

fried fresh chickpeas

Peanut or canola oil for deep-frying
Fresh chickpeas in the shell, rinsed and patted thoroughly dry
Ground fleur de sel or fine sea salt
Freshly ground black pepper

Set a cooling rack on a baking sheet and line the rack with paper towels.

Heat about 2 inches of peanut oil in a large deep pot over medium-high heat to 350°F. Add a handful of the chickpeas to the pot, not more than will fit in one layer; the chickpeas will rise to the top and the moisture in them will cause them to pop, so stand back. If you have a splatter screen, use it. Fry for 2 to 4 minutes, stirring occasionally, until the chickpeas stop popping and are golden brown. With a skimmer or slotted spoon, transfer the chickpeas to the paper towels to drain. Sprinkle immediately with fleur de sel and pepper. Fry any remaining chickpeas in batches, and serve while they are still warm. Eat them as you would edamame, removing the green chickpeas from the pods.

dressings A vinaigrette is a mixture of an oil and an acid—it's no more complicated than that. The acid can be any kind of vinegar—sherry, red wine, white wine—or lemon juice or lime juice, or a combination of citrus juices, or verjus. (If you aren't familiar with verjus, which we use in the garden vinaigrette, it is made from the juice of unripe grapes. It's acidic but not quite so strong as vinegar, so it doesn't overtake the sweet components of a vinaigrette the way a straight white wine vinegar can. It can also be used in sauces when you want a wine or grape flavor in your acidity, but not the alcohol.)

The oil can be vegetable or olive oil, or a flavorful nut oil, or even duck or bacon fat. Our workhorse vinaigrette is sherry vinaigrette, used when we want to feature delicate ingredients. When we have hearty ingredients, we use a vinaigrette with bigger flavors, such as the anchovy dressing (a Caesar-inspired anchovy aioli), or the bacon-mustard vinaigrette we pair with meaty fish and bitter greens. The blue cheese dressing is essentially a mayonnaise thinned with buttermilk and flavored with delicious Pt. Reyes blue cheese. The creamy pepper dressing is another mayonnaise-buttermilk combination, flavored by a pepper gastrique added when it's still warm. A straightforward red wine vinaigrette is used for sweeter greens such as romaine.

You can flavor the basic acid-fat mixture any way you wish—add some basil or oven-roasted tomatoes, flavor it with curry, fresh herbs, or smoky sweet piquillo peppers, or add mustard. Sometimes we sweeten a vinaigrette with honey (see page 143), perhaps for a cheese course salad, or make it very lemony for lighter greens or baby butter lettuces, mizuna, or tatsoi.

How you season a vinaigrette is important. Notice that some of these dressings are seasoned with salt and pepper and some are not. If the dressing has an assertive flavor that turns it into one of the main components of the salad, such as anchovy dressing or creamy pepper dressing, we season it before using. But if the dressing is more of a supporting player, we season the salad itself rather than the dressing.

simple vinaigrette

2 tablespoons Dijon mustard
¼ cup red wine vinegar
¾ cup canola oil

Whisk together the mustard and vinegar in a bowl. While whisking, pour in the canola oil in a thin stream until the dressing is emulsified and smooth. Refrigerate in a covered container for up to 2 weeks.

MAKES ABOUT 1 CUP

spicy herb vinaigrette

2 tablespoons spicy pimentón (Spanish smoked paprika;
    see Sources, page 346)
½ cup plus 3 tablespoons champagne vinegar
1½ cups extra virgin olive oil
½ cup finely chopped flat-leaf parsley
¼ cup finely chopped oregano
2 tablespoons minced chives
1 teaspoon red pepper flakes
Kosher salt and freshly ground black pepper

Combine the pimentón and vinegar in a Vita-Mix. Blend to combine, then, with the machine running, slowly drizzle in the olive oil until emulsified and smooth. Transfer to a bowl and whisk in the herbs and red pepper flakes. Season generously with salt and pepper to taste. Refrigerate in a covered container for up to 2 weeks (the herbs will darken after 1 day).

MAKES ABOUT 2 CUPS

sherry vinaigrette

¼ cup sherry wine vinegar
¼ cup red wine vinegar
1 to 1½ cups extra virgin olive oil

Whisk the two vinegars in a bowl, then whisk in about 1 cup of the olive oil in a steady stream. The vinaigrette should look broken (do not emulsify the dressing). Taste to check the balance of acid and oil, and add more olive oil as needed. Refrigerate in a covered container for up to 1 month.

MAKES 2 CUPS

mustard vinaigrette

½ cup champagne vinegar
2 teaspoons Dijon mustard
1½ cups extra virgin olive oil
1 teaspoon whole-grain mustard

Put the vinegar in a bowl and whisk in the Dijon mustard. Whisking constantly, slowly stream in the oil until emulsified and smooth. Whisk in the whole-grain mustard. Refrigerate in a covered container for up to 2 weeks.

MAKES ABOUT 2 CUPS

bacon vinaigrette

8 ounces applewood-smoked slab bacon (see Sources, page 346)
½ cup champagne vinegar
2 teaspoons Dijon mustard
1 teaspoon whole-grain mustard
1 cup canola oil
Kosher salt and freshly ground black pepper to taste

Cut the bacon cut into lardons 1 inch long and ½ inch thick (see page 150).

Put the lardons in a sauté pan in a single layer and cook over medium heat for 10 to 12 minutes, turning to color all sides and adjusting the heat as necessary, until crisp on the outside but still soft inside. Transfer to paper towels to drain; reserve the fat in the pan.

Combine the remaining ingredients in a Vita-Mix. With the machine running, pour in the bacon fat and blend until emulsified and smooth. Pour into a bowl, stir in the lardons, and use immediately.

MAKES ABOUT 2 CUPS

roasted garlic vinaigrette

½ cup champagne vinegar
2 to 3 tablespoons Garlic Puree (page 266)
1½ cups extra virgin olive oil

Whisk together the vinegar and garlic puree in a bowl. While whisking, slowly stream in the oil until emulsified and smooth. Refrigerate in a covered container for up to 2 weeks.

MAKES ABOUT 2 CUPS

GARDEN HERB

½ c. olive oil

¼ c. white verjus

¼ c. champagne vinegar

salt and pepper

VINAIGRETTE

1 Tbsp. minced shallot

2 Tbsp. chopped flat-leaf parsley

1 Tbsp. minced chives

1¹/₂ tsp. minced chervil

1¹/₂ tsp. minced tarragon

garden herb vinaigrette

¼ cup champagne vinegar
¼ cup white verjus (see Sources, page 346)
½ cup extra virgin olive oil
2 tablespoons coarsely chopped flat-leaf parsley
1 tablespoon minced chives
1½ teaspoons minced chervil
1½ teaspoons minced tarragon
1 tablespoon minced shallot
Kosher salt and freshly ground black pepper

Whisk together the vinegar and verjus in a medium bowl. Whisk in the oil, herbs, and shallot. Season to taste with salt and pepper. Refrigerate in a covered container for up to 2 weeks (the herbs will darken after 1 day).   **MAKES ABOUT 1¼ CUPS**

curry vinaigrette

2 teaspoons Madras curry powder
½ cup champagne vinegar
1½ cups canola oil
1 teaspoon minced garlic
Kosher salt and freshly ground black pepper

Preheat the oven to 250°F.

Spread the curry powder in a small pan and place in the oven, tossing occasionally, for about 15 minutes or until fragrant.

Put the vinegar in a bowl and whisk in the curry powder. Whisk in the oil. Stir in the garlic. Season to taste with salt and pepper. Refrigerate in a covered container for up to 2 weeks.

MAKES ABOUT 2 CUPS

lemon vinaigrette

¼ cup champagne vinegar
¼ cup fresh lemon juice, preferably from Meyer lemons, strained
¾ cup canola oil
1 teaspoon finely minced shallot
2 teaspoons finely minced chives

Whisk together the vinegar and lemon juice in a bowl. Slowly whisk in the canola oil. Stir in the shallot and chives. Refrigerate in a covered container for up to 2 weeks (the chives will darken after 1 day).

MAKES ABOUT 1¼ CUPS

buttermilk dressing

1 cup Aioli (page 333)
¼ to ½ cup buttermilk
½ cup crème fraîche
½ teaspoon onion powder
½ teaspoon garlic powder
¾ teaspoon fresh lemon juice
1 teaspoon minced chives
1 teaspoon minced flat-leaf parsley
1 teaspoon minced mint
Kosher salt

Put the aioli in a large bowl. Whisk in ¼ cup buttermilk and all the remaining ingredients. The dressing can be used now or refrigerated. Before serving, lift up a spoonful of dressing and pour it back into the bowl—it should run freely. If it is too thick, add additional buttermilk as necessary. Refrigerate in a covered container for up to 1 week (the herbs may darken after 1 day).

MAKES ABOUT 2 CUPS

BLUE CHEESE DRESSING Stir about 1½ cups crumbled blue cheese (about 8 ounces), preferably Pt. Reyes (see Sources, page 346), into the buttermilk dressing. Refrigerate in a covered container for up to 1 week.

piquillo pepper vinaigrette

2 cups piquillo peppers (see Lightbulb Moment, opposite)
¼ cup extra virgin olive oil
Kosher salt
1 to 2 tablespoons sherry vinegar

Preheat the oven to 300°F.

Remove any remaining seeds and skin from the peppers. Put the peppers in a small baking dish. Stir in the oil and a generous pinch of salt. Put in the oven and cook until the peppers are meltingly tender, 45 to 50 minutes.

Pour the peppers, with their liquid, into a Vita-Mix. Add 1 tablespoon sherry vinegar and blend until smooth. This will be thicker than a traditional vinaigrette. Season to taste with additional vinegar if necessary and salt. Refrigerate in a covered container for up to 2 weeks.

MAKES ABOUT 1¾ CUPS

anchovy dressing

1 salt-packed anchovy, filleted, or 2 oil-packed anchovy fillets, or to taste
¼ cup whole milk
1 garlic clove, crushed and peeled
2 tablespoons champagne vinegar
1 teaspoon Dijon mustard
1 cup Aioli (page 333)
2 tablespoons buttermilk
½ teaspoon fresh lemon juice
Kosher salt and freshly ground black pepper

Put the anchovies in a small bowl and pour the milk over them. Soak the anchovies for 30 minutes. (Soaking will give them a sweeter flavor.)

Drain the anchovies. Chop coarsely and transfer to a small food processor. Add the garlic, vinegar, and mustard and puree. Transfer to a bowl and fold in the aioli and buttermilk. Season with the lemon juice and salt and pepper to taste. Refrigerate in a covered container for up to 1 week. **MAKES ABOUT 1¼ CUPS**

creamy pepper dressing

½ teaspoon black peppercorns
¼ cup Banyuls vinegar (see Sources, page 346)
¼ cup honey
¾ cup Aioli (page 333)
¼ cup buttermilk
½ cup crème fraîche
Kosher salt and freshly ground black pepper

Crush the peppercorns in a mortar with a pestle (or put them in a heavy-duty plastic bag and crush with a meat mallet or the bottom of a heavy pan). The crushed peppercorns will be in the finished dressing, so they shouldn't be in large pieces. Transfer to a small saucepan, add the vinegar and honey, and bring to a simmer over medium-high heat. Skim and discard any foam that rises to the top and reduce the heat to keep at a gentle simmer. Simmer until the liquid is reduced to about ¼ cup. Remove from the heat.

Meanwhile, whisk together the aioli, buttermilk, and crème fraîche in a bowl. While the reduction is still warm, whisk it into the aioli mixture. Season to taste with salt and ground black pepper. Refrigerate in a covered container for up to 1 week. **MAKES ABOUT 1½ CUPS**

Piquillo peppers, stubby red peppers (their name means "little beak") grown in northern Spain and roasted over wood fires, are one of our few "prepared" foods. They have a wonderful smoky sweetness unlike anything else. We get jars of them from Basque Country and use them straight out of the jar (see Sources, page 346). They're already peeled, so once you scrape the seeds from them, they're ready to go. They're delicious served whole with roasted or grilled meats, diced in salads, or pureed for a vinaigrette for, say, crab cakes. We might fortify a lamb jus with piquillos and olives to serve with a lamb dish. We even line a baking dish with whole piquillo peppers, cover them with pureed piquillos, coat it all with olive oil, and roast until meltingly tender. Just delicious. Other prepared foods we love and rely on include Marcona almonds from Spain, honey from Marshall Farms, and Edmund Fallot Dijon mustard.

VEGGIES & SIDES

When I was growing up, we always had side dishes—meat came with two sides. Ham with scalloped potatoes and the green bean casserole. Remember the green bean casserole? But over the past decade or so, we've kind of lost our side dishes—or rather they've become less prevalent.

Vegetables and starches are often integrated into single dishes and they don't always get to stand out on their own. Here, in a book devoted to family meals and home-style cooking, we pull them out as traditional stand-alone side dishes. Some are as classic as can be—creamed spinach, roasted beets, corn on the cob. Others may be less familiar, but are just as easy—leek bread pudding, for example, or buttered farro (a wonderful grain). In either case, the vegetable, starch, or grain has the starring role in all of the following dishes.

Because these dishes are weighted toward vegetables, they tend to be the most seasonal recipes in the book. The proteins are available to us year-round whereas asparagus and tomatoes, corn, beets, and root vegetables each have their optimal times of year. So you may well want to plan a meal by choosing one or two side dishes, and then determining what meat or fish would go well with what you've chosen. Also, many of the side dishes here can be combined for a hearty vegetarian meal or simply enlarged into main-course size.

OVERLEAF: *Butter-Braised Radishes, Kohlrabi, and Brussels Sprouts (page 196).* **OPPOSITE:** *Creamed Summer Corn (page 189).*

corn two ways Both the corn on the cob and the creamed corn are seasoned with lime and salt. For the corn on the cob, we emulsify butter in a little of the corn cooking liquid, then swirl the ears of corn in the creamy butter and garnish with chives.

For the creamed corn, we cook the corn until most of the juices have evaporated, to concentrate the flavor, then we add the cream to give it a luxurious texture and cook until it is absorbed by the corn. Corn and lime are a natural pair, but you could use any acid—such as lemon juice or sherry vinegar—depending on your preference. We also add a little cayenne for spiciness.

I think of summer dishes when I think of corn—Buttermilk Fried Chicken (page 16), Rubbed and Glazed Pork Spareribs (page 66)—but corn also goes well with shellfish, especially scallops and lobster.

6 ears supersweet white or yellow corn, shucked
6 tablespoons (3 ounces) unsalted butter, cut into pieces, at room temperature
Lime Salt (recipe follows)
2 tablespoons finely chopped chives

Cut both ends off each ear of corn, and cut the ears in half.

Bring a large pot of well-salted water to a boil. Add the corn and cook for 5 to 7 minutes, or until the corn is tender.

Meanwhile, transfer about 2 tablespoons of the cooking water to a large wide heatproof bowl. Add the butter and swirl the bowl over the heat to emulsify. Add lime salt to taste, swirling the bowl to maintain the emulsification. Set aside in a warm spot.

Drain the corn well and add to the butter. Sprinkle in the chives. Swirl the bowl to coat the corn evenly. Sprinkle with additional lime salt, and serve the remaining salt on the side.   **SERVES 6**

lime salt

¼ cup Maldon sea salt or fleur de sel
Grated zest of 1 lime (use a Microplane)

Put the salt and lime zest in a small jar. Put on the lid, and shake to combine. Extra salt can be stored in the freezer.   **MAKES ¼ CUP**

creamed summer corn

6 ears supersweet white or yellow corn, shucked

1 large lime

3 tablespoons (1½ ounces) unsalted butter

Kosher salt

¾ to 1 cup heavy cream

⅛ teaspoon cayenne

1½ tablespoons finely chopped chives

With a sharp chef's knife, cut vertically down each ear of corn to slice off the kernels. (To remove any silk, see Lightbulb Moment, right.) Put the kernels in a large bowl, then hold each cob over the bowl and use a spoon or the back of a knife to scrape any remaining corn and the milk from the cob.

Grate the zest of the lime, preferably with a Microplane grater; set aside. Cut the lime in half.

Melt the butter in a large frying pan over medium heat. Add the corn, squeeze about 1 tablespoon lime juice, or to taste, over the corn, and season with salt. Reduce the heat to medium-low and cook until all the liquid has evaporated, concentrating the flavor, and the corn is beginning to sizzle, 15 to 17 minutes.

Stir in ¾ cup cream, the cayenne, and lime zest. Continue to cook for 6 to 8 minutes, until the cream is absorbed by the corn. Add up to ¼ cup more cream if desired for a creamier texture. Add salt to taste and stir in the chives.

PHOTOGRAPH ON PAGE 187   SERVES 6

After cutting the kernels from an ear of corn, put them in a large bowl. Set a medium bowl of water next to the large bowl. Swish your hand through the corn in a circular motion—any remaining corn silk will stick to your hand. Rinse your hand in the other bowl as you remove the silks.

nantes carrot stew

2 pounds sweet carrots, preferably Nantes

1 teaspoon coriander seeds

1 teaspoon caraway seeds

4 to 6 tablespoons (2 to 3 ounces) unsalted butter

Kosher salt

2 tablespoons dry sherry or Madeira

1 cup fresh carrot juice

Large pinch of Yellow Curry Powder (page 336) or Madras curry powder

Nantes carrots, which Tucker Taylor grows in the French Laundry garden, are a long cylindrical variety that's about the same diameter from end to end. Cut into oblique shapes or lengthwise into what we call icicles, they're small enough to stew quickly in carrot juice with a splash of sherry or Madeira and a sachet of coriander and caraway seeds, and they're finished with a touch of curry powder. Combined with Asparagus Coins (page 192), they make a vivid dish, great with a flaky white fish such as cod or bass. They'd also be excellent with a rack of lamb or Cornish game hens.

These can be cooked a day ahead, cooled in the liquid, and refrigerated. If you have a juicer, make your own carrot juice. The sauce will be thicker because of the natural starches in the juice, which store-bought carrot juice often lacks.

Peel the carrots and cut them into oblique shapes (see Lightbulb Moment, opposite).

Make a sachet of the coriander and caraway seeds by wrapping them in a piece of cheesecloth and tying it with kitchen twine.

Melt 2 tablespoons of the butter in a large sauté pan over medium heat. Add the carrots, season with salt, and cook, stirring often, until the carrots begin to give off their juices, about 7 minutes. Lower the heat as necessary to keep the carrots from browning. Add the sherry and cook for 2 minutes. Add the carrot juice, curry powder, and sachet and cook, swirling the pan, for 2 more minutes, or until the carrots are just tender. (The carrots can be cooled and refrigerated in the liquid overnight.) With a slotted spoon, transfer the carrots to a bowl. Discard the sachet.

Simmer the carrot juice until reduced to a light glaze. Whisk in the remaining 2 to 4 tablespoons of butter, depending on your preference, 1 tablespoon at a time. Season to taste with salt, add the carrots, and swirl to glaze the carrots. Transfer to a serving bowl.   SERVES 6

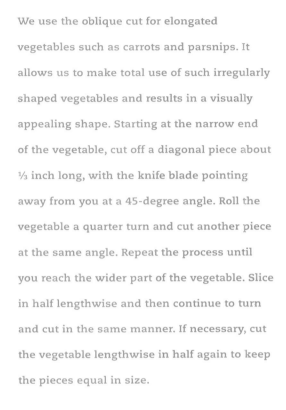

We use the oblique cut for elongated vegetables such as carrots and parsnips. It allows us to make total use of such irregularly shaped vegetables and results in a visually appealing shape. Starting at the narrow end of the vegetable, cut off a diagonal piece about ⅓ inch long, with the knife blade pointing away from you at a 45-degree angle. Roll the vegetable a quarter turn and cut another piece at the same angle. Repeat the process until you reach the wider part of the vegetable. Slice in half lengthwise and then continue to turn and cut in the same manner. If necessary, cut the vegetable lengthwise in half again to keep the pieces equal in size.

Using a Japanese mandoline or other vegetable slicer, you can slice asparagus stalks very thin. Hold a bundle, and run it across the blade to cut thin rounds; as you slice, turn the bunch slightly as necessary so the bottom end remains even, resulting in uniform slices. Move the rubber bands toward the tips as necessary. Stop when you have about 2½-inch tips remaining.

asparagus coins

1½ pounds pencil-thin asparagus
3 tablespoons Chive Oil (page 265)
Kosher salt and freshly ground black pepper
¼ cup Parsley Water (page 335)

Because the chemical that makes asparagus taste like asparagus is water-soluble, we gravitate to other ways to cook them besides blanching them in water, which diminishes some of their flavor (even though this method will retain their vibrant color). When they're very young and tender, asparagus can be cooked gently in a little liquid, and they're delicious. The liquid we use is a parsley water, which doesn't overpower them the way chicken stock might. For the parsley water, parsley is sautéed and pureed with some of its cooking water and a little honey. Parsley water has a lovely herbaceous flavor.

When they're tender, asparagus are also excellent grilled. We like the coins because they give an unusual bite.

Our favorite dishes to serve them with are cod (see Wild Cod en Persillade, page 95) and lamb.

Divide the asparagus in half and bundle each with a rubber band. Snap off the bottom of 1 stalk of asparagus to see where it breaks naturally. Cut across the bunches to trim all of the spears to the same length.

Slice on a Japanese mandoline (see Lightbulb Moment, left). Alternatively, you can slice the asparagus with a sharp chef's knife.

Put the tips in a large frying pan, add the chive oil, season with salt and pepper, and cook over medium heat, swirling the ingredients together, until the tips are coated with oil and beginning to sizzle, 1½ to 2 minutes. Add the asparagus rounds and cook until the edges look cooked but the centers are still raw. Add 3 tablespoons of the parsley water, stir to coat, and cook until the asparagus is tender, 1½ to 2 minutes. Remove the pan from the heat, add the remaining parsley water, and stir to coat.

SERVES 6

asparagus and tomato-bacon stew

3 ounces applewood-smoked slab or thick-sliced bacon (see Sources, page 346), cut into 1-inch by ¼-inch lardons (see page 150)

3 tablespoons coarsely chopped leeks (white and light green parts only)

2 tablespoons coarsely chopped onion

1 teaspoon finely chopped garlic

Kosher salt and freshly ground black pepper

One 14-ounce can San Marzano whole tomatoes

Canola oil (optional)

2½ pounds large asparagus, trimmed and peeled

¼ cup plus 2 tablespoons Chicken Stock (page 339)

Extra virgin olive oil

The grandmother of Josh Crain, one of our longtime chefs, used to cook green beans in a tomato sauce as a kind of stew. The notion of a tomato sauce served with a green vegetable struck us as interesting, and we developed this dish, tender asparagus with a sauce that is, in effect, stewed tomatoes and bacon (you can use pancetta if you wish). It's great for meaty fish, such as halibut, or with beef, such as the Marinated Skirt Steak (page 53).

Pour 2 tablespoons water into a medium saucepan and set over medium heat (the water will keep the bacon from crisping as the fat begins to render). Add the bacon, reduce the heat to medium-low, and let the bacon render its fat for 30 minutes. The bacon will color but not become completely crisp. Using a slotted spoon, transfer the bacon to paper towels to drain.

Pour off all but 1 to 2 tablespoons fat from the pan, reserving the extra fat. Set the pan over medium heat, add the leeks, onion, and garlic to the fat, stir to coat, and season with salt and pepper. Cook for 5 to 7 minutes, until the vegetables are soft. Add the tomatoes, with their juice, bring to a simmer, and simmer for 45 minutes.

Transfer half of the mixture to a food processor and puree. Stir the tomatoes back into the pan, return to a simmer, and cook until thickened, about 15 minutes. (The larger tomatoes will break down and the stew will have the texture of a thick tomato sauce.) Stir in the bacon and reduce the heat to low.

Heat a large frying pan that will hold half the asparagus in a single layer over medium-low heat. Pour a film of the reserved bacon fat or canola oil into the pan. Arrange half the asparagus in the pan, pour 3 tablespoons of the stock over it, and sprinkle with salt. Cook until the asparagus is tender but not limp, 6 to 7 minutes. Season with additional salt to taste and arrange the asparagus on a platter. Repeat with the remaining asparagus.

Spoon the sauce in a band across the asparagus. Drizzle with olive oil.

SERVES 6

baked beets

12 medium beets (about 12 ounces total), preferably 4 each red,
    Chioggia, and golden
3 tablespoons canola oil
Kosher salt and freshly ground black pepper
3 tablespoons (1½ ounces) unsalted butter

Beets get a bad rap—so many of us grew up thinking of beets only in canned form. But fresh, they're wonderfully sweet. I love to bake beets in foil with some salt and pepper and oil and eat them straight from the oven, sometimes even with a little maple syrup and vinegar. These beets would go well with salmon, duck, or the Peppercorn-Crusted Beef Tenderloin (page 47).

If you can't find beets that are similar in size, separate the beets by size as well as color and cook them in batches.

Preheat the oven to 350°F.

Trim the stems of the beets to about ½ inch and scrub the beets well.

Put each type of beet in a separate bowl, toss with 1 tablespoon of the oil, and sprinkle with salt and pepper. Put 3 pieces of aluminum foil large enough to enclose 4 of the beets on a work surface. Put 1 tablespoon butter in the center of each piece. Top each with one of the types of beets and any oil remaining in the bowl, fold over the sides, and crimp them to create a packet.

Put the packets on a baking sheet and bake until the beets are tender, 40 to 45 minutes. Carefully open the packets and let the beets cool, still in the packets, until they can be handled. Cut off the stem of each beet (reserve any juices in the foil packets) and wipe off the skin with a paper towel (see Lightbulb Moment, page 241). Cut the beets into ½-inch-wide wedges. Put each type of beet in a separate bowl and pour any cooking liquid from the packet over them. Season to taste with salt and pepper. **SERVES 6**

caramelized fennel

2 medium fennel bulbs
Kosher salt and freshly ground black pepper
Canola oil

Fennel is a great all-purpose vegetable that can be served shaved raw or braised, roasted, or sautéed. This preparation is good to do ahead of time. It goes well with roasted meats, such as Fig-Stuffed Roast Pork Loin (page 69). We first blanch wedges, then remove them from the water and allow them to cool. The wedges can be held until you're ready to reheat them, here by sautéing to give them some additional color and flavor.

Bring a large pot of salted water to a boil (see page 147). Meanwhile, cut off the fennel stalks and trim the core and the tough outer layer from each bulb. Cut the fennel lengthwise in half and then cut into ¼-inch-wide wedges.

Add the fennel to the boiling water and cook until crisp-tender, about 3 minutes. (The fennel will be cooked again, so be careful not to overcook it.) Drain the fennel and pat dry on paper towels. Season with salt and pepper.

Heat some canola oil over medium-high heat in a frying pan that will hold the fennel wedges in one layer (use two pans if necessary). Add the fennel, cut side down, and cook to caramelize the wedges, 2 to 3 minutes per each cut side. Drain on paper towels and serve.   **SERVES 6**

sautéed broccoli rabe
with garlic and chile flakes

4 bunches (about 18 ounces each) broccoli rabe

2 tablespoons canola oil

2 tablespoons finely sliced garlic

Red pepper flakes

Kosher salt and freshly ground black pepper

I love the bitterness of broccoli rabe, which comes with a touch of sweetness and works well here with the nutty notes of the sliced and sautéed garlic, and a little bit of heat from the dried red pepper. The technique of adding blanched vegetables to oil flavored with garlic and red pepper flakes also works well with broccolini, chard, and spinach. This versatile vegetable would be delicious with cod, grilled steak, roast pork, and chicken.

Cut away and discard the thicker part of the broccoli rabe stems, cutting about ½ inch below the smaller, more tender stems. Remove any torn or smaller greens.

Bring a large pot of salted water to a boil (see page 147). Set a cooling rack over a baking sheet and line with paper towels. Prepare an ice bath.

Add half of the broccoli rabe to the boiling water and cook until tender but slightly resistant to the tooth. Remove with a skimmer and chill in the ice bath, then drain on the paper towels. Repeat with the remaining broccoli rabe.

Heat the oil in a large frying pan over medium heat. Add the garlic and cook for about 1 minute, until lightly browned and crisp. Add a pinch of red pepper flakes and the broccoli rabe and cook, tossing often, for about 2 minutes, until heated through. Season to taste with salt and black pepper. **SERVES 6**

It's helpful to put a damp cloth or damp paper towel underneath your cutting board when you work, to prevent it from slipping.

butter-braised radishes, kohlrabi, and brussels sprouts

12 ounces Brussels sprouts

2 bunches (about 18) Easter or red radishes,
    about 1½ inches in diameter

8 tablespoons (1 stick; 4 ounces) unsalted butter

1 tablespoon minced shallot

½ teaspoon granulated sugar

½ teaspoon champagne vinegar, plus more to taste

Kosher salt and freshly ground black pepper

½ cup Chicken Stock (page 339) or Vegetable Stock (page 341),
    plus more if needed

6 kohlrabi, about 2½ inches in diameter

1 tablespoon finely chopped chives or mint

Brussels sprouts are more versatile than most people realize; they can be cooked whole or cut, or just their leaves can be quickly sautéed. Blanched in plenty of salted water as they are here, their sweetness is enhanced. Kohlrabi is in the cabbage family and has the flavor and texture of the inner broccoli stalk. Radishes, which we're most familiar with served raw, are gently cooked here in butter with a glaze of vinegar and sugar. These are fantastic with Pan-Roasted Duck Breasts (page 35).

Bring a large pot of salted water to a boil (see page 147). Prepare an ice bath. Meanwhile, trim the root ends of the Brussels sprouts and remove and discard any tough or bruised outer leaves. Cut the sprouts in half through the root end.

Blanch the sprouts until tender, about 4 minutes. Chill in the ice bath and drain. Transfer to a tray and put in the refrigerator to chill.

Trim the greens from the radishes and wash the radishes under cold water. Cut larger radishes into 6 wedges each, smaller radishes into quarters.

Melt 4 tablespoons of the butter over medium heat in a sauté pan big enough to hold the radishes in a single layer. Add the shallot and cook for 2 to 3 minutes, stirring often, until softened. Add the radishes, sugar, and vinegar, season generously with salt and pepper, and add ¼ cup of the stock. Bring to a simmer, cover the pan, and simmer gently for about 8 minutes, until the radishes are crisp-tender. Cook uncovered, swirling the pan, to glaze the radishes, about 4 minutes. Set aside.

Bring a large pot of salted water to a boil. Meanwhile, cut the stems and roots from the kohlrabi. Stand each kohlrabi on a cut end and peel it with a sharp knife, cutting deep enough to reach the tender flesh (see Lightbulb Moment, page 142). Cut lengthwise into slices about ½ inch thick. Trim the rounded sides of the slices and cut the kohlrabi into ½-inch-wide batons. You need 2 cups of batons (reserve any remaining kohlrabi for another use).

Add the kohlrabi to the boiling water and cook for 5 minutes, or until tender. Drain and transfer to paper towels to drain thoroughly.

Bring the remaining ¼ cup stock to a simmer in a large sauté pan. Whisk in the remaining 4 tablespoons butter until emulsified and smooth. Add the Brussels sprouts and kohlrabi and cook over high heat for 45 seconds. Add the radishes and any liquid remaining in the pan and heat through. If the butter begins to break, you can swirl in another couple of tablespoons of stock or water. Toss in the chives and season with salt and pepper and a few drops of vinegar, or to taste. Transfer the vegetables to a platter.

PHOTOGRAPH ON PAGE 185

SERVES 6

caramelized savoy cabbage

4½ pounds savoy cabbage

Canola oil

Kosher salt

¾ cup Chicken Stock (page 339) or Vegetable Stock (page 341), plus more if needed

3 tablespoons (1½ ounces) unsalted butter, cut into 3 pieces

¼ cup plus 2 tablespoons Melted Onions (page 337)

The savoy cabbage is cut into big pieces, blanched to tenderize the leaves, and then chilled to set their color. Then you quickly sauté it, adding a little chicken stock and butter so it becomes almost like a stew. It's wonderful with hearty meats—short ribs or pork belly, for instance. It would go well with poached salmon, grilled quail, or rack of pork. If you like, add pancetta or bacon lardons—sautéed until crisp and drained—to the cabbage before serving.

Cut the cabbage(s) in half through the core. Cut each in half again through the core. Cut out the core and discard. Turn a piece of cabbage cut side down and cut crosswise into 3 sections. Break apart the piece of cabbage over a bowl; cut out and discard any large tough ribs. Repeat with the remaining cabbage.

Bring a large pot of salted water to a boil (see page 147). Prepare an ice bath. Add the cabbage to the water and boil for 1½ to 2 minutes, until the leaves are wilted but still crisp. Drain, chill in the ice bath, and drain in a strainer. Place the strainer over a bowl and press down on the cabbage to drain excess moisture.

Shortly before serving, heat some canola oil in a large frying pan over medium-high heat. Add about one-third of the cabbage, lower the heat to medium, and cook for about 1 minute. Separate the cabbage leaves with a spoon or palette knife, so as to have as much of the surface against the hot pan as possible, season with a generous pinch of salt, and cook, without stirring, for 3 to 4 minutes, to evaporate any remaining water and caramelize the leaves. Watch carefully—you want the cabbage to brown but not to char or burn; adjust the heat as necessary. Then cook, turning the cabbage constantly, for another 2 to 3 minutes, until tender. Transfer to a bowl. Repeat with the remaining batches of cabbage, adding more canola oil to the pan as needed.

Combine all the cabbage and the stock in a large sauté pan and bring to a simmer over medium heat. Stir in the butter and onions and cook for about 3 minutes, tossing often, to heat the cabbage through. The butter should be creamy and not separated; if it has separated, stir in a bit more stock.

Spoon into a serving bowl. **SERVES 6**

sautéed red and green cabbage

¼ cup shelled pistachios

Canola oil or duck fat (see Sources, page 346)

4 cups ½-inch-wide strips savoy cabbage

4 cups ½-inch-wide strips purple cabbage

3 tablespoons finely chopped shallots

1½ cups Chicken Stock (page 339)

Kosher salt and freshly ground black pepper

Nutty flavors such as toasted sesame oil often are used with cabbage, but we prefer to add pistachios. This side dish is excellent with rich, hearty meats.

Preheat the oven to 350°F. Line a baking sheet with parchment paper.

Spread the nuts on the baking sheet and toast in the oven for 10 to 12 minutes, or until golden. Transfer to a plate to cool.

Heat some canola oil or duck fat in two large frying pans over medium-high heat. Put the green cabbage in one pan and the purple in the other, reduce the heat to medium, and cook, tossing often, until the cabbage has a touch of color, 3 to 4 minutes. (The green cabbage may cook more quickly than the red cabbage; finish each pan as the cabbage is cooked.)

Stir half the shallots into each pan. Pour ⅔ cup of the chicken stock into the green cabbage and the remaining stock into the red cabbage. Bring to a simmer and simmer, adjusting the heat as necessary and tossing the cabbage so it cooks evenly, until the stock has evaporated, 4 to 5 minutes. Lower the heat and continue to cook until the cabbage is tender but not mushy. Taste and season with salt and pepper.

Combine the cabbages in one pan. Stir in the pistachios and heat for several seconds to warm the pistachios. Transfer to a serving bowl.

SERVES 6

coleslaw

DRESSING

¾ cup sour cream

¼ cup mayonnaise, homemade (page 333) or store-bought

1½ teaspoons dry mustard

2 tablespoons granulated sugar

1½ teaspoons celery seeds

¼ cup champagne vinegar

Kosher salt to taste

1 large carrot, peeled

4 cups ¹⁄₁₆-inch-wide strips green cabbage

4 cups ¹⁄₁₆-inch-wide strips purple cabbage

2 teaspoons toasted sesame seeds

Fresh lemon juice

Kosher salt and freshly ground black pepper

This creamy dressing is sour cream based, and a little spicy from the mustard (it also works well as a potato salad dressing). The slaw is dressed at the last minute so that the purple cabbage doesn't tint the dressing. Serve with summer picnic food, such as the Maine Lobster Rolls (page 84), grilled chicken, or the Rubbed and Glazed Pork Spareribs (page 66).

Combine all of the dressing ingredients in a medium bowl, whisking to blend. Refrigerate until ready to use, or for up to 3 days.

Cut the carrot into 2½- to 3-inch-long pieces. Slice lengthwise on a Japanese mandoline or other vegetable slicer into very thin slices (the finished slices should be pliable). Stack a few slices at a time and cut lengthwise into ¹⁄₁₆-inch-wide strips. (The carrots may be grated, if you prefer.) You need about ½ cup (reserve any remaining carrot for another use).

Combine the cabbage and carrots in a large bowl. Add the sesame seeds and enough dressing to thoroughly coat the slaw. Season to taste with lemon juice and salt and pepper.

MAKES ABOUT 9 CUPS

celery root with melted onions

4 large celery root (about 4 pounds total)

8 tablespoons (1 stick; 4 ounces) unsalted butter, cut into 8 pieces

1 tablespoon thyme leaves

4 cloves garlic, crushed, skin left on

Kosher salt and freshly ground black pepper

1 cup Melted Onions (page 337)

½ cup Chicken Stock (page 339) or Vegetable Stock (page 341),
    plus more if needed

This is kind of a play on potatoes Lyonnaise, a classic potato and onion dish. Here celery root replaces the potatoes and is sautéed in brown butter and combined with "melted" onions. It's a wonderful side for Braised Beef Short Ribs (page 41) or Rack of Pork Arista (page 65).

Cut off the top and bottom of each celery root (see Lightbulb Moment, page 142). Stand each one up on a cut side and cut off the skin in strips from top to bottom, working around the celery root. Quarter each one lengthwise and then, with a Japanese mandoline or knife, cut crosswise into thin slices.

Heat two large sauté pans over high heat until hot. Add 2 tablespoons of the butter to each pan, then pull the pans off the heat and let the butter brown. Add one-quarter of the celery root to each pan and cook over medium heat for 1 minute, without stirring. Add one-quarter of the thyme and 1 garlic clove to each pan and cook, stirring from time to time, until the celery root is tender throughout, 9 to 10 minutes total cooking time. Season to taste with salt and pepper. Drain the celery root on paper towels. Pour off any excess fat from the pans (and remove any thyme); discard the garlic cloves. Repeat with the remaining celery root.

Add the melted onions to one of the pans and cook to give them a little color, about 3 minutes. Drain the onions to remove excess fat, and return them to the pan. Add the celery root, stir to combine, and season with salt and pepper as needed. Increase the heat to high and swirl in ½ cup stock. Bring to a simmer, adding additional stock or water if needed to create a creamy dish. Transfer to a serving bowl.   **SERVES 6**

An easy way to separate a head of garlic into individual cloves is to use something heavy, like a rolling pin, to hit the head of garlic on a hard surface. Individual cloves can be crushed with a rolling pin using lighter force, enabling the peel to come off easily.

SUMMER VEGETABLE GRATIN

1 medium yellow squash →

1 medium zucchini →

1 japanese eggplant →

pepper →

2 to 3 roma tomatoes

½ c. bread crumbs

2½ c. chopped onions

2 garlic cloves

½ c. grated parmigiano-reggiano

summer vegetable gratin

2 to 3 Roma (plum) tomatoes, 1½ to 2 inches in diameter

1 medium yellow squash

1 medium zucchini

1 Japanese eggplant or other small narrow eggplant

Canola oil

2½ cups coarsely chopped onions

2 garlic cloves, finely grated with a Microplane grater or minced

Kosher salt

1 tablespoon plus 1 teaspoon chopped thyme

¼ cup extra virgin olive oil, plus more for drizzling

Freshly ground black pepper

½ cup freshly grated Parmigiano-Reggiano

½ cup Dried Bread Crumbs (page 273)

Here, tomatoes, squash, and eggplant are layered on cooked onions and baked with a cheese-and-bread-crumb topping. If you have Soffritto (page 263) in your refrigerator, you can use it instead of the cooked onions. This is a good dish to assemble ahead and then bake before serving. Baking it the day before and then reheating it will enhance the flavor.

Pair this dish with Breaded Veal Cutlets (page 77) and serve with some crusty bread to soak up the delicious juices at the bottom of the baking dish.

Preheat the oven to 350°F. Set a cooling rack on a baking sheet.

Slice the vegetables to end up with slices as close in size as possible. Slice the tomatoes into ¼-inch slices (discard the end slices). Trim the yellow squash, zucchini, and eggplant and cut into ¼-inch-thick slices; if necessary, cut them on a slight diagonal so the slices are about the same size as the tomato slices.

Heat some canola oil in a large frying pan over medium heat. Reduce the heat to medium-low, add the onions and garlic, and season with salt. Cook without browning, stirring occasionally, until the onions are translucent, about 20 minutes. Stir in 1 tablespoon of the thyme.

Combine the yellow squash, zucchini, and eggplant in a large bowl, toss with the olive oil, and season with salt.

Drizzle the slices of tomato with olive oil and season with salt.

Combine the Parmesan, bread crumbs, and remaining 1 teaspoon thyme in a small bowl.

Spread the onion mixture in the bottom of a 13½-by-9½-inch gratin dish or 13-inch round shallow baking dish. Layer the vegetables in the dish, working on the diagonal. Arrange a layer of overlapping slices of one-third of the zucchini around the outside edge of the dish. Sprinkle 2 to 3 tablespoons of the cheese mixture over the top. Make a row of overlapping slices of yellow squash slightly overlapping the zucchini, and sprinkle 2 to 3 tablespoons of the cheese mixture over the top. Make a third row with overlapping slices of tomatoes, slightly overlapping the zucchini, and sprinkle with the cheese mixture. Make a fourth row with overlapping slices of eggplant, slightly overlapping the tomatoes, and sprinkle the cheese mixture over the top. Continue making overlapping rows of the remaining vegetables, and sprinkle the top with any remaining cheese mixture and a light sprinkling of salt.

Bake for 1 to 1½ hours until the vegetables are completely tender and offer no resistance when pierced with a knife. Remove from the oven and allow the gratin to rest for 10 minutes. Turn on the broiler.

Just before serving, place the gratin under the broiler to brown the top.   **SERVES 6**

honey-glazed cipollini onions

1¼ pounds cipollini onions (about 14), about 2 inches in diameter

1 tablespoon canola oil

2 garlic cloves, lightly crushed, skin left on

4 thyme sprigs

1 tablespoon honey

½ cup Chicken Stock (page 339)

Kosher salt and freshly ground black pepper

Cipollini onions are milder than yellow or Spanish onions, and smaller, so they cook relatively quickly and can be served whole, two or three to a plate. They're also a sweeter onion, so you can shave them raw over salads, and roasting or sautéing them intensifies their sweetness. In this dish the sweetness is heightened by glazing. These are delicious with any grilled meats.

Preheat the oven to 400°F.

Peel the onions. Cut off the top of each onion to create a flat surface for browning. Trim the root ends. If any of the onions are noticeably larger than the rest, peel off an outer layer so that they are closer in size.

Heat an ovenproof frying pan large enough to hold the onions in a single layer over medium heat. Add the canola oil and heat until warm. Add the onions cut-side-down and cook until browned, swirling the pan from time to time for even browning, about 6 minutes. Turn and cook to lightly brown the second side, about 4 minutes. Add the garlic, thyme, and honey to the pan. The honey will bubble up; once it stops, add the chicken stock and swirl the pan to incorporate. Increase the heat to medium-high and bring just to a boil.

Transfer to the oven and cook for 15 minutes, or until the onions are tender and the liquid has reduced to a thick glaze. Season to taste with salt and pepper.

Transfer the onions to a serving dish and spoon the glaze over the top.

SERVES 6

romano beans with mint

2 pounds romano beans, stem ends trimmed

2 tablespoons minced shallots

Canola oil

¼ cup Chicken Stock (page 339) or Vegetable Stock (page 341)

8 tablespoons (1 stick; 4 ounces) cold unsalted butter, cut into 8 pieces

Kosher salt and freshly ground black pepper

1 tablespoon finely chopped mint

Fleur de sel

Romano beans, also called Italian flat beans, are full of flavor, and part of the reason they're so special is that their season is so short. Here they're cut on an angle and tossed with sautéed shallots and mint. They are great with chicken or other poultry, including the Buttermilk Fried Chicken (page 16), Roast Poussins (page 26), and Sautéed Chicken Breasts with Tarragon (page 27).

Bring a large pot of salted water to a boil (see page 147). Set up an ice bath. Set a rack over a baking sheet and line the rack with paper towels. Blanch the beans in batches for about 4 minutes, or until just tender. Chill in the ice bath and drain.

Cut the beans on the bias in half or into thirds, depending on the length. Drain on the paper towels.

Heat some canola oil in a large sauté pan on medium-low heat. Add the shallots and cook gently over medium heat for about 3 minutes, until softened. Add the stock and bring to a simmer. Slowly whisk in the butter piece by piece to emulsify. Add the beans, season to taste with salt and pepper, and stir in the mint.

Transfer the beans to a serving bowl and sprinkle with fleur de sel.

SERVES 6

rainbow chard

with raisins, pine nuts, and serrano ham

2 tablespoons pine nuts

Kosher salt

4 to 5 pounds rainbow chard (see Note)

About ¼ cup canola oil

2 tablespoons finely chopped garlic

1 ounce thinly sliced serrano ham, cut crosswise into ¼-inch strips

2 tablespoons Wine-Steeped Golden Raisins (page 258)

Freshly ground black pepper

The addition of raisins, pine nuts, and dry-cured serrano ham speaks of our fondness for Spanish dishes as well as chard. We use two cooking methods for the chard after separating the stems from the leaves: we blanch the stems and sauté the leaves with garlic.

The chard can be cooked up to a day ahead and refrigerated, and finishing the dish is just a matter of a quick sauté. Try it as a side for Roasted Pork Short Ribs (page 66), Oil-Poached Sturgeon (page 100), or grilled quail (see page 31).

Preheat the oven to 350°F. Line 3 baking sheets with parchment paper.

Spread the nuts on one of the lined pans and toast in the oven for about 10 minutes, until evenly browned. Remove from the oven, transfer to a plate, sprinkle with salt, and let cool.

Cut out the thick stems from the leaves of chard and set aside. Stack the greens in batches and cut crosswise into thirds; set aside. Trim the stems and cut them on the diagonal into 1-inch slices. You need 2 cups stems for this recipe (reserve any remaining chard for another use).

Bring a large pot of salted water (see page 147) to a boil. Add the chard stems and blanch until tender but still slightly resistant to the tooth, 3 to 4 minutes. Drain and spread on the second parchment-lined baking sheet.

Pour 1½ tablespoons canola oil into each of two large sauté pans and heat over medium heat (if you have only one large pan, cook the greens in 2 batches). Add 1 tablespoon of the garlic to each pan, reduce the heat, and cook over medium-low heat until softened but not colored, about 1 minute. Add one-quarter of the chard greens to each pan, season with salt (salt lightly if your ham is very salty), and cook for 3 to 5 minutes over medium to medium-low heat, until the chard wilts to about half its original volume. Add the remaining chard and cook until wilted and tender, 15 to 20 minutes total. Spread the greens, with their liquid, on the third lined sheet.

To serve, heat some oil in a large frying pan over medium-high heat. Add the ham and sauté for about 45 seconds to crisp. Add the pine nuts and raisins and toss. Add the chard stems and greens, toss to combine, and heat through. Season to taste with salt and pepper. Transfer to a serving bowl.

SERVES 6

NOTE *If the chard you find has very large stems, buy 5 pounds to get enough greens.*

creamed baby spinach

4 tablespoons (2 ounces) unsalted butter

¼ cup finely chopped shallots

2 pounds baby spinach

Kosher salt

Freshly ground black pepper

Mornay Sauce (page 334)

½ cup grated Comté or Emmentaler cheese

We simply wilt the spinach in butter with shallots, then mix it with a Mornay, a béchamel flavored with Comté cheese, sprinkle more Comté over the top, and heat it in the oven. This goes well with rich meats, such as the Porterhouse Steak (page 51), Santa Maria–Style Tri-Tip (page 54), and Breaded Veal Cutlets (page 77).

Melt 2 tablespoons of the butter in a large sauté pan over medium heat. Add half of the shallots to the pan, then add a few handfuls of the spinach and stir to coat. As the spinach wilts, continue adding it by handfuls and wilting it until you've added about half of it, seasoning it with salt as you go, then cook until tender, about 4 to 5 minutes more. Transfer to a fine-mesh basket strainer to drain the excess liquid, then transfer to a bowl.

Cook the remaining spinach with the remaining butter and shallots, and drain. Taste for seasoning and add pepper and more salt if needed.

Preheat the oven to 350°F.

Stir the Mornay sauce into the spinach. Spread the spinach in a 9-inch square baking dish. Sprinkle the cheese over the top. (The spinach can be covered and refrigerated for several hours.)

Heat the spinach in the oven until it is hot and bubbling. Then turn on the broiler, put the spinach under the broiler, and melt and brown the cheese. **SERVES 6**

chanterelle mushrooms
with pea shoots

2 tablespoons (1 ounce) unsalted butter

2 tablespoons finely chopped shallots

3 thyme sprigs

8 ounces small chanterelles or other mushrooms in season, trimmed and washed

Kosher salt and freshly ground black pepper

¼ to ½ cup Chicken Stock (page 339)

1½ cups (2 ounces) pea shoots

Extra virgin olive oil

Fleur de sel

This is a simple and delicious dish that you'll like especially for its vivid yellow and green colors. If you can't find chanterelles, other mushrooms, preferably wild, will do. If you don't have access to pea shoots, you can substitute baby arugula or spinach. We use this as a bed for the Pan-Roasted Halibut (page 92).

Melt the butter in a medium sauté pan over medium-high heat. Add the shallots and cook for 2 to 3 minutes, until tender. Add the thyme and mushrooms, season with salt and pepper, and cook for 5 minutes, until the mushrooms are almost tender (if the pan becomes too dry, add a little of the chicken stock).

Add ¼ cup chicken stock and cook, adding more stock as needed, about 1 tablespoon at a time, until the mushrooms are tender. Continue to cook until the stock is reduced to a glaze. Discard the thyme.

Add the pea shoots and stir just to wilt and incorporate, about 30 seconds. Transfer to a serving bowl, drizzle with olive oil, and sprinkle with fleur de sel. **SERVES 6**

morels with madeira

1½ pounds morels, about 1½ inches long

4 tablespoons (2 ounces) unsalted butter

2 tablespoons finely chopped shallots

1½ teaspoons finely chopped thyme

¼ cup Madeira

Kosher salt

Morels are not a mushroom you want to sear—they're best cooked gently in butter. We flavor the butter with shallots, thyme, and Madeira, and the morels soak it all up. We serve these with Caramelized Sea Scallops (page 88). They're not only tasty, they have great visual appeal.

Using a paring knife, trim off the bottoms of the morel stems. Gently scrape off the outer layer of the remaining stem. Wash carefully in a bowl of warm water, making sure that any dirt inside the mushrooms or trapped in the crevices is removed. Drain the mushrooms and dry on paper towels. Repeat the washing as necessary until the water remains clear and all dirt is removed.

Melt the butter in a very large frying pan over medium heat. (If you don't have a very large pan, cook the mushrooms in 2 batches; clean the pan before cooking the second batch.) Add the shallots and cook until translucent, about 2 minutes. Add the thyme and Madeira, bring to a simmer, and simmer, adjusting the heat as necessary, for about 2 minutes to burn off the alcohol. Add the morels, sprinkle with salt, and cook over medium heat, stirring often, until tender, about 6 minutes.

Transfer to a bowl and serve.   SERVES 6

peperonata rustica

6 yellow bell peppers

6 red bell peppers

Canola oil

Kosher salt and freshly ground black pepper

8 ounces piquillo peppers (see Lightbulb Moment, page 183),
   drained, peeled, and seeded

About ½ cup Soffritto (page 263)

1⅓ cups Chicken Stock (page 339) or Vegetable Stock (page 341)

¾ teaspoon piment d'Espelette

1 tablespoon minced chives

The roasted peppers in this dish—red, yellow, and smoky piquillos—are torn by hand, not sliced, for a more rustic appearance, then stewed with soffritto, which makes the flavor very deep and sweet (this can be done a day ahead). They are seasoned with Espelette powder, another distinctive pepper flavor. Serve this with Oil-Poached Sturgeon (page 100), chop it and serve it over Garlic Toast (page 282), or use it to turn scrambled eggs into eggs flamenco for brunch.

Preheat the oven to 375°F. Line two baking sheets with parchment paper.

Cut the bell peppers lengthwise in half and remove the stems and seeds. Toss the peppers with oil to coat and salt and pepper to taste. Arrange the peppers cut side down on the baking sheets, the red peppers on one, the yellow peppers on the other.

Roast the peppers until the skin is blistering, 30 to 35 minutes for the red and 35 to 40 minutes for the yellow; do not allow the edges to blacken. Transfer the peppers to a bowl and cover with plastic wrap, or put in an airtight container with a lid.

When the peppers are cool enough to handle, peel them. Tear them lengthwise into strips about ¾ inch wide. Tear the piquillos into strips in the same way.

Combine all of the peppers, the soffritto, stock, and Espelette in a medium saucepan over medium heat, season with salt and pepper, and bring to a simmer. Cook for 30 minutes, to soften the peppers completely and meld the flavors.

Transfer to a bowl or platter, sprinkle with chives, and serve.

SERVES 6

EGGS FLAMENCO Combine the peperonata with a little stock in a sauté pan, add some fresh peas, and break a few eggs into it, then swirl the pan to incorporate the whites with the other ingredients but keep the yolks intact.

PIMENT D'ESPELETTE If you haven't tried piment d'Espelette (Espelette pepper), it's worth seeking out. These ground dried chile peppers, from the village of Espelette in Spain's Basque region, will give a fruity heat to any number of dishes. The powder is more flavorful and less hot than cayenne. For where to buy it, see page 346.

When mincing a long bunch of chives, it can be difficult to keep them together. Fold a small, slightly damp piece of paper towel into a strip and wrap it tightly around the center of the chives to keep them from separating as you mince. When you reach the paper towel, just slide it farther up the bunch of chives.

borlotti bean ragù

One 6-ounce piece salt pork or slab bacon

8 tablespoons (1 stick; 4 ounces) unsalted butter, at room temperature

¼ cup minced shallots

8 cloves Garlic Confit (page 266), crushed

3 to 4 teaspoons finely chopped thyme leaves

2 tablespoons red wine vinegar, plus additional to taste

7 cups cooked borlotti beans (see page 337)

Kosher salt and freshly ground black pepper

½ cup Chicken Stock (page 339), plus more if needed

¼ cup chopped chives

This bean dish can be made with any creamy bean, like navy beans or even the goat's eye beans we get from Rancho Gordo (see Sources, page 346). The beans are meltingly tender, but remain whole. The flavors get better over time, so you can make this a day ahead. With lamb or with pork, it's typically a winter dish.

Heat a large saucepan over medium-high heat until very hot; preheating the pan will prevent the pork from sticking. To test the heat, hold a corner of the pork against the pan; if it sticks, heat the pan a bit longer. Add the pork fat-side-down and lower the heat as necessary to render the fat without crisping and browning the meat. Turn the pork to cook all sides, about 15 minutes total.

Add the butter to the pan, increase the heat to medium-high, and cook, swirling the pan often, until the butter has browned and the bubbles begin to subside, about 2 minutes. Add the shallots, garlic confit, 3 teaspoons of the thyme, and the vinegar, then add the beans. Season with salt and with a generous amount of pepper, then add the chicken stock, stirring to emulsify the liquid and butter. Bring to a simmer to heat the beans through. Add the remaining 1 teaspoon thyme and additional salt, pepper, and/or vinegar to taste as necessary.

Serve immediately or keep in a warm spot for up to 1 hour. If the sauce begins to break and the beans look oily, stir in a small amount of chicken stock to re-emulsify it. Reheat gently before serving if necessary.

Stir in the chives and serve.   **SERVES 6**

leek bread pudding

2 cups ½-inch-thick slices leeks (white and light green parts only)

Kosher salt

4 tablespoons (2 ounces) unsalted butter

Freshly ground black pepper

12 cups 1-inch cubes crustless Brioche (page 272) or
    Pullman sandwich loaf

1 tablespoon finely chopped chives

1 teaspoon thyme leaves

3 large eggs

3 cups whole milk

3 cups heavy cream

Freshly grated nutmeg

1 cup shredded Comté or Emmentaler

Just as custards work well in the savory portion of the meal, although they're more often served as a dessert, so do bread puddings. This one is a great complement to the Blowtorch Prime Rib Roast (page 56) and Pan-Roasted Duck Breasts (page 35). But you could also top it with Oven-Roasted Tomatoes (page 262) and serve it as a vegetarian meal.

Preheat the oven to 350°F.

Put the leek rounds in a large bowl of tepid water and swish so that any dirt falls to the bottom of the bowl. Set a medium sauté pan over medium-high heat, lift the leeks from the water, drain, and add them to the pan. Season with salt and cook, stirring often, for about 5 minutes. As the leeks begin to soften, lower the heat to medium-low. The leeks will release liquid. Stir in the butter to emulsify, and season with pepper to taste. Cover the pan with a parchment lid (see page 120), and cook, stirring every 10 minutes, until the leeks are very soft, 30 to 35 minutes. If at any point the butter breaks or looks oily, stir in about a tablespoon of water to re-emulsify the sauce. Remove and discard the parchment lid.

Meanwhile, spread the bread cubes on a baking sheet and toast in the oven for about 20 minutes, rotating the pan about halfway through, until dry and pale gold. Transfer to a large bowl. Leave the oven on.

Add the leeks to the bread and toss well, then add the chives and thyme.

Lightly whisk the eggs in another large bowl. Whisk in the milk, cream, a generous pinch of salt, pepper to taste, and a pinch of nutmeg.

Sprinkle ¼ cup of the cheese in the bottom of a 9-by-13-inch baking pan. Spread half the leeks and croutons in the pan and sprinkle with another ¼ cup cheese. Scatter the remaining leeks and croutons over and top with another ¼ cup cheese. Pour in enough of the custard mixture to cover the bread and press gently on the bread so it soaks in the milk. Let soak for about 15 minutes.

Add the remaining custard, allowing some of the soaked cubes of bread to protrude. Sprinkle the remaining ¼ cup cheese on top and sprinkle with salt.

Bake for 1½ hours, or until the pudding feels set and the top is brown and bubbling.

PHOTOGRAPH ON PAGE 213

**SERVES 12 AS A SIDE DISH,
6 TO 8 AS A MAIN COURSE**

Leek Bread Pudding (page 211)

24 baby leeks, about ¾ inch in diameter

3 tablespoons Chicken Stock (page 339), Vegetable Stock (page 341),
   or water

8 tablespoons (1 stick; 4 ounces) unsalted butter, cut into small chunks

Kosher salt and freshly ground black pepper

These leeks, simply cooked until very tender and finished with butter, are a wonderful complement to any number of dishes. Very sweet and creamy, they're especially good with fish, particularly monkfish, skate, and salmon.

Bring a large pot of salted water to a boil (see page 147). Prepare an ice bath. Set a cooling rack on a baking sheet and line the rack with paper towels.

Meanwhile, trim the root ends of the leeks. Cut away the dark leaves, leaving the leeks 4 to 5 inches long. Rinse under warm water. Blanch the leeks for about 6 minutes, until just tender. Immediately transfer to the ice bath to cool. Drain the leeks on the paper-towel-lined rack.

Remove the outer layer from each leek. Bring the stock to a simmer in a medium sauté pan. Whisk in the butter one piece at a time to make an emulsification. Add the leeks and season to taste with salt and pepper.

Use immediately, or transfer to a container and refrigerate for up to 3 days. Reheat gently over low heat. As they are reheated, the leeks should look creamy at all times. If the butter separates or the pan appears dry, stir in a bit of cold water to re-emulsify the butter.

SERVES 6

Pasta Dough (page 338)

Tipo 00 flour (see Sources, page 346) for dusting

1 pound assorted wild mushrooms, such as small shiitakes, morels,
   chanterelles, small porcini, hen-of-the-woods, trumpet mushrooms,
   and/or oyster mushrooms

Canola oil

Kosher salt and freshly ground black pepper

⅓ cup minced shallots

4 tablespoons (2 ounces) unsalted butter, cut into 8 pieces

½ cup plus 2 tablespoons Chicken Stock (page 339) or Vegetable Stock
   (page 341)

1¼ teaspoons red wine vinegar

A chunk of Parmigiano-Reggiano for grating, plus grated cheese
   for serving

Homemade pasta has a delicate texture and flavor, and when you make your own pasta, you can cut it into any shape you want. Pappardelle are broad noodles. We cut them about an inch wide, and because they're hand cut, they're not exactly uniform, giving this dish an appealing rusticity. Because it's hearty and rich, it makes an excellent vegetarian entrée. To turn it into a bigger meal, serve it with our meatballs, as on page 50.

TO ROLL THE PASTA: Line a baking sheet with parchment paper.

Cut the dough into thirds. Work with one piece at a time, keeping the other pieces covered so the exterior does not dry out. Shape one piece of dough into a rectangle about ½ inch thick. Fold it into thirds, as if you were folding a business letter.

Set the rollers of the pasta machine at the widest setting and dust the rollers with flour. Roll the dough through the machine, and then run it through the same setting again. Repeat this procedure three or four more times, but the last time, fold the pasta sheet lengthwise in half to give you a narrower piece of pasta and run it through the machine. Lower the setting one notch and roll the dough through. Do not fold it over. Continue the process until the sheet of pasta is quite thin (there may be a recommended setting for your machine; if not, the second-to-the-last setting is usually best); sprinkle the dough lightly with the flour if it feels at all sticky or tacky. When the sheet becomes too long to work with, cut it in half, flour lightly, and continue to roll both pieces. Lay the dough on a floured surface, cover, and let it rest for a few minutes, then roll through the machine again. The pasta will be very thin.

Loosely roll up the dough and cut into 1- to 1¼-inch-wide strips. Spread the pappardelle on the prepared baking sheet and cover with another piece of parchment paper.

Repeat with the remaining 2 pieces of dough. The pasta can be covered tightly with plastic wrap and refrigerated for up to 2 days.

TO PREPARE THE MUSHROOMS: Remove any tough stems from the mushrooms, such as the stems of shiitake mushrooms, and discard. Trim the ends of the other mushrooms and trim any bruised areas. Rinse the mushrooms as necessary to remove any dirt. Small mushrooms can be left whole; larger mushrooms should be cut into pieces or slices. The size and shape will vary according to the variety of mushroom.

Fill a large pot, preferably a pot with a pasta insert, with salted water and bring to a boil. (A pasta insert is very handy, since the pasta will be cooked in two batches.) Put a large bowl on the back of the stove to warm.

Heat some canola oil in a large sauté pan over medium heat until hot but not smoking. Add only as many mushrooms as will fit in a single layer in the pan and cook, without moving the mushrooms, to brown them, about 2 minutes. Cook for another 2 minutes, stirring occasionally. Season with salt and pepper and transfer to a bowl. Heat more oil and cook the remaining mushrooms.

Return all the mushrooms to the sauté pan and set over medium heat. Add the shallots and cook until the shallots are softened, 1 to 2 minutes. Add 2 tablespoons of the butter and cook until the mushrooms are glazed, about 2 minutes. Add the stock, bring to a simmer, and whisk in the remaining 2 tablespoons butter until emulsified. If the sauce begins to break and looks oily, add a small amount of water to re-emulsify it. Stir in the vinegar, and pour the mushrooms into the warm bowl.

TO FINISH: Add half of the pasta to the boiling water, separating any pieces that are stuck together. Do not overcrowd the pot, which would cause the pasta to cook unevenly. Cook until tender, 2 to 3 minutes. Remove from the water with the pasta insert or a skimmer and stir into the mushroom sauce to coat. Cook the remaining pasta and add to the bowl, toss, then arrange in a serving bowl or on a platter.

Top the pasta with any mushrooms remaining in the bowl and grate Parmesan to taste over the top. Serve additional cheese on the side.

SERVES 6 TO 8 AS A SIDE DISH OR APPETIZER, 4 TO 6 AS A MAIN DISH

grits cakes

---

1 garlic clove

Kosher salt

3½ cups Chicken Stock (page 339) or Vegetable Stock (page 341)

2 cups coarse stone-ground white grits (see Sources, page 346)

8 tablespoons (1 stick; 4 ounces) unsalted butter, cut into 8 pieces, at room temperature

⅓ cup cream cheese, at room temperature

Freshly ground black pepper

About ½ cup all-purpose flour

3 large eggs

1½ cups finely ground panko crumbs

2 tablespoons coarsely chopped flat-leaf parsley

Canola oil

Oven-Roasted Tomato Sauce (page 333)

Deep-fried oregano (see page 342)

Crispy polenta is an easy, satisfying dish, and it gave us the idea of trying a similar preparation using grits instead of cornmeal. When we make polenta, we sometimes enrich it with Italian mascarpone. For these grits cakes, we replace it with all-American cream cheese, and the result is crispy on the outside and creamy in the middle. These will work as an appetizer as well, topped with a small dollop of Tomato-Basil Marmalade (page 248).

Line a 9-by-13-inch baking pan (or a quarter sheet pan; see Note, page 306) with parchment paper. Cut a second sheet of parchment the same size and set aside.

Finely chop the garlic. Sprinkle with ¼ teaspoon salt and work into a paste, chopping and scraping the garlic with the side of a chef's knife.

Combine the garlic paste and chicken stock in a medium saucepan, season with salt, and bring to a boil. Reduce the heat to medium-low and slowly whisk in the grits. Reduce the heat to low and cook, stirring occasionally to keep the grits from sticking to the bottom of the pan, for 25 to 30 minutes, or until all the stock has been absorbed and the grits are tender with just slight resistance; when a spoon is dragged through the grits, the bottom of the pan should remain visible.

Stir in the butter until it has absorbed, then stir in the cream cheese until well combined and smooth. Season to taste with salt and pepper.

Spread the grits evenly in the prepared pan. Cover with the second sheet of parchment paper. With your hands, smooth and compress the layer of grits. Top with a second baking sheet, weight with cans or foil-wrapped bricks, and refrigerate for at least 4 hours, until firm, or overnight.

Remove the top pan and the parchment from the grits. Run a knife around the edges of the pan to loosen them and invert the pan onto a cutting board. Peel off the parchment paper. Trim the edges and cut the grits into 12 equal pieces.

Preheat the oven to 200°F. Set a cooling rack over a baking sheet.

Spread the flour in a shallow bowl. Beat the eggs in a shallow bowl and season with salt and pepper. Combine the panko crumbs and parsley in a third shallow bowl.

Line another baking sheet with parchment paper. Dip each cake into the flour, turning to coat and patting off excess, then dip in the eggs, letting the excess drip off, and coat well in the panko crumbs. Set on the baking sheet.

Pour ¼ inch of oil into a large nonstick frying pan and heat over medium heat until the oil just begins to shimmer. Carefully add as many cakes as will fit in the pan comfortably and cook until golden on the first side, 1 to 2 minutes. Flip and cook until golden on the second side, 1 to 2 minutes. Transfer to the rack and put in the oven to keep warm while you cook the remaining cakes, adding more oil if needed. If at any point there are burned panko crumbs in the oil, discard the oil and replace it with fresh oil before continuing.

Coat a serving platter with some of the tomato sauce, arrange the grits cakes over the sauce, and sprinkle with the oregano leaves. Additional sauce can be served on the side.   **SERVES 6**

polenta

6 cups Chicken Stock (page 339) or Vegetable Stock (page 341)

2 tablespoons minced garlic

Kosher salt

1 pound (about 500 grams; 2¾ cups) polenta, preferably Moretti
   (see Sources, page 346)

2½ cups heavy cream

12 tablespoons (1½ sticks; 6 ounces) unsalted butter,
   cut into ½-inch pieces

Freshly ground black pepper

Extra virgin olive oil

Canola oil (for crispy polenta)

We serve polenta in two ways, creamy and crisp. For creamy polenta, we finish it almost like whipped potatoes—once it's cooked, we whip butter and cream into it. When we want to serve it crisp, we spread it in a baking sheet and chill it until it sets up, then cut it into shapes and sauté until golden brown. It needs to be at least an inch deep to ensure that the centers will remain creamy while the exterior crisps. You can also use leftover creamy polenta to make crisp polenta.

We use an extra-fine polenta called Moretti. Use whatever brand you like, but avoid quick-cooking polenta. Both the crispy and creamy version can take similar garnishes, such as rich tomato sauce and fried oregano sprigs. Either makes a great accompaniment to the Braised Beef Short Ribs (page 41) or Slow-Roasted Veal Shanks (page 76).

Combine the stock, garlic, and a sprinkling of salt in a large saucepan and bring to a boil. Pour in the polenta in a stream and cook over low heat, stirring often, for 17 to 20 minutes, until the polenta is quite dry and coats the bottom of the pan. The moisture must evaporate, because it will be replaced with fat; otherwise, the texture could be gummy.

Meanwhile, warm the cream in a small saucepan.

Increase the heat under the polenta to medium and stir in the butter. Add the cream about ½ cup at a time, letting the polenta absorb it each time before adding more. Season to taste with salt and pepper.

FOR CREAMY POLENTA: Pour the polenta into a bowl. Top with a drizzle of olive oil.

FOR CRISPY POLENTA: Pour the polenta (or any leftover creamy polenta) in a 1-inch-thick layer into a baking dish. Cover with a piece of plastic wrap pressed directly against the polenta. Refrigerate for several hours, until the polenta has set.

Cut the polenta into squares or other shapes. Heat some canola oil in a nonstick frying pan over medium heat. Add the polenta and cook, turning once, until a rich golden brown and crispy on both sides and hot throughout, about 12 minutes. Arrange on a serving platter.

SERVES 6 TO 8

buttered farro

3 tablespoons canola oil

½ cup finely diced onion

1 pound (2¾ cups) farro (see Sources, page 346, and Note below)

8 cups Chicken Stock (page 339), Vegetable Stock (page 341), or water

1 Sachet (page 342)

Kosher salt

8 tablespoons (1 stick; 4 ounces) cold unsalted butter, cut into 8 pieces

Freshly ground black pepper

2 tablespoons coarsely chopped flat-leaf parsley leaves

2 tablespoons minced chives

Farro is a large, sturdy grain. There are two kinds, long-cooking farro and semipearled farro, which will cook in about half the time. We prefer the long-cooking variety because it has a nuttier flavor and firmer texture.

Heat the canola oil in a wide pot (about 11 inches in diameter) over medium heat. When the oil is hot, add the onion and cook over medium-low heat, stirring from time to time, about 10 minutes, until softened but not colored. Add the farro, turn the heat to medium, and cook, stirring often, for about 5 minutes, to toast the farro and bring out its nuttiness.

Add the stock or water and sachet and bring to a simmer over medium-high heat. Partially cover, reduce the heat to maintain a gentle simmer, and simmer for 25 to 50 minutes (see Note). The farro should be tender but not at all mushy.

Add salt to taste to the farro, turn off the heat, and allow it to sit for 2 or 3 minutes. Place a colander over a large bowl and drain the farro, reserving the liquid.

Return the farro and ¾ cup of the reserved liquid to the pot and add the butter. Set over medium heat and heat, stirring constantly to emulsify the butter with the liquid and give the farro a creamy consistency. Season to taste with salt and pepper, remove from the heat, and stir in the parsley and chives.　SERVES 6

NOTE *Most farro is semipearled, which means that part of the hull has been removed and the grain will cook more quickly. Farro that is not pearled will take about twice as long to cook. Because farro is often sold without labeling that specifies cooking times, it is important to check it frequently during cooking.*

saffron rice

¼ cup canola oil

¾ cup finely chopped onion (cut just smaller than a grain of cooked rice)

Kosher salt

1 teaspoon saffron threads

2 cups (about 14 ounces) short-grain rice, preferably Calasparra
(see Sources, page 346)

2¾ to 3½ cups Chicken Stock (page 339) or Vegetable Stock (page 341)

Calasparra is a Spanish rice that's ideal for paella. It has short plump grains, like Carnaroli, the Italian risotto rice. Though this saffron rice can be served as a simple side dish, it also works well as a bed for fish—with Roasted Monkfish (page 96), for instance—or for paella. The onion is cut into pieces just smaller than the grains of cooked rice. And be sure to use a wide pan rather than a saucepan, so that the rice is spread out in a thinner layer for more rapid evaporation of the liquid, which will keep the kernels distinct and separate.

Heat the oil in a large sauté pan over medium heat until hot. Add the onion and season with a sprinkling of salt. Reduce the heat and cook gently for 3 minutes. Add the saffron. Reduce the heat to very low, and cook for another 2 minutes; do not brown the onions and saffron. Add the rice and cook over medium heat, stirring often, to toast the rice for 1 to 2 minutes.

Add 2½ cups of the stock, stir once, scraping the sides of the pan if necessary, and cover with a parchment lid (see page 120). Bring the stock to a simmer and simmer, adjusting the heat as necessary, for about 8 minutes, until most of the stock has been absorbed. The rice will still be firm. Gently stir the rice, scraping it up from the bottom, and reduce the heat to very low. Add an additional ¼ cup of stock, cover with the lid, increase the heat, and bring to a simmer. Simmer for about 3 minutes, until the stock is absorbed. Taste the rice and, if necessary, continue cooking, adding up to ¾ cup more stock ¼ cup at a time, as necessary, until the rice is almost tender and the final addition of liquid is almost absorbed. Turn the heat to low to allow the rice to absorb the remaining liquid, stirring occasionally. Season with salt and serve hot. Or, if the rice is to be served cold in the Saffron Rice Salad (page 166), spread it on a parchment-lined baking sheet to cool, then refrigerate.

SERVES 6

braised artichokes

1 anchovy fillet, salt-packed or oil-packed (optional)

¼ cup whole milk (if using the anchovy)

4 cups Chicken Stock (page 339) or Vegetable Stock (page 341)

2 cups dry white wine, such as Sauvignon Blanc

2 cups water

1½ cups olive oil

8 large artichokes (about 10 ounces each) or 16 small artichokes (5 ounces each)

2 lemons, halved

1 cup chopped carrots

1 cup sliced fennel

2 cups chopped onions

3 tablespoons minced shallots

1 tablespoon plus 1 teaspoon minced garlic

¾ teaspoon kosher salt

1 Sachet (page 342)

Artichokes add a fantastic sweet undertone to many dishes— you can pair them with olives, fennel, carrots, lamb, or hearty fish like monkfish, Arctic char, and salmon. We cook them most often using this technique, stewing them gently in olive oil and stock with aromatic herbs and vegetables.

If using the anchovy, soak it in the milk for 30 minutes.

Drain the anchovy, rinse under cold water, and coarsely chop. Set aside.

Meanwhile, mix the stock, wine, water, and 1 cup of the olive oil in a large bowl.

Hold an artichoke with the stem end toward you and pull off the very small bottom leaves. Working your way around the artichoke, break off the larger leaves, pushing with your thumb against the bottom of each leaf as you snap it off about ½ inch above its base, so you are well above the meaty portion (the heart). Continue removing the tougher outer leaves until you reach the line of tender, yellow leaves. Cut off the top two-thirds of the artichoke at the point where the meaty heart begins. Using a paring knife, cut away the tough dark green parts of the leaves to expose the tender heart: first cut around the artichoke bottom to remove a strip of dark green. Then, holding the knife at a 45-degree angle, trim the base of the artichoke above the stem. Trim off the bottom of the stem and peel the stem. Remove the fuzzy choke, using a sharp spoon to scrape the heart clean. Squeeze some lemon juice over the artichoke and submerge it in the stock mixture. Repeat with the remaining artichokes.

Warm the remaining ½ cup olive oil in a pot large enough and deep enough to hold the standing artichokes in one layer. Add the carrots and cook over medium heat for 2 to 2½ minutes until they begin to sweat. Add the fennel, onions, shallots, and garlic and cook for 4 minutes, or until the vegetables have softened. Remove the artichokes from the liquid, reserving the liquid, and put the artichokes stem side up on the vegetables. Sprinkle with the salt, cover the pot, and cook for 10 minutes. (Cooking the artichokes without liquid to start will help prevent the discoloration that normally occurs when artichokes cook in a liquid.)

Pour the reserved liquid over the vegetables and add the sachet. Lay a clean dampened kitchen towel over the artichokes to keep them submerged, bring just to a simmer, and cook at a gentle simmer for 15 minutes. If using the anchovy, add it. Continue to cook the artichokes until there is no resistance when a heart is poked with the tip of a sharp knife, 10 to 15 minutes, depending on the size.

Serve the artichokes, or transfer them with their liquids to a container (the artichokes should be submerged in the liquid) and cool to room temperature, then cover and refrigerate. The artichokes can be refrigerated for up to 1 week; reheat in the braising liquid.

MAKES 8 LARGE OR 16 SMALLER ARTICHOKES

potato hash
with bacon and melted onions

12 ounces applewood-smoked slab bacon (see Sources, page 346)

Canola oil

3 pounds Yukon Gold potatoes

Kosher salt

1 thyme sprig, leaves only

1 cup Melted Onions (page 337)

Freshly ground black pepper

1 tablespoon minced chives

I love hash so much I've even served this diner staple at The French Laundry. It's a great Sunday brunch dish, with poached eggs, but could also be served as a side dish at dinner. Don't hold the cubed potatoes in water—cut them just before cooking so that they are very dry and will become very crisp. The cooked potatoes are tossed with bacon and melted onions.

Preheat the oven to 200°F.

Cut the bacon into lardons about 1 inch long and ½ inch thick (see page 150). Set aside.

Pour about 1½ inches of oil into a large saucepan and heat to 300°F. Set a cooling rack over a baking sheet and line the rack with paper towels.

Meanwhile, square off the sides of the potatoes to give them a rectangular shape and cut into ½-inch dice. They may not all be perfectly square, and a bit of skin left on the cubes is also fine.

Add half the potatoes to the hot oil and cook for about 8 minutes, until tender and a rich golden brown; they will not be crisp. Remove from the oil with a wire skimmer or slotted spoon and drain on the paper towels. Repeat with the remaining potatoes.

Pour 2 tablespoons water into a medium saucepan and set over medium heat (the water will keep the bacon from crisping as the fat begins to render). Add the bacon, reduce the heat to medium-low, and let the bacon render its fat for 30 minutes. The bacon will color but not become completely crisp. Using a slotted spoon, transfer the bacon to paper towels to drain. Drain the excess fat from the pan, leaving just a film of fat to cook the potatoes; reserve the extra fat.

Add half the potatoes to the pan, sprinkle with salt, and add half the thyme. Cook for 3 to 4 minutes to crisp the potatoes and heat through. Add half the onions and fold in one-quarter of the bacon. Transfer the potatoes to a large bowl and keep warm in the oven while you cook the remaining potatoes (add some of the reserved fat to the pan if necessary) with the remaining ingredients. Season to taste with salt and pepper.

Transfer the potatoes to a serving bowl, add the minced chives, and garnish with the remaining bacon. **SERVES 6**

butter-poached marble potatoes

2 pounds marble potatoes, about 1½ inches in diameter

1 Sachet (page 342)

About 2½ cups Emulsified Butter (page 335)

Kosher salt and freshly ground black pepper

Herb leaves for garnish (optional)

As good as marble potatoes are roasted, we also like to cook them slowly, submerged in creamy melted butter in a low oven until tender. We often finish them with fresh herbs. These would go well with Pan-Roasted Halibut (page 92) or Roasted Spring Leg of Lamb (page 60).

Preheat the oven to 200°F.

Cut the potatoes in half. Put them in a medium ovenproof saucepan with the sachet, add enough emulsified butter to cover the potatoes, and heat over medium-high heat until the butter just begins to simmer.

Cover, transfer to the oven, and cook for 1 hour and 45 minutes to 2 hours, until the potatoes are completely tender. Season to taste with salt and pepper

Transfer to a bowl, garnish with fresh herbs if desired, and serve.

SERVES 6

puree of garlic potatoes

4 pounds large Yukon Gold potatoes, about 2 inches in diameter

Kosher salt

2 cups heavy cream

8 tablespoons (1 stick; 4 ounces) cold unsalted butter, cut into 8 pieces, plus a piece of butter for garnish

¼ cup Garlic Confit (page 266)

Freshly ground black pepper

1 tablespoon minced chives

These are our basic potatoes—simmered, then passed through a ricer or a food mill with butter and garlic confit. It's important to cook the potatoes gently, just at a simmer, so the outer layer doesn't disintegrate. I love these with the Buttermilk Fried Chicken (page 16), but they go with many other things, from the Sautéed Chicken Breasts with Tarragon (page 27) to the Braised Beef Short Ribs (page 41) or a big meaty fish such as monkfish.

Put the potatoes in a large pot and cover by at least 2 inches of cold water. Season the water with about ¼ cup salt and bring to a simmer over medium-high heat.

Adjust the heat as necessary to maintain a very gentle simmer, and cook for about 20 minutes, until tender enough to purée. Drain the potatoes in a colander and let them steam to evaporate excess water for 1 to 2 minutes. Then quickly peel them.

Meanwhile, heat the cream in a heavy saucepan; keep warm.

Set a food mill fitted with the medium blade over a pot. Add about one-quarter of the potatoes, top with 2 pieces of the butter and one-quarter of the garlic, and purée. Repeat with the remaining potatoes, butter, and garlic in 3 batches. (The potatoes can be puréed up to 3 hours ahead and held at room temperature.)

To serve, warm the potatoes in a saucepan over medium heat. As they heat, whip the cream into the potatoes. Season to taste with salt and pepper. Transfer to a serving bowl, sprinkle with the chives, and top with a spoonful of butter.

SERVES 6

smashed roasted marble potatoes

2¼ pounds marble potatoes, washed and dried

About ¼ cup canola oil

4 thyme sprigs, plus a few sprigs for garnish

Kosher salt

4 tablespoons (2 ounces) unsalted butter

8 cloves Garlic Confit (page 266), or to taste

2 tablespoons minced chives

Fleur de sel

I like the very small marble-sized potatoes, especially when we can find them in a variety of colors. We toss them with salt, olive oil, garlic, and herbs and roast them until they're tender. Sometimes we serve them whole; sometimes we smash them lightly with a fork and finish them with some garlic confit, butter, and chives. And sometimes we crush them gently and brown them in hot oil. These would go well with the Marinated Skirt Steak (page 53). When looking for little potatoes, remember that the smallest potatoes tend to fall to the bottom of the bin, so reach down there and pick out ones similar in size.

Preheat the oven to 375°F.

Toss the potatoes with oil to coat, the thyme, and salt to taste in a large bowl.

Melt 2 tablespoons of the butter in a large ovenproof frying pan. Spread the potatoes in the pan, transfer to the oven, and roast for 15 to 30 minutes, depending on the size, until the potatoes are completely tender when pierced with the tip of a paring knife.

Drain the potatoes, discard the thyme sprigs and garlic, and transfer the hot potatoes to a bowl. Add the remaining 2 tablespoons butter, the garlic confit, and chives and, using the back of a fork, smash the potatoes to combine them with the other ingredients. Serve garnished with thyme sprigs and a sprinkling of fleur de sel.

SERVES 6

CRISPED ROASTED MARBLE POTATOES Omit the garlic confit and chives. You will need a little more canola oil. When tossing the uncooked potaotes, toss with 12 unpeeled garlic cloves.

After the potatoes have cooked, discard the 4 thyme springs and allow the potatoes to cool enough to handle. One at a time, place each potato on a board and crush the potato lightly (with the heel of your hand or a meat mallet); the sides should split, but try to keep the potato whole.

Heat some canola oil in a large frying pan over medium-high heat until hot. Add the potatoes and garlic cloves and sauté, turning to brown both sides. Remove any excess oil in the pan, then swirl in the remaining 2 tablespoons butter to glaze the potatoes. Serve garnished with thyme sprigs and a sprinkling of fleur de sel.

Crisped Roasted Marble Potatoes

potato pavé

1 cup heavy cream

Kosher salt and freshly ground black pepper

3 pounds russet potatoes (three 1-pound potatoes if possible)

5 tablespoons (2½ ounces) unsalted butter, 1 tablespoon softened and
   4 tablespoons (2 ounces) cut into ½-inch cubes

Canola oil

2 thyme sprigs

2 garlic cloves, lightly crushed, skin left on

Minced chives

For a more refined version of scalloped potatoes, we cook russet potatoes, then cool them and cut them into rectangles. *Pavé* is the French word for "paving stones," and we use it to describe any such rectangular or square preparation.

What's fun is that when you reheat the potatoes, you sauté them on their cut sides so that all the layers of the potatoes become crisp, and you get some crunch in every bite. You can vary this by adding some onion confit or fresh herbs to the layers. In the winter, you might layer sweet potatoes in among the russets. It's easiest to use the largest potatoes you can find. It's a very versatile dish and can be served hot, at room temperature, or even cold. Try it with Herb-Crusted Rack of Lamb with Honey Mustard Glaze (page 59) or the Peppercorn-Crusted Beef Tenderloin (page 47).

Preheat the oven to 350°F.

Pour the cream into a large bowl and season with 1 teaspoon salt and ½ teaspoon pepper. Peel the potatoes. Cut a thin lengthwise slice off one side of a potato so it will rest flat on the mandoline. Lay a Japanese mandoline or other vegetable slicer over the bowl of cream and slice the potato lengthwise into very thin (about ¹⁄₁₆ inch) slices, letting them drop into the cream. (If you can't lay your mandoline across the bowl, slice the potatoes, adding the slices to the cream as you go.) Stop from time to time to toss the slices in the cream to keep them coated and prevent them from oxidizing. Repeat with the remaining potatoes.

Brush a 10-by-6½-by-3-inch-high pan with half the softened butter. (Don't use a shallower pan—you need the depth this size pan gives the pavé.) Line with parchment paper, leaving a 5-inch overhang on the two long sides. These extensions will be used to cover the potatoes as they cook and later serve as handles when unmolding. Brush the parchment with the remaining softened butter and sprinkle with salt and pepper.

Trim the potato slices to form a solid even layer in the bottom of the pan and lay them in the direction that works best to fill the pan. Repeat to form a second layer. Dot with a few cubes of butter and sprinkle lightly with salt and pepper. Continue layering the potatoes, adding butter and seasonings after each two layers. Fold over the sides of the parchment to cover the potatoes. Cover tightly with a piece of aluminum foil (to allow the potatoes to steam as they bake).

Bake the potatoes for 1 hour and 50 minutes, or until completely tender when pierced with the tip of a knife or a wire cake tester. Remove from the oven and let cool for 15 minutes. Put a weight on top of the potatoes (see Note), cool to room temperature, wrap well, and refrigerate for at least 6 hours, or up to 2 days.

To serve, run a palette knife around the two longer sides of the pavé to release it from the pan, and use the parchment handles to lift the potatoes from the pan, or invert onto a cutting surface. Trim all sides of the pavé. Cut the pavé into 12 equal pieces and let sit at room temperature for 30 minutes.

Heat some canola oil in a large frying pan over medium-high heat. Add the potatoes cut-side-down, add the thyme and garlic, and cook, basting with the liquid in the pan, until browned on the first side, then turn carefully and brown the opposite side.

Arrange the potatoes on a serving platter, browned side up. Put a small piece of butter on each piece to melt, and sprinkle with chives.

PHOTOGRAPH ON PAGE 227   SERVES 6

NOTE *The easiest way to weight the pavé is to cut a piece of cardboard just smaller than the top of the pan, so that it will cover the top of the pavé without resting on the sides of the pan. Wrap the cardboard in aluminum foil, set it on top of the pavé, and place a few cans or other weights on the cardboard for even weight distribution.*

on using fats

My primary cooking oil is canola oil, the most economical of the best neutral cooking oils. I often deep-fry in peanut oil because of its flavor and high smoke point. But I never cook with olive oil, because high temperatures affect its flavor—and why use a more expensive oil for a poor result?

Butter is my favorite fat. It can be a cooking medium and a sauce base, a finishing fat, or a condiment. In *Ma Gastronomie,* my favorite cookbook, Fernand Point wrote, "Butter! Give me butter! Always butter!" I can't say it any better than that.

When you cook the water out of butter, the solids are able to brown and give the resulting brown butter a delicious nutty flavor. It can be used to flavor many dishes, savory or sweet.

If you slowly melt butter in a pan, the fat will separate from the milk solids and the water. This fat, when separated from the solids and water, is called clarified butter (see page 335) and is an extraordinary cooking fat.

If you whisk chunks of butter into a small amount of simmering liquid, a tablespoon or two of water, for instance, the butter will melt but the solids and water will remain emulsified, so that the butter is liquid but still creamy and opaque—not translucent like butter that is simply melted. In professional kitchens we call this *beurre monté,* but in this book it's referred to simply as emulsified butter. This creamy melted butter allows you to coat food plentifully

and evenly—see, for example, Butter-Braised Radishes, Kohlrabi, and Brussels Sprouts (page 196). And I also use it for basting. But knowing that butter will emulsify naturally if there's a hot water-based liquid in the pan is useful. Any time you add butter to such a pan, you are in effect making *beurre monté,* which does a better job of coating food, such as corn on the cob (see page 188), than solid butter.

I also use flavorful animal fats, such as beef fat and duck fat, which flavor potatoes beautifully and make them very crisp. Marrow fat, the fat that melts out of beef marrow bones, is delicious—I might use it to make a bone marrow vinaigrette. I especially like duck fat and use it to sauté cabbage. It's wonderful added to braised collards instead of bacon, and, of course, I use duck fat to confit duck legs.

Potato Pavé (page 225)

To drain vegetables after blanching or deep-frying them, set a cooling rack over a baking sheet, line the rack with paper towels, and drain them on the towels. The excess water or oil will drip through the towel onto the pan, so that the vegetables won't sit in the liquid or oil. We use the same technique when frying fish.

red potato and green bean salad
with creamy pepper dressing

2 pounds new potatoes, about 1½ inches in diameter

1 Sachet (page 342)

Kosher salt

1 pound thin green beans (haricots verts)

2 heads Bibb lettuce

Creamy Pepper Dressing (page 183)

2 tablespoons minced shallots

1 tablespoon 1-inch pieces chives

Freshly ground black pepper

Small tarragon and chervil sprigs

This is a wonderful side dish—a hearty, nutritious, and satisfying combination of familiar vegetables: green beans and potatoes. The peppery buttermilk dressing is based on a black pepper gastrique, an intense sweet-sour sauce, made with Banyuls vinegar (which is made from a French fortified red wine) and sugar.

This hearty salad can turn the Braised Oxtail and Mushroom Tartine (page 55) into a dinner. It also makes a good accompaniment to Buttermilk Fried Chicken (page 16) or Roast Poussins (page 26).

Put the potatoes, sachet, and 2 teaspoons salt in a large saucepan, add cold water to cover, bring to a simmer, and cook until the potatoes are just tender, about 10 minutes. Drain and spread on a tray to cool; discard the sachet. Once they are cool, cut the potatoes in half.

Bring a large pot of salted water to a boil (see page 147). Prepare an ice bath. Set a cooling rack over a baking sheet and line the rack with paper towels.

Hold the beans a handful at a time with the ends all facing one direction and use scissors to cut off the stem ends (see photo). Blanch the beans for 2 to 3 minutes, until tender but still slightly resistant to the tooth. Drain and put in the ice bath just until cold, then drain on the paper towels.

Cut out the cores of the heads of lettuce. Separate the leaves, wash, and dry in a salad spinner. Stack several leaves at a time, roll up, and cut crosswise into strips about ¾ inch wide (this is called a chiffonade). Separate the chiffonade and put into a bowl. Toss with enough of the dressing to coat lightly.

Transfer the beans to a large bowl and toss with the potatoes, shallots, and chives. Spoon about ¼ cup of the dressing around the sides of the bowl and toss the ingredients to lightly coat. Season to taste with salt and pepper.

Spread half the lettuce on a serving platter. Arrange about half the vegetables in a layer over the greens. Top with another layer of lettuce and the remaining vegetables. Garnish with the herb sprigs, and serve the remaining dressing on the side.　　　　**SERVES 6**

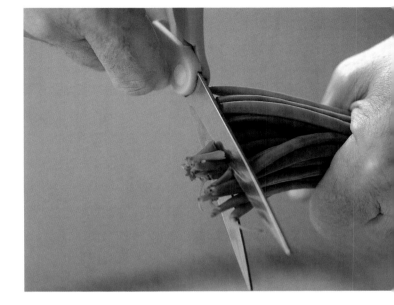

Keep a good pair of scissors in your kitchen. Sometimes they are better for a job than a knife. To trim green beans, gather a bunch in your hand, with the stems facing the same direction, and snip off the ends.

scallion potato cakes

5 scallions

3 pounds large russet potatoes

½ cup cornstarch

Canola oil

Kosher salt and freshly ground black pepper

While potato pancakes can be made by grating potatoes straight into the pan, we grate and rinse them, squeeze them dry, and toss them with cornstarch. The cornstarch prevents the potatoes from discoloring and helps to bind the cakes (they don't contain any eggs) and make them crisp. These can be served with duck or with corned beef, and topped with a poached egg. You could make smaller individual cakes to serve as an appetizer with smoked salmon and Horseradish Cream (page 57) or Slow-Cooker Apple Butter (page 249) and sour cream.

These are best eaten immediately, but you can keep the first and second batches warm in the oven while you cook the final one.

Preheat the oven to 200°F. Set a cooling rack on a baking sheet.

Cut away the ends of the scallions on a severe diagonal and discard, then cut the dark greens into very thin slices. (Reserve the remaining scallions for another use.) Set aside.

Set up a food processor with the coarse shredding blade. Peel the potatoes and shred them. Immediately transfer them to a large bowl of cold water and swirl and rinse the potatoes. Lift them from the water and dry in a salad spinner. Transfer to another large bowl. Spoon the cornstarch around the sides of the bowl and toss the potatoes with it (adding the cornstarch this way will help to coat the potatoes evenly). Do not let the potatoes sit for too long, or they will release their starch and the centers of the potatoes can become sticky.

Heat some canola oil in a 10-inch nonstick frying pan over medium-high heat until the oil is shimmering. Turn down the heat to medium. Add one-sixth of the potatoes, gently spreading them into an 8- to 9-inch circle. Keep the potato cake light and airy; do not press down on the potatoes. Season with a generous pinch each of salt and pepper. Reserve ¼ cup of the scallion greens for garnish, and sprinkle one-third of the remaining scallion greens over the potatoes. Carefully spread another one-sixth of the potatoes on top; again, do not press down on them. Season with salt and pepper. Cook for 6 to 7 minutes, to brown the bottom. You should hear the potatoes sizzling in the oil; if the potatoes get quiet and are not sizzling, or the pan looks dry, add a bit more oil. Turn the pancake over to brown the second side. The pancakes are somewhat fragile and can be difficult to flip with a spatula; if you don't feel comfortable turning them, invert the pancake onto the back of a baking sheet, held tilted over a second baking sheet, as some oil may seep out, then return the pan to the heat and slide the potato cake into the pan browned side up. Cook until the second side is browned and crisp, then transfer to the rack and keep warm in the oven while you cook the remaining 2 pancakes.

Cut each pancake into 4 wedges, stack on a platter, and garnish with the reserved scallion greens. SERVES 6

glazed sweet potatoes

2½ pounds large sweet potatoes (two 1¼-pound potatoes, if possible), scrubbed

8 tablespoons (1 stick; 4 ounces) unsalted butter, cut into 12 pieces, at room temperature

Kosher salt

About ½ cup packed light brown sugar

These are a variant of big steak fries, sweet potatoes cut into wedges and roasted in a covered baking dish until tender. Before serving them, we sprinkle the flesh with brown sugar and broil the potatoes to caramelize the sugar. Because of their sweetness, we often pair them with bitter greens, such as Rainbow Chard with Raisins, Pine Nuts, and Serrano Ham (page 205). Try them with Hamburgers (page 48) or Fig-Stuffed Roast Pork Loin (page 69).

Preheat the oven to 450°F.

Cut the ends from the potatoes. Cut each potato lengthwise in half, and cut each half into 1-inch-wide lengthwise wedges. Put them in a large baking dish that will hold them in a single layer. Spread the softened butter over the top of the potatoes. Sprinkle with salt.

Cover the pan tightly with foil and bake until the potatoes are tender when pierced with a paring knife, about 35 minutes. Remove from the oven and let cool until you're able to handle them.

Preheat the broiler. Spread the sugar in an even layer in a shallow bowl. One at a time, remove the potato wedges from the pan, brush the cut sides with some of the butter in the pan, and dip the cut sides into the sugar, then return to the pan. Sprinkle the potatoes with salt.

Just before serving, place the potatoes under the broiler until caramelized and heated through. Serve immediately. **SERVES 6**

fingerling or sweet potato chips

1 pound large fingerling potatoes, scrubbed, or 1 large sweet potato, peeled

Peanut or canola oil for deep-frying

Kosher salt

Fingerling potatoes sliced lengthwise make visually unusual, appealing chips. For bigger chips, we like to fry sweet potatoes, which are very crunchy and flavorful. These go perfectly with the Grilled Cheese Sandwich (page 288) and Hamburgers (page 48), but they'd also be an elegant side for either of the quail dishes (see page 31).

Set up a Japanese mandoline or other vegetable slicer to make very thin slices. Cut off the end of the potato(es) on a slight diagonal, which will give you a better angle for slicing the potato, and cut a few slices on the mandoline. The slices should be as thin as possible but not so thin that the edges become uneven; adjust the blade as necessary, and continue slicing the potatoes.

Pour 3 inches of oil into a Dutch oven or deep pot and heat over medium-high heat to 350°F for fingerlings, 325°F for sweet potatoes.

Preheat the oven to 200°F. Set a cooling rack on a baking sheet and line the rack with paper towels.

Add about one-quarter of the potatoes to the hot oil and cook, turning once with a wire skimmer, until golden brown, about 2½ minutes. Turning the potatoes helps prevent air pockets from developing in the chips, which would keep the centers from crisping. Transfer to the paper towels to drain and immediately season with salt. **SERVES 6**

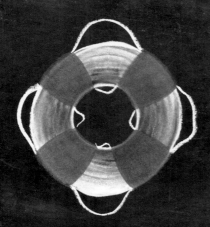

LIFESAVERS

Having a few staples on hand gives you incredible versatility in the kitchen, allowing you to transform an ordinary preparation into an extraordinary one. For instance, say you have an olive or artichoke tapenade. Add it to some red wine vinegar and oil, and suddenly you have an artichoke vinaigrette for a salad, or an olive vinaigrette for a piece of fish or sautéed lamb. Or a spread for toast to serve as a last-minute

canapé or alongside a bowl of soup. Similarly, a kumquat marmalade works as well as a sauce for roasted duck breast as it does as a condiment for a creamy cheese.

If you're shopping and see a beautiful piece of halibut for sale, and if you have a couple of these staples on hand, the soffritto, say, or the mushroom conserva, you'll have an instant dish. Want to enliven your basic roasted chicken? Serve it with some artichoke or fennel mustard. The following recipes open up your repertoire and allow you to be spontaneous.

There are many different kinds of staples here, but the majority are sweet, acidic, or spicy condiments that include chutneys, compotes, jams, jellies, and marmalades.

The savory counterparts include garlic puree, a variety of mustards, mushroom conserva, tapenades, and loads of pickles, which can be used as seasoning devices or garnishes in salads, sides, and main courses. While we preserve fruits and vegetables for their taste—that intense balance of sweetness and acidity—as well as for their texture, preservation is also important to us. Often we'll have abundant quantities of fresh carrots, for instance, more than we can serve in an evening to, say, accompany braised beef. To avoid wasting any, we'll pickle what's left over so that they can be used differently later in the week. Pickles can garnish a charcuterie platter, be chopped and used in a dressing, added to a mayonnaise, sliced and served on a sandwich, or tossed with a salad.

OVERLEAF, FROM LEFT: *Potted Rainier Cherries with Rum and Vanilla Bean (page 242); Potted Bing Cherries with Cherry Balsamic Vinegar and Tarragon (page 242).*
OPPOSITE: *Mushroom Conserva (page 260).*

nuts *Candied and seasoned nuts are fantastic in so many ways, especially given how easy they are to make. Generally speaking, you can toast them and toss them with whatever seasonings you choose—here, honey, fresh herbs, or paprika and Espelette pepper. They can be served as an hors d'oeuvre with cocktails, of course. But they give a whole new dimension to salads and offer the perfect contrast to cheeses. And vanilla ice cream with caramel sauce is a new dessert when you top it with candied pecans.*

candied pecans

3 cups raw pecan halves
3 tablespoons clover honey
¾ teaspoon ground fleur de sel or fine sea salt, plus a pinch

Position the racks in the lower and upper thirds of the oven and preheat the oven to 250°F.

Line a baking sheet with parchment paper and spread the nuts on the pan. Warm in the oven for 5 minutes (warming the nuts helps prevent them from crystallizing the honey).

Meanwhile, pour the honey into a small saucepan and warm over medium heat.

Pour the nuts into a bowl, add the honey, and sprinkle with a pinch of salt. Stir to coat the nuts evenly with the honey.

Line two baking sheets with Silpats and spread the nuts on the sheets. Sprinkle with the remaining ¾ teaspoon salt. Bake for 2 hours, rotating the pans halfway through baking.

Remove the pans from the oven and separate any nuts that cling together. Let the nuts cool on the pans.

Store in an airtight container for up to 1 week.

PHOTOGRAPH ON PAGE 239   MAKES 3 CUPS

herbed toasted walnuts

3 cups raw walnut halves
2 tablespoons (1 ounce) unsalted butter
¾ teaspoon finely chopped rosemary
¾ teaspoon finely chopped oregano
¾ teaspoon finely chopped thyme
¾ teaspoon finely chopped flat-leaf parsley
Pinch of ground fleur de sel or fine sea salt

Preheat the oven to 350°F. Line a baking sheet with parchment paper. Set a cooling rack on a second baking sheet.

Spread the nuts on the lined baking sheet and toast in the oven for 7 minutes. Rotate the pan and toast for 5 to 8 minutes longer, until the nuts are fragrant and lightly colored.

Meanwhile, combine the butter and herbs in a small saucepan over medium heat. As soon as the butter begins to bubble, remove from the heat and set aside to infuse while the nuts toast.

Pour the butter mixture into a medium bowl, add the salt, and swirl the butter around the sides of the bowl. Add the nuts and toss to coat. Transfer the nuts to the rack and drizzle any remaining butter over them. Let cool slightly. Since these are coated in butter, they are best served warm.

To store, cool the nuts completely, then store in an airtight container for up to 1 week. Reheat on a baking sheet in a warm oven before serving.

PHOTOGRAPH ON PAGE 239   MAKES 3 CUPS

spiced mixed nuts

1 cup raw hazelnuts
1 cup raw pecan halves
1 cup raw walnut halves
½ teaspoon sweet paprika
½ teaspoon piment d'Espelette (see page 208)
2 tablespoons extra virgin olive oil
¼ teaspoon ground fleur de sel or fine sea salt

Preheat the oven to 350°F. Line two baking sheets with parchment paper.

Spread the hazelnuts on one pan and toast until a rich golden brown, 15 to 20 minutes. If the skins are still on the hazelnuts, the nuts may take longer; toast until the skins have split and become papery. Remove the nuts from the oven. If they still have the skins on, wrap in a kitchen towel and rub vigorously to remove as much of the skins as possible.

Meanwhile, spread the pecans and walnuts on the second baking pan and toast as above. While the pecans and walnuts toast, combine the paprika, Espelette, oil, and salt in a medium bowl. Set a cooling rack on a baking sheet.

Add all the nuts to the oil and toss to coat evenly. Transfer the nuts to the rack to cool.

Store the nuts in an airtight container for up to 1 week.

PHOTOGRAPH ON PAGE 239   MAKES 3 CUPS

TOP: *Apple-Beet Chutney (page 241).* **ABOVE (CLOCKWISE FROM UPPER LEFT):** *Candied Pecans (page 238), Herbed Toasted Walnuts (page 238),*

and Spiced Mixed Nuts (page 238). **RIGHT (FROM TOP):** *Pistachio Butter (page 240), Marcona Almond Butter (page 240), and Hazelnut Butter (page 240).*

nut butters *We cook almonds, pistachios, or hazelnuts in milk or cream until soft and then puree them to a paste that can be used to add flavor and texture in vinaigrettes or butter sauces. They can be used as a condiment alongside any cooked whitefish, such as John Dory, codfish, or halibut, whether sautéed, roasted, or fried. Or they can be thinned with stock, milk, cream, or even water, and spooned over the fish as an instant sauce. And they're great folded into ice cream along with pieces of chocolate or spread on brioche.*

marcona almond butter

2 cups salted roasted Marcona almonds
4 cups whole milk
Kosher salt

Put the almonds in a saucepan, cover with the milk, and bring to a simmer. Simmer gently for about 1½ hours, until the nuts are soft enough to puree in a Vita-Mix. If the liquid reduces below the level of the nuts before they are soft, just add enough water to keep them covered.

Drain the almonds, reserving the liquid. Put the nuts in a Vita-Mix and, with the machine running on medium speed, begin adding enough liquid to allow the nuts to spin. Blend on high speed for several minutes, adding more liquid as necessary and scraping down the sides from time to time, until you have a silky-smooth puree.

Transfer to a bowl and refrigerate until ready to use, or for up to 2 weeks. The butter will stiffen in the refrigerator; bring to room temperature before using.

PHOTOGRAPH ON PAGE 239   **MAKES ABOUT 3 CUPS**

pistachio butter

1½ cups shelled raw pistachios, preferably bright green Sicilian pistachios (see Sources, page 346)
2 to 3 cups whole milk
2 cups heavy cream
Kosher salt

Preheat the oven to 350°F. Line a baking sheet with parchment paper.

Spread the pistachios on the pan and toast until a rich golden brown, about 12 minutes.

Transfer the nuts to a saucepan, cover with 2 cups of the milk and the cream, and bring to a simmer. Simmer gently for about 1½ hours, until the nuts are soft enough to puree in a Vita-Mix. If the liquid reduces too much, add up to 1 cup more milk to keep the nuts covered.

Drain the pistachios, reserving the liquid. Put the nuts in a Vita-Mix and, with the machine running on medium speed, begin adding enough liquid to allow the nuts to spin. Blend on high speed for several minutes, adding more liquid as necessary and scraping down the sides from time to time, until you have a silky-smooth puree.

Transfer to a bowl and refrigerate until ready to use, or for up to 2 weeks. The butter will stiffen in the refrigerator; bring to room temperature before using.

PHOTOGRAPH ON PAGE 239   **MAKES ABOUT 2½ CUPS**

hazelnut butter

1½ cups raw hazelnuts
2 to 3 cups whole milk
2 cups heavy cream
Kosher salt

Preheat the oven to 350°F. Line a baking sheet with a piece of parchment paper.

Spread the hazelnuts on the pan and toast until a rich golden brown, 15 to 20 minutes. If the skins are still on the hazelnuts, they may take longer: toast until the skins have split and become papery. Remove the nuts from the oven. If they still have the skins on, wrap in a kitchen towel and rub vigorously to remove as much of the skins as possible.

Transfer the hazelnuts to a saucepan, cover with 2 cups of the milk and the cream, and bring to a simmer. Simmer gently for about 1½ hours, until the nuts are soft enough to puree in a Vita-Mix. If the liquid reduces too much, add up to 1 cup more milk to keep the nuts covered.

Drain the hazelnuts, reserving the liquid. Put the nuts in a Vita-Mix and, with the machine running on medium speed, begin adding enough liquid to allow the nuts to spin. Blend on high speed for several minutes, adding more liquid as necessary and scraping down the sides from time to time, until you have a silky-smooth puree.

Transfer to a bowl and refrigerate until ready to use, or for up to 2 weeks. The butter will stiffen in the refrigerator; bring to room temperature before using.

PHOTOGRAPH ON PAGE 239   **MAKES ABOUT 2½ CUPS**

chutneys *We use chutneys, the chunky sweet-sour-spicy condiments of cooked fruits, and sometimes vegetables, to complement cheese, but they are excellent in place of a sauce for meat or fish. The cipollini onions are particularly good with chicken, quail, duck, lamb, salmon, and monkfish— actually, with any proteins that go well with other preparations of onions. We primarily use the apple-beet chutney with our cheeses.*

apple-beet chutney

8 ounces small to medium Chioggia beets, as close in size as possible
8 ounces small to medium golden beets, as close in size as possible
2 tablespoons canola oil
4 Fuji apples (about 2 pounds), stemmed and cored
½ cup apple juice
¼ cup apple cider vinegar
½ teaspoon Dijon mustard
½ teaspoon whole-grain mustard
4 large mint leaves
Maldon salt or other flaky sea salt

When we have a lot of beets in a variety of colors, we turn them into a vivid compote that's great with roasted vegetables and meats, as well as salmon.

Preheat the oven to 350°F.

Wash the beets, cut off the stems, and trim away any roots. Place each type of beet on a separate sheet of aluminum foil. Drizzle with the oil. Fold up the edges and crimp each to create a packet.

Put the packets on a baking sheet. Cook until tender when pierced with a knife, about 50 minutes for smaller beets and 1 hour to 1 hour 15 minutes for the larger beets. Remove from the oven and let cool slightly.

Once the beets are cool enough to handle, peel (see Lightbulb Moment, right) and cut into ½-inch dice.

Peel the apples and cut into ½-inch dice. Combine the apples, apple juice, and vinegar in a medium saucepan, simmer over medium heat for 10 minutes, or until the apples are crisp-tender. Remove from the heat and stir in the beets and mustards.

With a slotted spoon, transfer the apples and beets to a 1½-quart canning jar or other storage container, interspersing the mint leaves as you spoon in the fruit. Press down slightly on the compote and top with enough liquid to cover. Cover with the lid and cool to room temperature, then refrigerate for up to 1 week (it may discolor if stored any longer).

Serve sprinkled with Maldon salt.

PHOTOGRAPH ON PAGE 239   MAKES ABOUT 4 CUPS

A paper towel works perfectly for peeling cooked beets. Once the beets are cool enough to handle, cut off the tops and use a paper towel to lightly rub the beet from the cut end toward the root; the skin will come right off.

cipollini onion chutney
with almonds

3 small (about 2-inch-long) sweet red peppers, such as Red Fresno
Canola oil
30 medium (1½ to 2 inches wide) cipollini onions, peeled and root ends
    trimmed flush with onions
¼ cup honey, or to taste
1 cup white wine vinegar, or to taste
1 cup slivered almonds

Cut the ends from 2 of the peppers and cut lengthwise in half. Run a paring knife around the core of seeds to remove it. Cut the peppers into ⅛-inch-wide julienne. Leave the remaining pepper whole, but cut a slit down one side. Set aside.

Heat some oil in a large frying pan over medium heat until hot. Working in batches (use two pans if you have them), add the cipollini, root end up, in a single layer, and cook, swirling the pan from time to time, for 5 to 7 minutes, until the onions are a rich golden brown. Drain off any excess oil, turn the onions over, and brown on the second side for about 4 minutes. Transfer to a bowl.

Return all the onions to the pan, add the honey, all of the peppers, and the vinegar, and swirl to distribute the ingredients. Raise the heat to medium-high, to bring the liquid to a boil, stirring to dissolve the honey, and cook until the cipollini are tender, about 3 minutes; lower the heat as necessary so the honey and vinegar don't reduce too quickly. Taste the liquid and add honey or vinegar to taste if necessary; if you add more, cook for another minute. Remove the pan from the heat.

With a slotted spoon, transfer the onions and peppers to a 1-quart canning jar or other storage container. Press down slightly on the onions and add enough of the cooking liquid to cover them. Put the lid on the jar and let cool to room temperature, then refrigerate until ready to serve, or for up to 1 month.

Preheat the oven to 350°F. Line a baking sheet with parchment paper.

Spread the nuts on the pan and toast for 7 minutes, or until golden. Remove from the heat. Serve the onions sprinkled with the toasted almonds.

PHOTOGRAPH ON PAGE 244   **MAKES 4 CUPS**

---

compotes *Compotes are fruits or vegetables that are slowly cooked, usually in a sugar syrup, sometimes with sweet spices. As with the other condiments in this section, many can be used as a finishing sauce or an accompaniment, as well as a dessert, as a complement to harder cheeses, or as part of a charcuterie platter.*

potted rainier cherries
with rum and vanilla bean

1 pound Rainier cherries with stems
⅓ cup light rum
1 cup granulated sugar
1 cup water
2 vanilla beans, split

This cherry and vanilla compote is versatile enough to pair with pork in a savory course or spoon over ice cream for dessert.

Wash and pit the cherries (see Lightbulb Moment, page 243), then trim the stems to about 1½ inches.

Pour the rum into a small saucepan and bring to boil over medium-high heat. Carefully light the rum with a match, or by tilting the pan toward the burner if using a gas stove, to burn off the alcohol. Remove from the heat.

Add the sugar and water to the pan. Scrape the vanilla seeds from the beans and add to the pan, then add the pods. Return to the heat, bring to a simmer, and simmer for 2 minutes, stirring to dissolve the sugar. Remove from the heat and let the syrup steep for 30 minutes.

Using a slotted spoon, transfer the cherries and vanilla beans to a canning jar or other storage container (do not press down on the cherries). Pour the liquid over the cherries, cover with the lid, and let cool, then refrigerate for up to 2 weeks.

PHOTOGRAPH ON PAGES 234–35   **MAKES ABOUT 4 CUPS**

potted bing cherries
with cherry balsamic vinegar and tarragon

1 pound Bing cherries with stems
Two 4-inch tarragon sprigs
¾ cup granulated sugar
¾ cup Cherry Balsamic Vinegar (see Note) or balsamic vinegar
1½ cups water
30 black peppercorns

This cherry and tarragon compote is excellent as part of a charcuterie platter.

Wash and pit the cherries (see Lightbulb Moment, right), then trim the stems to about 1½ inches. Put the cherries and tarragon in a canning jar or other storage container (do not press down on the cherries).

Combine the sugar, vinegar, water, and peppercorns in a medium saucepan and bring to a boil over medium-high heat, stirring to dissolve the sugar. Strain the liquid, cool, pour it over the cherries, and cover with the lid. Let cool, then refrigerate for up to 2 weeks.

PHOTOGRAPHS ON PAGES 235 AND 244   **MAKES ABOUT 4 CUPS**

NOTE *To make Cherry Balsamic Vinegar, reserve the pits from 1 pound of cherries. Bring ¾ cup of balsamic vinegar to a simmer, pour over the pits, and let steep for 1 hour. Drain.*

apricot-currant compote

2 cups granulated sugar
1½ tablespoons apple pectin (see Sources, page 346)
½ teaspoon coriander seeds
1 cinnamon stick, broken in half
1 star anise
2¼ pounds ripe apricots, cut in half and pitted
¼ cup dried currants
1 teaspoon fresh lemon juice

Apricots are so plentiful in the the late spring and early summer that we can hardly find enough uses for them. We stew them in a sweet spiced liquid with currants for a compote that can be used as a glaze for roasted pork or poultry or as a condiment on a cheese board. Usually we rein in the seasonings so that we can highlight the fruit, but occasionally we'll add a sachet of coriander, cinnamon, and star anise for some spice.

Combine ⅓ cup of the sugar and the pectin in a small bowl, mixing well so that the pectin will dissolve smoothly; set aside. Make a sachet (see page 342) containing the coriander, cinnamon, and star anise.

Put the apricots in a large bowl, add the remaining 1⅔ cups sugar, and toss to coat the apricots in sugar. Let stand for 10 minutes to draw out some of the juices from the apricots.

Transfer the apricots and any sugar and juices to a medium saucepan and attach a candy thermometer to the pan. Add the sachet and bring to a simmer over medium-high heat. The apricots will release more liquid as they cook; stir to submerge the apricots in the liquid. Adjust the heat

We pit cherries from the bottom so they keep their shape. They can be pitted using a small paring knife, but the easiest way is to use a very small (#12) parisienne melon baller. Scoop out a small circle from the bottom of a cherry, then gently push the melon baller into the cherry and pull out the pit. Repeat with the remaining cherries; it will get easier as you go. (If you'd like to make Cherry Balsamic Vinegar [see Note, left], reserve the pits.)

OPPOSITE (CLOCKWISE FROM TOP): *Apricot-Currant Compote (page 243), Potted Bing Cherries with Cherry Balsamic Vinegar and Tarragon (page 242), Cipollini Onion Chutney with Almonds (page 242), and Tomato-Basil Marmalade (page 248).* **THIS PAGE (FROM LEFT):** *Tangerine-Kumquat Marmalade (page 249), Red Pepper Jelly (page 247), and Fig and Balsamic Jam (page 246) on crackers.*

as necessary to keep the apricots at a simmer, and cook until they are tender but not mushy, about 15 minutes.

Stir in the currants and cook for about 5 minutes, or until the currants are tender. Slowly whisk in the sugar and pectin mixture and continue to cook until the syrup registers 215° to 220°F. Remove from the heat. (See Note, page 249.)

Remove the sachet and stir in the lemon juice. Spoon the compote into a canning jar or other storage container, cover, and let cool to room temperature, then refrigerate for up to 1 month.

PHOTOGRAPH ON PAGE 244   MAKES ABOUT 2½ CUPS

pear with vanilla bean compote

2 pounds Comice pears
2 cups dry white wine, such as Sauvignon Blanc
½ cup granulated sugar
2 whole cloves
1 vanilla bean, split

Peel the pears and quarter them lengthwise. Remove and discard the core from each quarter and cut the pears lengthwise into slices just over ½ inch thick. You need 3 cups pear slices for this recipe.

Combine the wine, sugar, and cloves in a medium saucepan. With a paring knife, scrape the seeds from the vanilla bean and add them to the pan, along with the pod. Bring to a boil over medium heat, stirring occasionally until the sugar dissolves. Add the pears; they should just be covered with liquid. If not, add just enough water to cover. Bring to a simmer and simmer, stirring gently from time to time, until the pears are tender and completely translucent (any patches of white are an indication that the pears are not fully cooked). The cooking time will vary according to the ripeness of the pears: it may take only about 6 minutes for ripe pears and as long as 15 to 20 minutes for hard pears. As they become tender, remove the individual slices with a slotted spoon and place in an even layer in a storage container. Cover.

Once all of the slices are cooked, pour any liquid accumulated in the container back into the saucepan. Boil to reduce the liquid to about ½ cup; it should be a light amber in color with the consistency of a medium-bodied syrup (like maple syrup).

Pour the liquid over the pears. For a deeper vanilla flavor, leave the bean in the compote. Cover with the lid and refrigerate for at least 1 hour, or, preferably, overnight. The pears can be refrigerated for up to 1 month.

MAKES ABOUT 2 CUPS

jams and jellies *We make a red pepper jelly to serve on brioche with a creamy cheese, such as Camembert, and some almonds. It's also good with Flatbread (page 280) and would go well with a softer pita-style bread or even potato pancakes. It makes a delicious glaze for pork spareribs.*

We also serve jams with desserts—as a garnish for a parfait or cupcake, or a side for beignets. Figs make great jam, as do plums. We add Zinfandel to the plum jam because this wine is often described as having plum flavors, and the two go well together. And raspberry is, of course, a standard that is especially valuable in desserts.

fig and balsamic jam

2 pounds figs, preferably Black Mission or Kadota, stems removed and coarsely chopped
1½ cups granulated sugar
½ cup balsamic vinegar
1 teaspoon black peppercorns, tied into a sachet (see page 342)
Fresh lemon juice

Combine the figs, sugar, balsamic vinegar, and sachet in a large saucepan and attach a candy thermometer to the pan. Bring to a simmer over medium-high heat, then lower the heat to maintain a gentle simmer and cook, stirring to break up the larger pieces of fig, keeping a chunky consistency, until the jam reaches 215° to 220°F. Remove from the heat. (See Note, page 249.)

Remove the sachet and stir in lemon juice to taste. Spoon the jam into a canning jar or other storage container, cover, and let cool to room temperature, then refrigerate for up to 1 month.

PHOTOGRAPH ON PAGE 245   MAKES 2½ CUPS

plum zinfandel jam

2 pounds Santa Rosa plums
1 cup Zinfandel
¾ cup granulated sugar, or to taste

Cut the flesh of the plums away from the pits and cut into ¾-inch pieces.

Combine the plums, wine, and sugar in a large saucepan and attach a candy thermometer to the pan. Bring to a simmer over medium-high heat, then lower the heat to maintain a gentle simmer and cook, skimming off any foam that rises to the top, until the jam reaches 215° to 220°F. Remove from the heat. (See Note, page 249.)

Taste the jam and add additional sugar as needed, stirring to dissolve it. Spoon into a canning jar or other storage container, cover, and let cool to room temperature, then refrigerate for up to 1 month.

MAKES 1½ CUPS

raspberry jam

2 cups granulated sugar, or to taste
1 tablespoon plus 1 teaspoon apple pectin (see Sources, page 346)
4 cups raspberries
¼ cup water
1 teaspoon fresh lemon juice, or to taste

Combine the sugar and pectin in a small bowl, mixing well so that the pectin will dissolve smoothly. Combine the raspberries, pectin mixture, and water in a large saucepan, attach a candy thermometer to the pan, and bring to a simmer over medium-high heat, stirring occasionally to dissolve the sugar. Reduce the heat and simmer until the mixture reaches 215° to 220°F. Remove from the heat. (See Note, page 249.)

Taste the jam and add additional sugar if needed, stirring to dissolve the sugar. Add the lemon juice. Spoon into a canning jar or other storage container, cover, and let cool to room temperature, then refrigerate for up to 1 month.

MAKES 2¾ CUPS

red pepper jelly

7 medium red bell peppers (4 to 6 ounces each), seeded
1 serrano pepper, halved lengthwise and seeded
2 cups apple cider vinegar
½ teaspoon kosher salt
2 cups granulated sugar
1 tablespoon apple pectin (see Sources, page 346)
1 tablespoon canola oil

Cut enough of the bell peppers into ¼-inch dice to make 1 cup; reserve. Cut the remaining peppers into ½-inch pieces, place in a medium saucepan with the serrano pepper, vinegar, and salt, and bring to a simmer over medium heat. Cook, stirring occasionally, for 15 to 20 minutes, until the peppers are tender.

Line a fine-mesh basket strainer with dampened cheesecloth and set it over a deep bowl. Strain the pepper mixture through the cheesecloth. Do not push on the solids (that would cloud the jelly). Twist the cheesecloth and let it sit in the strainer for about 15 minutes, lightly twisting and pressing gently from time to time to extract all of the liquid. You should have about 1¾ cups liquid. Discard the peppers.

Combine the sugar and pectin in a small bowl, mixing well so that the pectin will dissolve smoothly.

Heat the canola oil in a small frying pan over low heat. Add the diced peppers and cook slowly to soften them without coloring them, about 5 minutes. Drain the peppers on paper towels, then place them in a clean large saucepan. Add the pepper liquid, increase the heat to medium, and heat until the liquid is warm. Slowly add the pectin mixture, whisking until dissolved, then attach a candy thermometer to the pan. Increase the heat, bring to a simmer, and simmer until the jelly reaches 215° to 220°F. Remove from the heat. (See Note, page 249.)

Pour the jelly into a canning jar or other storage container, cover, and let cool to room temperature, then refrigerate for up to 1 month.

PHOTOGRAPH ON PAGE 245   **MAKES ABOUT 2 CUPS**

marmalades *These marmalades are fresh, sweet, tart, and bright and can work with savory items—the red onion–cranberry marmalade with duck confit, for instance—and many kinds of cheese. The only cheeses we don't recommend pairing with preserves are pungent cheeses such as Époisses and Taleggio; for these, we prefer salty, savory pairings such as a salad with dry-cured ham.*

red onion–cranberry marmalade

¼ cup canola oil
3 cups diced (¼-inch) red onions
1 cup chopped dried cranberries
3 cups apple juice
½ cup apple cider vinegar
½ cup packed dark brown sugar
½ cup granulated sugar
1 tablespoon apple pectin (see Sources, page 346)
1 tablespoon plus 1 teaspoon grated orange zest
Fresh lemon juice for serving

Red onion and cranberry is a wonderful combination, with the sweetness of the onions intensified by cooking and the tartness of the fruit balanced with brown sugar. Acid—cider vinegar—along with apple juice and orange zest, round it all out.

Heat the oil in a large saucepan over low heat. Add the red onions and cook very slowly for about 30 minutes, until the onions have softened but not colored.

Add the cranberries and cook for 5 minutes. Stir in the apple juice and cider vinegar. Combine both sugars and the pectin in a small bowl, mixing well so that the pectin will dissolve smoothly, and add to the pan, along with the orange zest. Attach a candy thermometer to the pan, bring to a simmer, and cook until the marmalade registers 215° to 220°F. (See Note, page 249.)

Transfer the marmalade to a canning jar or other storage container, cover and let cool, then refrigerate for up to 3 months.

Just before serving, squeeze a bit of lemon juice over the marmalade.

MAKES ABOUT 2½ CUPS

tomato-basil marmalade

½ cup coarsely chopped fennel
½ cup coarsely chopped onion
½ cup coarsely chopped leeks (white and light green parts only)
2 medium garlic cloves, thinly sliced
Canola oil
Kosher salt
½ cup lightly packed light brown sugar
1 cup red wine vinegar
8 slightly underripe beefsteak tomatoes (about 5 ounces each), cored and cut into ½-inch dice
2 cups loosely packed large basil leaves, plus (optional) small basil leaves for garnish

This tomato-basil marmalade is, in essence, a variation of our Oven-Roasted Tomato Sauce (page 333), made with slow-roasted fennel and onions, with some brown sugar and red wine vinegar added. After it's cooked, we add large leaves of basil to perfume it.

This marmalade goes well with sausages and prosciutto, or even just spread on toast. It is also extraordinary with lamb. Remove the basil (which will have turned brown) before serving, and garnish the marmalade with small fresh basil leaves if you wish. We don't peel the tomatoes, but you can for a more refined marmalade.

Preheat the oven to 375°F.

Toss the fennel, onion, leeks, and garlic with enough oil to coat, put in a large ovenproof saucepan, and sprinkle with salt. Put in the oven and cook for 45 minutes to 1 hour, stirring every 15 minutes, until soft and lightly caramelized. (There should be some caramelization on the vegetables, but if any become charred remove them and discard.)

Stir in the brown sugar and vinegar. Cook for another 20 minutes, to absorb the liquid.

Stir in the tomatoes and cook for another 1½ hours, stirring every 30 minutes. Taste the marmalade. Rather than tasting of vinegar, it should have a full, rich flavor. Cook for a little longer if the vinegar flavor is still too sharp.

With a slotted spoon, transfer the tomatoes to a 1-quart canning jar or other storage container, interspersing the large basil leaves as you spoon in the tomatoes. Press the tomatoes down slightly and add enough of the cooking liquid to cover. Cover and let cool to room temperature, then refrigerate for up to 1 month.

Remove the large basil leaves when serving, and garnish the marmalade with small basil leaves if desired.

PHOTOGRAPH ON PAGE 244

MAKES 4 CUPS

tangerine-kumquat marmalade

1½ pounds kumquats
6 tangerines or other mandarin oranges
2½ cups granulated sugar

This tangerine-kumquat marmalade—chewy from the kumquats and just enough rind—is as good with duck as it is with a bagel and cream cheese.

Cut the kumquats lengthwise in half. Remove all the seeds and the small stems. Put the kumquats in a large bowl, cover by 2 inches with cold water, and refrigerate for at least 18 hours, or up to 24 hours, to remove some of the bitterness from the rind.

Drain the kumquats and return to the bowl. The halved kumquats are the right size for serving the marmalade as an accompaniment to meat or cheese. If you will be using the marmalade to spread on toast, cut the kumquats into smaller pieces.

Quarter the tangerines, reserving the juices. Cut the flesh of the tangerine wedges away from the pith and skin and remove and discard any seeds. Squeeze the juice from the tangerines into a measuring cup and add the juice from the cutting board. Set aside 1 cup of the juice for this recipe, and reserve any remaining juice for another use.

Chop the remaining tangerine flesh and add to the bowl of kumquats. Transfer the kumquats and tangerines to a pot, add the juice and sugar, and attach a candy thermometer to the pot. Bring to a simmer, skimming off any foam that rises to the top, until the marmalade registers 215° to 220°F. Remove from the heat. (See Note.)

Spoon the marmalade into a jar or other storage container. Cover and let cool to room temperature, then refrigerate for at least 2 hours, or, preferably, for 24. The marmalade can be refrigerated for up to 1 month.

PHOTOGRAPHS ON PAGE 245 AND 271   **MAKES ABOUT 2½ CUPS**

NOTE ON PLATE TESTING *To check that compotes, jams, and jellies are at the right consistency, put a tablespoonful of what you're cooking on a plate and chill it in the refrigerator for 10 minutes. If it is too thin, return to the heat, cook a few more minutes, and retest.*

peach puree

2 pounds ripe peaches
2 cups granulated sugar
1 tablespoon fresh lemon juice
⅛ teaspoon ground cinnamon
¼ teaspoon freshly grated nutmeg

A simple peach puree is a versatile condiment. It can be used in salads, mixed in some lemon or lime juice and a bit of Grand Marnier to toss with fresh fruit, or used to sweeten a bowl of plain yogurt.

Unless you can peel the peaches easily with a paring knife, bring a pot of water to a boil. Prepare an ice bath. Cut an X in the bottom of each peach, extending the cuts two-thirds of the way up the sides (this will make it easier to peel the peaches). Drop them into boiling water for 30 to 60 seconds, just until the skin pulls away easily from the flesh, then plunge them into the ice bath to cool.

Drain the peaches and peel them. Halve, pit, and cut into ½-inch pieces. Transfer to a Vita-Mix and puree until smooth. Strain through a fine-mesh basket strainer.

Combine the peach puree, sugar, lemon juice, cinnamon, and nutmeg in a large saucepan, attach a candy thermometer to the pan, and bring to a simmer over medium heat. Reduce the heat if necessary and simmer, skimming the foam occasionally, until the puree reaches 215° to 220°F. Remove from the heat. (See Note, left.)

Pour the puree into a canning jar or other storage container, cover and let cool to room temperature, then refrigerate for up to 1 month.

MAKES ABOUT 2½ CUPS

slow-cooker apple butter

2 pounds Gravenstein apples
2 pounds Pink Lady apples
1 cup champagne vinegar
2 cups water
About 4 cups granulated sugar
2 teaspoons ground cinnamon
½ teaspoon ground cloves
½ teaspoon ground allspice
Grated zest and juice of 1 lemon

This apple butter is fantastic with potato pancakes or simply spread on toast. We use Gravenstein and Pink Lady apples, but you could also use a combination of Sierra Beauty, Golden Delicious, Honeycrisp, and/or Fuji apples.

continued

Heat a slow cooker to high.

Remove the apple stems and cut the apples, including the cores, into 1-inch-wide wedges. Put the apples in the slow cooker, add the vinegar and water, cover, and cook for 2½ to 3 hours, stirring every hour until the apples are soft enough to puree through a food mill.

Set a food mill fitted with a medium screen over a large bowl and puree the apples. (Discard what remains in the food mill.) Weigh or measure the puree. You should have about 4 pounds or 8 cups of puree. Use 1 cup of sugar for each pound or 2 cups of puree.

Stir in the remaining ingredients and return the apple puree to the slow cooker. Turn the heat to low, cover, and cook the apples for another 8 hours.

Remove the lid, stir the apple puree, and continue to cook uncovered for another 3 to 4 hours, stirring every 30 minutes, until the apple butter is thicker than applesauce but not as thick as a jam.

Spoon into jars or other storage containers, cover, and let cool, then refrigerate for up to 1 month. **MAKES ABOUT 6 CUPS**

tapenades *Here are three tapenades: a traditional olive tapenade, an artichoke tapenade, and an onion tapenade, all of which include capers, garlic, anchovy, and, of course, olives. In the end, a tapenade is about the olive—get good olives, and you can't make a bad tapenade.*

sweet onion tapenade

3 tablespoons canola oil
2 cups chopped red onions
1 salt-packed or oil-packed anchovy
¼ cup whole milk
1 cup (4 ounces) pitted Kalamata olives, rinsed and drained
1 teaspoon capers, rinsed and drained
1 medium garlic clove
¼ cup plus 2 tablespoons extra virgin olive oil

We like to leave this onion tapenade a little chunkier than the others. It's more mellow with the sweetness of slow-cooked red onions; and excellent with whitefish or with crudités, or as the basis for a vinaigrette.

Heat the canola oil in a large frying pan over medium heat. Add the onions, reduce the heat to medium-low, and cook slowly, adjusting the heat as necessary to keep the onions from coloring, for about 30 minutes, until very soft. Transfer to a Vita-Mix.

Meanwhile, soak the anchovy in the milk for 30 minutes. Drain and rinse under cold water.

Add the anchovy, olives, capers, garlic, and olive oil to the blender and blend, scraping down the sides as necessary, to a coarse puree.

Refrigerate in a covered container for up to 1 week.

MAKES ABOUT 1½ CUPS

artichoke tapenade

1 salt-packed or oil-packed anchovy
¼ cup whole milk
8 large or 16 small Braised Artichokes (page 221), drained, cooking liquid reserved, and cut into pieces
1 cup (4 ounces) pitted Niçoise or tournant olives, rinsed and drained
1 teaspoon capers, rinsed and drained
1 medium garlic clove
1 cup extra virgin olive oil

Soak the anchovy in the milk for 30 minutes. Drain and rinse under cold water.

Combine the artichokes, olives, anchovy, capers, and garlic in a Vita-Mix. With the machine running on low speed, slowly add in the olive oil and blend to a chunky puree (overprocessing it can darken and dull the color). The tapenade will have a slightly broken look.

Refrigerate in a covered container for up to 1 week. Just before serving, stir the tapenade quickly to emulsify. **MAKES ABOUT 2 CUPS**

olive tapenade

1 salt-packed or oil-packed anchovy
¼ cup whole milk
1½ cups (6 ounces) pitted Niçoise olives, rinsed and drained
1 teaspoon Dijon mustard
1 teaspoon minced capers, rinsed and drained
1 medium garlic clove
¼ cup extra virgin olive oil

Soak the anchovy in the milk for 30 minutes. Drain and rinse under cold water.

Combine the anchovy, olives, mustard, capers, garlic, and olive oil in a Vita-Mix. Begin blending on low and gradually increase the speed, blending until the mixture just comes together. Do not overprocess; the tapenade should still have some texture.

Refrigerate in a covered container for up to 1 week.

MAKES ABOUT 1¼ CUPS

mustards *Pureeing vegetables with some form of mustard and some seasoning is an easy way to turn them into an intriguing condiment. We've made mustards with artichokes, eggplant, and fennel, but any vegetable that makes a smooth, creamy puree can be transformed into a mustard. The artichoke mustard is excellent as a dip for fritto misto, and the eggplant-raisin mustard is an unusual condiment for simple light poultry dishes or Salt-Crusted Striped Bass (page 98). We serve the fennel mustard with pork tenderloin, but you could also use it with corned beef.*

artichoke mustard

8 large or 16 small Braised Artichokes (page 221), drained,
    cooking liquid reserved, and cut into pieces
½ teaspoon dry mustard
1 teaspooon champagne vinegar
1 teaspoon Dijon mustard, or to taste
Kosher salt

Combine the artichokes, 2 tablespoons of their cooking liquid, the dry mustard, vinegar, and Dijon mustard in a Vita-Mix and blend on medium speed for 30 seconds to 1 minute, until smooth; scrape down the sides as necessary. If the mustard seems too thick, add small amounts of water to thin. Do not overprocess the mustard, or the color could darken and become dull.

Press the mustard through a fine-mesh conical strainer if you would like a more refined mustard. Season with salt to taste and additional Dijon mustard if necessary. Refrigerate in a covered container for up to 1 week. **MAKES ABOUT ¾ CUP**

eggplant-raisin mustard

1 pound Japanese eggplants
Kosher salt
¼ cup golden raisins, plumped in warm water
2 teaspoons Dijon mustard
1 teaspoon whole-grain mustard

Set a cooling rack on a baking sheet.

Cut the eggplants lengthwise in half. Score the flesh ¼ inch deep in a crosshatch pattern. Sprinkle generously with salt and put cut side down on the rack. Let stand at room temperature for 30 minutes. The salt will pull out some of the moisture and reduce the bitter flavor of the mustard.

Preheat the oven to 425°F.

Pat the eggplants dry with paper towels. Clean the rack and baking sheet, return the eggplants to the rack, and bake until tender, about 15 minutes.

Scrape the flesh from the eggplants into a Vita-Mix. Discard the skins. Add the raisins and both mustards and blend until smooth, using the plunger and scraping down the sides as needed. Season to taste with salt. Refrigerate in a covered container for up to 1 week. **MAKES 1 CUP**

fennel mustard

3 pounds fennel (about 4 bulbs)
Canola oil
½ cup white wine vinegar
1 teaspoon dry mustard
1 tablespoon water, if needed
2 teaspoons whole-grain mustard

Cut away the stalks and fronds from the fennel and trim the bottoms. Remove the outer layers of each bulb (see photo, page 30), and reserve the small inner portion for another use. Coarsely chop the fennel into ½-inch pieces. You need 3 cups; if you don't have enough, use some of the center portions.

Toss the fennel with about 1 tablespoon canola oil to coat and spread in a large sauté pan that holds the fennel in a single layer. Cook over very low heat for 25 minutes, or until it has softened, but not browned; it should still have some bite left to it. Add the vinegar and cook over medium-low heat until the fennel is very tender, about 15 minutes longer. Remove from the heat.

Transfer the fennel to a Vita-Mix—if there is any liquid remaining in the pan, use a slotted spoon to remove the fennel, reserving the liquid. Add the dry mustard and blend on low speed for about 30 seconds. Add just enough of the reserved liquid or water to allow the fennel to spin and blend on medium speed to a puree, scraping down the sides of the blender as necessary. Once blended add the whole-grain mustard. Refrigerate in a covered container for up to 1 week. **MAKES ABOUT 1 CUP**

TAPENADE

ARTICHOKE TAPENADE

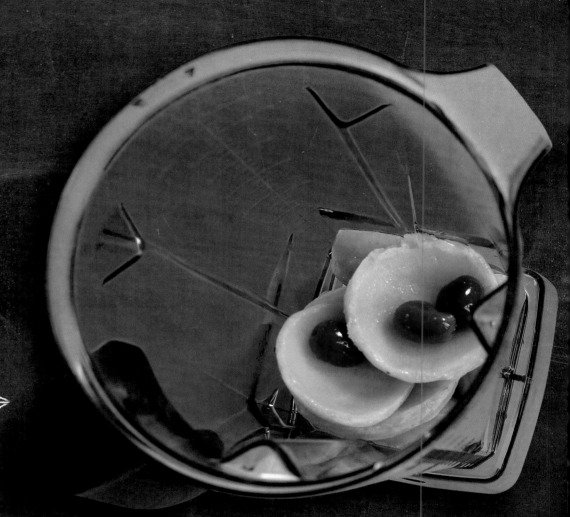

8 large braised artichokes →

1 anchovy →

¼ c. whole milk →

1 c. niçoise or tournant olives

1 c. olive oil

1 tsp. capers

1 medium garlic clove

quince paste

4 pounds quinces
About 8 cups water
1 vanilla bean, split
1 sachet made with 1 star anise, 2 whole cloves,
    and 1 cinnamon stick
About 4 cups granulated sugar
2 tablespoons fresh lemon juice
Canola oil

While you can't eat quince raw, when cooked it's like a cross between a pear and an apple—floral, perfumey, jammy in flavor and texture. When quinces come in from Jacobsen Farm, we use them to make this quince paste (*membrillo*). It's a great transformation of the fruit—to take something that's inedible in its raw state and cook it for hours and hours, until it is thick and deep burnt orange to red and delicious, is a satisfying process. I like to serve the paste with a tangy Spanish cheese such as Garrotxa or Manchego, or as a garnish for a main course.

Peel the quinces. Cut each one into quarters, and cut out and discard the stems and cores. Cut the quinces into ½-inch pieces.

Put the quinces in a large saucepan and add cold water to cover. Add the vanilla bean and sachet, and bring to a simmer. Cover and cook for 30 to 40 minutes, or until the quinces are pink and soft enough to puree.

Drain the quinces in a colander and discard the vanilla bean and sachet. Transfer the quinces to a Vita-Mix and puree.

Measure the quince puree, transfer to a large saucepan, and stir in an equal amount of sugar (by volume: you should have 4 cups of puree, so use 4 cups of sugar). Add the lemon juice. Bring to a simmer over medium heat, stirring to dissolve the sugar. Reduce the heat and simmer very gently, stirring occasionally, for 3 hours, or until the quince paste is very thick and a deep burnt orange to red. Remove from the heat.

Preheat the oven to the lowest temperature possible (approximately 125°F). Line an 8-inch square baking dish with parchment and oil the parchment.

Spoon the cooked quince paste into the baking dish and smooth the top. Put in the oven and let the paste dry for 1½ hours.

Remove the quince paste from the oven and cool to room temperature, then cover and refrigerate. The paste will become firm enough to be sliced. It can be refrigerated for up to 6 months.

MAKES ONE 8-INCH SQUARE

red-wine-poached prunes

2 cups dry red wine, such as Cabernet Sauvignon
2 star anise
1 cinnamon stick
¼ cup wildflower honey
1 pound prunes, with pits or without

Try these poached prunes with a charcuterie or cheese plate, or with duck. Or spoon over vanilla ice cream.

Combine the wine, star anise, cinnamon stick, and honey in a medium bowl. Stir in the prunes, cover, and refrigerate overnight.

Transfer the prune mixture to a saucepan, bring just to a simmer, and simmer for 15 minutes, stirring occasionally. Remove from the heat and let cool.

Transfer the prunes, with the liquid and spices, to a storage container. Cover and refrigerate for up to 2 weeks. Discard the star anise and cinnamon stick before serving. **MAKES ABOUT 3 CUPS**

pickled vegetables and fruits
With their sweet-sour flavors, pickled fruits and vegetables add vibrancy to many dishes, whether it's pickled red onions on a hamburger or curried champagne grapes with poultry or fish. The pickles help balance rich items, such as the Braised Oxtail and Mushroom Tartine (page 55) or the Crispy Fried Fish (page 100). They add a vivid visual component to any plate.

basic pickling liquid

1 cup champagne vinegar
½ cup granulated sugar
½ cup water

Our basic pickling liquid is 2 parts vinegar to 1 part sugar to 1 part water; it can be scaled up easily for larger quantities of vegetables.

Combine all the ingredients in a saucepan, and process with one of the following vegetables. **MAKES ABOUT 1¾ CUPS**

pickled garlic

¾ cup garlic cloves, peeled, very large cloves halved or quartered
½ recipe Basic Pickling Liquid

Put the garlic cloves in a small saucepan, cover with salted water, bring to a simmer, and simmer for 2 to 3 minutes. Drain and repeat; drain. Repeat again, simmering until the garlic is tender but is still slightly resistant to the tooth. Drain and transfer the garlic to a canning jar or other storage container.

Bring the pickling liquid to a boil, stirring to dissolve the sugar. Pour the pickling liquid over the garlic. Cool to room temperature, then cover and refrigerate for up to 1 month.

PHOTOGRAPH ON PAGE 256   MAKES ABOUT ¾ CUP

pickled carrots

10 medium carrots or 20 baby carrots, peeled
½ teaspoon Yellow Curry Powder (page 336) or Madras curry powder
¼ jalapeño, seeded
Basic Pickling Liquid

Cut medium carrots on the diagonal into 2-inch sections and then cut the sections lengthwise in half (or into quarters at the thicker end). Trim the green tops of baby carrots to about ¼ inch and cut the carrots lengthwise in half.

Put the curry powder in a medium saucepan and heat over medium heat, stirring constantly, for 1 to 1½ minutes or until fragrant. Be careful—the curry can burn easily.

Add the carrots, jalapeño, and pickling liquid to the curry, bring to a simmer, stirring from time to time to dissolve the sugar, and simmer for 2 minutes. Pour into a container and let the carrots cool in the liquid, then cover and refrigerate for up to 1 month.

PHOTOGRAPH ON PAGE 256   MAKES ABOUT 2 CUPS

pickled cauliflower

½ teaspoon piment d'Espelette (see page 208)
Basic Pickling Liquid
4 cups ¾-inch cauliflower florets (about the diameter of a quarter) from about 1½ pounds cauliflower

Add the Espelette to the pickling liquid and bring to a boil, stirring to dissolve the sugar. Remove from the heat and let cool to room temperature.

Bring a large pot of salted water to a boil. Add the cauliflower and blanch for 4 to 5 minutes, until crisp-tender; it should still be slightly resistant to the tooth. Drain and transfer the cauliflower to a canning jar or other storage container. Pour the pickling liquid over the top. Let cool to room temperature, then cover and refrigerate for up to 1 month.

PHOTOGRAPH ON PAGE 256

MAKES ABOUT 4 CUPS

pickled green beans

1 teaspoon black peppercorns
1 shallot, peeled and cut lengthwise into quarters
Basic Pickling Liquid
4 cups trimmed thin green beans (haricots verts)

Add the peppercorns and shallot to the pickling liquid and bring to a boil, stirring to dissolve the sugar. Pour into a bowl and let cool to room temperature, then chill in the refrigerator.

Bring a large pot of salted water to a boil (see page 147). Blanch the beans until crisp-tender. Drain and dry on paper towels.

Stand the beans in a canning jar or other storage container that holds them in a very tight fit and pour the cold pickling liquid over the top. Cover and refrigerate for up to 1 month.

PHOTOGRAPH ON PAGE 256   MAKES ABOUT 4 CUPS

pickled baby leeks

10 baby leeks
20 black peppercorns
Basic Pickling Liquid

Cut off the root ends of the leeks. Cut off the dark greens ¼ inch below the point where the leaves begin to separate. Rinse well.

Bring a large pot of salted water to a boil (see page 147).

Meanwhile, add the peppercorns to the pickling liquid and bring to a boil, stirring to dissolve the sugar. Pour into a bowl.

Tie the leeks in a bundle and blanch until just tender, about 2 minutes. Drain and add to the warm pickling liquid. Let cool in the liquid.

Transfer the leeks to a canning jar or other storage container and pour the pickling liquid over the top. Cover and refrigerate for up to 1 month.   MAKES 10 PICKLED LEEKS

CLOCKWISE FROM RIGHT: *Pickled Cauliflower (page 255), Pickled Red Onions (page 257), Pickled Watermelon Rind (page 257) with cinnamon stick,*

Pickled Green Beans (page 255), Pickled Garlic (page 255), and Pickled Carrots (page 255).

pickled radishes

½ recipe Basic Pickling Liquid (use red wine vinegar if pickling watermelon radishes)
1 cup icicle radishes, trimmed and thinly sliced on a diagonal; watermelon radishes, trimmed, halved lengthwise, and cut into thin half circles; or red radishes, trimmed and thinly sliced

Bring the pickling liquid to a boil, stirring to dissolve the sugar. Remove from the heat and let cool to room temperature, then chill in the refrigerator.

Put the radishes in a canning jar or other storage container and pour the pickling liquid over them. Let stand for 20 to 30 minutes, then cover and refrigerate for up to 1 month. **MAKES ABOUT ¾ CUP**

pickled red onions

2 large red onions (about 1¼ pounds each)
1½ cups red wine vinegar
¾ cup granulated sugar

Cut off the top and bottom of each onion and cut lengthwise in half. Remove and discard the outer layer. Cut a V-shaped wedge from the bottom of each half to remove the roots and the very center pieces of onion. Put the onions cut side down on a cutting board and slice lengthwise into ⅛-inch-thick slices, following the natural lines on the outside of the onion; cutting with the lines, or grain, rather than across them will help the onions soften more quickly in the pickling liquid. Pack the onions into a 1-quart canning jar; reserve any slices that don't fit.

Combine the vinegar and sugar in a small saucepan and bring to a boil, stirring to dissolve the sugar. Pour the hot vinegar mixture over the onions. Once the onions begin to wilt, you can add any remaining onion slices to the jar, gently pushing them down into the liquid to submerge them. Let cool to room temperature, then cover and refrigerate for at least 24 hours, or for up to 1 month.

PHOTOGRAPH ON PAGE 256   **MAKES ABOUT 4 CUPS**

pickled watermelon rind

½ small watermelon (not a baby watermelon)
4 cups water
¼ cup kosher salt
1 cup apple cider vinegar
2 cups granulated sugar
2 cinnamon sticks
⅛ teaspoon yellow mustard seeds

Put the watermelon cut side down on the cutting board. Cutting from the top center toward the bottom, cut away and discard the thin dark green skin, leaving behind the pale green rind. Cutting in the same way, cut off the rind in strips about 1½ inches wide, following the shape of the watermelon (reserve the flesh for another use). Trim any uneven edges from the strips of rind, and cut into pieces about 1-inch square. You need about 1½ cups of rind.

Pour the water into a storage container and add the salt, stirring to dissolve. Add the rind and refrigerate for at least 12 hours, or up to 24 hours.

Combine the vinegar, sugar, cinnamon, and mustard seeds in a small saucepan and bring to a boil, stirring to dissolve the sugar. Transfer to a canning jar or other storage container and let stand for 15 minutes.

Meanwhile, drain the rind, transfer to a medium saucepan, and cover with cold water. Bring to a boil over medium-high heat and boil for about 1 minute; the pieces should be tender but still have some crunch.

Drain the watermelon, add to the vinegar mixture, and let cool to room temperature, then cover and refrigerate for up to 1 month.

PHOTOGRAPH ON PAGE 256   **MAKES 1½ CUPS**

marinated cucumbers

6 small cucumbers (5 to 6 ounces each) or 2 pounds medium cucumbers
¾ cup champagne vinegar
1½ cups extra virgin olive oil
½ teaspoon red pepper flakes
2 teaspoons granulated sugar
Kosher salt and freshly ground black pepper

Cut off the ends of the cucumbers and peel them. Seed the cucumbers if desired: cut the cucumbers lengthwise in half and use a small spoon to scrape out the seeds. Cut the cucumbers into half rounds, or into rounds (if you didn't seed them), batons, wedges, or any shape you like.

Combine the vinegar, oil, red pepper, and sugar in a small bowl, stirring to dissolve the sugar. Season to taste with salt and pepper. Put the cucumbers in a canning jar or other storage container and pour the liquid over the top. Refrigerate for at least 1 day, or for up to 2 weeks.

Before serving, remove any solidified oil from the top of the liquid and discard. Serve cold. **MAKES ABOUT 3 CUPS**

wine-steeped golden raisins

¾ cup golden raisins
¼ star anise
1 whole clove
½ cup dry white wine, such as Sauvignon Blanc

Combine the raisins, star anise, and clove in a jar.

Bring the wine to a boil in a small saucepan. Pour over the raisins and let cool to room temperature. Let stand for 30 minutes, or cover and refrigerate for up to 1 month. Remove the star anise and clove before serving.   **MAKES ABOUT ¾ CUP**

champagne grapes
with yellow curry

3 tablespoons Yellow Curry Powder (page 336) or Madras curry powder
1 lemon
1 pound champagne grape clusters, rinsed
1½ cups dry white wine, such as Sauvignon Blanc
1½ cups water
3 tablespoons granulated sugar

Preheat the oven to 275°F.

Spread the curry powder on a small ovenproof tray and place in the oven to toast for 15 minutes, or until it is fragrant and the color has deepened from the oil in the spices—be careful, the curry can burn easily.

Using a vegetable peeler, peel off the lemon zest in long strips. If any white pith remains on the zest, use a paring knife to scrape it away.

Put the grape clusters in a canning jar or other storage container, interspersing the lemon zest strips with the grapes.

Place the wine, water, sugar, and curry powder in a medium saucepan and bring to a boil, stirring to dissolve the sugar, then lower the heat and simmer for 2 minutes.

Strain the liquid through a fine-mesh conical strainer and pour the hot liquid over the grapes. Cool, then cover and refrigerate for at least 1 day, or for up to 1 week.

Before serving, shake the container to mix in the curry powder that has settled on the bottom.

PHOTOGRAPH ON PAGE 259   **MAKES ABOUT 6 CUPS**

green grapes
with green curry

GREEN CURRY
One 3½-inch piece lemongrass stalk, coarsely chopped
1 tablespoon coarsely chopped peeled galangal
    (see Sources, page 346) or ginger
3 tablespoons fish sauce
1 teaspoon granulated sugar
1 small serrano chile, seeded and coarsely chopped
3 garlic cloves, coarsely chopped
3 fresh kaffir lime leaves (see Sources, page 346)
1 cup small cilantro sprigs
2 teaspoons dark soy sauce
⅓ cup unsweetened coconut milk
1 tablespoon coriander seeds
½ cup water

3 cups seedless green grapes (see Note)
1 lime

These beautiful curried grapes have the big flavors of galangal, a pungent relative of ginger, and kaffir lime leaves, both of which are available in Asian markets and through mail-order sources.

Combine all of the ingredients for the curry except the water in a Vita-Mix and blend to a coarse puree. Add the water and blend until smooth. Strain through a fine-mesh basket strainer into a small bowl. You need ¾ cup curry for this recipe.

Process 1 cup of the grapes through a juicer. Stir into the green curry.

Peel the remaining 2 cups grapes and put in a medium bowl. Toss with enough curry to coat. Using a vegetable peeler, peel off 3 strips of lime zest in long strips. If any white pith remains on the zest, use a paring knife to scrape it away.

Using a slotted spoon, transfer the grapes to a canning jar, interspersing the strips of lime zest with the grapes. Pour in enough of the curry mixture to fill the jar, cover, and refrigerate for 24 hours, or for up to 1 week.

PHOTOGRAPH ON PAGE 259   **MAKES ABOUT 3 CUPS**

NOTE *If you don't have a juicer, you can substitute 1 cup white grape juice for 1 cup of the grapes.*

LEFT: *Champagne Grapes with Yellow Curry (opposite).* **RIGHT:** *Green Grapes with Green Curry (opposite).*

mushroom conserva

2 pounds assorted wild mushrooms such as small shiitakes, morels, chanterelles, porcini, hen-of-the-woods, trumpet, and/or oyster mushrooms
2 cups extra virgin olive oil
2 bay leaves
4 thyme sprigs
One 6-inch rosemary sprig
1 teaspoon piment d'Espelette (see page 208)
3 tablespoons sherry vinegar
Kosher salt and freshly ground black pepper

Dave Cruz learned this technique for preserving mushrooms from a chef in the Basque region of Spain, and it's so tasty and versatile that you'll find many uses for it. The method is simple—mushrooms are steeped in medium-hot aromatic oil for 5 minutes and then seasoned with vinegar and salt. Mushrooms prepared this way are both earthy and acidic, excellent served hot with meats (the Santa Maria–Style Tri-Tip [page 54], for example), or as a base for fish. They are also good cold, as a condiment, as a component of a salad (Mushroom and Leek Salad with Oven-Roasted Tomatoes and Radishes [page 160], or even as the main component, garnished with shaved radishes and similarly preserved tomatoes). Use a variety of mushrooms for textural and taste contrast—oyster, hen-of-the-woods, trumpet, shiitake, chanterelle, porcini, and morels. Strain and save the oil when you're finished with the mushrooms to use in vinaigrettes or as a flavored oil.

Just before cooking, rinse the mushrooms to remove any dirt. Remove the shiitake stems and any other stems that are tough and discard, or reserve for another use (such as vegetable stock). Trim the ends of the other stems, as well as any bruised areas. Leave small mushrooms whole. Cut larger mushrooms into pieces or into slices; or slice mushrooms with meaty stems, such as porcini or trumpet mushrooms, lengthwise in half, then use the tip of a paring knife to score the inside of the stem in a crosshatch pattern. The pieces of mushroom will shrink as they cook, but the finished pieces should not be larger than one bite. You should have about 10 cups of trimmed mushrooms.

Combine the olive oil, bay leaves, thyme sprigs, rosemary, and Espelette in a large wide pot, put a deep-frying thermometer in the pot, and heat over medium to medium-high heat until the oil reaches 170°F (it may be necessary to tilt the pot and pool the oil to get a correct reading on the thermometer). Add the mushrooms to the pot and gently turn them in the oil. When the oil reaches 170°F again, adjust the heat as necessary to maintain the temperature and cook for 5 minutes, gently turning the mushrooms from time to time. The mushrooms will not initially be submerged in the oil, but they will wilt as they steep.

Remove from the heat, stir in the vinegar and salt and pepper to taste, and let the mushrooms steep in the oil for 45 minutes.

Transfer the mushrooms, oil, and herbs to a covered storage container; the mushrooms should be covered by the oil. The mushrooms will keep for up to 1 month in the refrigerator. Serve hot or at room temperature.

PHOTOGRAPH ON PAGE 237   MAKES ABOUT 3 CUPS

The first step in preparing a tomato for peeling is to cut out the stem and cut an X in the bottom of the tomato. Rather than making a small X, we extend the X so that the cuts run down the sides of the tomato. Then the tomatoes are blanched in boiling water just until the skin starts to pull away. The long X allows the skin to come away from the fruit much more readily.

oven-roasted tomatoes

12 plum tomatoes
½ cup extra virgin olive oil
3 thyme sprigs
Kosher salt and freshly ground black pepper

Roasting tomatoes slowly cooks out the moisture and intensifies their flavor. The tomatoes bring a sweet, tangy flavor to meat, fish, and vegetables. Put them in sandwiches, or finely chop them and use them to flavor vinaigrettes. Pencil asparagus are great with a roasted tomato vinaigrette, and so is fresh mozzarella. They're so versatile you can use them as garnish for a rich meat, such as lamb, or in a salad.

Preheat the oven to 200°F. Line a baking sheet with aluminum foil.

To peel the tomatoes, bring a large pot of water to a boil. Prepare an ice bath. With a paring knife, cut out the core of each tomato. Score an X on the bottom of each tomato, extending the cuts about two-thirds of the way up the tomato.

Drop the tomatoes into the water and simmer just until the skins are starting to pull away from the tomato. This may take only a few seconds, depending on the ripeness of the tomato. With a skimmer or slotted spoon, immediately transfer the tomatoes to the ice bath. Remove them as soon as they are cold and peel them.

Cut the tomatoes lengthwise in half and place cut side up on the lined baking sheet. Drizzle a little olive oil over each one, letting it run into any crevices. Scatter the thyme sprigs over the top and season with salt and pepper.

Put in the oven and cook for 5 to 6 hours, until the tomatoes have shrunk but are still moist. Let cool on the baking sheet.

Transfer the tomatoes to a storage container and pour any oil from the pan over them. The tomatoes can be refrigerated for up to a week.

MAKES 24 TOMATO HALVES

preserved lemons *Here are two kinds of preserved lemons: one uses salt and aromatics to confit whole lemons, and the other uses a combination of salt and sugar to cure slices of lemon. Unlike the preserved lemons, from which we take only the peel, the cured lemons are sliced before being cured and then we use whole slices, which have a sweetness from the absorbed sugar.*

Both preparations can be used instead of lemon rind in many dishes. If oil is appropriate in a dish, the peel of the preserved lemon lends an interesting note. We use it in marinades, mixed with salt as a rub on lamb or chicken before roasting, or in a compound butter that melts over hot meat, fish, or vegetables. The cured lemons can be added to vanilla ice cream for a salty lemon ice cream. We use them when sautéing bass or skate and as a garnish to Brined Pork Tenderloin (page 64), where they caramelize in the hot oil, adding a whole new layer of flavor to the dish.

preserved whole lemons

1½ cups kosher salt
6 lemons (3 to 4 ounces each), scrubbed
1 teaspoon black peppercorns
3 bay leaves
Juice of 2 lemons, or as needed
½ cup extra virgin olive oil

Pour ½ inch of salt into a 1-pint canning jar.

Cut each lemon lengthwise into quarters, stopping about ⅜ inch from the stem end so that the lemon wedges stay attached. Spread the lemons open. Salt the inside of 1 lemon generously, then push the wedges together to "close" the lemon and place it in the jar, pressing it down slightly. Repeat with another lemon, and add ⅓ teaspoon peppercorns, 1 bay leaf, and one-third of the remaining salt. Repeat with 2 more lemons. Add ⅓ teaspoon peppercorns, 1 bay leaf, and half of the remaining salt. Repeat with the last 2 lemons and the remaining ⅓ teaspoon peppercorns, bay leaf, and salt.

The lemons will have released some juice. Add enough additional juice to cover the lemons, pressing down slightly on them to compress them. Top with the olive oil and cover the jar.

Put the jar in a pantry or other cool, dark spot and let stand for at least 1 month, or for up to 6 months. Refrigerate the jar after opening, and use the lemons within 1 month.

PHOTOGRAPH ON PAGE 264   MAKES 6 LEMONS

cured lemons

8 lemons (3 to 4 ounces each), scrubbed
1¾ cups plus 1 tablespoon granulated sugar
1½ cups plus 2 tablespoons kosher salt

Cut ½ inch from one end of a lemon, leaving you with the nicest, widest portion, and slice the lemon into ⅛-inch rounds, removing the seeds as you go and stopping ½ inch from the other end. Repeat with the remaining lemons.

Combine the sugar and salt in a large bowl.

Sprinkle just under ½ inch of the sugar mixture in the bottom of a storage container that is about 6 inches square. Arrange a row of slightly overlapping lemon slices on top, and top with a layer of the sugar mixture that just covers the lemon slices completely. As you layer the lemons, the goal is to have enough of the sugar and salt mixture evenly distributed on the slices so that when it dissolves, all of the lemon slices will be covered with the liquid. (It is better to use too much sugar and salt than too little, because any exposed areas of lemon can mold.) Continue the process, alternating the lemon slices and sugar mixture, and ending with a layer of the sugar mixture on top.

Put the lid on the container and wrap the container tightly in plastic wrap. Refrigerate for at least 2 weeks, or for up to 1 month.

PHOTOGRAPH ON PAGE 264   MAKES ABOUT 125 SLICES

soffritto

3 cups finely diced Spanish onions (about 1 pound)
1 cup extra virgin olive oil
Kosher salt
1 pound plum tomatoes (about 6)
½ teaspoon minced garlic

Soffritto is an onion-tomato mixture that's cooked low and slow and is used to add depth of flavor and intense savory sweetness to numerous dishes, including soups and stews. It can also be used as a condiment or sauce. It's an ingredient in the Catalan Beef Stew (page 46) and the Peperonata Rustica (page 208), but it's also great tossed with pasta or with scrambled eggs. Soffritto is a common technique in Spanish and Italian traditions, and it is found in various forms throughout the Mediterranean.

Combine the onions, oil, and a pinch of salt in an 8- to 9-inch-wide saucepan and set over medium heat. As soon as the oil starts to simmer, reduce the heat to low and set the saucepan on a diffuser (such as a Flame-Tamer) to maintain an even low heat. The onions should stew

LEFT: *Preserved Whole Lemons (page 263).* **RIGHT:** *Cured Lemons (page 263).*

slowly but eventually caramelize; adjust the heat as necessary so that the oil continues to bubble gently. As the onions release their liquid, the oil will become cloudy, but once the moisture has evaporated, the oil will clear. Cook for about 2½ hours, or until the onions are a rich golden brown (a shade darker than a golden raisin) and the oil is perfectly clear. Check the pan often; if any of the onions have caramelized against the sides of the pan, scrape them back into the oil.

Meanwhile, for a quick tomato puree, cut the tomatoes lengthwise in half. Gently squeeze out the seeds and discard. Hold the cut side of each half against the large holes of a box grater and grate the tomato flesh; discard the skin. You will have about 1 cup of tomato puree.

Add the tomatoes to the caramelized onions and cook for 2 to 2½ hours longer, or until the onions and tomatoes begin to fry in the oil: the mixture will sizzle and small bubbles will cover the entire surface. Gently stir the mixture—the tomatoes and onions will separate from the clear oil. Turn off the heat, add another pinch of salt and the garlic, and let the soffritto cool in the pan.

The soffritto will keep covered in the refrigerator for up to 1 week. Drain it before using. The oil can be used to start another soffritto.

MAKES 1 CUP

oils *When the summer garden provides an abundance of chives and basil, infusing them into oils is a wonderful way to take advantage of the bounty. Basil and olive oil are of course a lovely pairing, but the chive oil uses canola oil and so has a very pure, clean flavor. You can use these oils as we do in our recipes but they are delicious simply drizzled on, say, a sautéed fillet of fish.*

chive oil

1 cup ½-inch pieces chives
1 cup canola oil

Put the chives in a fine-mesh basket strainer and run under hot tap water to soften them and remove any chlorophyll taste. Drain them and squeeze as dry as possible.

Put half the chives in a Vita-Mix, add oil just to cover, and blend for 2 minutes. Add half the remaining chives and oil to cover and blend for another 2 minutes. Add the remaining chives and oil and blend for 2 minutes. Pour into a container and refrigerate for 24 hours.

Place a piece of cheesecloth over a bowl and secure with a rubber band to make a smooth, tight surface. Pour the chive oil onto the cheesecloth and let sit for an hour to allow the oil to drip through.

Remove and discard the cheesecloth; do not wring out the cheesecloth, or it may cloud the oil. Refrigerate the oil in a covered container for 2 days, or freeze for up to 1 month.   **MAKES ABOUT ⅓ CUP**

basil oil

3 packed cups basil leaves
¾ cup olive oil

Bring a large pot of salted water to a boil (see page 147). Prepare an ice bath. Put the basil in the water for about 15 seconds, keeping the water at a strong boil, then drain and immediately plunge the blanched basil into the ice water. Once it is cold, drain the basil and squeeze as dry as possible. Use scissors to cut the leaves into small pieces (chopping basil can cause it to oxidize and darken).

Put half the basil in a Vita-Mix, add oil just to cover, and blend for 2 minutes. Add half the remaining basil and oil to cover and blend for another 2 minutes. Add the remaining basil and oil and blend for 2 minutes. Pour into a container and refrigerate for 24 hours.

Place a piece of cheesecloth over a bowl and secure with a rubber band to make a smooth, tight surface. Pour the basil oil onto the cheesecloth and let sit for an hour to allow the oil to drip through.

Remove and discard the cheesecloth; do not wring out the cheesecloth, or it may cloud the oil. Refrigerate the oil in a covered container for 2 days, or freeze for up to 1 month.   **MAKES ABOUT ⅓ CUP**

garlic *Garlic confit, garlic slow-cooked in oil until meltingly tender, has a mild, subtle, sweet flavor and a rich texture, wholly different from what we tend to think of when we hear the word garlic. And it's a preparation that gives us several products: the confited garlic cloves can be pureed and stirred into soups, sauces, butter, vinaigrettes, and legumes and grains, and to marinades.*

They can be lightly mashed into boiled new potatoes or added to boiled russets when you pass them through a ricer or food mill for garlic mashed potatoes. Sometimes we don't bother to peel them but just make a slit down their flat side, then confit them and serve them whole in the skins as a garnish—they're fun to pop out of the skin and eat whole.

Garlic confit is a great staple that will keep in your refrigerator for up to a week.

The oil that the garlic is confited in can be used in vinaigrettes or for aioli. Brush the oil on toasted baguette slices, or spread the mashed cloves on toast.

garlic confit and oil

1 cup peeled garlic cloves
About 2 cups canola oil

Cut off and discard the root ends of the garlic cloves. Put the cloves in a small saucepan and add enough oil to cover them by about 1 inch—none of the garlic cloves should be poking through the oil.

Set the saucepan on a diffuser over medium-low heat. The garlic should cook gently: very small bubbles will come up through the oil, but the bubbles should not break the surface; adjust the heat as necessary and/or move the pan to one side of the diffuser if it is cooking too quickly. Cook the garlic for about 40 minutes, stirring every 5 minutes or so, until the cloves are completely tender when pierced with the tip of a knife. Remove the saucepan from the heat and allow the garlic to cool in the oil.

Refrigerate the garlic in a covered container, submerged in the oil, for up to 1 week.   **MAKES 1 CUP**

garlic puree

¼ cup Garlic Confit cloves

Put the garlic in a small food processor and blend, scraping down the sides often, to puree. For a finer texture, press through a small fine-mesh basket strainer.   **MAKES 3 TABLESPOONS**

garlic chips

Garlic cloves
Whole milk, cold
Canola oil for deep-frying

Garlic chips are crisp, something you don't normally associate with garlic. Blanching the garlic cloves in milk before frying them leaches out some of the pungency and makes them sweeter.

Slice the garlic cloves as thin as possible on a Japanese mandoline or other vegetable slicer.

Put the slices in a small saucepan, cover with the milk, and bring to a boil. Drain the garlic slices in a fine-mesh basket strainer (discard the milk) and rinse under cold water. Return the slices to the pan and repeat the process 3 times, using fresh milk. Pat the garlic slices dry on paper towels.

Heat 2 inches of oil to 300°F in a deep saucepan. Add the garlic in batches, without crowding, and fry for 12 to 15 minutes, or until the bubbles around the chips have subsided (signifying that all the moisture has evaporated) and the chips are a light golden brown. Transfer the garlic chips to paper towels to drain.

Store in an airtight container at room temperature for 1 to 2 days.

BREADS, CRACKERS, CHEESE

We pick up breads and crackers at the store almost without thinking, and yet the pleasures and fantastic tastes you can achieve by making them yourself are enormous. You'll be amazed by the soup crackers. They're so easy and good; to serve a soup along with crackers you made yourself is a really special experience.

And the torn croutons, slowly cooked in garlic oil until they're very crisp, are more addictive than salted nuts. I'd rather you didn't serve croutons at all than use store-bought ones. Biscuits too—you can't buy biscuits of the same quality as homemade ones. Also, there's an emotional connection to buttery homemade biscuits that's important. Next time you need a flatbread or crackers, I hope you'll consider making these simple, satisfying recipes rather than buying lesser versions at the store.

Crunchy bread with cheese is a natural, so we decided to talk about our favorite cheeses in this chapter, and close the chapter with a recipe for the perfect marriage of bread and cheese: a grilled cheese sandwich made with homemade brioche. We love the photograph of the groaning board of cheeses on pages 290–91 and hope it will make identifying and recognizing cheeses easier.

Lastly, the fresh cow's and goat cheeses with their creamy texture and refreshing taste find their way into desserts. You'll find them in the recipes for Peaches and Cream (page 297) and Cheesecake (page 313). And always simple and very satisfying is a portion of fresh cheese with fruit and a drizzle of honey at the end of a meal.

OVERLEAF: *Flatbread (page 280).* **OPPOSITE:** *Tangerine-Kumquat Marmalade (page 249) served with baguette toasts and Inverness, a soft young cow's-milk cheese.*

brioche

⅓ cup very warm water (110° to 115°F)

One ¼-ounce package (2¼ teaspoons) active dry yeast (not quick-rising)

2⅓ cups cake flour

2 cups all-purpose flour

⅓ cup granulated sugar

2½ teaspoons fleur de sel or fine sea salt

6 large eggs, at room temperature

2½ sticks (10 ounces) unsalted butter, cut into 1-inch cubes,
   at room temperature

I've put this recipe in all our books as a tribute to the late Jean-Louis Palladin, my friend and colleague, because his brioche is so good, and so versatile. If you haven't ever made brioche, you should—it's a cross between bread and cake, a yeast bread loaded with eggs and butter. It's delicious and has many uses in both savory and sweet courses. We cut it up and crisp it for croutons and use it as the toast for grilled cheese.

The dough must rest overnight in the refrigerator, so start at least a day before you need it. Brioche freezes well, so that's an option when making it in advance.

Combine the water and yeast in a small bowl. Let stand for 10 minutes, then stir until the yeast is completely dissolved. Set aside.

Sift together the flours, sugar, and salt into the bowl of a stand mixer fitted with the dough hook. Add the eggs and beat for 1 minute at low speed, scraping down the sides with a rubber spatula as needed. Slowly add the dissolved yeast and continue beating at low speed for 5 minutes. Stop the machine, scrape any dough off the dough hook, and beat for another 5 minutes.

Add the butter cubes, about one-quarter of them at a time, beating for about 1 minute after each addition. Once all the butter has been added, beat for 10 minutes more, until the dough is smooth and silky.

Transfer the dough to a large floured bowl and cover with plastic wrap. Let stand in a warm place until doubled in size, about 3 hours.

Turn the dough out onto a generously floured work surface and gently work out the air bubbles by folding the dough over several times while lightly pressing down on it. Return the dough to the bowl, cover with plastic wrap, and refrigerate overnight.

Generously butter two 8½-by-4½-by-3-inch loaf pans or one 15¾-by-4½-by-3¾-inch Pullman loaf pan (see Sources, page 346). Turn the dough out onto a floured work surface. With floured hands, divide the dough in half, shape it into 2 rectangles that fit into the loaf pans, and put the dough in the pans. Or shape it into 1 loaf and put it in the Pullman pan (if using a Pullman pan, cover with the lid once the dough reaches ½ inch from the top). Let the dough rise, uncovered, in a warm place until it is about ½ inch above the top of the pans, about 3 hours.

Preheat the oven to 350°F.

Bake the brioche until it is well browned on top and sounds hollow when tapped on the bottom, 35 to 40 minutes for 2 loaves, 45 to 50 minutes for a Pullman loaf. Remove from the oven and immediately turn the brioche out onto a cooling rack.

If serving immediately, let the bread cool for 10 minutes, then slice. If serving within a few hours or up to 2 days, promptly wrap the hot bread in aluminum foil and set aside at room temperature until ready to use. To freeze, wrap the hot bread in foil and promptly freeze. The bread can be frozen for up to 2 months; when ready to use, reheat (without thawing, and still wrapped in the foil) in a 250°F oven until heated through, 20 to 25 minutes.

If using the brioche for croutons or bread pudding, let sit at room temperature, uncovered, to dry for a day.

MAKES 2 STANDARD LOAVES OR 1 PULLMAN LOAF

brioche croutons

2 cups ¼- to ½-inch crustless cubes Brioche (opposite)

These brioche croutons are best served warm, but they can be made ahead and rewarmed before serving.

Preheat the oven to 350°F. Line a baking sheet with parchment paper.

Spread the brioche cubes in a single layer on the parchment-lined pan. Toast in the oven for 5 minutes. Turn the croutons and toast for another 5 minutes, or until a rich golden brown. The croutons can be cooled and then stored in an airtight container for up to a week; rewarm them in a low oven before serving.   **MAKES ABOUT 1¾ CUPS**

dried bread crumbs

1 loaf country bread

While we often use panko, the very hard Japanese bread crumbs (because they result in a crispy coating), we also use bread crumbs we dry ourselves. It's always better to make your own bread crumbs because they're very easy to make and taste so much better than store-bought bread crumbs.

Preheat the oven to 250°F.

Cut away the crusts from the bread. Tear the bread into small pieces or pulse to coarse crumbs in a food processor. Spread the crumbs on a baking sheet and toast in the oven for 30 minutes. Toss the crumbs to redistribute, and toast for about another 30 minutes, or until the crumbs are completely dried out (they should not have changed color).

If you want a finer texture, the crumbs can be processed in the food processor again. Store in an airtight container for up to 1 month.

I've found that a lot of people are afraid to touch food, and this always takes me aback, because our hands are our most important tool. Touching food is good. It brings you closer to the food itself and gives you results impossible to achieve when you're using long metal utensils. The closer you are to the food, the more control you have. Learn to handle food in your hands—don't be afraid of it, and don't be afraid you're going to get burned laying a fillet into hot oil. When you have better control of the food, you can work closer to the heat.

torn croutons

1 loaf country bread

Garlic Oil from Garlic Confit (page 266; see Note)

2 tablespoons (1 ounce) unsalted butter

Cooking the torn pieces of bread very, very slowly is the key to these garlicky croutons. When toasted over high heat, croutons become a little dry; these absorb the oil and butter through the slow cooking, and the result is croutons that are very crunchy but bursting with the flavor of the oil when you bite into them. We serve these in many salads.

Cut the crusts off the loaf of bread. Tear the bread into irregular pieces no larger than 2 inches. You need about 3 cups of croutons; reserve any remaining bread for another use.

Pour ⅛ inch of the garlic oil into a large sauté pan and heat over medium heat until hot. Spread the bread in a single layer in the pan (if your pan is not large enough, these can be cooked in two smaller pans). Add the butter. The oil and butter should be bubbling, but if you hear sizzling, the heat is too high. Adjust the heat as necessary, and stir the croutons often as they cook. Cook until the croutons are crisp and a beautiful rich golden brown on all sides, 15 to 20 minutes. Move the croutons to one side of the pan and keep warm until ready to serve. (Do not drain on paper towels; you want the flavors of the oil intermingled with the other ingredients as you eat the croutons in a salad.) Torn croutons should be used the day they are made; you can reheat them in a low oven before serving if necessary.   MAKES 3 CUPS

NOTE *If you don't have any garlic oil on hand, pour ⅛ inch of canola oil into a sauté pan, add 5 crushed, peeled garlic cloves, and heat over low heat until the garlic cloves are golden brown, flipping the cloves from time to time. Remove the garlic cloves and use the oil for the croutons.*

buttermilk biscuits

2 cups cake flour

2 cups all-purpose flour

1 tablespoon plus 1 teaspoon kosher salt

1 tablespoon baking powder

1 teaspoon baking soda

½ pound (2 sticks) unsalted butter, cut into ½-inch cubes and chilled

1½ cups buttermilk, plus 1 to 2 tablespoons for brushing

2 to 3 tablespoons (1 to 1½ ounces) unsalted butter, melted

These biscuits bake up light and fluffy. It's important not to overwork the dough, which would make the biscuits tough. To that end, we pulse the butter and dry ingredients together in a food processor, then turn them out into a bowl and gradually work in the liquids by hand. You can serve them with some good butter and raspberry jam, and perhaps a sprinkle of fleur de sel, but they're so good you might want to eat them as is, straight out of the oven. We serve these with fried chicken, but they make a good brunch accompaniment and also work as a strawberry shortcake biscuit for dessert (see page 2).

Preheat the oven to 425°F. Line a baking sheet with parchment paper.

Combine the flours, salt, baking powder, and baking soda in the bowl of a food processor and pulse a few times to blend. Add the chilled butter and pulse several times, until the pieces of butter are no bigger than small peas. Do not overprocess; the dough should not come together.

Transfer the dough to a large bowl and make a well in the center of the flour mixture. Pour in the buttermilk. Stir and lift the mixture with a sturdy spoon, gently working the flour into the buttermilk. The dough should begin to come together but not form a solid mass, or the biscuits may be tough.

Dust a work surface with flour and turn out the dough. Pat the dough into a ¾-inch-thick rectangle. Using a 2½-inch round cutter, cut out the biscuits. (If the cutter sticks to the dough, dip the cutter in flour before cutting.) Place the biscuits on the baking sheet. The dough trimmings can be gently pushed together, patted out, and cut one more time; do not overwork the dough.

Brush the tops of the biscuits lightly with buttermilk. Bake for 15 to 18 minutes, rotating the pan halfway through baking, until a rich golden brown. As soon as you remove the biscuits from the oven, brush the tops with melted butter. Serve warm. **MAKES 12 BISCUITS**

soup crackers

¼ cup warm water (110° to 115°F)

¾ teaspoon active dry yeast (not quick-rising)

¾ cup plus 2 tablespoons all-purpose flour, plus more for dusting

1 teaspoon kosher salt

2 tablespoons plus 2 teaspoons unsalted butter (1⅔ ounces),
   at room temperature

Ground fine fleur de sel or fine sea salt

This recipe comes from Matthew McDonald, head baker at Bouchon Bakery. The simple buttery yeast dough is rested for only 10 minutes, then rolled out as thin as possible, cut into crackers, and seasoned with ground fleur de sel before baking. These are a must-have with the Clam Chowder with Bacon (page 126).

Position the oven racks in the lower and upper thirds of the oven and preheat the oven to 350°F. Line two baking sheets with parchment paper or Silpats.

Combine the water and yeast in a small bowl. Let stand for 10 minutes, then stir until the yeast is completely dissolved. Combine the flour and salt in a medium bowl. Using a fork or your hands add the butter and yeast mixture and mix until the dough comes together.

Transfer the dough to a lightly floured work surface and knead until completely smooth, about 10 minutes. Shape the dough into a ball, put on a board, cover with a towel, and let rest for 10 minutes.

Lightly dust the work surface. Cut the dough in half. Put 1 piece of the dough on the surface and dust it lightly with flour. Using a floured rolling pin, roll out the dough to just over ⅛ inch thick. Transfer the dough to one of the baking sheets. Repeat with the second piece of dough.

Put about ¼ inch of flour in a small bowl. Dip a fluted round ¾-inch cutter in the flour and then cut out the crackers, reflouring the cutter each time. (Or cut smaller or larger, as you like.) Once all the crackers are cut, lift the excess dough off the pans. (Any trimmings can be pushed together and rerolled once.)

Using a pin or a cake tester, prick the top of each cracker in 3 to 5 spots. Sprinkle the crackers with fleur de sel. Bake for about 10 minutes, until the crackers are crisp and golden brown. Let cool on the pans on a cooling rack. Store in an airtight container for up to 2 weeks.

MAKES ABOUT 200 CRACKERS

garlic toast

½ cup extra virgin olive oil or Garlic Oil from Garlic Confit (page 266)

Three 1-inch-thick slices large country bread

1 large garlic clove, peeled

Nothing fancy here—nice crusty slices of bread, brushed with olive oil or garlic oil, toasted in a frying pan, and then rubbed with a raw garlic clove. As with the Torn Croutons (page 274), you get a burst of flavorful oil with each bite. We typically serve garlic toast with cheese or soup.

Pour the oil onto a rimmed plate or into a baking dish. Put the bread in the oil and turn until the slices are evenly moistened and all of the oil is absorbed.

Heat a large frying pan over medium heat. Add the bread in a single layer and cook for about 3 minutes, until the toasts are golden brown on the bottom, then turn to brown the second side.

Remove the toasts from the pan and, using some pressure, rub the garlic clove on both sides of the bread. (Don't drain the bread on paper towels—you want to taste the oil when you bite into the toast.) Slice each piece of bread in half on the diagonal and serve warm. **SERVES 6**

flatbread

¼ cup warm water (110° to 115°F)

1 tablespoon plus 2 teaspoons active dry yeast (not quick-rising)

1 large egg, lightly beaten

½ cup room-temperature water

3¼ cups all-purpose flour

2 teaspoons kosher salt

1 tablespoon plus 1 teaspoon granulated sugar

¼ cup Clarified Butter (page 335), at room temperature

Canola oil

Extra virgin olive oil

Maldon salt or fleur de sel

Piment d' Espelette (optional; see page 208)

I roll our flatbread dough through a pasta machine so that it's very thin. It can be seasoned however you'd like, with piment d'Espelette and Maldon salt, black pepper, or dried herbs. You can bake the sheets of dough whole, then break them into large pieces and serve.

Combine the warm water and yeast in a small bowl. Let stand for 10 minutes, then stir to dissolve the yeast. Mix the egg with the water and stir to combine with the yeast mixture.

Combine the flour, salt, and sugar in the bowl of a stand mixer fitted with the dough hook. With the mixer on low speed, add the butter, followed by the egg mixture, and mix until the dough comes together on the hook.

Transfer the dough to a lightly floured board and knead for 5 minutes, or until smooth. Fold the edges under to form a round dough. Lightly oil a large bowl with canola oil and put the dough in the bowl. Brush a piece of plastic wrap with canola oil and press it directly onto the surface of the dough. Cover the bowl with a kitchen towel and let sit in a warm place until doubled in size, about 2 hours.

Position the oven racks in the lower and upper thirds of the oven and preheat the oven to 350°F. Line two baking sheets with parchment paper and brush with olive oil. (If you have a third rack in the oven, line another baking sheet and bake three pans at a time.)

Open the rollers of a pasta machine to the widest setting and flour the rollers. Cut the dough into quarters. Work with one quarter at a time, keeping the other pieces covered so they do not dry out. Lightly flour the piece of dough and, using the heel of your hand, press the dough down to a rectangle about ½ inch thick. Trim off one end so there is a straight edge, and roll the dough through the machine. Roll again through the widest setting. Continue to roll the dough twice through each setting, lightly flouring it as needed to keep it from sticking, until it is paper-thin; we roll ours to the second-to-last setting.

The piece of dough will be about 36 inches long. Trim the ends. Cut lengthwise in half and then cut crosswise in half to make 4 sheets about 3 inches by 15 inches. Place 3 sheets on one of the lined baking sheets, and roll out a second piece of dough. (If you don't have three baking sheets, put the extra sheets of dough on a sheet of parchment paper until ready to bake.)

Brush the flatbreads lightly with olive oil and sprinkle with Maldon salt and, if using, piment d'Espelette. Bake for 12 to 15 minutes, switching the position of the pans and rotating them halfway through baking, until crisp and golden. Let the flatbreads cool on the pans on cooling racks.

Repeat with the remaining dough. Leave the breads whole or break into pieces to serve. Store in an airtight container for up to 1 week.

PHOTOGRAPH ON PAGE 269

**MAKES 16 SHEETS OF FLATBREAD
ABOUT 15 INCHES BY 3 INCHES**

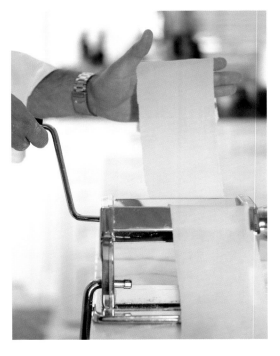

Of course I use a pasta machine for rolling out pasta dough, but I've found it to be an invaluable tool with other doughs that I want rolled into thin even sheets, such as flatbread.

grissini

½ cup warm water (110° to 115°F)

1 tablespoon active dry yeast (not quick-rising)

1½ cups all-purpose flour, plus additional as needed

⅓ cup fine semolina flour

¼ cup freshly grated Parmigiano-Reggiano

1 teaspoon ground fleur de sel or fine sea salt

2 tablespoons olive oil, plus additional for brushing

Coarsely ground black pepper

Simple breadsticks, fun to hold, satisfyingly crunchy. You can take these breadsticks in numerous directions, flattening them for a different texture, or using different oils—garlic rather than plain olive oil, for instance—different seasonings, or chopped herbs. These go well with salads, such as a tomato salad where you want some contrasting texture.

Combine the water and yeast in a small bowl. Let stand for 10 minutes, then stir until the yeast is completely dissolved.

Combine the flours, cheese, and salt in a large bowl. Make a well in the center of the dry ingredients. Stir the oil into the yeast mixture, then pour into the well and mix together with a fork. Once the dough comes together, transfer to a lightly floured board and knead, adding a dusting of all-purpose flour as necessary (depending on the flours and humidity, you may need up to an additional ¼ cup), until a smooth dough forms. Shape the dough into a ball and roll on the board to coat very lightly with flour.

Transfer the dough to a medium bowl, cover with a damp towel, and let rest in a warm place for about 15 minutes, or until it has risen slightly.

Position the oven racks in the lower and upper thirds of the oven and preheat the oven to 400°F. Line two baking sheets with parchment paper.

Turn the dough out onto the floured work surface and, using a dough scraper or sharp knife, cut the dough in half. Cut one half into 12 pieces for short grissini, or 6 pieces for long grissini. Roll each piece into a rope about 9 inches long for short grissini, or about 15 inches long for long grissini. You can leave them round or twist or flatten them, or a combination of the two. The thinner or flatter they are, the crispier the result; thicker grissini may be doughier, if that is your preference. Transfer to one of the parchment-lined baking sheets as you form them.

Coarsely grind a light dusting of pepper onto a section of the work surface; it is easier to control the amount of pepper that will be rolled onto the grissini by keeping the area small. (Alternatively, omit the pepper and sprinkle the grissini with fleur de sel or seeds.) Lightly brush the grissini with olive oil. One at a time, roll in the pepper and return to the parchment; grind additional pepper as needed. Repeat with the remaining dough. (The grissini can be held for up to an hour on the baking sheets in a cool spot. Or, to hold them longer, cover with parchment paper, wrap the baking sheets in plastic wrap, and refrigerate for up to 6 hours.)

Bake the grissini, switching the position of the pans and rotating them halfway through baking, until golden and crisp, 16 to 18 minutes. Cool on the pans on a rack. Store in an airtight container for up to 1 week.

MAKES 24 SMALL OR 12 LARGE GRISSINI

on cheese

I've always loved a cheese course, though it's not part of American culinary tradition. When I was writing the first French Laundry menus, for a room where a cheese cart was impractical, I chose to serve a composed cheese course. It also works perfectly in a family-style meal. Serving a cheese course is probably not something we want to do every night at home, but definitely now and then, because it stretches out the meal, allowing us the pleasure of more conversation and another glass of wine, and of being in one another's company a little while longer.

And what a time to do it: never before has there been such a range of outstanding artisanal cheeses available in this country. Cheeses can be as complex as wine and the *affineurs,* the people in charge of aging the cheese, can be every bit as dedicated to and as articulate about their work as winemakers. Cheeses, like wines, are infinitely nuanced, with a complex range of flavors and textures, and I encourage you to explore cheese the way you might explore wine. Go to a local cheesemonger and taste and try different cheeses to find what you like. Do you like blue cheeses? Intensely aromatic cheeses like Époisses or Taleggio? Perhaps you like cheeses wrapped in fig leaves or misted with ash. Or the wonderful double- and triple-creams. There are no rules except to eat with pleasure and attention and to gain an understanding of the broad categories, which are these: cheeses made from cow's milk,

sheep's milk, or goat's milk; soft, medium, or hard; young or old; and cheeses with natural, bloomed, washed, or flavored rinds. A natural rind is one that forms as the cheese ages; the tough dry exterior of Parmigiano-Reggiano is an example. For a bloomed rind, mold spores are sprayed on cheeses; they develop a soft white exterior (Camembert is a good example). A washed rind indicates a cheese that has been bathed, often in wine or beer, facilitating the growth of beneficial bacteria. The washed-rind cheeses are typically very pungent, such as Taleggio. Other cheeses are coated in ash or in herbs to introduce different flavors.

I regret the tendency of wine aficionados to overvalue pairings—you *must* have the 1945 Huet Moelleux with cold foie gras, and such. That thinking distances people from wine. But the broad strokes are another story. Say you had a Cabernet Sauvignon with steak frites and loved it—that's a pairing most people can relate to. The same goes for cheeses in my opinion. You might really love a goat cheese paired with sweet vegetables such as beets, onions, or leeks to balance the cheese's acidity; a rich pungent cheese, such as Taleggio, with pickled vegetables and the sweet-tart crunch of Granny Smith apples; and the rich aromatic complexity of blue cheese with dates and nuts. We serve cheeses simply, often just a wedge of cheese along with some nuts and a preserved fruit: Humboldt Fog goat cheese with figs and honey, and some crusty bread, for example. Sweet, creamy cheeses usually get some form of fruit, fresh or dried or cooked: pears, apples, grapes, apricots, peaches, tangerines, dates, and raisins, to name several. We always include a crunchy component, whether toast, flatbread, or nuts—candied, herbed, or toasted. We may pair some of the more pungent cheeses with something savory, such as prosciutto or salami. There's a lot of flexibility here and the opportunity for combining many different flavors and textures.

Below are ten cheeses we love, followed by a few of the ways we serve them. These are just a few examples—we could serve 365 different cheeses a year!

Point Reyes Original Blue cheese with a spoonful of blue cheese dressing

Humboldt Fog goat's-milk cheese served with honey and almonds

SHEEP'S-MILK CHEESES

hudson valley camembert This lovely sheep's-milk Camembert (it contains some cow's milk too) is from Old Chatham Sheepherding Company, a small sheep farm with a well-known inn and restaurant in New York's northern Hudson Valley. It has a creamy texture, a buttery flavor, and a bloomed rind; it is aged for 2 to 4 weeks.

We serve it with nuts and honey, or perhaps a pear jam or jelly. We've also served it with warm Mushroom Conserva (page 260) on top, so the flavors combine when you cut into the cheese.

idiazábal This is a Basque Country cheese that, traditionally, the shepherds aged in their chimneys so that the cheese picked up a smoky flavor. Ours is made in the Navarra region from raw sheep's milk, aged 6 months or more, and is smoked over beech, birch, or cherry wood. It has a hard rind, a firm texture, and a buttery, nutty flavor.

We dice it and marinate it in olive oil with aromatics for 24 hours, then drain it and serve it in a bowl with olives and Marcona almonds, the delicious roasted Spanish variety.

GOAT'S-MILK CHEESES

pug's leap bûche This cheese, made by Pascal Destandau across the Napa Valley, in Healdsburg, from pasteurized goat's milk, is very soft, and is aged for just 3 to 4 weeks. It has a distinct tanginess but is smooth and creamy, within a bloomed rind. We serve it with crunchy toasted country bread to balance its creaminess and accompany it with olive oil and Tomato-Basil Marmalade (page 248), a rich, sweet, acidic condiment.

wabash cannonball This is a soft, very young (1 week old) goat cheese, dusted with ash, which contributes to the flavor. It's made by Judith Schad at her Capriole Dairy in Greenville, Indiana. It's shaped into small balls and is soft, a little chalky, with a high level of acidity.

We serve it simply with honey to balance the acidity, and maybe some nuts.

garrotxa Garrotxa is a Spanish cheese from Catalonia. It's a semi-hard cheese with a natural rind. The deep rich flavor is buttery, a little tangy, but not overly so.

We serve it with Quince Paste (page 254) and some crusty bread.

humboldt fog This soft, dense goat's-milk cheese (see photo, left) with a bloomy rind has a vein of ash running through the center, which adds to the subtle tangy flavor. It's made at Cypress Grove Creamery in Arcata, California, by Mary Keehn.

We serve it with figs and honey, or maybe some fresh fruit or nuts.

COW'S-MILK CHEESES

burrata Burrata, a wonderful creamy mozzarella, is bundled up in a pouch around a center of mozzarella trimmings, mixed with cream, and sealed. Traditionally, the cheese is wrapped in fresh asphodel leaves, which should still be green, as an indication of freshness. Our burrata is made in California, and we serve it with broccolini as a special salad (see page 144).

pierce pt. We buy many of our cheeses from the well-known Cowgirl Creamery in Point Reyes Station, California. We adore the proprietors, Sue Conley and Peggy Smith, and are glad to contribute to their success and promote their cheeses. They not only make cheese but are purveyors as well (all the cheeses discussed here are available through their company, at www.cowgirlcreamery.com). Pierce Pt. is a firm but creamy cheese from pasteurized cow's milk with a bloomy rind that is washed in a Moscato wine and rolled in herbs. It's available only in the fall and winter.

We serve it with a little frisée and fennel salad with currants and pine nuts.

taleggio Italian Taleggio is a great washed-rind cheese that can get really funky with age, with a sticky orange exterior and strong aroma. But the flavor is rich and delicious and the texture is soft and velvety. The Taleggio we serve is aged for 40 days.

We serve this with a crunchy toasted bread. Taleggio goes beautifully with mushrooms, so we sometimes melt the cheese on flatbread and cover it with sautéed mushrooms.

parmigiano-reggiano This revered cheese from the Emilia-Romagna region of Italy is made from April through November from the raw milk of cows that graze on local grasses. Transformed into 80-pound wheels, true Parmigiano-Reggiano is aged for at least 2 years, and the longer it goes, the more complex it becomes. It's a hard cheese with a natural rind and a great texture that can seem almost crystallized.

When we serve Parmigiano for a cheese course, we may just do abundant shavings of the cheese over an arugula salad. We love the salty cheese with a good aged balsamic.

This sheep's-milk cheese with peppercorns, Pepato from Bellwether Farms, is served with breadsticks and a salad of frisée, olives, and melon.

the grilled cheese sandwich

Twelve ¼-inch-thick slices Brioche (page 272)

8 to 10 ounces thinly sliced Gruyère

6 tablespoons (3 ounces) unsalted butter, at room temperature

Sweet Potato Chips (page 232)

This iconic lunchtime staple, often accompanied by a can of Campbell's tomato soup, was a fixture of my youth, and it still factors in my cooking, whether as a course at The French Laundry or a family meal.

Here, we sandwich a Roth Käse special reserve Gruyère (see Sources, page 346), though any good Gruyère will do, between thin slices of brioche, cook them in good butter, and pop them into the oven until the cheese is melted. We serve them simply with a side of sweet potato chips. If you want to make this more special, serve it with Sun Gold Tomato Gazpacho (page 114), a perfect pairing and a reminder of the innocent comforts of youth.

Preheat the oven to 350°F.

Lay 6 slices of the bread on a work surface. Divide the cheese evenly among them and top with the remaining pieces of bread.

Heat a medium skillet over medium heat. Add 2 tablespoons of the butter and cook to brown the butter. Add half the sandwiches and cook until browned on the first side, about 1½ minutes. Turn the sandwiches over and brown the second side for 30 to 45 seconds. Transfer to a baking sheet, and spread 1 teaspoon of the remaining butter over the top of each sandwich. Put the baking sheet into the oven to finish cooking and melting the cheese, about 2 minutes. Cook the remaining sandwiches in the same way, and finish in the oven.

Transfer the sandwiches to a cutting board, cut off the crusts, and cut each sandwich into quarters. Stack on a serving plate and serve with the chips.　　　　SERVES 6

There's such an enduring quality to fried buttered bread and melted cheese.

1

2

3

4

5

6

7

8

9

10

11

12

14

15

16

17

SHEEP

1. Sottocenere
2. Winchester Super Aged Gouda
3. Browning Gold
4. Stichelton
5. St. George Matos
6. Dorset
7. Inverness
8. Vella Reserve Dry Aged Jack
9. Westcombe Red
10. Pierce Pt.
11. Garrotxa
12. Crocodile Tears
13. Humboldt Fog
14. Pug's Leap Bûche
15. Hubbardston Blue
16. Humbug Mountain
17. Wabash Cannonball
18. Tomette d'Helette
19. Sally Jackson Sheep
20. Ocooch Mountain
21. Idiazábal
22. Nancy's Camembert
23. Manchego el Trigal

DESSERTS

I, for one, don't feel a meal is complete until I've had at least a bite of something sweet. It doesn't have to be substantial—it can be as small as some peanut butter and chocolate on a cracker. Or it can be something special, like an ice cream sundae.

We all have our favorites. For some people it's brownies; for others, it's apple pie or a piece of cake. What we hope to do here with these family-style desserts is to touch on all those desires. One of my favorites as a kid was lemon meringue pie. My grandmother would take me to the drugstore for lunch—back when drugstores had lunch counters—and all their desserts would be sitting there in front of you, under glass domes, from the moment you sat down. They didn't have vegetable soup in there, they had pie! And I'd eye that lemon meringue the whole time, the finish line, the goal, the reward. We have it here in the form of lemon bars topped with meringue (see page 304). And when I have a bite of Coconut Cake (page 309), I'm returned to a time when my mother, long deceased, baked me cakes and I didn't have a care in the world.

Dessert is by far the most child-connected course. And what I hope comes forward in these desserts—besides their ease and comfort—is that childhood sense of reward.

OVERLEAF: *Ice Cream Sandwiches (page 325);* **OPPOSITE:** *Blueberry Cobbler (page 296).*

blueberry cobbler

TOPPING

1¾ cups all-purpose flour

½ teaspoon baking powder

½ teaspoon baking soda

6 tablespoons (3 ounces) unsalted butter, at room temperature

¾ cup granulated sugar

2 large eggs

½ cup buttermilk

FILLING

4 pints (8 cups) blueberries

¼ cup granulated sugar

2 tablespoons all-purpose flour

1 tablespoon grated lemon zest

CINNAMON SUGAR

1 tablespoon granulated sugar

¼ teaspoon ground cinnamon, or to taste

Having a cobbler in your repertoire gives you great versatility, because cobblers can be made with so many fruits and are easy to prepare. Some have a biscuit-like topping; ours is more cake-like, so it really soaks up all the fruit juices. Serve it warm with Vanilla Ice Cream (page 319) or whipped cream. With any luck, there will be leftovers—I love it warmed, with my morning coffee.

Preheat the oven to 350°F.

Sift together the flour, baking powder, and baking soda; set aside.

Put the butter and sugar in the bowl of a stand mixer fitted with the paddle and mix on low speed to combine, then beat on medium speed for about 3 minutes, until the mixture is light and creamy, scraping down the sides as necessary. Beat in the eggs one at a time until fully incorporated. Add the dry ingredients in 3 batches, alternating with the buttermilk in 2 batches. Scrape down the sides and mix again to be certain that all the ingredients are combined.

Put the blueberries in a large bowl and toss with the sugar, flour, and zest. Spread in an 11-inch square baking dish or a 9-by-13-inch baking pan. Spoon mounds of the batter over the berries, leaving space between the mounds.

Combine the sugar and cinnamon and sprinkle over the batter.

Bake for about 40 minutes, or until the juices are bubbling and the topping is golden brown and cooked through. If the top becomes too brown before it is cooked, lay a piece of aluminum foil over the top of the cobbler.

Let the cobbler stand for at least 10 minutes before serving. (Any leftover cobbler can be refrigerated for up to 2 days.)

PHOTOGRAPH ON PAGE 295

SERVES 6

peaches and cream

MASCARPONE CREAM

4 large eggs, separated

½ cup granulated sugar

½ cup mascarpone cheese, at room temperature

1 cup heavy cream

2 pounds ripe peaches, preferably freestone

1 teaspoon grated lemon zest

1½ teaspoons fresh lemon juice

2 tablespoons Tondo balsamic (see Sources, page 346)

I never get tired of this classic pairing. What's special about this version is the lightness of the mascarpone cream, which is almost mousse-like. Make the cream up to a day in advance; then it's simply a matter of slicing the peaches and tossing them with lemon and balsamic to balance the sweetness. Tondo balsamic vinegar has a syrupy consistency that can be used straight out of the bottle, with no reduction necessary as you would do with "ordinary" balsamic. We use it to adorn many foods, both savory and sweet.

This is a wonderfully light dessert, a perfect choice to serve after a filling meal. Its success depends on the quality of the peaches, so be sure to make it when peaches are at their peak.

In the bowl of a stand mixer fitted with the whisk, whisk the egg whites until foamy. Gradually add ¼ cup of the sugar and continue to whisk until stiff peaks form. Transfer to a bowl. (It is not necessary to wash the bowl or the whisk.)

Add the egg yolks and the remaining ¼ cup sugar to the mixer bowl and whisk until pale and thick. Whisk in the mascarpone cheese. Transfer to a large bowl.

Wash the bowl and whisk, using cold water to chill them. Dry and return to the mixer stand. Add the heavy cream and whisk until medium peaks form. Fold one-third of the cream into the yolk mixture to lighten it, then fold in another third and then the remaining cream. Fold in the whites one-third at a time just until combined. Cover with plastic wrap and refrigerate for at least 2 hours, or for up to 1 day.

Just before serving, slice each peach in half, twist the halves to separate, and remove and discard the pits. Cut each peach half into 4 to 5 slices. Put in a bowl and toss with the lemon zest, lemon juice, and balsamic.

Spoon some of the cream into a serving bowl. Top with the peaches and garnish the top with more cream. Serve the remaining cream on the side.

SERVES 6

apple fritters

1 cup all-purpose flour

2 tablespoons granulated sugar

1½ teaspoons baking powder

⅛ teaspoon ground cinnamon

½ teaspoon kosher salt

1 large egg

½ cup plus 1 tablespoon whole milk

3 large Fuji, Gala, or Golden Delicious apples

Canola oil for deep-frying

Powdered sugar for dusting

I love the casualness and ease of this great finger food dessert—a plate of hot apple fritters, dusted with powdered sugar, passed around the table is a satisfying end to a meal. While these fritters are a wonderful dessert to make when seasonal apples are abundant, you can also vary the fruit, using pears instead of apples, for example. If you like, serve them with Vanilla Ice Cream (page 319) and a drizzle of honey. They're best immediately after they are fried, so serve them hot.

Whisk together the flour, sugar, baking powder, cinnamon, and salt in a medium bowl. Lightly beat the egg and milk in a small bowl. Whisk into the dry ingredients until combined. The batter can be covered and refrigerated for up to 3 hours.

Peel the apples and slice the fruit from the core. Cut the apples into 2-inch-long, ¼-inch-thick matchsticks. Fold into the batter.

Heat about 1½ inches of oil to 325°F in a wide deep pot. Set a cooling rack over a baking sheet and line with paper towels. Using two forks, lift up about 5 to 6 of the apple matchsticks from the batter, allowing the excess batter to drip back into the bowl—the fritter should be irregular in shape, with just a very light coating of batter—and add to the hot oil. Add a few more fritters to the pot, without crowding, and fry for about 5 minutes, turning the fritters from time to time, until crisp and golden brown. Use a skimmer or slotted spoon to transfer them to the paper towels, and fry the remaining fritters in batches.

Stack the fritters on a serving platter, sprinkle generously with powdered sugar, and serve immediately.   SERVES 6

banana bread pudding

2¼ cups whole milk

2¼ cups heavy cream

1 cup granulated sugar

1 tablespoon vanilla paste (see Sources, page 346) or pure vanilla extract

One 14-inch Brioche Pullman loaf (page 272) or *pain de mie*

10 large eggs

3 bananas

About ½ cup Clarified Butter (page 335)

This is a great dessert for entertaining that would also be a perfect brunch dish. It's very basic—custard-soaked bread— yet rich and elegant, and it can be made up to 2 days in advance. We bake the bread pudding and then chill it, cut it into squares, and cook it in butter, so it's almost like French toast. We use brioche for its flavor, but any good white sandwich bread will work; look for the long rectangular loaf called a Pullman loaf or *pain de mie,* which has a soft, uniform interior, or crumb. The bananas can be replaced with a similar quantity of dried fruit or omitted altogether—this is a delicious bread pudding without any fruit. It's excellent topped with ice cream and chocolate sauce, mascarpone cheese, maple syrup, honey, or even a berry sauce.

Combine the milk, cream, ½ cup of the sugar, and the vanilla paste (not extract) in a large saucepan and bring to a boil, stirring to dissolve the sugar. Remove from the heat and stir in the vanilla extract, if using.

Preheat the broiler. Cut the crusts from the loaf of bread. Cut the bread in half, then cut lengthwise into slices that are about ½ inch thick; you will need 8 slices of bread (reserve the remaining bread for another use).

Put the slices on a baking sheet and toast on both sides under the broiler until golden brown. Remove from the broiler.

Lightly whisk the eggs in a large bowl. Whisk in the remaining ½ cup sugar. Whisk several ladles of the milk mixture into the yolk mixture, then whisk the yolk mixture back into the milk. Strain through a fine-mesh basket strainer into a bowl and let the custard cool completely.

Spread about ¼ inch of the custard in the bottom of a 9-by-13-inch baking pan. Lay 2 slices of the bread in a baking dish and pour in enough of the egg mixture to cover. Soak them, turning once, for about 1 minute; do not soak too long, or they will be difficult to move. Lay the slices of bread crosswise in the baking pan. Repeat with 2 more slices.

Cut the bananas crosswise in half, then cut each half lengthwise into 3 slices. Lay the banana slices side by side, running lengthwise in the pan, to cover the bread. Soak the remaining 4 pieces of bread in 2 batches, laying them crosswise over the bananas. Pour the remaining egg mixture over the top.

Cover the bread pudding with a piece of plastic wrap and press down gently. Let stand for 20 minutes to allow the egg mixture to soak into the bread.

Preheat the oven to 300°F.

Bring a large saucepan of water to a simmer. Remove the plastic wrap and place a piece of parchment paper over the top of the bread pudding. Cover the pan with aluminum foil.

Put the baking pan in a larger pan, such as a roasting pan. Carefully pour enough hot water into the roasting pan to come about two-thirds up the sides of the baking pan. Bake for 1 hour, or until an instant-read thermometer inserted in the center of the pudding registers 180°F; a knife inserted in the pudding should come out clean. Carefully remove the baking pan from the water bath (using a turkey baster or a ladle to remove some of the water from the roasting pan first will make this easier), set on a cooling rack, and let cool, still covered, to room temperature.

Refrigerate for at least 6 hours, or for up to 2 days.

Preheat the oven to 275°F. Set a cooling rack over a baking sheet and put it in the oven.

Cut the bread pudding into 24 squares and remove them from the pan. Trim them as necessary and scrape off any custard from the bottom of the squares.

Heat about ¼ inch of clarified butter in a large nonstick frying pan over medium-high heat. Add several pieces of the bread pudding, cut side down, without crowding. Reduce the heat to medium, and cook for 2 to 3 minutes on each side, to warm and brown the pieces. Put the browned pieces on the rack to keep warm as you continue to brown the remaining pieces. **SERVES 12**

panna cotta

1½ teaspoons powdered gelatin

1 tablespoon water

2 cups sour cream

½ cup plus 1 tablespoon buttermilk

1¼ teaspoons vanilla paste (see Sources, page 346) or pure vanilla extract

⅔ cup granulated sugar

1 cup crème fraîche

*P*anna cotta means, literally, "cooked cream." To make this Italian dessert, cream is usually cooked, flavored, and lightly jelled. There are any number of variations, but I like it best with a subtly acidic element, here sour cream and buttermilk. Panna cotta can be served plain or enhanced with a compote or a sauce, such as the Blackberry Sauce (page 343).

Put the gelatin in a small cup and add the water. Let stand for about 5 minutes to soften.

Meanwhile, whisk together the sour cream, buttermilk, vanilla, and sugar in a medium bowl.

Spoon about ½ cup of the mixture into a small saucepan and heat over medium-low heat, stirring, just to warm. Add the softened gelatin, stirring to dissolve. Rub a bit of the mixture between your fingers; it should not feel gritty. Remove from the heat and let cool for 5 minutes, then stir the gelatin mixture into the sour cream mixture.

Whisk the crème fraîche in a medium bowl until it thickens and holds a shape. Fold in the sour cream mixture. Strain through a fine-mesh conical strainer into a bowl with a spout or liquid measuring cup. Pour the mixture into six 4- to 5-ounce ramekins or molds. Refrigerate for at least 5 hours until set, or up to 2 days.

To unmold, run the tip of a paring knife about ¼ inch deep around the edges of each panna cotta. Fill a bowl with very hot tap water. Dip one mold quickly two-thirds of the way into the water; you want to soften the panna cotta just enough to unmold it. If the mold is held in the water too long, the outside of the panna cotta will liquefy. Invert onto a serving plate. Repeat with the remaining panna cotta. **SERVES 6**

brownies

¾ cup all-purpose flour

1 cup unsweetened alkalized cocoa powder (see Sources, page 346)

1 teaspoon kosher salt

¾ pound (3 sticks) unsalted butter, cut into 1-tablespoon pieces

3 large eggs

1¾ cups granulated sugar

½ teaspoon vanilla paste (see Sources, page 346) or pure vanilla extract

6 ounces 61 to 64% chocolate (see Sources, page 346), chopped into chip-sized pieces (about 1½ cups)

Powdered sugar for dusting

Brownies embody so much of what I love about dessert generally—they remind me of family, comfort, childhood. They draw you to them. You can turn these into a special dessert by serving them alongside Caramel Ice Cream (page 321) or with Vanilla Ice Cream (page 319) and Caramel Sauce (page 344), but they're great with just a little whipped cream or powdered sugar—or all by themselves.

Preheat the oven to 350°F. We use a 9-inch square silicone mold (see Sources, page 346), because it keeps the edges from overcooking; if you use a metal or glass baking pan, butter and flour it. Set aside.

Sift together the flour, cocoa powder, and salt; set aside.

Melt half the butter in a small saucepan over medium heat, stirring occasionally. Put the remaining butter in a medium bowl. Pour the melted butter over the bowl of butter and stir to melt the butter. The butter should look creamy, with small bits of unmelted butter, and be at room temperature.

In the bowl of a stand mixer fitted with the paddle, mix together the eggs and sugar on medium speed for about 3 minutes, or until thick and very pale. Mix in the vanilla. On low speed, add about one-third of the dry ingredients, then add one-third of the butter, and continue alternating the remaining flour and butter. Add the chocolate and mix to combine. (The batter can be refrigerated for up to 1 week.)

Spread the batter evenly in the pan. Bake for 40 to 45 minutes, until a cake tester or wooden skewer poked into the center comes out with just a few moist crumbs sticking to it. If the pick comes out wet, test a second time, because you may have hit a piece of chocolate chip; then bake for a few minutes longer if necessary. Cool in the pan until the brownie is just a bit warmer than room temperature.

Run a knife around the edges if not using a silicone mold, and invert the brownie onto a cutting board. Cut into 12 rectangles. Dust the tops with powdered sugar just before serving. (The brownies can be stored in an airtight container for up to 2 days.) **MAKES 12 BROWNIES**

lemon bars with meringue

CRUST

10½ tablespoons (5¼ ounces) unsalted butter, at room temperature

¼ cup plus 1 tablespoon granulated sugar

½ teaspoon vanilla paste (see Sources, page 346) or pure vanilla extract

1¾ cups all-purpose flour

FILLING

1 cup fresh lemon juice

6 large eggs

6 large egg yolks

1¼ cups granulated sugar

9 tablespoons (4½ ounces) unsalted butter, cut into small chunks,
    at room temperature

Meringue (page 344)

Lemon bars and their cousins, lemon tart and lemon meringue pie, are among my favorite desserts. After assembling the bars, we freeze them. This makes them easy to slice and serve, and it also gives the lemon curd a great texture—somewhat firm but amazingly creamy—and the bars deliver a pleasing chill on the palate. You can make these several days ahead and keep them frozen.

We usually finish the bars with piped meringue, but you can omit that and just serve them with some sweetened whipped cream or a dusting of powdered sugar. If you are making the meringue, you'll need a propane torch to brown the top—a broiler just doesn't give you the kind of control you need. Miniature kitchen torches are available at specialty stores, but regular all-purpose propane torches are inexpensive and available at any hardware store—you'll find lots of uses for one in the kitchen besides browning meringue, such as melting the sugar for crème brûlée or developing a great browned crust on a roast (see page 56).

Put the butter and sugar in the bowl of a stand mixer fitted with the paddle and mix on low speed to combine. Increase the speed to medium and beat for 3 minutes, until the mixture is light and creamy, scraping down the sides as necessary. Add the vanilla. Then add the flour about ¼ cup at a time, mixing until just incorporated. The dough should not form a mass, but it should hold together if you squeeze it with your hands.

Transfer the dough to a large piece of parchment paper and pat it into a rectangle. Wrap the dough in plastic and refrigerate for at least 30 minutes, or for up to 2 days; let stand at room temperature to soften slightly before rolling.

Cover the dough with another piece of parchment paper and roll it out to a 12-by-16-inch rectangle. If at any point the dough is too soft to work with, slide it onto a baking sheet and refrigerate briefly.

Set out a quarter sheet pan (see Note). Remove the top piece of parchment and invert the dough into the pan. Fit into the pan, pressing it evenly over the bottom and up the sides; lift the edges to ease the dough into the corners, and let the excess dough hang over the sides of the pan. (The overhanging dough will help anchor the crust and keep it from shrinking as it bakes.) If you see any cracks in the dough, use small pieces from the overhang to patch them. Prick the bottom and sides of the crust with a fork, and refrigerate for 5 minutes.

Preheat the oven to 350°F.

Bake the crust until golden brown, 15 to 20 minutes, rotating the pan halfway through baking for even browning. Transfer to a cooling rack and let cool to room temperature.

Combine the lemon juice, eggs, yolks, and sugar in the top of a double boiler or in a large metal bowl set over a saucepan of simmering water and whisk for about 5 minutes, or until the mixture thickens and holds a shape when the whisk is lifted. Remove from the heat and whisk in the butter bit by bit.

Strain the curd through a fine-mesh basket strainer into the crust. Shake the pan gently to distribute the filling evenly.

continued

Pipe the meringue, working in a circular motion, to form lengthwise coils.
Just before serving, use a kitchen torch or propane torch to brown the top of the meringue.
Because the bars have been precut, they can easily be lifted with a spatula.

Cut a piece of parchment paper the size of the pan, spray it with nonstick spray, and lay it over the lemon filling. Cover the pan with plastic wrap and freeze for at least several hours, until frozen solid.

Using a paring knife, scrape off the pastry overhang. Run a palette knife or narrow spatula between the pastry and the sides of the pan to loosen the bars. With a wide spatula, lift the sheet of lemon bars and place on a cutting surface. Slice off the crusts on all four sides. Cut the sheet of bars lengthwise in half and then cut crosswise into quarters to make a total of 8 squares. Use the palette knife to transfer the lemon bars to a large rectangular serving platter, reassembling them into a rectangle. The lemon bars can be returned to the freezer for up to 2 days on the serving platter or refrigerated for up to 1 day.

Just before serving, beginning in an upper corner of the rectangle of bars, pipe a vertical coil of meringue, working in a circular motion, down the length of the bars. Turn the platter around and pipe a second coil of meringue touching the first. Continue until the lemon bars are covered in meringue.

Using a blowtorch, carefully brown the meringue, adjusting the flame and/or moving the torch closer or farther away from the meringue to ensure even browning. Serve immediately.

MAKES 8 LARGE BARS

NOTE ON QUARTER SHEET PANS *Quarter sheet pans, which measure 9 by 13 by 1 inch, are useful especially for their shallow depth. While a 9-by-13-inch baking dish can work, a sheet pan allows you to have perfectly uniform depth for dishes such as the grits cakes and for lemon and pecan bars. It also allows you to overhang dough, preventing its shrinking and cracking (eventually, what's left of the overhang is trimmed away). A standard baking dish would be too deep.*

pecan-walnut bars

CRUST

1 cup powdered sugar

⅓ cup almond flour

1⅔ cups all-purpose flour

11 tablespoons (5½ ounces) unsalted butter, at room temperature

½ teaspoon vanilla paste (see Sources, page 346) or pure vanilla extract

1 large egg

FILLING

2 cups pecans

1 cup walnuts

6 large eggs

¼ cup unsulphured molasses

2 teaspoons vanilla paste (see Sources, page 346) or pure vanilla extract

½ teaspoon kosher salt

1½ cups lightly packed light brown sugar

1 cup light corn syrup

12 tablespoons (1½ sticks; 6 ounces) unsalted butter, melted and cooled

This is just like a pecan pie—butter, brown sugar, eggs, and nuts combined in a wonderful caramelly, nutty, crunchy filling—in bar form with a delicious sweet shortbread crust flavored with almond and vanilla. These are great 30 minutes out of the freezer, with a cold and chewy consistency, but I also love them warm from the oven. Serve them with whipped cream or ice cream if you like.

Put ⅓ cup of the powdered sugar and the almond flour in a food processor and pulse to combine. Transfer to a bowl and stir in the flour.

Put the butter and the remaining ⅔ cup powdered sugar in the bowl of a stand mixer fitted with the paddle and mix on low speed to combine. Increase the speed to medium and beat for 3 minutes, until the mixture is light and creamy, scraping down the sides as necessary. Add the vanilla and then the egg, beating on medium speed until incorporated. Turn the speed to low and slowly add the dry ingredients.

Remove the bowl from the mixer and turn the dough a few times with a rubber spatula to be sure that everything is evenly incorporated. Transfer the dough to a large piece of parchment paper and pat it into a rectangle. Wrap the dough in plastic and refrigerate for at least 30 minutes, or for up to 2 days; let stand at room temperature to soften slightly before rolling.

Coarsely chop the nuts into about 3 or 4 pieces per nut. If the nuts are chopped too fine, they will rise to the top of the filling.

Lightly whisk the eggs in a large bowl. Add the molasses, vanilla, salt, brown sugar, and corn syrup. Whisk in the melted butter. Stir in the nuts, and let stand for 30 minutes.

Meanwhile, cover the dough with another piece of parchment paper and roll out to a 12-by-16-inch rectangle. If at any point the dough is too soft to work with, slide it onto a baking sheet and refrigerate briefly.

Set out a quarter sheet pan (see Note, opposite). Remove the top piece of parchment and invert the dough into the pan. Fit it into the pan, pressing it evenly over the bottom and up the sides; lift the edges to ease the dough into the corners, and let the excess dough hang over the sides of the pan. (The overhanging dough will help anchor the crust and keep it from shrinking as it bakes.) If you see any cracks in the dough, use small pieces from the overhang to patch them. Prick the bottom and sides of the crust with a fork, and refrigerate for 5 minutes.

Preheat the oven to 350°F.

Bake the crust until golden, 25 to 30 minutes, rotating the pan halfway through baking for even browning. Remove from the oven, immediately pour in the filling, and return the pan to the oven. Bake for 15 minutes, or until the top is evenly browned. To be sure that it is done, shake the pan gently: the center of the filling should not move. Transfer to a rack and let cool to room temperature.

Wrap the pan in plastic wrap and freeze for at least several hours, until solid, or up to 2 days.

Using a paring knife, scrape off the pastry overhang. Run a palette knife or narrow spatula between the pastry and the sides of the pan to loosen the bars. With a wide spatula, lift the sheet of bars and place on a cutting surface. Slice off the crusts on all four sides. Cut the sheet of bars lengthwise in half and then cut crosswise into quarters to make a total of 8 squares. Transfer the bars to a serving platter.

Serve the bars cold or at room temperature.   **MAKES 8 LARGE BARS**

cherry pie

FILLING

2 tablespoons cornstarch

2 tablespoons water

7 cups sweet cherries, such as Bing, pitted

¾ to 1 cup granulated sugar

1 tablespoon vanilla paste (see Sources, page 346) or pure vanilla extract

Basic Pie Crust (page 338)

1 large egg, beaten

Granulated sugar for sprinkling (optional)

My dad's parents had a huge cherry tree in their yard in Monroeville, Pennsylvania, and when I was very young, my grandmother would make the most amazing cherry pies. When it's the height of summer, and the cherries are ripe, there is nothing better than this American classic.

Combine the cornstarch and water in a small bowl, stirring to dissolve the cornstarch (this is called a slurry).

Put 5 cups of the cherries in a large bowl; set aside. Put the remaining 2 cups cherries in a Vita-Mix and blend to a puree; don't worry if there are some small pieces of cherry remaining. Taste the puree to check how sweet it is.

Combine the puree, sugar (¾ cup if the cherries are sweet, up to 1 cup if the cherries are tart), and vanilla paste (not the extract) in a medium saucepan, bring to a simmer over medium heat, and simmer for about 30 minutes, stirring often to prevent the bottom from burning, until the mixture has reduced to 1¼ to 1½ cups. Reduce the heat to medium-low and, stirring constantly, add the cornstarch slurry.

Bring to a boil, stirring, and cook until the mixture becomes translucent again. Remove from the heat, spoon a little of the puree mixture onto a plate, and let cool slightly, then rub it between your fingertips to feel for any remaining grains of cornstarch. If necessary, cook slightly longer to dissolve the cornstarch. Transfer the filling to a medium bowl and stir in the vanilla extract, if using. Let cool completely.

Roll out the dough, place one piece in a pie plate and the other on a baking sheet, and refrigerate as directed on page 338.

Remove both doughs from the refrigerator.

Position one oven rack in the bottom of the oven and the other in the center and preheat the oven to 400°F.

Stir the puree into the whole cherries and pour into the pie shell. At this point, if the top crust is too hard to shape, let it rest at room temperature for a few minutes. Moisten the rim of the pie shell with some of the beaten egg. Cover the filling with the top crust and press the edges together to seal (see photo, page 24).

At the rim of the pie plate, pinch the top and bottom crusts together to seal and create a raised edge to the crust. Trim away the excess dough that overhangs the rim.

Brush the top crust with the beaten egg and sprinkle with sugar if desired. Using a paring knife, cut a few slits in the top of the pie for steam vents. Put on the bottom rack of the oven and bake for 20 minutes.

Lower the heat to 375°F, move the pie to the center rack, and bake until the crust is golden and the filling is bubbling, 20 to 30 minutes.

Transfer the pie to a cooling rack to cool.

The pie is best served 2 to 3 hours after it is baked, but it can be kept at room temperature the day it is baked or wrapped and refrigerated for up to 3 days. To reheat, warm in a 325°F oven for about 15 minutes.

SERVES 6 TO 8

coconut cake

One 15-ounce can coconut milk (not "lite")

1½ teaspoons pure vanilla extract

3 cups cake flour

1 tablespoon baking powder

¾ teaspoon kosher salt

¾ cup egg whites (from about 6 large eggs)

2 cups granulated sugar

12 tablespoons (1½ sticks; 6 ounces) unsalted butter, at room temperature

2 cups dried shredded unsweetened coconut

Meringue (page 344)

This is dear to me because it's a cake my mom used to make, and so I love it for that emotional connection. It's a simple white cake, kind of like an angel food cake, but I add butter for richness and flavor. And I use vanilla extract rather than vanilla paste, because it helps to keep the cake very white.

Pour the coconut milk into a small saucepan and whisk to blend. Bring to a simmer over medium heat and simmer gently, stirring occasionally, until the milk has reduced to 1 cup.

Meanwhile, prepare an ice bath in a medium bowl and set a small metal bowl on top.

Pour the coconut milk into the small bowl. Once the milk is cool, remove from the ice bath and stir in the vanilla.

Preheat the oven to 350°F. Butter two 9-inch round cake pans. Line with parchment paper, butter the parchment, and coat with flour, tapping out the excess.

Sift the cake flour and baking powder together into a bowl. Stir in the salt. Set aside.

In the bowl of a stand mixer fitted with the whisk attachment, whip the whites on medium speed, until they begin to froth. With the mixer running, slowly add ¾ cup of the sugar, then increase the speed to medium-high and continue to whip until medium peaks form. Remove from the mixer. (If you have only one bowl, transfer the whites to another bowl and wash out the mixer bowl.) Switch to the paddle attachment.

Put the butter in the mixer bowl and beat on medium-low to medium speed to soften, about 1 minute. Scrape down the sides of the bowl with a rubber spatula, add the remaining 1¼ cups sugar, and mix on medium speed until light and creamy, stopping to scrape the sides as needed, 3 to 4 minutes.

From this point, it is important not to overmix the batter. Each addition does not have to be completely incorporated before you add the next; there may be some visible streaks remaining. Add half the dry ingredients to the butter and mix on medium-low to medium speed. Add half of the coconut milk and mix. Add half of the remaining dry mixture, then the remaining milk and finally the remaining dry mixture. Remove the bowl from the mixer. Scrape down the sides and the bottom to incorporate any ingredients that may have settled in the bottom of the bowl, and mix with the spatula so there are no longer any streaks.

Top the batter with one-third of the whites and fold in gently. Gently fold in another third of the whites and finally the remaining whites.

Divide the batter evenly between the pans and gently smooth the tops. Bake until a cake tester or wooden skewer inserted in the center comes out clean, 26 to 28 minutes. Let the layers cool on a cooling rack for about 10 minutes, then turn out of the pans and let cool completely.

Meanwhile, spread the coconut on a baking sheet and toast lightly in the oven, 6 to 8 minutes. Transfer to a small bowl and let cool completely.

Lay strips of parchment paper around the edges of a cake stand or serving plate to catch any excess frosting or coconut when you decorate the cake. Position one of the cake layers in the center. Spread a ⅓-inch-thick layer of meringue evenly over the cake layer. Sprinkle a light layer of the coconut over the meringue. Top with the second cake layer. Spread the remaining meringue evenly over the sides and top of the cake. Sprinkle the remaining coconut on the sides and the top. Pull away and discard the pieces of parchment paper. This cake is best served the day it is made. **SERVES 10 TO 12**

pineapple upside-down cake

PAN SCHMEAR

8 tablespoons (1 stick; 4 ounces) unsalted butter, at room temperature

1½ tablespoons honey

½ teaspoon dark rum

1 cup packed light brown sugar

¼ teaspoon vanilla paste (see Sources, page 346) or pure vanilla extract

Kosher salt

1 Gold (extra-sweet) pineapple

CAKE

1⅓ cups cake flour

2 teaspoons baking powder

8 tablespoons (1 stick; 4 ounces) unsalted butter, at room temperature

½ cup plus 2 tablespoons granulated sugar

½ teaspoon vanilla paste (see Sources, page 346) or pure vanilla extract

2 large eggs

1 tablespoon plus 1 teaspoon milk

H ere is another slightly quirky entry from the American tradition, pineapple upside-down cake. I have some affection for canned pineapple for nostalgic reasons, but we use fresh pineapple here for a more elegant dessert. Again, think of this as a general template that you can use for different fruits, and they all work wonderfully. We make what we call a "pan schmear" of butter and brown sugar, top it with the fruit, and pour the cake batter over the top. The recipe makes more schmear than you need, but it is difficult to make less. It will keep for a couple of weeks in the refrigerator, ready when you want to make another cake, or it can be frozen.

Preheat the oven to 350°F.

In the bowl of a stand mixer fitted with the paddle, combine the butter, honey, rum, brown sugar, and vanilla and beat until smooth and well blended. Spread ⅓ cup of the schmear over the bottom of a 9-inch silicone cake pan. Sprinkle lightly with salt. (The remaining schmear can be refrigerated for up to 2 weeks or frozen for up to 1 month; bring to room temperature before using.)

Cut the top and bottom from the pineapple and cut away the peel. Cut the pineapple lengthwise into quarters, and cut off the core from each section. Cut each piece crosswise into ⅛-inch-thick slices. Beginning at the perimeter of the pan, make an overlapping ring of pineapple slices with the curved side facing out. Make a second ring inside the first one, overlapping the slices in the opposite direction, working toward the center of the pan (see photo below). Reserve any extra pineapple for another use.

Sift the flour and baking powder together; set aside.

Put the butter and sugar in the bowl of a stand mixer fitted with the paddle and mix on low speed to combine, then beat on medium speed for about 3 minutes, until light and creamy, stopping to scrape down the sides as necessary. Mix in the vanilla. Add the eggs one at a time, beating until the first one is incorporated before adding the second and scraping down the sides as necessary. Beat in the milk. Add the flour mixture in 3 batches, beating just until combined.

Pour the batter into the pan and spread over the pineapple. Bake for 15 minutes. Rotate the pan for even browning and bake for another 20 to 25 minutes, until a cake tester or wooden skewer inserted in the center of the cake comes out clean. Cool the cake in the pan on a cooling rack for 20 to 30 minutes.

Run a knife around the edges of the cake, invert onto a serving platter, and serve warm. (Leftover cake can be stored at room temperature for up to 2 days.) **SERVES 8**

grapefruit cake

CAKE

2 cups all-purpose flour

1¾ teaspoons baking powder

1 teaspoon kosher salt

1⅔ cups granulated sugar

2 large eggs

1 cup whole milk

¾ cup canola oil

1 tablespoon grated pink grapefruit zest

1 teaspoon vanilla paste (see Sources, page 346) or pure vanilla extract

GRAPEFRUIT SYRUP

1 cup strained fresh pink grapefruit juice

⅔ cup granulated sugar

GRAPEFRUIT ICING

¾ cup powdered sugar

1 tablespoon plus 1 teaspoon fresh pink grapefruit juice

This is an all-purpose cake, simple but versatile. Its texture is a cross between a sponge cake and a quick bread or muffin. Here we flavor it with grapefruit—I love the bittersweetness of this citrus. But you could change the fruit to lemon, with some additional sugar added to the syrup and icing (to compensate for the tartness of the lemon), and have a fantastic lemon cake. When I've got wonderful strawberries, I omit the citrus entirely and use the cake in place of a shortcake. I also make these in individual loaves and serve them with a simple sauce.

Preheat the oven to 350°F. Spray a 10-by-4-inch loaf pan or other loaf pan with a 7-cup capacity, such as a 9-by-5-inch pan, with nonstick spray, or lightly oil it.

Sift the flour and baking powder together and stir in the salt. Set aside.

Combine the sugar and eggs in the bowl of a stand mixer fitted with the whisk attachment and beat at medium speed for about 3 minutes, until the mixture is thickened and the whisk leaves a trail. Beat in the milk, then the oil, grapefruit zest, and vanilla. Reduce the speed to low and add the flour mixture, mixing just to incorporate; scrape the sides of the bowl as needed.

Spread the batter in the pan. Spray or lightly oil a paring knife and run the knife lengthwise down the center of batter, about ½ inch deep; this will give the baked cake a beautiful top with an even crack down the center.

Put the pan on a small baking sheet and bake for 30 minutes. Turn the pan around so the cake will color evenly and bake for another 30 minutes, or until a cake tester or wooden skewer inserted in the center comes out with just a few moist crumbs clinging to it. Transfer the pan to a cooling rack.

Meanwhile, combine the grapefruit juice and sugar in a small saucepan, bring to a simmer, stirring to dissolve the sugar, and simmer for 1 minute. Set aside.

As soon as you have removed the cake from the oven, using a long skewer, poke deep holes every ¾ inch or so all over the top of the cake. Immediately begin brushing the syrup over the cake. It may be necessary at times to wait for the syrup to soak in, but continue until you've used all the syrup. Let the cake cool for about 10 minutes.

Unmold the cake onto a cooling rack, turn it right side up, and let cool to room temperature.

Stir the powdered sugar and grapefruit juice together in a bowl until smooth. Using a spoon, drizzle the icing on a diagonal over the top of the cake, allowing it to drip down the sides. Slice the cake and serve. (The cake keeps well, loosely covered at room temperature, for up to 2 days.) **SERVES 8 TO 10**

cheesecake

CRUST

1 cup graham cracker crumbs

3 tablespoons granulated sugar

5 tablespoons (2½ ounces) unsalted butter, melted

FILLING

1 pound cream cheese (not reduced-fat), room temperature

8 ounces mascarpone cheese

1 cup granulated sugar

4 large eggs

2 large egg yolks

2 teaspoons vanilla paste (see Sources, page 346) or pure vanilla extract

1 teaspoon fresh lemon juice

¼ cup plus 2 tablespoons heavy cream

Grated zest of 1 lemon

Please don't substitute low-fat anything here—fat is what makes this rich and satisfying dessert such a pleasure. If you want to reduce fat, cut a smaller piece! One of the glories of a great cheesecake is its texture, and baking the cheesecake in a water bath makes it very, very creamy—and it won't crack along the top when it cools, as cheesecakes tend to do. Garnish it with fresh berries or serve it with Strawberry Coulis (page 343), Blackberry Sauce (page 343), or Apricot-Currant Compote (page 243).

Preheat the oven to 325°F.

Combine the graham crackers and sugar in a bowl. Stir in the melted butter to moisten the crumbs evenly. Press the crumbs over the bottom and about ½ inch up the sides of a 9-inch springform pan.

Bake for 8 to 10 minutes, until the crust is evenly browned and set. Remove from the oven and set on a cooling rack.

Bring a large pot of water to a simmer for the water bath.

Meanwhile, in the bowl of a stand mixer fitted with the paddle, combine the cream cheese, mascarpone, and sugar and beat at low speed to mix, then raise the speed to medium and beat for about 3 minutes, scraping down the sides as necessary, until the mixture is lightened and smooth.

In a small bowl, lightly beat the eggs, egg yolks, and vanilla together with a fork. Add the lemon juice. Slowly add the mixture to the cream cheese mixture, beating until smooth and well combined. Slowly pour in the cream. (If there are any lumps in the batter, strain it through a fine-mesh basket strainer into another bowl, pressing on any solids left in the strainer to force them through the strainer.) Stir in the lemon zest.

Wrap the springform pan in foil to prevent leaks: put the pan on a double layer of aluminum foil that is large enough to come up to the rim of the pan. Fold the foil up around the pan and crimp any foil that extends above the rim. Put the pan in a deep larger pan, such as a roasting pan. Pour the cheesecake batter into the springform pan.

Place the larger pan in the oven and pour enough simmering water into the larger pan to come halfway up the sides of the cheesecake. Bake for 1 hour, or until the cheesecake is set and a light golden brown. To check the cheesecake, wiggle the pan gently: the cheesecake filling should look set, even in the center. Remove from the oven and let the cheesecake cool in the water bath until the water is at room temperature.

Remove the springform pan from the water and discard the foil. Refrigerate, in the springform pan, for at least several hours, to chill completely, or for up to 2 days.

To serve, remove the ring of the springform and cut the cheesecake into wedges.

SERVES 8

IN THE FOREGROUND, FROM LEFT: *Carrot Cake Cupcake (page 317), Devil's Food Cupcake (page 316), and White Cupcake (opposite).*

white cupcakes

3 cups all-purpose flour

2 teaspoons baking powder

¾ teaspoon kosher salt

12 tablespoons (1½ sticks; 6 ounces) unsalted butter, cut into 12 pieces,
    at room temperature

2¾ cups granulated sugar

1 teaspoon pure vanilla extract

1¼ cups whole milk

¾ cup egg whites (from about 6 large eggs), at room temperature

Vanilla Buttercream Frosting (recipe follows)

White chocolate shavings (optional; see Note)

Cupcakes make a festive dessert, especially when there are a few different kinds on the same plate. Here, and on the next few pages, we offer white cupcakes and chocolate cupcakes, each with a different buttercream frosting, and carrot cupcakes with a cream cheese frosting. You can use fancy toppings such as shaved chocolate, and that's delicious, but frankly, I like sprinkles too.

Preheat the oven to 350°F. Line 24 cupcake cups with paper liners.

Sift together the flour and baking powder into a bowl. Stir in the salt. Set aside.

In the bowl of a stand mixer fitted with the paddle, beat the butter and 1½ cups of the sugar at medium speed to combine. Increase the speed to medium-high and beat, scraping down the sides as necessary, until the mixture is pale and thick, about 5 minutes. Beat in the vanilla, then add the dry ingredients in 3 additions, alternating with the milk in 2 additions. The batter will be thick. Transfer to a large bowl.

Put the egg whites in the clean mixer bowl and whisk on medium speed until the whites begin to foam. Increase the speed to medium-high and slowly add the remaining 1¼ cups sugar, then beat on high speed until the meringue is thick and glossy and holds almost-stiff peaks. Fold one-third of the whites into the batter to lighten it, then fold in the remaining whites.

Use a ⅓-cup dry measuring cup to scoop up the batter, then smooth the top and scrape the batter into one of the 24 lined cups. Repeat with the remaining batter.

Bake for 10 minutes. Rotate the pan and bake for another 10 minutes, or until a cake tester or a wooden skewer inserted in the center of a cupcake comes out clean. Remove the cupcakes from the tins and let cool to room temperature on a cooling rack.

Using a pastry bag fitted with a star tip, pipe a spiral mound of buttercream on top of each cupcake, or simply spread the frosting with a small palette knife or icing spatula. Garnish with the chocolate shavings, if using.

The cupcakes are best frosted and eaten the day they are baked, but they can be refrigerated for up to 2 days; bring to room temperature before serving.   **MAKES 24 CUPCAKES**

NOTE *To make chocolate shavings, run a vegetable peeler across a thick bar of chocolate.*

vanilla buttercream frosting

1¾ cups plus 2 tablespoons granulated sugar

¾ cup egg whites (from about 6 large eggs)

3½ sticks (14 ounces) unsalted butter, cut into ½-inch pieces,
    at room temperature

1 tablespoon vanilla paste (see Sources, page 346) or pure vanilla extract

Fill a medium saucepan halfway with water and bring to a simmer over medium heat. Combine the sugar and egg whites in the bowl of a stand mixer, set over the simmering water, and whisk constantly until the sugar has dissolved and the mixture is hot to the touch (150° to 160°F).

Remove the bowl from the heat, immediately place on the mixer stand, and, using the whisk attachment, whip on high speed until the whites are thick and hold stiff peaks and the whites and the bowl are cool to the touch, 10 to 12 minutes.

Switch to the paddle attachment. Beating on medium speed, add the butter 2 or 3 pieces at a time, being sure each batch is incorporated before adding more. If at any point the mixture looks broken, increase the speed to medium-high and beat to bring it back together, then reduce the speed and continue adding the butter.

Once all of the butter has been added, check the consistency. If the frosting is too thin to hold its shape, beat for a few more minutes to thicken. Turn the mixer speed to low and add the vanilla.

MAKES ABOUT 5 CUPS

CHOCOLATE BUTTERCREAM FROSTING Omit the vanilla. Beat 5 ounces 61 to 64% chocolate (see Sources, page 346), melted and cooled, into the finished frosting.

devil's food cupcakes

1⅔ cups cake flour

⅓ cup plus 1 tablespoon unsweetened alkalized cocoa powder (see Sources, page 346)

1 teaspoon baking powder

1 teaspoon baking soda

1½ cups granulated sugar

½ teaspoon kosher salt

1 cup buttermilk

1 cup sour cream

3 large eggs, lightly beaten

6 tablespoons (3 ounces) unsalted butter, melted

Chocolate Buttercream Frosting (left)

Semisweet chocolate shavings (optional; see Note, page 315)

Preheat the oven to 350°F. Line 24 cupcake cups with paper liners.

Sift the cake flour, cocoa powder, baking powder, baking soda, and sugar into the bowl of a stand mixer. Stir in the salt. Place the bowl on the mixer stand and fit the mixer with the paddle.

Combine the buttermilk and sour cream in a large measuring cup or a bowl. Stir the eggs and melted butter together in a bowl.

With the mixer on medium-low speed, add the buttermilk and egg mixtures alternately, scraping down the sides often to prevent any lumps in the mixture.

Divide the batter among the lined cupcake cups. Bake for 10 minutes. Rotate the pan and bake for another 10 minutes, or until a cake tester or a wooden skewer inserted in the center of a cupcake comes out clean. Remove the cupcakes from the tins and let cool to room temperature on a cooling rack.

Use a pastry bag fitted with a star tip to pipe rosettes of buttercream on top of the cupcakes, or simply spread the frosting with a small palette knife or icing spatula. Garnish with the chocolate shavings, if using.

The cupcakes are best frosted and eaten the day they are baked, but they can be refrigerated for up to 2 days; bring to room temperature before serving.

PHOTOGRAPH ON PAGE 314

MAKES 24 CUPCAKES

carrot cake cupcakes

CUPCAKES

2 cups cake flour

1 teaspoon baking powder

1 teaspoon baking soda

2 teaspoons ground cinnamon

4 large eggs

¼ cup whole milk

1 teaspoon vanilla paste (see Sources, page 346) or pure vanilla extract

1 cup granulated sugar

1 cup packed light brown sugar

1 cup canola oil

3 cups finely shredded carrots

1½ cups coarsely chopped toasted walnuts

CREAM CHEESE FROSTING (MAKES ABOUT 3¾ CUPS)

1½ pounds cream cheese, at room temperature

½ pound (2 sticks) unsalted butter, cut into chunks, at room temperature

1½ cups powdered sugar, sifted

1 teaspoon vanilla paste (see Sources, page 346) or pure vanilla extract

Preheat the oven to 350°F. Line 24 cupcake cups with paper liners.

Sift together the flour, baking powder, baking soda, and cinnamon; set aside.

In the bowl of a stand mixer fitted with the paddle, beat the eggs, milk, vanilla, and both sugars until smooth. Beat in the oil. Slowly add the dry ingredients. Mix in the carrots and 1 cup of the chopped walnuts.

Divide the batter among the lined cupcake cups. Bake for 10 minutes. Rotate the pan and bake for another 10 minutes, or until a cake tester or wooden skewer inserted in the center of a cupcake comes out clean. Remove the cupcakes from the tins and let cool to room temperature on a cooling rack.

Meanwhile, in the bowl of a stand mixer fitted with the paddle, beat the cream cheese at medium speed until smooth. Add the butter and mix until smooth. Beat in the powdered sugar, then add the vanilla. Scrape down the sides and beat for 30 seconds on high speed.

Spread the tops of the cupcakes with the cream cheese frosting and sprinkle with the remaining chopped walnuts.

The cupcakes are best frosted and eaten the day they are baked, but they can be refrigerated for up to 2 days; bring to room temperature before serving.

PHOTOGRAPH ON PAGE 314   **MAKES 24 CUPCAKES**

ice creams

All of these ice creams use essentially the same base, so when you know one of these ice creams, you know many. The best ice creams all start from a cooked custard, which is very easy: combine the sugar and egg yolks, slowly whisk in the hot cream and/or milk to temper (or warm) the yolks, return the mixture to the pan, cook until it thickens, and strain it into a bowl set in an ice bath to halt the cooking. It shouldn't take more than 10 minutes once you've gathered the ingredients. Just be sure to use a heavy-bottomed pan, so the custard doesn't scorch. And be sure the base is thoroughly

chilled—the less time it takes to freeze in the ice cream machine, the better the texture will be.

Chocolate, cherries, caramel, or many other ingredients can be added to this base. For coffee ice cream, we infuse the cream with coffee beans. I particularly love the mint variation because it's a pure vanilla white, not artificially green, so that the minty punch is surprising.

If you don't freeze this basic base, it's the sauce known as crème Anglaise, or vanilla sauce. Serve it over fresh berries.

Note: While the general ratio here is 10 egg yolks for a quart of liquid, large eggs vary in size, with the yolks ranging from 0.5 to 0.7 ounces (15 to 20 grams), West Coast eggs being on the smaller side, East Coast on the larger. If you own a scale, I recommend that you weigh your yolks for consistency, using 5.2 ounces (150 grams) for each quart of liquid.

vanilla ice cream

2 cups whole milk

2 cups heavy cream

¾ cup plus 2 tablespoons granulated sugar

1 vanilla bean, split lengthwise, or 1 tablespoon vanilla paste
   (see Sources, page 346)

10 large egg yolks

Pinch of kosher salt

Pour the milk and cream into a large saucepan, and add ½ cup of the sugar. With a paring knife, scrape the seeds from the vanilla bean, if using, and add them to the liquid, along with the pod. Or stir in the vanilla paste. Bring to just below a simmer over medium-high heat, stirring to dissolve the sugar; a skin will form on top and the liquid should just begin to bubble. Remove the pan from the heat and let steep, uncovered, for 20 minutes.

Remove the vanilla bean from the pan, if you used it. Return the pan to the heat and heat until the milk is just below a simmer.

Meanwhile, whisk the remaining 6 tablespoons sugar and the yolks in a bowl until slightly thickened and the whisk leaves a trail. Slowly, while whisking, add about ½ cup of the hot milk mixture to the yolks, then whisk in the remaining milk mixture. Set a fine-mesh basket strainer over a clean saucepan and strain the liquid into the pan.

Prepare an ice bath in a large bowl and set a medium bowl in the ice bath; have a strainer ready.

Put the saucepan over medium heat and cook, stirring constantly and scraping the bottom and sides often with a wooden spoon, until steam begins to rise from the surface and the custard thickens enough to coat the spoon. Strain into the bowl, add the salt, and let cool, stirring from time to time.

Refrigerate until cold or, preferably, overnight.

Pour the custard into an ice cream maker and freeze according to the manufacturer's instructions. When the texture is "soft serve," transfer to a storage container and freeze to harden. (The ice cream is best eaten within a day, but it can be made several days ahead.)

MAKES A GENEROUS 1 QUART

chocolate ice cream

7 ounces 55% chocolate (see Sources, page 346), cut into ½-inch pieces

2 cups whole milk

2 cups heavy cream

1½ cups granulated sugar

10 large egg yolks

Pinch of kosher salt

Melt the chocolate in the top of a double boiler or a metal bowl set over a saucepan of barely simmering water.

Pour the milk and cream into a large saucepan and heat over medium-high heat until warm. Reduce the heat to medium, whisk in the melted chocolate, and heat until just below a simmer.

Meanwhile, whisk the sugar and yolks in a medium bowl until slightly thickened and the whisk leaves a trail. Slowly, whisking constantly, add about ½ cup of the hot liquid to the yolks, then whisk in the remaining liquid. Set a fine-mesh basket strainer over a clean saucepan and strain the liquid into the pan.

Prepare an ice bath in a large bowl. Set a medium bowl in the ice bath; have a strainer ready.

Put the saucepan over medium heat and cook, stirring constantly and scraping the bottom and sides often with a wooden spoon, until steam begins to rise from the surface and the custard thickens enough to coat the spoon. Strain into the bowl, add the salt, and let cool, stirring from time to time.

Refrigerate until cold or, preferably, overnight.

Pour the custard into an ice cream maker and freeze according to the manufacturer's instructions. When the texture is "soft serve," transfer to a storage container and freeze to harden. (The ice cream is best eaten within a day, but it can be made several days ahead.)

MAKES A GENEROUS 1 QUART

mint chocolate chip ice cream

2 cups whole milk

2 cups heavy cream

½ cup (½ ounce) loosely packed mint leaves

1⅓ cups granulated sugar

10 large egg yolks

3 ounces 55% chocolate (see Sources, page 346), cut into very small chips (about ⅛ inch; about 1¼ cups)

Pour the milk and cream into a large saucepan, add the mint, and bring to a simmer over medium heat. Remove from the heat and let sit at room temperature for 20 minutes to infuse the mint flavor.

Strain the milk through a fine-mesh basket strainer into a clean saucepan. Add ⅔ cup of the sugar and heat over medium-high heat to just below a simmer, whisking to dissolve the sugar.

Meanwhile, whisk the remaining ⅔ cup sugar and the yolks in a medium bowl until slightly thickened and the whisk leaves a trail. Slowly, while whisking, add about ½ cup of the hot milk mixture to the yolks, then whisk in the remaining milk mixture. Set a fine-mesh basket strainer over a clean saucepan and strain the liquid into the pan.

Prepare an ice bath in a large bowl. Set a medium bowl in the ice bath; have a strainer ready.

Put the saucepan over medium heat and cook, stirring constantly and scraping the bottom and sides often with a wooden spoon, until steam begins to rise from the surface and the custard thickens enough to coat the spoon. Strain into the bowl and let cool, stirring from time to time.

Refrigerate until cold or, preferably, overnight.

Pour the custard into an ice cream maker and freeze according to the manufacturer's instructions. When the texture is "soft serve," fold in the chocolate chips, transfer to a storage container, and freeze to harden. (The ice cream is best eaten within a day, but it can be made several days ahead.) **MAKES A GENEROUS 1 QUART**

cherry ice cream

2⅔ cups cherry puree, preferably Boiron (see Sources, page 346)

1 cup whole milk

1 cup heavy cream

⅓ cup granulated sugar

12 large egg yolks

Pour the cherry puree into a medium saucepan and simmer gently over medium heat, stirring from time to time and lowering the heat as necessary, until reduced to 1⅓ cups, 20 to 25 minutes. As the puree reduces, it can be transferred to a smaller pan, to help prevent scorching. Remove from the heat and let cool completely.

Pour the milk and cream into a large saucepan, add about half of the sugar, and heat to just below a simmer, stirring to dissolve the sugar.

Meanwhile, whisk the yolks and the remaining sugar in a medium bowl until slightly thickened and the whisk leaves a trail. Slowly, while whisking, add about ½ cup of the hot milk mixture to the yolks, then whisk in the remaining milk mixture. Set a fine-mesh basket strainer over a clean saucepan and strain the liquid into the pan.

Prepare an ice bath in a large bowl. Set a medium bowl in the ice bath; have a strainer ready.

Put the saucepan over medium heat and cook, stirring constantly and scraping the bottom and sides often with a wooden spoon, until steam begins to rise from the surface and the custard thickens enough to coat the spoon. Strain into the bowl and let cool, stirring from time to time.

Whisk the cherry puree into the custard. Refrigerate until cold or, preferably, overnight.

Pour the custard into an ice cream maker and freeze according to the manufacturer's instructions. When the texture is "soft serve," transfer to a storage container and freeze to harden. (The ice cream is best eaten within a day, but it can be made several days ahead.) **MAKES A GENEROUS 1 QUART**

caramel ice cream

1¾ cups granulated sugar

½ cup water

2 cups whole milk, warm

2 cups heavy cream, warm

10 large egg yolks

¾ teaspoon kosher salt

Put 1½ cups plus 2 tablespoons of the sugar in a deep heavy saucepan and stir in the water to moisten the sugar and make a mixture that resembles wet sand. (This will help the sugar caramelize evenly.) Bring to a simmer over medium heat, stirring to dissolve the sugar, then simmer, without stirring, for 15 minutes, or until the sugar melts into a rich amber caramel. If any sugar crystallizes on the sides of the pan, brush with a wet pastry brush.

Remove the pan from the heat and slowly (to prevent bubbling up) stir in the milk and cream. Should the caramel seize and harden, return the mixture to the heat and stir to dissolve the caramel, then remove from the heat.

Whisk the remaining 2 tablespoons of sugar and yolks in a medium bowl until slightly thickened and the whisk leaves a trail. Slowly, while whisking, add about ½ cup of the hot liquid to the yolks, then whisk in the remaining liquid. Set a fine-mesh basket strainer over a clean saucepan and strain the liquid into the pan.

Prepare an ice bath in a large bowl. Set a medium bowl in the ice bath; have a strainer ready.

Place the saucepan over medium heat and cook, stirring constantly and scraping the bottom and sides often with a wooden spoon, until steam begins to rise from the surface and the custard thickens enough to coat the spoon. Strain into the bowl, add the salt, and let cool, stirring from time to time.

Refrigerate until cold or, preferably, overnight.

Pour the custard into an ice cream machine and freeze according to the manufacturer's instructions. When the texture is "soft serve," transfer to a storage container and freeze to harden. (The ice cream is best eaten within a day, but it can be made several days ahead.)

MAKES A GENEROUS 1 QUART

coffee ice cream

3 tablespoons coffee beans

2 cups whole milk

2 cups heavy cream

¾ cup plus 2 tablespoons granulated sugar

10 large egg yolks

Pinch of kosher salt

Using the bottom of a heavy pot or a rolling pin, lightly crush the coffee beans, splitting each one into 2 or 3 pieces. Pour the milk and cream into a large saucepan, add the coffee beans and ½ cup of the sugar, and bring to just under a simmer over medium-high heat, stirring to dissolve the sugar; a skin will form on top and the liquid should just begin to bubble. Remove the pan from the heat and let steep, uncovered, for 1 hour.

Return the pan to the heat and heat until the milk is just below the simmer.

Meanwhile, whisk the remaining 6 tablespoons sugar and the yolks in a bowl until slightly thickened and the whisk leaves a trail. Slowly, while whisking, add about ½ cup of the hot milk mixture to the yolks, then whisk in the remaining milk mixture. Set a fine-mesh basket strainer over a clean saucepan and strain the liquid into the pan; discard the coffee beans.

Prepare an ice bath in a large bowl. Set a medium bowl in the ice bath; have a strainer ready.

Put the saucepan over medium heat and cook, stirring constantly and scraping the bottom and sides often with a wooden spoon, until steam begins to rise from the surface and the custard thickens enough to coat the spoon. Strain into the bowl, add the salt, and let cool, stirring from time to time.

Refrigerate until cold or, preferably, overnight.

Pour the custard into an ice cream machine and freeze according to the manufacturer's instructions. When the texture is "soft serve," transfer to a storage container and freeze to harden. (The ice cream is best eaten within a day, but it can be made several days ahead.)

MAKES A GENEROUS 1 QUART

banana split

½ cup heavy cream

1½ tablespoons granulated sugar

¼ teaspoon vanilla paste (see Sources, page 346) or pure vanilla extract

2 ripe bananas, cut lengthwise in half

⅓ cup finely chopped fresh pineapple or canned crushed pineapple

About ¼ cup Cherry Compote (page 343)

About ¼ cup Chocolate Sauce (page 344)

2 scoops Vanilla Ice Cream (page 319)

2 scoops Cherry Ice Cream (page 320)

2 scoops Chocolate Ice Cream (page 319)

2 tablespoons chopped Candied Pecans (page 238) or pecans

2 cherries

This is an over-the-top dessert, an ode to American innocence and abundance—three different kinds of ice cream, nuts, whipped cream, both bananas and pineapple, cherry compote, and chocolate sauce. This is a recipe for two to share.

Combine the cream, sugar, and vanilla in a medium bowl and whip until the cream holds medium peaks. Put the cream in a large pastry bag fitted with a medium star tip.

Arrange the bananas in a large serving dish. Spoon the pineapple, cherry compote, and chocolate sauce into three separate areas. Top the pineapple with the vanilla ice cream, the cherry compote with the cherry ice cream, and the chocolate sauce with the chocolate ice cream. Pipe the whipped cream over the top and garnish with the pecans and cherries.

SERVES 2

ice cream sandwiches

1 quart homemade ice cream (pages 319–22), just spun,
    or store-bought ice cream, softened
Twenty-four 2- to 3-inch cookies

My fondness for this American classic is so well-known that my French pastry chef at per se created a four-star version. But here's a simple version that's hard to beat. You can use any kind of cookie and any kind of ice cream. Simply spread the soft ice cream on a quarter sheet pan (see Note, page 306) and freeze it until firm, then use the same cutter you used for the cookies to cut out squares or rounds of ice cream and sandwich them between the cookies. Kids love this, but it's also a fabulous adult dessert.

You can use just one kind or a variety of ice cream flavors and cookies. Some of our favorite combinations are Chocolate Chip Cookies (page 326) with Vanilla Ice Cream (page 319), Chocolate Shortbread Cookies (page 327) with Mint Chocolate Chip Ice Cream (page 320), and Linzer Cookies (page 331) with Chocolate Ice Cream (page 319).

Line a quarter sheet pan with a piece of plastic wrap, leaving an overhang on both long sides. Spread the ice cream in an even layer in the pan. Fold over the plastic and freeze until firm.

Lift up the edges of the plastic wrap to remove the ice cream. Have a bowl of hot water at your side. Using the cutter you used to make the cookies or a knife, cut squares or rounds of ice cream slightly smaller than the cookies, dipping the cutter or knife in the hot water and drying it with a towel before making each cut. Assemble the sandwiches and serve immediately, or wrap in plastic wrap and freeze for up to 3 days.

MAKES 12 ICE CREAM SANDWICHES

cookies *A crème brûlée is something you get introduced to, often when you're eating out: "Oh, this is a crème brûlée." But unlike crème brûlée, cookies have been there from the beginning. There's a comfort in things that are with us all our lives. My favorite? Without hesitation: chocolate chip. Ideally, crunchy on the outside, chewy on the inside.*

chocolate chip cookies

2⅓ cups plus 1 tablespoon all-purpose flour

¾ teaspoon baking soda

1 teaspoon kosher salt

5 ounces 55% chocolate (see Sources, page 346), cut into chip-sized pieces (about 1¼ cups)

5 ounces 70 to 72% chocolate (see Sources, page 346), cut into chip-sized pieces (about 1¼ cups)

½ pound (2 sticks) cold unsalted butter, cut into small pieces

1 cup packed dark brown sugar, preferably molasses sugar (see Sources, page 346, and Note)

¾ cup granulated sugar

2 large eggs

This is our version of what is arguably the best cookie ever. I like to use different chocolates, one sweeter, one with a more complex bittersweet balance. After you chop the chocolate, sift it to remove any tiny fragments to give the cookies a cleaner look. If you like softer cookies, don't underbake them, just mist them with water before baking.

Of course, chocolate chip cookies are great on their own, but you could also break some up and add them to Vanilla Ice Cream (page 319) about halfway through the freezing process.

Position the oven racks in the lower and upper thirds of the oven and preheat the oven to 350°F. Line two baking sheets with Silpats or parchment paper.

Sift the flour and baking soda into a medium bowl. Stir in the salt.

Put the chips in a fine-mesh basket strainer and shake to remove any chocolate "dust" (small fragments).

In the bowl of a stand mixer fitted with the paddle, beat half the butter on medium speed until fairly smooth. Add both sugars and the remaining butter, and beat until well combined, then beat for a few minutes, until the mixture is light and creamy. Scrape down the sides of the bowl. Add the eggs one at a time, beating until the first one is incorporated before adding the next and scraping the bowl as necessary. Add the dry ingredients and mix on low speed to combine. Mix in the chocolate.

Remove the bowl from the mixer and fold the dough with a spatula to be sure that the chocolate is evenly incorporated. The dough or shaped cookies can be refrigerated, well wrapped, for up to 5 days or frozen for up to 2 weeks. Freeze shaped cookies on the baking sheets until firm, then transfer to freezer containers. (Defrost frozen cookies overnight in the refrigerator before baking.)

Using about 2 level tablespoons per cookie, shape the dough into balls. Arrange 8 cookies on each pan, leaving about 2 inches between them, because the dough will spread. Bake for 12 minutes, or until the tops are no longer shiny, switching the position and rotating the pans halfway through baking.

Cool the cookies on the pans on cooling racks for about 2 minutes to firm up a bit, then transfer to the racks to cool completely. Repeat to bake the remaining cookies. (The cookies can be stored in an airtight container for up to 2 days.) **MAKES ABOUT THIRTY 3-INCH COOKIES**

NOTE *If your brown sugar has hardened, soften it in the microwave for 15 to 30 seconds.*

shortbread cookies

14 tablespoons (1¾ sticks; 7 ounces) unsalted butter, at room temperature

½ cup granulated sugar, plus extra for sprinkling

1 teaspoon vanilla paste (see Sources, page 346) or pure vanilla extract

2 cups all-purpose flour

These are wonderful, simple cookies. They're a perfect cookie to cut into festive shapes, and you can decorate them during the holidays. They also make great gifts. And they're very satisfying, not too sweet.

In the bowl of a stand mixer fitted with the paddle, mix the butter and sugar on low speed to combine, then increase to medium speed and beat for about 3 minutes until light and creamy. Scrape down the sides of the bowl, and mix in the vanilla. On the lowest speed, mix in the flour to combine, then increase the speed to medium and beat until the dough begins to cling to the paddle and no longer looks dry; do not wait for it to form a solid mass.

Transfer the dough to a board and use the heel of your hand or a pastry scraper to bring the dough together. Put the dough on a large piece of plastic wrap and pat it into a rectangle ½ to ¾ inch thick. Refrigerate the dough for 30 minutes. (The dough can be refrigerated for up to 5 days or frozen for up to 2 weeks; defrost frozen dough overnight in the refrigerator.)

Roll out the dough between two pieces of parchment paper to about ¼ inch thick. Remove the top sheet of parchment and reserve. Cut the cookies into 2-inch squares, leaving them on the parchment. The dough will have softened; cover with the reserved parchment, slide onto a baking sheet, and refrigerate for about 15 minutes, or until the cookies are firm enough to remove from the parchment.

Position the racks in the lower and upper thirds of the oven and preheat the oven to 350°F. Line two baking sheets with Silpats or parchment paper.

Remove the top sheet of parchment. Using a small offset spatula, transfer the cookies to the baking sheets, arranging them 1 inch apart. The trimmings can be pressed together and rerolled once for additional cookies. Sprinkle the cookies with sugar.

Bake for about 12 minutes, switching the position and rotating the sheets halfway through baking, until crisp and light golden brown. Remove the sheets from the oven and cool for 2 to 5 minutes on cooling racks to firm the cookies up a bit. Transfer the cookies directly to the racks to cool completely. (The cookies can be stored in an airtight container for up to 2 days.) **MAKES ABOUT TWENTY-FOUR 2-INCH COOKIES**

CHOCOLATE CHIP

2¹/₃ c. plus 1 Tbsp. flour ⟶

³/₄ tsp. baking soda ⟶

1 tsp. salt ⟶

¹/₂ lb. butter ⟶

COOKIES

1 c. dark brown sugar

2 large eggs

1 TBSP

VALRHON

5 oz. 70% chocolate

5 oz. 55% chocolate

3/4 c. granulated sugar

on chocolate The quality of chocolate ranges from poor to fantastic, and happily, more of the fantastic chocolate is available than ever before. Chocolates are composed of cocoa (which provides the flavor and fat) and sugar (which gives chocolate its sweetness). The higher the percentage of cocoa, the less sugar it will contain. If you love chocolate, try different brands and pay attention to their differing percentages of cocoa to see what balance you prefer.

I've really come to appreciate the bitterness of chocolate, the ones with the least amount of sugar. That's where you see the true flavor of chocolate; moreover, if you're cooking with it, it allows you to add your own sugar.

What type of chocolate you use should depend on what you're using it for. If you're making chocolate truffles, or a chocolate icing, you want high quality because the focus is on the taste of the chocolate. If you're using it in a cake or in a cookie—anything in which there are other flavors, such as molasses, brown sugar, eggs, and butter—the quality of the chocolate may be less important.

¾ cup granulated sugar

1½ cups plus 3 tablespoons all-purpose flour

¾ cup plus 1 tablespoon unsweetened alkalized cocoa powder (see Sources, page 346)

½ teaspoon baking soda

1½ teaspoons kosher salt

15 tablespoons (7½ ounces) unsalted butter, cut into ¾-inch cubes, at room temperature

Chocolate shortbread cookies are a little different from our other shortbread cookie in that they have a little leavening in them in addition to the cocoa powder. The latter gives the cookie a deep mahogany color and a robust flavor. Meanwhile, the salt enhances the chocolate. If you ever need a chocolate crust, pulverize this cookie in a food processor and use it as the base.

In the bowl of a stand mixer fitted with the paddle, mix the sugar, flour, cocoa powder, baking soda, and salt on low speed. Slowly mix in the butter, a few pieces at a time; the dough will have a sandy texture, then form pebble-sized pieces. Continue to beat just until the dough begins to cling to the paddle and no longer looks dry; do not wait for it to form a solid mass.

Transfer the dough to a board and use the heel of your hand or a pastry scraper to bring the dough together. Shape into a block about

5 by 7 inches. Wrap in plastic wrap and refrigerate for 1 hour. (The dough can be refrigerated for up to 5 days or frozen for up to 2 weeks; defrost frozen dough overnight in the refrigerator.)

Cut the block of dough in half. One at a time, roll each piece of dough out between two pieces of parchment paper to ¼ inch thick. Remove the top piece of parchment and reserve. Using a knife, cut the dough into 1¾-by-3-inch rectangles, or use a cookie cutter to cut into 2-inch rounds (or any shape you like), leaving the dough on the parchment. The dough will have softened; cover with the reserved parchment, slide onto a baking sheet, and refrigerate for about 15 minutes, or until the cookies are firm enough to remove from the parchment.

Position the racks in the lower and upper thirds of the oven and preheat the oven to 350°F. Line two baking sheets with Silpats or parchment paper.

Remove the top sheets of parchment. Using a small offset spatula, transfer the cookies to the baking sheets, arranging them 1 inch apart. The trimmings can be pressed together and rerolled once for additional cookies.

Bake for 10 to 12 minutes, until the tops are no longer shiny, switching the position and rotating the sheets halfway through baking.

Remove the sheets from the oven and cool for 2 to 5 minutes on cooling racks to firm the cookies up a bit. Transfer the cookies directly to the racks to cool completely. (The cookies can be stored in an airtight container for up to 2 days.)

MAKES ABOUT TWENTY-FOUR 1¾-BY-3-INCH RECTANGLES OR 3-INCH ROUNDS

1 cup ground peeled hazelnuts

1½ cups all-purpose flour

¼ teaspoon ground cinnamon

½ teaspoon unsweetened alkalized cocoa powder (see Sources, page 346)

12 tablespoons (1½ sticks; 6 ounces) unsalted butter, at room temperature

1 teaspoon grated lemon zest

½ teaspoon fresh lemon juice

¾ cup powdered sugar

Linzer dough can be made with almonds or, as here, hazelnuts, and it can be used to make cookies or a crust for a tart. The cookies are great by themselves but even better sandwiched with a filling of Raspberry Jam (page 247).

Whisk together the hazelnuts, flour, cinnamon, and cocoa powder in a medium bowl; set aside.

In the bowl of a stand mixer fitted with the paddle, mix the butter, lemon zest, and lemon juice on medium speed. Add the sugar and beat for 2 to 3 minutes, until light and fluffy. Add the dry ingredients, and mix on low speed to combine, then increase the speed to medium and beat to incorporate, scraping down the sides as necessary.

Transfer the dough to a work surface and form into a 7-inch square. Wrap in plastic wrap and refrigerate for at least 30 minutes, or up to 5 days.

Position the racks in the lower and upper thirds of the oven and preheat the oven to 350°F. Line two baking sheets with Silpats or parchment paper.

Cut the dough in half. Roll each piece out between two pieces of parchment paper to just under ¼ inch thick. Cut out cookies with a 3-inch square cutter (or any other shape) and transfer to the prepared sheets, leaving about 1 inch between them. Bake for 18 to 20 minutes, switching the position and rotating the sheets halfway through, until light golden. Remove the sheets from the oven and cool for 2 to 5 minutes to firm the cookies up. Transfer the cookies directly to the racks to cool completely. (The cookies can be stored in an airtight container for up to 2 days.) **MAKES ABOUT TWENTY-FOUR 3-INCH COOKIES**

BASICS

mayonnaise

4 large egg yolks
2 cups canola oil
1 tablespoon plus 1 teaspoon fresh lemon juice
2 teaspoons kosher salt

Mayonnaise is extremely versatile and can be flavored in any number of directions. We use aioli, mayonnaise flavored with garlic, for sandwiches or tartines, and it is also wonderful with cooked vegetables and as a condiment for fish. Homemade mayonnaise tastes better, you can control the flavor and consistency, and you can enhance it as you wish. And it's not at all difficult to do—we make it in the food processor.

Put the egg yolks in a food processor and process to combine. With the motor running, begin adding the oil very, very slowly (if your processor has a tube with a small hole in the center to control the stream, this is the time to use it), blending until emulsified and thickened. Add the lemon juice and salt. Refrigerate in a covered container for up to 1 week.

MAKES ABOUT 2 CUPS

AIOLI Substitute Garlic Oil from Garlic Confit (page 266) for the canola oil.

PIMENT D'ESPELETTE AIOLI Whisk 1 teaspoon piment d'Espelette (see page 208) into the aioli.

LEMON AIOLI Add finely minced Preserved Whole Lemon peel (page 263) to taste to the aioli.

oven-roasted tomato sauce

2 tablespoons canola oil
1 cup finely chopped yellow onion
1 cup minced leeks (white and pale green parts only)
1 cup finely chopped fennel
1 tablespoon plus 1 teaspoon minced garlic
Kosher salt
2 tablespoons light brown sugar
2 tablespoons red wine vinegar
Two 28- to 32-ounce cans San Marzano whole peeled tomatoes
1 Sachet (page 342)
Freshly ground black pepper

This is a convenient tomato sauce because it's all done in the oven—you don't need to spend time tending the pot on the stovetop. Use San Marzano tomatoes, from the eponymous region in Italy that grows the best plum tomatoes for sauces. This version is excellent with grits, polenta, or meatballs.

Preheat the oven to 350°F.

Combine the oil, onion, leeks, fennel, and garlic in a large ovenproof Dutch oven or a baking dish and sprinkle with salt. Put in the oven and cook for 45 minutes to 1 hour, until the vegetables are tender and beginning to caramelize.

Stir in the brown sugar and vinegar and return to the oven for another 20 minutes, or until the liquid is absorbed. Remove from the oven.

Meanwhile, drain the canned tomatoes and remove the seeds. Coarsely chop half the tomatoes. Puree the other half in a food processor.

Add the tomatoes to the vegetables along with the sachet, season with salt and pepper to taste, and return to the oven for 1½ hours, stirring every 30 minutes. The sauce should be thick and have a full rich flavor. Run the side of a spoon through the sauce—if it runs back together immediately, it is too thin. Return it to the oven and cook until thickened.

Discard the sachet and let the sauce cool to room temperature. Refrigerate in a covered container for up to 1 week.

MAKES ABOUT 2½ CUPS

romesco sauce

3 dried Nora chiles (see Sources, page 346) or other dried sweet chiles, such as pasillas
6 plum tomatoes, cored and halved lengthwise
1 red bell pepper, halved lengthwise, cored, and seeded
½ large onion, cut in half
1 large garlic clove
¼ cup extra virgin olive oil
Kosher salt and freshly ground black pepper
Canola oil
6 crustless 2-inch cubes country bread
¼ cup slivered almonds
2 tablespoons plus 1 teaspoon sherry vinegar
1 teaspoon sweet paprika
1½ teaspoons piment d'Espelette (see page 208)

Romesco is a fantastic all-purpose sauce that goes well almost across the board, with vegetables, meat, and fish. Toss roasted potatoes with it, spoon it over steak, serve with fish, or add it as a garnish for scrambled eggs.

continued

Preheat the oven to 400°F.

Remove the stems and seeds from the chiles. Put the chiles in a small bowl, cover with hot water, and let soak for 30 minutes.

Meanwhile, put the tomatoes, bell pepper, onion, and garlic in a 9-by-13-inch baking dish. Toss with the olive oil and season with salt and pepper. Turn the tomatoes and peppers cut side down. Roast for 1 hour, until the vegetables are well browned with some charring on the edges. Remove from the oven and let cool slightly.

Remove the skins from the tomatoes and the peppers. Remove the outer layer from the onion. Reserve any liquid in the roasting pan.

Heat some canola oil in a medium frying pan over medium heat until warm. Add the bread and toast, turning to toast on all sides, for 2 to 3 minutes. Transfer the bread to a plate. Add the nuts to the pan and toast for 30 seconds to 1 minute, until fragrant. Transfer to a plate.

Drain the chiles and transfer to a Vita-Mix. Add the roasted vegetables, as well as any liquid from them, and blend until smooth. Break up the bread slightly and add to the blender, along with the nuts, vinegar, paprika, and Espelette. Blend until smooth. Season with salt to taste.

Refrigerate in a covered container for up to 2 weeks.

MAKES ABOUT 2 CUPS

mornay sauce

1½ tablespoons (¾ ounce) unsalted butter
¼ cup diced (¼-inch) Spanish onion
Kosher salt
1½ tablespoons all-purpose flour
1 cup whole milk
½ cup heavy cream
1 small bay leaf
2 black peppercorns
2 whole cloves
Freshly grated nutmeg
Freshly ground white pepper
3 tablespoons grated Comté or Emmentaler cheese

Mornay is simply a béchamel sauce into which you whisk grated cheese. Traditional uses for it are as a sauce for steamed broccoli, cauliflower, or spinach (see page 206).

Melt the butter in a medium saucepan set on a diffuser over medium heat. Add the onion and a pinch of salt and cook slowly, stirring occasionally, for 2 to 3 minutes, until the onion is translucent. Sprinkle in the flour and cook, stirring constantly so the roux does not color, for 3 minutes. Whisking constantly, add the milk and cream and whisk until fully incorporated. Bring to a simmer, whisking, and add the bay

leaf, peppercorns, and cloves. Move the pan to one side of the diffuser, away from direct heat, to prevent scorching, and simmer gently, whisking occasionally, for 30 minutes; lower the heat as necessary to keep the sauce at a very low simmer. (If the sauce does begin to scorch, immediately pour it into a clean pan—don't scrape the bottom of the pan—and continue.)

Remove the sauce from the heat and season with salt to taste, a grating of nutmeg, and a pinch of white pepper. Strain the sauce through a fine-mesh conical strainer into a bowl, add the cheese, and whisk to melt. Use immediately, or transfer to a storage container, press a piece of plastic wrap against the surface to keep a skin from forming, and refrigerate for up to 3 days. If the sauce is too thick after refrigeration, it can be thinned with a little heavy cream when you reheat it.

MAKES 1 CUP

roux

8 tablespoons (1 stick; 4 ounces) unsalted butter
½ cup plus 3 tablespoons all-purpose flour

We use roux, the traditional thickener made by cooking equal parts by weight butter and flour, for sauces and other dishes. For the smoothest sauces, add room-temperature or cold roux to a simmering liquid, or add cold liquid to a hot roux, to prevent the roux from seizing up.

Put the butter in a small skillet or saucepan and set it over medium heat. When it is almost melted, whisk in the flour and cook, whisking constantly and adjusting the heat as necessary so the roux bubbles but does not brown, 3 to 4 minutes. Transfer to a bowl or other container to cool, then store in the refrigerator for up to 2 weeks.

MAKES ⅔ CUP

herb and shallot butter

⅔ cup minced shallots
12 tablespoons (1½ sticks; 6 ounces) plus 1 teaspoon unsalted butter, at room temperature
1 tablespoon finely chopped flat-leaf parsley
1 tablespoon fresh lemon juice
¾ teaspoon kosher salt
¾ teaspoon sweet paprika

Use this compound butter for brushing on meat or fish as it grills, or place a slice of butter atop cooked meat or fish to melt as it is served. Pieces can also be added to melt over clams or mussels after they have opened, or melted on omelets or roasted potatoes. Although traditionally shallots are used raw in this preparation, we sauté them to develop their sweetness.

Combine the shallots and 1 teaspoon of the butter in a small saucepan and cook over very low heat until the shallots are tender but have not browned, about 10 minutes. Remove from the heat and let cool.

Put the remaining 12 tablespoons butter in a small bowl, add the parsley, lemon juice, salt, and paprika, and stir to incorporate. Stir in the shallots. Shape into a log, wrap tightly in plastic wrap, put in a resealable bag, and refrigerate until ready to use; or freeze for up to 1 week. **MAKES A GENEROUS 1 CUP**

clarified butter

1 pound (4 sticks) unsalted butter, cut into pieces

While clarified butter is something that is less commonly needed at home, it does have good uses there. When you clarify butter, you remove all the milk solids that can burn at high temperatures, so clarified butter can be used for sautéing meat and fish (see Caramelized Sea Scallops, page 88) or brushing on Flatbread (page 280). Of course there are few things better to dip some lobster or clams into than hot clarified butter. If you wish, you can clarify more butter than you need and freeze it. It will keep frozen for several months if wrapped airtight.

Put the butter in a small saucepan and melt it over low heat, without stirring. Skim off the foamy layer that has risen to the top and discard. Carefully pour off the clear yellow liquid, the clarified butter, into a container, leaving the white milky layer behind. Cover tightly and refrigerate for up to 1 month, or freeze. **MAKES ABOUT 1½ CUPS**

emulsified butter

Water
Unsalted butter, cut into chunks

Emulsified butter—butter that is liquid but opaque, with the water and milk solids suspended in the fat—is an all-purpose tool. It adds flavor and sheen to a dish. We toss it into vegetables just before serving, use it for basting meat and fish as they sauté, and use it to enrich sauces. It's known as *beurre monté* in French. What's so wonderful about it is its texture, thick and creamy, not oily, so it coats a vegetable like corn on the cob and adheres to it, giving it a rich silky coating.

Make the emulsified butter close to the time it will be used and keep it in a warm place.

No matter the quantity of emulsified butter you will be making, a couple of tablespoons of water helps the emulsion process. Pour the water into a saucepan and bring to a boil. Reduce the heat to low and begin whisking in the butter bit by bit to emulsify. Once you have established the emulsion, continue to add pieces of butter until you have the quantity of emulsified butter that you need. It is important to keep the level of heat gentle and consistent in order to maintain the emulsification. Emulsified butter cannot be stored. Extra can be used as you would melted butter or it can be clarified and used in recipes calling for clarified butter.

parsley water

6 tablespoons water
1 teaspoon canola oil
1 tablespoon honey
3 cups flat-leaf parsley leaves and tender stems,
    washed and patted thoroughly dry

We use parsley water to cook some vegetables when a chicken stock would be too powerful a flavor (see Asparagus Coins, page 192). Parsley is sautéed quickly with some honey, shocked in ice water, then thoroughly pureed with water and strained.

Pour the water into a small bowl and freeze until the water is ice-cold.

Heat a medium frying pan over medium-high heat until hot. Add the oil and swirl to coat the pan. Add the honey and heat to melt and lightly caramelize it for a few seconds. Add the parsley and stir to coat the parsley with the honey and wilt it, about 30 seconds. Transfer the contents of the pan to the ice-cold water to chill the parsley leaves.

Transfer the parsley and liquid to a Vita-Mix and blend until smooth. Strain through a fine-mesh basket strainer into a storage container. The parsley water can be refrigerated for up to 2 days or frozen for up to 1 month. **MAKES A SCANT ½ CUP**

cherry gastrique

22 Bing cherries (about 9 ounces), stems removed
1 cup Banyuls vinegar (see Sources, page 346)
1 cup honey

Gastrique is the French term for a sweet-sour reduction, and it
can be as basic as sugar or honey cooked down with vinegar. It's
customarily used as a sauce base for deeply savory dishes—roasted
duck or venison, for instance—and often includes fruit. But it might
also be the base for a vinaigrette (see Creamy Pepper Dressing, page
183). Part of the nature of the gastrique is its thick, almost honey-
like texture; this is a result of cooking the sugar or honey and the
reduction of the vinegar, which makes it a flavorful sauce. We use it
with the soft-shell crabs (see page 82), and it also makes a perfect
condiment for a cheese board.

Pit 7 of the cherries and coarsely chop. Set aside.

Combine the remaining cherries, the vinegar, and honey in a large
saucepan and bring to a simmer over medium heat, and simmer,
adjusting the heat as necessary (the mixture can easily boil over and/or
burn) and skimming off any foam, for about 45 minutes, until the
gastrique has reached a syrupy consistency and measures about $2/3$ to $3/4$
cup. The bubbles will cluster together like they do on the end of a kid's
bubble wand. To check the consistency, remove from the heat and put a
tablespoon of the gastrique on a cold plate. Refrigerate until cold. The
gastrique should hold its shape when the plate is tilted. If necessary,
return the pan to the heat and continue to cook.

Strain the gastrique through a basket strainer into a bowl, pressing
on the cherries with a wooden spoon to push the pulp through. Stir
in the chopped cherries. Refrigerate in a covered container for up to
1 month; bring to room temperature before serving.

MAKES ABOUT ½ CUP

yellow curry powder

½ teaspoon ground allspice
2 teaspoons anise seeds
1 bay leaf
1 tablespoon brown mustard seeds
1 teaspoon ground cardamom
Two 2-inch pieces cinnamon stick
½ teaspoon whole cloves
2 tablespoons ground coriander
1 tablespoon plus ½ teaspoon ground cumin
1½ tablespoons fennel seeds
1 tablespoon plus 1 teaspoon fenugreek seeds
1 teaspoon freshly grated nutmeg
1 teaspoon whole mace
1¾ teaspoons black peppercorns, preferably Tellicherry
1¾ teaspoons powdered ginger
2 medium star anise
1 tablespoon yellow mustard seeds
2 tablespoons ground turmeric
1¼ teaspoons sweet paprika
1¼ teaspoons Maldon salt or other flaky sea salt

Freshness is the reason to make your own curry powder. If you
have a container of it in your cupboard, I'll bet you wouldn't be
able to tell me when you bought it. The spices that go into a curry
powder are volatile and diminish rapidly with age (see Lightbulb
Moment, page 17). Making your own ensures that your curry will be
powerfully flavored and carry all the nuances that make it such an
exciting ingredient to work with.

Combine all the ingredients in a Vita-Mix. Start the machine on the
lowest speed to break up the cinnamon stick and star anise. After about
30 seconds, gradually increase the speed, eventually grinding at the
highest setting. (Or grind in batches in a spice grinder.)

Set a fine-mesh basket strainer over a medium bowl and add the
ground spices to the strainer. Tap the side of the strainer to shake the
fine powder through. Return the spices left in the strainer to the Vita-
Mix and regrind. Strain again. If there are any unground spices in the
strainer, they can be ground a final time.

Store in a covered container for up to 3 months. **MAKES ABOUT 1 CUP**

melted onions

8 cups sliced onions (about 3 large onions)
Kosher salt
8 tablespoons (1 stick; 4 ounces) unsalted butter, cut into 8 pieces
1 Sachet (page 342)

It's difficult to overstate the power of this simple preparation. Onions, aggressively flavored when raw, acquire a wonderful creamy sweetness when they're cooked slowly, until they're so tender they virtually melt into one another. They can be added to almost anything and make it better. Their sweetness will enhance soups and stews, they can be a garnish on any meat or fish—monkfish, skate, and salmon are especially enhanced with melted onions—or, at room temperature, they can top a lamb sandwich, be added to salads, or stirred into a sauce. Butter is added to these to make them very flavorful and creamy.

Put the onions in a large sauté pan, set over medium-low heat, sprinkle with 2 generous pinches of salt, and cook, stirring from time to time, for about 20 minutes, until the onions have released much of their liquid.

Stir in the butter, add the sachet, cover with a parchment lid (see page 120), and cook slowly over low to medium-low heat for another 30 to 35 minutes. The onions should look creamy at all times; if the butter separates, or the pan looks dry before the onions are done, add a bit of cold water and stir well to re-emulsify the butter. The onions should be meltingly tender but not falling apart or mushy. Season to taste with salt.

Once cooled, the onions can be refrigerated for up to 3 days.

MAKES 2 CUPS

melted leek rounds

8 large leeks (about 1½ pounds)
3 tablespoons Chicken Stock (page 339), Vegetable Stock (page 341), or water
8 ounces (2 sticks) unsalted butter, cut into small chunks
Kosher salt and freshly ground black pepper

Bring a large pot of salted water to a boil (see page 147). Prepare an ice bath. Set a cooling rack over a baking sheet and line it with paper towels.

Meanwhile, cut off the dark green leaves of the leeks, leaving the pale green and tender white parts. Remove and discard the tough outer layer and cut the light green sections into ½-inch rounds.

Put the leeks in a large bowl of warm water and swish them gently to remove any dirt, being careful not to separate the rounds. Lift them from the water. Repeat as needed.

Add half the leeks to the boiling water, and blanch for about 5 minutes, until tender. Remove the leeks with a skimmer and submerge them in the ice bath for no more than 15 seconds, just to chill quickly and preserve their color. Drain on the paper-towel-lined rack, and repeat with the remaining leeks.

Bring the stock to a simmer in a medium sauté pan. Whisk in the butter one piece at a time to emulsify. Add the leeks and season to taste with salt and pepper.

Use immediately, or transfer to a container and refrigerate for up to 3 days. Reheat gently over low heat. As they are reheated, the leeks should look creamy at all times. If the butter breaks, or the pan appears dry, stir in a bit of cold water to re-emulsify the butter.

SERVES 6

traditional and slow-cooker beans

1 pound (about 2½ cups) dried borlotti beans (see Sources, page 346)
1 medium leek, trimmed, split lengthwise, and rinsed
½ onion
½ large carrot, peeled
1 Sachet (page 342)
8 cups water
1 tablespoon red wine vinegar
Kosher salt

The key to cooking beans well is to cook them gently. If you boil them, they begin to fall apart before they're cooked through. The rule is the gentler the better. I'm a huge fan of using slow cookers for beans. The newer models have much better temperature controls and so can cook legumes perfectly every time.

Put the beans in a large bowl, add enough cold water to cover them by at least 2 inches. Let soak overnight.

FOR TRADITIONAL STOVETOP BEANS: Drain the beans. Put them in a large saucepan, add the leek, onion, carrot, and sachet, and pour in the water. Bring to a simmer and simmer for 50 minutes to 1 hour. The beans should be tender but not falling apart. Remove from the heat.

FOR SLOW-COOKER BEANS: Drain the beans. Put in the slow-cooker insert, add the leek, onion, carrot, and sachet, and pour in the water. Turn the slow cooker onto low, cover, and cook for 6 hours, or until tender but not falling apart; stir after 1 hour and then every hour to hour and a half after that.

continued

TO FINISH: Using a slotted spoon, spoon the beans into a bowl or container, discarding the vegetables and sachet. Strain the liquid over the beans. Season with the red wine vinegar and salt. The beans can be refrigerated in their liquid for about 3 days; drain before serving.

MAKES 7 CUPS

pasta dough

2¾ cups (13 ounces) Tipo 00 flour (see Sources, page 346)
1 large egg
14 large egg yolks
1½ teaspoons extra virgin olive oil
1½ teaspoons whole milk

Pasta dough is such an elementary and satisfying process with so many applications that I always try to encourage people to make it at home. You can't achieve the same effects with store-bought fresh pasta, and it's a completely different product from dried pasta.

It's also a wonderful way to get kids into the kitchen and cooking. This is a very rich egg-yolk pasta. Try to find Tipo 00 flour, the "00" designating a finely ground flour; it's usually available in Italian markets and results in a pasta with a soft silky texture.

Mound 2½ cups of the flour on a board. Create a well about 8 inches across in the center by pushing the flour out from the center, leaving some flour at the bottom of the well.

Pour the egg, yolks, olive oil, and milk into the well. Using a fork, mix the ingredients together in the well. Then, little by little, begin to bring in some of the flour from the sides of the well. Continue to bring in the flour until all of it is incorporated and the mixture has a paste-like texture. Using a dough scraper, starting at the outermost part of the well, make chops across from left to right and then top to bottom. Then use the dough scraper to lift the dough from the board and fold it over itself until it completely comes together.

Begin to knead the dough and use the scraper to clean the board. Sprinkle the board with some of the remaining ¼ cup flour. Continue to knead the dough on the floured surface for about 15 minutes, adding flour as needed, until very smooth and elastic.

Lightly dust the dough with flour and wrap tightly in plastic wrap. Refrigerate for at least 12 hours, or up to 24. (Freezing the dough is not recommended; it is better to roll out and dry, or freeze the pasta itself.)

MAKES ABOUT 1½ POUNDS

basic pie crust

2½ cups all-purpose flour, plus additional for rolling
1¼ teaspoons kosher salt
2½ sticks (10 ounces) unsalted butter, cut into ½-inch pieces and chilled
About 5 tablespoons ice water

The secret to a great pie is a great dough that bakes into a flaky, crispy crust. It's not difficult—the key is to avoid overworking the dough. I prefer mixing the dough by hand, but you can use a mixer if you like. As I mentioned earlier, I believe that feeling comfortable making a pie dough is one of those essential skills any cook should have, and it's another technique that gives you versatility in the kitchen. When you know how to make a good pie dough, you can use it for Chicken Potpie (page 24), Cherry Pie (page 308), a blueberry pie, a lemon tart, or a tarte tatin.

Combine the flour and salt in a large bowl, then add the butter and toss to coat with flour. With your hands or a pastry blender, work the butter into the flour, tossing and incorporating any pieces of butter that have settled at the bottom of the bowl, until the butter pieces are no larger than a pea. Drizzle ¼ cup of the water over the top and, using a fork, mix the dough until it just holds together when pinched; add the remaining tablespoon of water if the dough is very dry. Knead the dough until it is completely smooth and the butter is incorporated.

Divide the dough in half, with one piece slightly larger than the other (the larger piece will be for the bottom crust). Shape each half into a 1-inch-thick disk, wrap tightly in plastic wrap, and refrigerate for at least 1 hour, or for up to a day. (If the dough does not rest, it will shrink as it bakes.)

If the dough is too hard to roll, let it rest at room temperature for a few minutes or pound it a few times with a rolling pin. Lightly flour the work surface and a rolling pin. Lightly dust the top of the larger disk of dough with flour and roll it out to a 13- to 14-inch round, about ⅛ inch thick: roll outward from the center, rotating the dough frequently and adding a little flour to the work surface or dough as needed to prevent sticking. Fold the dough in half and transfer to a 9- to 10-inch pie plate, gently easing the dough into the corners and up the sides.

Roll out the second piece of dough in the same manner, to a 12-inch round, about ⅛-inch thick. Place on a parchment-lined baking sheet. Refrigerate both doughs for 15 minutes.

MAKES ONE 9- TO 10-INCH DOUBLE-CRUST PIE

chicken brine

5 lemons, halved
12 bay leaves
1 bunch (4 ounces) flat-leaf parsley
1 bunch (1 ounce) thyme
½ cup clover honey
1 head garlic, halved through the equator
¼ cup black peppercorns
2 cups (10 ounces) Diamond Crystal kosher salt
2 gallons water

The key ingredient here is the lemon, which goes wonderfully with chicken, as do the herbs: bay leaf, parsley, and thyme. This amount of brine will be enough for 10 pounds. (See Brining Meats & Fish, page 75.) If using another brand of kosher salt, use exactly 10 ounces—see page 52.

Combine all the ingredients in a large pot, cover, and bring to a boil. Boil for 1 minute, stirring to dissolve the salt. Remove from the heat and cool completely, then chill before using. The brine can be refrigerated for up to 3 days.   **MAKES 2 GALLONS**

pork brine

¼ cup plus 2 tablespoons honey
12 bay leaves
3 large rosemary sprigs
½ bunch (½ ounce) thyme
½ bunch (about 2 ounces) flat-leaf parsley
½ cup garlic cloves, crushed, skin left on
2 tablespoons black peppercorns
1 cup (5 ounces) Diamond Crystal kosher salt
8 cups water

It's almost always a good idea to brine your pork. Brining it makes it flavorful and keeps it juicy. This brine is distinguished by its use of garlic and rosemary, but you can flavor your brine with almost anything. This amount of brine is ideal for up to 4 pounds of pork. (See Brining Meats & Fish, page 75.) If using another brand of kosher salt, use exactly 5 ounces—see page 52.

Combine all the ingredients in a large pot, cover, and bring to a boil. Boil for 1 minute, stirring to dissolve the salt. Remove from the heat and cool completely, then chill before using. The brine can be refrigerated for up to 3 days.   **MAKES 2 QUARTS**

chicken stock

5 pounds chicken bones, necks, and backs
1 pound chicken feet (optional)
About 4 quarts cold water
About 8 cups ice cubes
1¾ cups carrots cut into 1-inch cubes
2 heaping cups leeks cut into 1-inch pieces
  (white and light green parts only)
1½ cups Spanish onions cut into 1-inch pieces
1 bay leaf

This is a very light stock, appropriate for a variety of uses—from the braising liquid for meats and beans to the base for soups and sauces. For a stronger chicken flavor, reduce the finished stock by one-third or use more bones.

As with all stocks, you're looking to remove impurities—fats and food particles—while extracting as much flavor and gelatin as possible from the bones, and the maximum flavor from the vegetables and aromatics. You do this not only through gentle heat, but through gradual heat transitions as well; in other words, you don't start with hot water, you begin with cold and bring it slowly up to heat. Skim often throughout the cooking process—especially in the beginning, when a lot of impurities will rise to the surface. You can't skim too much. I add ice cubes after the stock has come up to a simmer; this chills any remaining fat and makes it easier to remove. Maintain a gentle heat over a long time, continuing to skim, and then carefully strain the stock. All the steps are simple, but each one is essential.

Rinse the bones, necks, backs, and chicken feet, if using, thoroughly under cold water to remove all visible blood. Remove and discard any organs still attached to the bones. (Rinsing the bones and removing any organs is an essential first step in the clarification of the stock, as this removes any blood proteins that would coagulate when heated and cloud the stock.)

Put all the bones and the feet, if using, in a very large stockpot and add 4 quarts cold water, or just enough to cover the bones. Set the pot to one side of the burner (see Note). Slowly bring the liquid to a simmer, beginning to skim as soon as any impurities rise to the top. (It is important to keep skimming as the stock comes to a simmer, because impurities could otherwise be pulled back into the liquid and cloud the finished stock.) Once the liquid is at a simmer, add the ice cubes (ice will solidify the remaining fat and make it easier to remove), and then remove the fat. Skim off as much of the impurities as possible. (Once the vegetables have been added, skimming will be more difficult.)

Add the remaining ingredients and slowly bring the liquid back to a simmer, skimming frequently. Simmer for another 40 minutes, skimming often. Turn off the heat and let the stock rest for 10 minutes (this allows any particles left in the stock to settle at the bottom of the pot).

Prepare an ice bath. Set a fine-mesh conical strainer over a container large enough to hold at least 6 quarts liquid. Use a ladle to transfer the stock from the pot to the strainer. (It is important to ladle the stock rather than pour it, as the force of pouring it out all at once would carry impurities through the strainer.) Do not press on the solids in the strainer or force through any liquid, or the stock will be cloudy. Discard any stock that is cloudy with impurities at the bottom of the pot.

Measure the stock. If you have more than 4½ quarts, pour it into a saucepan, bring it to a simmer, and simmer to reduce. Strain into a clean container before measuring again.

Put the container in the ice bath to cool the stock rapidly. Stir occasionally until there are no longer any traces of steam and the stock is cool. Store in the refrigerator for up to 3 days, or freeze in smaller containers for up to 2 months. **MAKES 4½ QUARTS**

NOTE *By setting your pot half off the burner, you'll create a natural convection current that pushes the impurities to one side of the pot. Then you can skim them away—it's kind of a natural clarification process.*

beef stock

2 tablespoons canola oil
5 pounds meaty beef neck or leg bones, cut into 2- to 3-inch sections
    (by the butcher)
2 small Spanish onions
About 5 quarts cold water
½ teaspoon kosher salt
1 large carrot, peeled and cut into 1-inch pieces
1 large leek, root end trimmed, split lengthwise, rinsed well,
    and cut into 2-inch pieces
1 large thyme sprig
1 large flat-leaf parsley sprig
3 bay leaves
¼ teaspoon black peppercorns
½ head garlic, cut in half through the equator

The bones for this stock are roasted first to give the stock a deeper flavor, then simmered with caramelized vegetables for a rich brown stock.

Preheat the oven to 475°F. Put a large roasting pan in the oven to preheat for about 10 minutes.

Add 1 tablespoon of the oil to the hot pan, add the bones, and spread them in a single layer. Roast, turning occasionally, for about 45 minutes, until richly browned on all sides.

Meanwhile, cut 1 onion crosswise in half. Heat a small heavy sauté pan over medium-high heat for 2 to 3 minutes. Place 1 onion half cut side down to one side of the sauté pan, so that it is not over direct heat, and let it brown and char black, about 30 minutes. (This will add color to the stock.) Set aside.

Remove the roasting pan from the oven and reduce the oven temperature to 400°F. Transfer the bones to a large colander set over a baking sheet to drain. Drain the fat from the roasting pan, add about 1 cup of water to the pan, and deglaze over medium heat, scraping up the brown bits. Put the liquid and browned bits into a large stockpot.

Transfer the bones to the stockpot and add 5 quarts water, or enough to just cover the bones. Set the pot to one side of the burner (see Note, left). With a skimmer, skim off any fat, then add the charred onion half and the salt. Bring to a simmer over medium heat, then reduce the heat and simmer gently, skimming often, for 5 hours. Add water if necessary to keep the bones covered.

Meanwhile, cut the remaining 1½ onions into quarters. Put the onions, carrot, and leek in a roasting pan that will hold them in a single layer, toss with the remaining 1 tablespoon oil, and roast for 20 minutes. Stir, and roast for another 20 minutes, or until the vegetables are richly caramelized. Set aside.

After 5 hours of simmering, add the caramelized vegetables, herbs, peppercorns, and garlic to the stockpot, and simmer for 1 hour longer. Turn off the heat and allow the stock to rest for 10 minutes.

Prepare an ice bath. Set a fine-mesh conical strainer over a container large enough to hold at least 6 quarts. Use a ladle to transfer the stock from the pot to the strainer. (It is important to ladle the stock rather than pour it, as the force of pouring it out all at once would carry impurities through the strainer.) Do not press on the solids in the strainer or force through the liquid, or the stock will be cloudy. Discard any stock that is cloudy with impurities at the bottom of the pot.

Strain a second time through a fine-mesh conical strainer lined with a dampened cheesecloth.

Measure the stock. If you have more than 3½ quarts, pour it into a saucepan, bring it to a simmer, and simmer to reduce, then strain into a clean container. Put the container in the ice bath to cool rapidly. Stir occasionally until there are no longer any traces of steam and the stock is cool. Store in the refrigerator for up to 3 days, or freeze in smaller containers for up to 2 months. **MAKES 3½ QUARTS**

mushroom stock

4 pounds button mushrooms or mushroom stems, washed

1 medium onion, coarsely chopped

1 large carrot, peeled and coarsely chopped

Greens from 1 leek, coarsely chopped and washed well

6 quarts cold water

½ head garlic (cut in half through the equator), separated into cloves and crushed, skin left on

½ bunch flat-leaf parsley, coarsely chopped

½ bunch thyme, coarsely chopped

4 bay leaves

1 tablespoon black peppercorns

Mushroom stock is very easy to make and has a more focused, savory flavor than a vegetable stock made without mushrooms.

Finely chop the mushrooms, onion, carrot, and leek in a food processor, working in batches.

Put the vegetables in a large stockpot, add the cold water, and bring to a boil. Add the garlic, herbs, bay leaves, and peppercorns, return to a simmer, and simmer uncovered for 45 minutes.

Prepare an ice bath. Set a fine-mesh conical strainer over a container large enough to hold at least 6 quarts.

Strain the stock through a colander, then strain through the strainer into the container.

Measure the stock. If you have more than 4 quarts, pour it into a saucepan, simmer to reduce, and strain again into a clean container. Put the container in the ice bath to cool rapidly. Stir occasionally until there are no longer any traces of steam and the stock is cool. Store in the refrigerator for up to 3 days, or freeze in smaller containers for up to 2 months. **MAKES 4 QUARTS**

vegetable stock

1 large bunch (1½ pounds) leeks, white parts only, coarsely chopped and washed well

1 pound carrots, peeled and coarsely chopped

1½ pounds Spanish onions (about 2 large), coarsely chopped

1 small fennel bulb, trimmed and coarsely chopped

¼ cup canola oil

2 bay leaves

2 thyme sprigs

1 bunch flat-leaf parsley

3 to 4 quarts cold water

Vegetable stock loses its flavor quickly, so it's best to make it as close to the time of use as possible. Make it in small quantities, or make it in large batches and freeze immediately. We finely chop the vegetables or grind them so we can extract maximum flavor in the shortest time.

Finely chop all the vegetables in a food processor, working in batches.

Cook the vegetables in the canola oil in a medium stockpot over low heat for 5 to 8 minutes, or until softened. Add the bay leaves, thyme, parsley, and enough water to cover. Bring to a gentle simmer, skimming frequently, and cook for 45 minutes.

Prepare an ice bath. Set a fine-mesh conical strainer over a container large enough to hold at least 6 quarts.

Strain the stock, and put the container in the ice bath to cool rapidly. Stir occasionally until there are no longer any traces of steam and the stock is cool. Store in the refrigerator for up to 3 days, or freeze in small containers for up to 2 months. **MAKES 3 TO 4 QUARTS**

court bouillon

4 leeks (white and light green parts only), split lengthwise, washed well, and cut crosswise into ½-inch pieces

4 large carrots, peeled and cut into ½-inch-thick rounds

3 cups coarsely chopped onions

2 medium fennel bulbs, trimmed and coarsely chopped

1 Sachet (page 342)

4 quarts water

2 cups dry white wine, such as Sauvignon Blanc

1 cup white wine vinegar

2 lemons, halved

Court bouillon literally translates as "quick stock" and that's what it is, a stock made when you need it. Court bouillons are usually used for cooking seafood, adding delicious flavor to sole or salmon or any shellfish. They use plenty of aromatic vegetables and also include acidic components, such as wine and vinegar.

Combine the vegetables and sachet in a large stockpot, add the water, and bring to a boil. Reduce to a simmer and add the wine and vinegar. Squeeze in the lemon juice and add the lemon halves to the pot. Return to a simmer.

Use as directed in the recipe. **MAKES ABOUT 5 QUARTS**

sachet

1 bay leaf
3 thyme sprigs
10 black peppercorns
1 garlic clove, smashed and peeled

Sachets are used to flavor cooking liquids. A cheesecloth sachet encloses small herbs and spices such as peppercorns and cloves, and works like a tea bag. Once the contents have added their flavors to the cooking liquid, the sachet can easily be removed and discarded.

Lay out a 7-inch square of cheesecloth. Put the bay leaf, thyme, peppercorns, and garlic near the bottom of the square and fold the bottom edge up and over them. Roll once, tuck in the two ends of the cheesecloth, and continue to roll. Tie the cheesecloth at both ends with kitchen twine. **MAKES 1 SACHET**

preparing lobsters

Court Bouillon (page 341)
1- to 1½-pound live lobsters

When preparing lobsters that will be used cold, it's best to cook them in a court bouillon. Steeping the lobsters in the flavored liquid adds much more flavor and complexity to the meat than cooking them in plain water or steaming them.

Bring the court bouillon to a boil in a large pot. Cook 1 or 2 lobsters at a time. Add the lobster(s) headfirst and cover the pot to return the liquid to a gentle boil, then remove the lid and boil for 1 minute. Remove the pot from the heat, cover, and let the lobster(s) steep in the liquid for 10 minutes.

Transfer the lobster(s) to a tray to cool for about 15 minutes. Remove the meat from the shells: Working over the tray, twist off and remove the tail from each lobster body. Then twist and pull off each of the claws.

TO REMOVE THE TAIL MEAT: Hold each tail flat, back shell facing up, and, using a sharp chef's knife, cut lengthwise in half. With a pair of tweezers, pull out and discard the vein that runs the length of the tail.

For the Maine Lobster Rolls (page 84) and Saffron Rice Salad with Summer Squash and Maine Lobster (page 166), cut the tail into pieces about ¾ inch in size. If there is any roe (bright red coral), it can be finely chopped and added to the lobster salad.

For the Shellfish Salad (page 170), cut the tail meat into 6 pieces.

TO REMOVE THE KNUCKLE AND CLAW MEAT: Twist off each knuckle from the claw. Hold the claw in your hand and pull down to loosen the lower pincer, then push it to either side to crack it and pull it straight off. Still holding the claw, crack the top of the shell with the heel of a knife, about ¾ inch from the joint where the knuckle was attached, and wiggle your knife to loosen and crack open the shell. Shake the claw to remove the meat.

For the lobster rolls and saffron rice salad, cut the claw meat into ¾-inch pieces.

For the shellfish salad, cut each claw into 2 pieces; discard any pieces of cartilage.

Cut off the top joint, the one that was attached to the body, of each knuckle. Use scissors to cut open the shell along the smooth outside edge of each knuckle. Pry open the shell and remove the meat.

Cover all the lobster meat and refrigerate until completely chilled.

deep-fried herbs

Peanut oil or canola oil for deep-frying
Fresh herb sprigs (thyme, rosemary, or oregano) or flat-leaf parsley leaves, patted thoroughly dry
Kosher salt

Herbs take on a great flavor when they're fried. Those that aren't palatable whole and raw, such as rosemary and oregano, become delicate and flavorful.

Heat at least 1 inch of oil to 350°F in a small pot. (The exact quantity of oil depends on how much you will fry; you need to be able to turn and move the sprigs as they cook.) Add the herbs, in batches as necessary. They will be done in a few seconds, so move them in the oil and remove them as soon as they are crisp. Drain briefly on paper towels and use as soon as possible. Season with salt.

cooking eggs

Firm soft-cooked: yolks are just firm enough to handle but still slightly runny, whites are set
Medium-cooked: center of the yolks are soft with a slightly darker color
Hard-cooked: yolks are completely set

It is always a good idea to cook a couple of extra eggs so that you are able to test them during the cooking.

It's best to use a timer when cooking eggs. Prepare an ice water bath.

FOR FIRM SOFT-COOKED EGGS: Bring a saucepan filled with at least 4 inches of water to a rapid simmer. One at a time, put the eggs on a slotted spoon and lower into the water. Cover the pot, remove from the heat, and let stand for 7 minutes. Transfer the eggs to the ice bath. When the eggs have cooled, tap them on the counter to crack the shells and carefully peel them under cold running water.

FOR MEDIUM-COOKED AND HARD-COOKED EGGS: Put the eggs in a saucepan filled with at least 4 inches of cold water and bring to a rapid simmer over medium-high heat and cook for 4 minutes (timing from the beginning of the simmer) for medium-cooked eggs, 7 minutes for hard-cooked eggs. Transfer the eggs to the ice bath to stop the cooking. When the eggs have cooled, tap them on the counter to crack the shells and carefully peel them under cold running water.

For poached eggs, see page 156.

dessert basics

blackberry sauce

½ cup Banyuls wine (see Sources, page 346), late-harvest Zinfandel, or tawny port
2 cups (8 ounces) blackberries
½ cup granulated sugar
1 tablespoon fresh lemon juice
1 tablespoon cornstarch

Pour the wine into a medium saucepan and bring to a boil over medium heat, then reduce the heat to a simmer and reduce the wine to ¼ cup.

Stir the berries and sugar into the wine. Increase the heat to medium-high, bring to a simmer and cook, stirring, for about 5 minutes, until the sugar is dissolved.

Combine the lemon juice and cornstarch in a small bowl, stirring until smooth (this is called a slurry). Add enough of the berry liquid, 2 to 3 tablespoons, to the slurry to make it more fluid, then stir it into the berry mixture and simmer for 1 to 2 minutes to cook the cornstarch and thicken the sauce. Remove from the heat.

Put a tablespoon of the sauce on a plate and refrigerate for about 10 minutes to test the consistency. If the sauce is looser than you would like, return it to the heat and cook for a few minutes longer. Remove from the heat and let cool, then refrigerate in a covered container for up to 1 week.

MAKES ABOUT 1½ CUPS

strawberry coulis

3 cups strawberries, hulled and quartered
¼ cup plus 2 tablespoons granulated sugar
2 tablespoons water

Combine all the ingredients in a medium saucepan, bring to a boil over medium heat, and cook until the berries are soft, about 4 minutes.

Remove from the heat, pour into a Vita-Mix, and puree, scraping down the sides as necessary. Strain through a fine-mesh conical strainer and refrigerate in a covered container for up to 3 days.

MAKES ABOUT 1 CUP

STRAWBERRY SAUCE Add 8 ounces strawberries, sliced.

cherry compote

2½ cups pitted cherries
2 tablespoons granulated sugar, or to taste
About 1 teaspoon fresh lemon juice

Chop ¾ cup of the cherries, put in a Vita-Mix, and blend to puree; if necessary, add a very small amount of water to allow the cherries to spin.

Cut the remaining cherries into rough pieces, about 4 per cherry.

Combine the cherries, cherry puree, and sugar in a medium saucepan, bring to a simmer over medium heat, and cook for 30 minutes, or until the compote has thickened to the consistency of a sauce. Add lemon juice to taste and additional sugar if needed.

Let cool, then refrigerate in a covered container for up to 1 week.

MAKES ABOUT 1 CUP

chocolate sauce

7 ounces 55% chocolate (see Sources, page 346), chopped into
    ¼-inch pieces
¾ cup heavy cream
¼ cup light corn syrup

Put the chocolate in a medium bowl. Pour the cream and corn syrup into a medium saucepan and heat over medium-high heat until a skin forms and the cream is just below a boil. Pour over the chocolate and let stand for 1 minute, then stir until smooth.

    Serve, or cool and refrigerate in a covered container for up to 1 week. Rewarm before serving.   **MAKES ABOUT 1¾ CUPS**

caramel sauce

¾ cup plus 2 tablespoons granulated sugar
¼ cup plus 2 tablespoons light corn syrup
¼ cup water
1½ cups heavy cream, warmed
2 tablespoons (1 ounce) unsalted butter, at room temperature

Combine the sugar and corn syrup in a medium saucepan and stir in the water. Set over medium-high heat and bring to a simmer, then adjust the heat as necessary to simmer and cook without stirring, for 30 to 35 minutes, until the caramel is a rich amber color; if you want to check the color, use a small spoon to drop a small amount on a white plate. You want a dark caramel so the finished sauce will be a rich caramel color.

    Remove from the heat and slowly whisk in the cream, being careful, as the mixture will bubble up. If the sauce seizes, stir it over the heat to slowly remelt any hardened caramel. Whisk in the butter.

    Serve, or cool and refrigerate in a covered container for up to 1 month. Warm before serving.   **MAKES ABOUT 2½ CUPS**

CARAMEL PECAN SAUCE Add 1½ cups toasted pecans to the finished caramel sauce. The nuts can be left whole or chopped; if you chop them, put them in a fine-mesh basket strainer and shake to remove the fine dust. Stir the nuts into the sauce. **(MAKES 4 CUPS)**

meringue

1¼ cups plus 2 tablespoons plus 1 teaspoon granulated sugar
¼ cup plus 1 tablespoon water
3 large egg whites, at room temperature
½ teaspoon pure vanilla extract (if using meringue for Coconut Cake)

Meringue has many uses in the dessert kitchen. It can be baked, poached, or used, as we do here, as a topping for Lemon Bars (page 304) and Coconut Cake (page 309). This meringue is made with a syrup—sugar dissolved in a little water and heated to 220°F. It's then added to the egg whites as they're being whipped. It's best to make meringue right before you need it and to eat it the day it's made.

Combine 1¼ cups of the sugar and the water in a medium saucepan and heat over medium heat to 220°F, stirring at first to dissolve the sugar.

    Meanwhile, in the bowl of a stand mixer fitted with the whisk attachment, whip the egg whites on medium speed until they begin to look foamy, then gradually add the remaining 2 tablespoons plus 1 teaspoon sugar. Increase the speed to medium-high and whip until the whites form soft peaks.

    With the mixer running, slowly add the sugar syrup, pouring it down the side of the bowl to avoid the whisk. Add the vanilla, if using, and continue to whip until stiff peaks form and the bowl is cool.

    Use as directed in the recipe.   **MAKES ABOUT 3½ CUPS**

grilling basics

grilling with a charcoal grill

I love grilled foods but it's important to pay attention to flames and charring. Flames ignited by rendering fat can char the meat too much and make it bitter.

Light the charcoal about 45 minutes before you plan to grill.

TO LIGHT THE CHARCOAL: Add crumpled newspaper to the bottom of a chimney (see Sources, page 346) and set it on the bottom rack of the grill. Fill the chimney with charcoal, preferably hardwood charcoal. Light the newspaper and let burn until all the coals are covered with light gray ash. This will take about 30 minutes, depending on the type of charcoal.

Wearing heatproof gloves or oven mitts, lift the chimney and pour the coals onto the bottom grill rack.

FOR SINGLE-TEMPERATURE COOKING: Spread the coals out in an even layer. Put the top grill grate on the grill, cover with the lid, and let the rack heat for 10 to 15 minutes.

FOR MULTIPLE-TEMPERATURE COOKING: The coals need to be arranged to set up two cooking zones. The higher the mound of coals is, the higher the temperature will be (see How Hot Is It? right). Spread out about half of the coals on one side of the bottom rack of the grill. Arrange the remaining coals on the other side of the grill, mounding them so that they are 2 to 3 inches higher than the other coals. If necessary, add more coals to this high side and let them burn until covered by ash, about 10 minutes. Put the grill grate on the grill, cover with the lid, and let the rack heat for 10 to 15 minutes.

FOR DIRECT-HEAT COOKING FOLLOWED BY INDIRECT-HEAT COOKING: The coals can be set up in two different ways. You can spread all the coals out on one side of the lower rack, leaving the other side empty. Or you can spread the coals in two piles on either side, leaving the center empty. Put the grill grate on the grill, cover with the lid, and let the rack heat for 10 to 15 minutes.

ADDING MORE CHARCOAL: For recipes requiring a longer cooking time, add new coals every 30 to 40 minutes, putting them on top of the burning coals, to keep the fire going.

grilling with gas

The heating elements in a gas grill can run from left to right or from front to back. Most gas grills have two or three heating elements. Follow the general instructions below, but consult the manufacturer's instructions for specifics. Turn on your grill about 30 minutes before you plan to grill.

FOR SINGLE-TEMPERATURE COOKING: Turn on the grill, close the lid, and preheat for 20 to 30 minutes.

FOR MULTIPLE-TEMPERATURE COOKING: Turn one of the burners to one of the temperatures needed and the other one to the other temperature needed. (If you have a three-burner grill, you may choose to set two to the higher temperature for the initial searing/cooking and then turn one of the burners down to the lower temperature.) Close the lid and preheat for 20 to 30 minutes.

FOR DIRECT-HEAT COOKING FOLLOWED BY INDIRECT-HEAT COOKING: How you set up your grill for indirect heat depends on how many burners your grill has, but the basic principle is that the area receiving indirect heat is surrounded by direct heat. For a three-burner grill, turn on the left and right burners (or the front and back ones) to the desired temperature, leaving the center burner off. For a four-burner grill, turn on the outer burners and leave the two center ones off. For a two-burner grill, turn on one burner and leave the other one off. In all cases, close the lid and preheat for 20 to 30 minutes.

HOW HOT IS IT? *The best way to gauge the temperature of your grill, whether using charcoal or gas, is to monitor the heat by holding your hand about 6 inches above the cooking grate. For high heat, you will only be able to hold your hand over the flame for about 2 seconds; for medium-high, 3 to 4 seconds; medium, 5 to 6; medium-low, about 7; and low, about 8.*

sources

FOR FOOD

ANSON MILLS
803-467-4122
www.ansonmills.com
Grits

CIA INSTITUTE OF AMERICA AT GREYSTONE
888-424-2433
www.prochef.com
Apple pectin

COWGIRL CREAMERY
866-249-7833
www.cowgirlcreamery.com
Artisanal cheeses

D'ARTAGNAN
800-327-8246
www.dartagnan.com
Rendered duck fat

DIBRUNO BROS.
888-322-4337
www.dibruno.com
Fresh mozzarella curd

FRA' MANI
510-526-7000
www.framani.com
Sweet Italian sausage

GUITTARD
800-468-2462
www.guittard.com
Cocoa rouge, cocoa powder, 61% semisweet and 72% bittersweet chocolate

HOBBS' APPLEWOOD SMOKED MEATS
510-232-5577
Applewood smoked bacon

IMPORTFOOD
888-618-8424
www.importfood.com
Kaffir lime leaves and galangal

K&L WINE MERCHANTS
877-559-4637
www.klwines.com
Banyuls wine by Cornet et Cie

LA TIENDA
800-710-4304
www.tienda.com
Calasparra rice, ibérico ham, dried Nora chiles, pardina lentils, pimentón, piquillo peppers

LE SANCTUAIRE
415-986-4216
www.le-sanctuaire.com
Don Millan Pedro Ximenez sherry vinegar

LE VILLAGE
888-873-7194
www.levillage.com
Edmond Fallot mustards

MANCHESTER FARMS
800-845-0421
www.manchesterfarms.com
Quail

MARKET HALL FOODS
888-952-4005
www.markethallfoods.com
Banyuls vinegar, farro, Maldon sea salt, Moretti polenta, piment d'Espelette, smoked salmon, Tipo oo flour, white verjus

MARSHALL'S FARM NATURAL HONEY
800-624-4637
www.marshallshoney.com
Honey

MONTEREY AQUARIUM SEA WATCH
www.montereybayaquarium
.org/cr/seafoodwatch.aspx
Resource for sustainable seafood purchases

NIELSEN MASSEY VANILLAS
800-525-7873
www.nielsenmassey.com
Vanilla paste and extract

THE PERFECT PUREE OF NAPA VALLEY
800-556-3707
www.perfectpuree.com
Cherry puree

PURCELL MOUNTAIN FARMS
208-267-0627
www.purcellmountainfarms.com
Asian black rice

PURE BRED
724-852-2535
www.purebredlamb.com
Lamb

RANCHO GORDO
707-259-1935
www.ranchogordo.com
Heirloom beans

RÖTH KASE
www.rothkase.com
Gruyère cheese

SABATINO TARTUFI
www.sabatinotartufi.com
Tondo balsamic vinegar

SONOMA COUNTY POULTRY
800-953-8257
www.libertyducks.com
Pekin Long Island duck

SPARROW LANE
866-515-2477
www.sparrowlane.com
Assorted vinegars

VALRHONA
www.valrhona.com
Cocoa powder, 55% Le Noir, 64% Manjari, and 70% Guanaja chocolate

WHOLESOME SWEETENERS
800-680-1896
www.wholesomesweeteners.com
Billington's molasses sugar

ZINGERMAN'S
888-636-8162
www.zingermans.com
Pomegranate molasses

FOR EQUIPMENT

ALL-CLAD
800-255-2523
www.allclad.com
Cookware and small appliances, including slow-cookers

CUCINA PRO
216-351-3002
www.cucinapro.com
Pasta machines

CUISIPRO
302-326-4802
www.cuisipro.com
Kitchen accessories and utensils, including skimmers

EMILE HENRY
302-326-4800
www.emilehenry.com
Cookware and Urban Colors Collection

HOME DEPOT
800-553-3199
www.homedepot.com
Store locator information available for purchasing propane torches and chimney starters

JB PRINCE
800-473-0577
www.jbprince.com
Professional cooking equipment and supplies, including a #12 parisienne scoop (also called 7/16-inch melon baller), Pullman loaf pan

KUHN RIKON
800-662-5882
www.kuhnrikon.com
Kitchen accessories and utensils, including the Flame Tamer heat diffuser

RÖSLE USA
302-326-4801
www.rosleusa.com
Kitchen accessories and utensils

STAUB
866-782-8287
www.staubusa.com
Cast-iron cookware

SUR LA TABLE
800-243-0852
www.surlatable.com
Cookware and kitchen tools, including Japanese mandoline, 9-by-13-inch baking sheets, silicone baking pans

WILLIAMS-SONOMA
877-812-6235
www.williams-sonoma.com
Cookware and kitchen tools, including palette knife, baking sheets, cooling racks

VITA-MIX
800-848-2649
www.vitamix.com
Vita-Mix

FOR PRESENTATION PIECES

HEATH CERAMICS
415-332-3732
www.heath.com
Ceramic tableware

ILEONI
707-762-9611
www.ileoni.com
Dining and culinary pieces

MATCH
201-792-9444
www.match1995.com
Pewter table service pieces and Berti cutlery

SAGAFORM
www.sagaform.se
Presentation pieces, including woods

VANDERBILT & CO.
707-963-1010
Presentation pieces, including Vietri

FOR ANTIQUES

HERITAGE CULINARY ARTIFACTS
707-224-2101
www.oxbowpublicmarket.com

SONOMA COUNTRY ANTIQUES
707-938-8315
www.sonomacountryantiques.com

acknowledgments

On behalf of myself, Ad Hoc chef de cuisine Dave Cruz, and our co-authors, I would like to thank the many colleagues behind the scenes who helped to make this book happen. First and foremost, the whole team of Ad Hoc has established a restaurant that has inspired the food in this book; a few of them deserve special mention: Jeff Cerciello, culinary director for Bouchon; chefs Josh Crain and Jonathan Watsky; and, in the dining room, Nick Didier. Chefs Brandon Olsen and Michael Kalhorn from Ad Hoc were instrumental in recipe development, testing, and photography. We'd like to thank our assistants, who help us to manage our busy days, Molly Fleming, Simran Winkelstern, and Kim Schager. Deborah Jones is grateful to her assistants, Jeri Jones and Gene Lee.

For the beautiful props for photography, we're grateful to many companies. For the beautiful presentation pieces: Heath Ceramics, iLeoni, Match, Sagaform, and Vanderbilt & Co. For antiques: Heritage Culinary Artifacts and Sonoma Country Antiques. And for cookware, cutlery, and utensils: All-Clad, Berti, Cucina Pro, Cuisipro, Emile Henry, Kuhn Rikon, Rösle USA, and Staub.

The team at Artisan has once again pulled out all the stops to produce a book that I'm immensely proud of: Trent Duffy, Nancy Murray, Jan Derevjanik, Amy Corley, Erin Sainz, Barbara Peragine, and our fantastic copy editor, Judith Sutton.

Finally, I want to say a personal thanks to my book team. We have worked together now on four books and truly are a family. We love the process of making a book as much as we do holding the finished product. They are: Deborah Jones, our brilliant photographer, who brings the food to life on the pages; Susie Heller, Michael Ruhlman, and Amy Vogler, who pull together all our thoughts, from the recipes to the essays; the creative team of David and Joleen Hughes at Level Design; and, of course, my publisher at Artisan, Ann Bramson, who has believed in me for more than ten years.

index